PRIDE, PREJUDICE, AND POLITICS

PRIDE,
PREJUDICE,
and POLITICS

Roosevelt versus Recovery, 1933–1938

GARY DEAN BEST

PRAEGER

New York
Westport, Connecticut
London

Library of Congress Cataloging-in-Publication Data

Best, Gary Dean.
    Pride, prejudice, and politics : Roosevelt versus recovery,
1933–1938 / Gary Dean Best.
        p.   cm.
    Includes bibliographical references and index.
    ISBN 0-275-93524-8 (alk. paper)
    1. New Deal, 1933–1939.   2. Roosevelt, Franklin D. (Franklin
Delano), 1882–1945.   3. United States—Economic policy—1933–1945.
4. United States—History—1933–1945.   I. Title.
E806.B494   1991
973.917—dc20   90-38841

Library of Congress Catalog Card Number: 90–38841
ISBN: 0-275-93524-8

First published in 1991

Praeger Publishers, One Madison Avenue, New York, NY 10010
An imprint of Greenwood Publishing Group, Inc.

Printed in the United States of America

The paper used in this book complies with the
Permanent Paper Standard issued by the National
Information Standards Organization (Z39.48-1984).

10 9 8 7 6 5 4 3 2 1

Copyright Acknowledgments

The author and publisher gratefully acknowledge permission to use the following copyrighted materials:

Excerpts from Pierre S. DuPont Papers, Lammot DuPont (from E.I. DuPont De Nemours & Co.,
Administrative Papers), and John Raskob Papers, courtesy of Hagley Museum and Library, Wil-
mington, Delaware.

Excerpts from Rexford Tugwell Papers and Diaries, courtesy of Mrs. Rexford Tugwell.

For my best friend and wife,
Lani,
and her two great kids,
Kehau and Grad

Contents

Preface

This book had its genesis in the fact that I have for a long time felt uncomfortable with the standard works written about Franklin Delano Roosevelt and the New Deal, and with the influence those works have exerted on others writing about and teaching U.S. history. Although I approach the subject from a very different perspective, Paul K. Conkin's preface to the second edition of *The New Deal* (1975) expressed many of my own misgivings about writings on the subject. Conkin wrote that "pervading even the most scholarly revelations was a monotonous, often almost reflexive, and in my estimation a very smug or superficial valuative perspective—approval, even glowing approval, of most enduring New Deal policies, or at least of the underlying goals that a sympathetic observer could always find behind policies and programs."

Studies of the New Deal such as Conkin described seemed to me to be examples of a genre relatively rare in U.S. historiography—that of "court histories," such as those that put the hump on the back of poor Richard III. Like the New Dealers themselves, the authors of these histories seemed to show a contempt toward critics of the New Deal akin to that of the Duchess in *Alice in Wonderland* in her dialogue with Alice:

"I've a right to think," said Alice. . . .
"Just about as much right," said the Duchess sharply, "as pigs have to fly."

But, like most historians teaching courses dealing with the Roosevelt period, I was captive to the published works unless I was willing and able to devote the time to pursue extensive research in the period myself. After some years that became possible, and this book is the result.

My principal problem with Roosevelt and the New Deal was not over his specific reforms or his social programs, but with the failure of the United States to recover from the depression during the eight peacetime years that he and his policies governed the nation. I consider that failure tragic, not only for the 14.6 percent of the labor force that remained unemployed as late as 1940, and for the millions of others who subsisted on government welfare because of the prolonged depression, but also because of the image that the depression-plagued United States projected to the world at a crucial time in international affairs. In the late 1930s and early 1940s, when U.S. economic strength might have given pause to potential aggressors in the world, our economic weakness furnished encouragement to them instead.[1] From the standpoint, then, not only of our domestic history, but also of the tragic events and results of World War II, it has seemed to me that Roosevelt's failure to generate economic recovery during this critical period deserved more attention than historians have given it.

Most historians of the New Deal period leave the impression that the failure of the United States to recover during those eight years resulted from Roosevelt's unwillingness to embrace Keynesian spending. According to this thesis, recovery came during World War II because the war at last forced Roosevelt to spend at the level required all along for recovery. This, however, seemed to me more an advocacy of Keynes' theories by the historians involved than an explanation for the U.S. failure to recover during those years. Great Britain, for example, managed to recover by the late 1930s without recourse to deficit spending. By that time the United States was, by contrast, near the bottom of the list of industrial nations as measured in progress toward recovery, with most others having reached the predepression levels and many having exceeded them. The recovered countries represented a variety of economic systems, from state ownership to private enterprise. The common denominator in their success was not a reliance on deficit spending, but rather the stimulus they furnished to industrial enterprise.

What went wrong in the United States? Simplistic answers such as the reference to Keynesianism seemed to me only a means of avoiding a real answer to the question. A wise president, entering the White House in the midst of a crippling depression, should do everything possible to stimulate enterprise. In a free economy, economic recovery means *business* recovery. It follows, therefore, that a wise chief executive should do everything possible to create the conditions and psychology most conducive to business recovery—to encourage business to expand production, and lenders and investors to furnish the financing and capital that are required. An administration seeking economic recovery will do as little as possible that might inhibit recovery, will weigh all its actions with the necessity for economic recovery in mind, and will consult with competent business and financial leaders, as well as economists, to determine the best policies to follow. Such a president will seek to promote cooperation between the federal government and business, rather than conflict, and will seek to introduce as much consistency and stability as possible into government economic policies so that businessmen and investors can plan ahead. While obviously the destitute must be cared for, ultimately the most humane contribution a liberal government can make to the victims of a depression is the restoration of prosperity and the reemployment of the idle in genuine jobs.

In measuring the Roosevelt policies and programs during the New Deal years against such standards, I was struck by the air of unreality that hung over Washington in general and the White House in particular during this period. Business and financial leaders who questioned the wisdom of New Deal policies were disregarded and deprecated because of their "greed" and "self-interest," while economists and business academicians who persisted in calling attention to the collision between New Deal policies and simple economic realities were dismissed for their "orthodoxy." As one "orthodox" economist pointed out early in the New Deal years,

economic realism . . . insists that policies aiming to promote recovery will, in fact, retard recovery if and where they fail to take into account correctly of stubborn facts in the existing economic situation and of the arithmetic of business as it must be carried out in the economic situation we are trying to revive. The antithesis of this economic realism is the vaguely hopeful or optimistic idealism in the field of economic policy, as such, which feels that good intentions, enough cleverness, and the right appeal to the emotions of the people ought to insure good results in spite of inconvenient facts.[2]

Those "inconvenient facts" dogged the New Deal throughout these years, only to be stubbornly resisted by a president whose pride, prejudices, and politics would rarely permit an accommodation with them.

Most studies of the New Deal years approach the period largely from the perspective of the New Dealers themselves. Critics and opponents of Roosevelt's policies and programs are given scant attention in such works except to point up the "reactionary" and "unenlightened" opposition with which Roosevelt was forced to contend in seeking to provide Americans with "a more abundant life." The few studies that have concentrated on critics and opponents of the New Deal in the business community have been by unsympathetic historians who have tended to distort the opposition to fit the caricature drawn by the New Dealers, so that they offer little to explain the impact of Roosevelt's policies in delaying recovery from the depression.

The issue of *why* businessmen and bankers were so critical of the New Deal has been for too long swept under the rug, together with the question of *how* Roosevelt and his advisers could possibly expect to produce an economic recovery while a state of war existed between his administration and the employers and investors who, alone, could produce such a recovery. Even a Keynesian response to economic depression is ultimately dependent on the positive reactions of businessmen and investors for its success, as Keynes well knew, and those reactions were not likely to be as widespread as necessary under such a state of warfare between government and business. Businessmen, bankers, and investors may have been "greedy" and "self-interested." They may have been guilty of wrong perceptions and unfounded fears. But they are also the ones, in a free economy, upon whose decisions and actions economic recovery must depend. To understand their opposition to the New Deal requires an immersion in the public and private comments of critics of Roosevelt's policies. The degree and nature of business, banking, and investor concern about the direction and consequences of New Deal policies can be gleaned from the hundreds of banking and business periodicals representative of every branch of U.S. business and finance in the 1930s, and from the letters and diaries of the New Deal's business and other critics during the decade.

In the course of the research and writing involved in this book I have incurred many obligations. My late wife, Matsue, endured a year of sharing motel and hotel rooms with me as we moved from library to library during a year of manuscript research. That year of research would have been impossible but for a fellowship from the National Endowment for the Humanities for 1982–1983. I renewed old acquaintances among the staffs of the Hoover Institution on War, Revolution and Peace, the Hoover Presidential Library, and the Library of Congress, and received wonderful cooperation from new acquaintances in the Roosevelt Presidential Library, as well as the libraries of Syracuse, Cornell, and Harvard universities and the Hagley Museum and Library. I owe a special debt of gratitude, as always, to Ken Herrick and the staff of the University of Hawaii at Hilo Library for their constant support. Finally, this book would never have been completed had it not been for the encouragement and patience of my wife, Lani.

Introduction

Statistics are useful in understanding the history of any period, but particularly periods of economic growth or depression. Statistics for the Roosevelt years may easily be found in *Historical Statistics of the United States* published by the Bureau of the Census, U.S. Department of Commerce (1975). Some of the trauma of the depression years may be inferred from the fact that the population of the United States grew by over 17 million between 1920 and 1930, but by only about half of that (8.9 million) between 1930 and 1940.

Historical Statistics gives the figures shown in Table 1 for unemployment, 1929–1940. These figures are, however, only estimates. The federal government did not monitor the number of unemployed during those years. Even so, these figures are shocking, indicating as they do that even after the war had begun in Europe, with the increased orders that it provided for U.S. mines, factories, and farms, unemployment remained at 14.6 percent.

One characteristic of the depression, to which attention was frequently called during the Roosevelt years, was the contrast between its effects on the durable goods and consumer goods industries. Between 1929 and 1933, expenditures on personal durable goods dropped by nearly 50 percent, and in 1938 they were still nearly 25 percent below the 1929 figures. Producers' durable goods suffered even more, falling by nearly two-thirds between 1929 and 1933, and remaining more than 50 percent below the 1929 figure in 1938. At the same time, expenditures on nondurable, or consumer, goods showed much less effect. Between 1929 and 1933 they fell only about 14.5 percent, and by 1938 they exceeded the 1929 level. These figures indicate that the worst effects of the depression,

Table 1
Unemployment, 1929–1940

Year	Unemployment Rate	Number Unemployed (in millions)
1929	3.2	1,550
1930	8.9	4,340
1931	16.3	8,020
1932	24.1	12,060
1933	25.2	12,830
1934	22.0	11,340
1935	20.3	10,610
1936	17.0	9,030
1937	14.3	7,700
1938	19.1	10,390
1939	17.2	9,480
1940	14.6	8,120

Table 2
Balance of Trade, 1929–1940 (millions of dollars)

1929	+686
1930	+514
1931	+186
1932	+729
1933	+358
1934	−742
1935	−1,839
1936	−1,254
1937	−1,400
1938	−1,063
1939	−2,786
1940	−3,403

and resultant unemployment, were being felt in the durable goods industries. Roosevelt's policies, however, served mainly to stimulate the consumer goods industries where the depression and unemployment were far less seriously felt.

One consequence of Roosevelt's policies can be seen in the U.S. balance of trade during the New Deal years. By a variety of devices, Roosevelt drove up the prices of U.S. industrial and agricultural products, making it difficult for these goods to compete in the world market, and opening U.S. markets to cheaper foreign products, as can be seen from Table 2. With the exception of a $41 million deficit in 1888, these were the only deficits in U.S. trade for a century, from the 1870s to the 1970s.

One curious aspect of the statistics of the Roosevelt years can be seen by pairing the figures in Table 3. Thus, while suicides during the Roosevelt years

Table 3
Suicides and Deaths by Accidental Falls, 1929–1940

Year	SUICIDES (number)	DEATHS BY ACCIDENTAL FALLS (rate)
1929	16,045	14.5
1930	18,323	14.7
1931	19,807	14.6
1932	20,646	14.8
1933	19,993	15.1
1934	18,828	18.8
1935	18,214	19.2
1936	18,294	20.8
1937	19,294	20.4
1938	19,802	19.5
1939	18,511	17.5
1940	18,907	17.2

remained about the same as during the Hoover years, the death rate by "accidental falls" increased significantly. In fact, according to *Historical Statistics*, the death rate by "accidental falls" was higher in the period 1934–1938 than at any other time between 1910 and 1970 (the years for which figures are given).

Interestingly, the number of persons arrested grew steadily during the depression years. In 1938 nearly twice as many (554,000) were arrested as in 1932 (278,000), and the number continued to increase until 1941. And, while the number of telephones declined after 1930 and did not regain the 1930 level until 1939, the number of households with radios increased steadily during the depression years. And Americans continued to travel. Even in the lowest year, 1933, 300,000 Americans visited foreign countries (down from 517,000 in 1929), while the number visiting national parks, monuments, and such, steadily increased during the depression—in 1938 nearly five times as many (16,331,000) did so as in 1929 (3,248,000).

Comparisons of the recovery of the United States with that of other nations may be found in the volumes of the League of Nations' *World Economic Survey* for the depression years. Table 4 (from the volume of 1938/39) shows comparisons of unemployment rates. From this it can be seen that in 1929 the United States had the lowest unemployment rate of the countries listed; by 1932 the United States was midway on the list, with seven nations reporting higher unemployment rates and seven reporting lower unemployment. By mid–1938, however, after over five years of the New Deal, only three nations had higher unemployment rates, while twelve had lower unemployment. The United States, then, had lost ground in comparison with the other nations between 1932 and 1938.

The *World Economic Survey* for 1937/38 compared the levels of industrial

Table 4
Percentage of Workers Unemployed, 1929–1938, Selected Years

	1929	1932	1937	1938
World Index	5.4	21.1	10.1	11.4
Australia	11.1	29.0	9.3	8.7
Austria	12.3	26.1	20.4	15.3
Belgium	1.9	23.5	13.1	17.6
Canada	4.2	26.0	12.5	15.1
Czechoslovakia	2.2	13.5	8.8	8.5
Denmark	15.5	31.7	21.9	21.4
France	n/a	n/a	n/a	8.0
Germany	9.3	30.1	4.6	2.1
Japan	4.0	6.8	3.7	3.0
Netherlands	5.9	25.3	26.9	25.0
Norway	15.4	30.8	20.0	22.0
Poland	4.9	11.8	14.6	12.7
Sweden	10.7	22.8	11.6	11.8
Switzerland	3.5	21.3	12.5	13.1
United Kingdom	10.4	22.1	10.5	12.6
United States	1.0	24.9	13.2	19.8

Table 5
Industrial Production in 1937 (1929 = 100)

United States	92.2
Belgium	93.6
Czechoslovakia	96.3
Canada	99.5
Netherlands	90.9
Roumania	131.7
France	82.8
Austria	106.0
Hungary	137.3
Denmark	134.0
United Kingdom	124.0
Japan	170.8
Norway	127.6
Sweden	149.0
Finland	149.2
Chile	131.6
Italy	99.6
Germany	117.2
Poland	85.3
Estonia	138.7
Latvia	155.9
Greece	151.2
U.S.S.R.	424.0

production for 23 nations in 1937, expressed as a percentage of their industrial production in 1929 (see Table 5). It must be remembered that the figures for the United States reflect the level of industrial production reached just before the collapse of the economy later that year. Of the 22 other nations listed, 19 showed a higher rate of recovery in industrial production than the United States, while only 3 lagged behind. One of these, France, had followed policies similar to those of the New Deal in the United States. As the *World Economic Survey* put it, both the Roosevelt administration and the Blum government in France had "adopted far-reaching social and economic policies which combined recovery measures with measures of social reform." It added: "The consequent doubt regarding the prospects of profit and the uneasy relations between business-men and the Government have in the opinion of many, been an important factor in delaying recovery," and the two countries had, "unlike the United Kingdom and Germany," failed to "regain the 1929 level of employment and production." The *World Economic Survey* the following year (1939) pointed out that industrial production in the United States had fallen from the 92.2 in Table 5 to 65 by June 1938, and hovered between 77 and 85 throughout 1939. Thus, by the end of 1938 the U.S. record was even sorrier than revealed by the table.

Chapter 1

Dramatis Personae

THE PRESIDENT

It was very difficult not to like Franklin Delano Roosevelt. By all accounts he could display immense personal charm, and his radio voice, especially, was nearly irresistible. Caricaturist Peggy Bacon described Roosevelt as follows: "Head like a big trunk, battered by travel and covered with labels, mostly indecipherable. . . . Bright, direct look, the frank, clear gaze of craft. Clever as hell but so innocent."[1] Florence Kerr recalled her first meeting with Roosevelt, how he had instantly put her at ease by calling her by her first name and bantering with her.

Seated at the desk he was a handsome man, broad shouldered, big head, strong arms and so on. None of his weakness and fraility was visible. . . . and, of course, a voice which was really Heaven's gift. What a voice! And the only person I know who could read as though he were talking. The Fireside Chats were read. But they sound as though he was just talking to you.[2]

Roosevelt projected a gaiety, an enthusiasm, and a zest for life that was infectious.

One cannot say too much about the appeal of Roosevelt's voice and his skillful use of radio. A New Dealer recalled of the 1932 campaign:

Late one night I turned on my radio, which I didn't listen to very much. Everybody else in the house was in bed, and in the far distance I heard a clear, beautiful voice which attracted my attention. I sat down and waited until the end of the apparently political speech to find out who in the world had such a nice voice. It turned out to be a man named Franklin Delano Roosevelt.[3]

Political columnist Mark Sullivan, a frequent critic of the New Deal, wrote in 1936 of Roosevelt's radio voice: "If the President's addresses were delivered in the Czechoslovakian tongue they would be listened to with pleasure. He could recite the Polish alphabet and it would be accepted as an eloquent plea for disarmament."[4] After the first fireside chat, *Barron's* wrote that Roosevelt had delivered it "with a technique that would have made the best 'announcers' tear their hair in impotent envy. If there be any 'voice' better upon the air than that of the President, it has not yet been heard."[5] *Fortune* wrote that Roosevelt was "by all odds the best actor in talking pictures and the best voice in radio. Until Mr. Roosevelt taught the world how that titanic trombone of tubes and antenna could be played no one had any idea of the possible range of virtuosity."[6] He was, New York mayor Fiorello LaGuardia would observe, a "verbal necker."[7]

The result was that Roosevelt projected what one observer called an "intimate hearthstone psychology," which led the people to develop a sense of personal relationship with their president that was unique in U.S. political history.[8] Roosevelt was not simply the man in the White House, or a politician, but a personality. As the *American Mercury* put it, "the President is liked in much the same way that a popular movie-star is liked; that is, he is liked for reasons which have nothing to do with conduct or character, but only with what is vaguely called 'personal charm.' "[9] A survey of public opinion published in January 1938 found Roosevelt ranked eleventh among radio personalities, just behind Edgar Bergen's wooden dummy Charlie McCarthy and ahead of George Burns' wife and comedic foil Gracie Allen.[10]

The term most often used to describe Roosevelt's temperament by his intimates was "adolescent" or "boyish." His physician described Roosevelt's "sanguine temperament, almost adolescent in its buoyancy," while others found him "as rich in enthusiasm and interest as a boy," or "somewhat like a boy, a freshman in college."[11] Where the terms were not used, the behavior described fit them. Thus, observers noted Roosevelt's delight in springing surprises, in dramatic behavior, his erratic and impulsive nature, and other qualities generally associated with adolescence rather than with the mature mind. Hugh Johnson, who headed the National Recovery Administration under Roosevelt, profiled him as delighting "in surprises—clever, cunning and quick."[12] Recalling his cousin, Theodore Roosevelt, H. L. Mencken found FDR sharing "the common Roosevelt quality of being somewhat theatrical; he is only too often the actor far more than he is a statesman."[13] Mark Sullivan observed of Roosevelt that "if something dramatic, sensational occurs to him, he just can't help doing it."[14] A critic wrote that Roosevelt was "flamboyant, theatrical, striving always to create a startling effect." He added:

When Roosevelt smokes a cigaret it is an act. He waves his arms above his head as though the thing were a conductor's baton. He puffs out his cheeks; throws back his head and blows the smoke toward the ceiling; then laughs and smirks and winks; waves his arms and blows again. One moment he has a cigaret holder and the next his cigaret is held in his fingers. The ashes are constantly being flicked even when there is no ash.[15]

Roosevelt insisted on being at center stage. A critic observed that "Roosevelt uses the pronoun 'I' until his papers and speeches take on the appearance of a picket fence."[16] Conversations with him tended to be interminable monologues by Roosevelt, in which he frequently embellished his experiences and accomplishments.[17] He could not brook competition for the limelight. Perhaps partly for this reason, Roosevelt did not surround himself with a cabinet of distinguished individuals such as one might expect under the circumstances. Instead, his cabinet and other advisers consisted of people who had little standing in the world other than that which they acquired from their association with him. He apparently found it difficult to take advice from men of stature, who were his equals or had exceeded him in their achievements. As Mark Sullivan put it, "toward equals Mr. Roosevelt has perpetually the manner of having a chip on his shoulder."[18] Hugh Johnson said of his former boss that: "He seeks complete subservience. He thrives on adulation and submission."[19]

This Rooseveltian quality was manifested, too, in his deprecation of people of greater accomplishments than his own. Businessmen, for example, who headed giant corporations, were belittled for lack of intelligence.[20] At the same time, Roosevelt delighted in showing off his limited knowledge and in claiming expertise. Columnist Raymond Clapper, who was as friendly to the Roosevelt administration as any newsman in Washington, found many in the capital appalled by Roosevelt's personality, including columnist Joseph Alsop, who was "disgusted at [the] unmitigated gall and excessive ego" of the president.[21] Others complained that Roosevelt was "always trying to show off—[he] reels off details to show his knowledge."[22] Mark Sullivan described a masterful press conference performance in which Roosevelt analyzed a complicated bill for the assembled reporters, but Sullivan added: "And yet there was something a little unassuring about it. I felt that he was enjoying what he was doing as a show; that he was getting pleasure and delight out of proving to the newspaper men how clever he is and how able he is in the field of finance."[23]

While deprecating the intelligence and abilities of others, Roosevelt apparently recognized no limits on his own. Because his maternal grandfather, Warren Delano, had made a fortune in the China trade, Roosevelt claimed expertise concerning that part of the world. He wrote Treasury Secretary Morgenthau in 1934: "Please remember that I have a background of a little over a century in Chinese affairs," and on the basis of his assumed knowledge dictated the continuance of a policy that was disastrous to the Chinese economy.[24] Roosevelt also assumed for himself a vast knowledge of economics, even suggesting to Morgenthau at one point that he should act as an economic consultant to the various nations of the world.[25] This, despite the fact that his economic policies had failed to produce recovery in the United States, and that this nation lagged behind most of the nations of the world in progress toward recovery.

In fact, Roosevelt was particularly weak in his understanding of economics, which made him fair game for many of the crackpot economic theories that surfaced during the depression. Economists as diverse as Guido Jung, the Italian finance minister, and John Maynard Keynes came away from talks with Roosevelt appalled by his lack of knowledge of the subject.[26] His understanding of the workings of business was likewise almost nonexistent. Labor Secretary Frances Perkins noted that "Roosevelt never understood the point of view of the business community, nor could he make out why it didn't like him."[27] These deficiencies would have been unfortunate even in the best of times, but they were particularly lamentable for a nation mired in the depths of depression.

It is difficult, in fact, to imagine that anyone could reach the White House with so scant a grasp of business and economics as Roosevelt possessed. But Roosevelt's background was rather unique. As his critics were fond of pointing out, he had never been obliged to earn a living, and his few attempts at doing so were not marked by success. The Roosevelt family fortune had already been made before Franklin was born, and his efforts to "get on" in the world were more in the nature of a light-hearted hobby than from necessity. One of his law professors at Columbia University recalled that Roosevelt "was no good as a student. He didn't appear to have any aptitude for law, and [exerted] no effort to overcome that handicap by hard work." Moreover, as a lawyer, Roosevelt "didn't bring in any business and he didn't do any business."[28] In common with those he would criticize during his presidency, Roosevelt succumbed to the "get rich quick" fever of the 1920s and participated in several speculative ventures that fell far short of their promoters' extravagant hopes and promises.[29]

Some Roosevelt watchers early came to the conclusion that he could best be understood by reference to his "landed gentry" or "rentier" background. Columnist Walter Lippmann wrote in 1936 that Roosevelt exhibited

the typical prejudices of the landed gentry; a love of the land and sympathy with agriculture—a distrust of new wealth based on enterprise or speculation, and of those whom Jefferson's friends used to call somewhat snobbishly the "paper aristocracy"—a considerable tolerance for old landed property—a feeling not unlike that of the Virginia planters who disliked Hamilton's finance, or even of the English country gentry who disliked the Bank of England—a sympathy for the poor, plenty of courage, an aristocratic disdain of prudence—no great understanding of industry or finance, and a taste for the kind of civilized leisure of country life rather than for the restlessness of the big industrial and financial centers.[30]

It was from this background, then, that the sympathies and prejudices of the president were formed. More so than might be expected in a mature mind, these sympathies and prejudices dictated Roosevelt's attitudes and policies during his presidency.

To these must be added the effect of the New York experience. Most of

Roosevelt's adult life was spent in or near New York City, and most of the advisers with whom he surrounded himself likewise came from the New York City environment. It was New York City, of course, that exhibited most of the worst features of the 1920s and of the early depression years—whether it was the wild speculation in Wall Street or the "sweating" of workers by cutthroat manufacturers. For those whose experience with the business and financial world was limited largely to the excesses of that city, it was all too easy to conclude that what was true of the business morality and conditions in New York was equally true of the rest of the country. As one critic observed:

One reason, and an important one, for the resentment that the New Deal has aroused outside New York is its assumption that all business and all finance in the country are as inhuman and dishonorable as were New York's business and finance in the decade of the "mad chase." The drastic treatment which may be a purge for New York is poison to the rest of the country.[31]

In his political career, and no less in the White House, Roosevelt clearly sought not only to emulate, but to surpass his cousin Theodore's achievements in the presidency.[32] This meant that he must be an active executive seeking an ever larger arena in which to exercise authority. Under such circumstances, the adolescent qualities, the deficiencies, and the prejudices and sympathies of Roosevelt would exert a greater influence on the United States than in the case of, for example, a Calvin Coolidge. His volatile mind and intolerance of criticism and opposition, when combined with his lack of understanding of the economy (and a similar deficiency on the part of his most trusted advisors), led Roosevelt to embrace economic policies that were frequently not only contradictory but even foolish or dangerous, against the advice of businessmen and economists better able to assess their consequences.

Roosevelt had scarcely settled into the White House before the drive for executive power began. Less than two months after Roosevelt's inauguration, columnist Arthur Krock wrote:

A poetic statistician has estimated that, after forty-nine and one-half days in office, Franklin D. Roosevelt possesses, is seeking, and has been offered more absolute power than the sum of the arbitrary authority exercised at various times in history by Generals Washington, Lee, Grant and Sherman, Presidents Jackson, Lincoln and Wilson, and all the Emperors of the Ming dynasty.

The Constitution, Krock concluded, had been "republished on India rubber" so that it could be stretched to meet Roosevelt's desires.[33]

This early grasp for power was widely supported as necessary under the emergency conditions that seemed to prevail in the days immediately following Roosevelt's inauguration. Disgust with Congress for its inability to replace petty partisan bickering with constructive action during the final months of the Hoover presidency led many to feel that the situation cried out for a strong president who would force Congress to act. As a result, there was almost no journalistic criticism of Roosevelt or his legislation in the early weeks of his administration. Mark Sullivan expressed what was probably a widespread view when he wrote that, despite his own misgivings about Roosevelt's policies, it was "too dangerous from the point of view of the country" to oppose them. "Roosevelt," he wrote, "is the only President we have . . . the only symbol through which the country can think and act and feel . . . the only one in whom the people now have faith. And it would be much too dangerous to destroy that faith."[34]

Even when Roosevelt's programs and policies began to attract increasing criticism in late 1933, the president himself remained remarkably free from it. In part, this was because of his popularity, which remained high until well into 1935, and which meant that his advisers bore the brunt of any criticism rather than Roosevelt. As columnist Frank Kent put it early in 1935, "the brain-trust is denounced; the professors indicted; the NRA and AAA ridiculed, and the 'Administration' scored. But the one man who creates, continues and controls all these things is treated by those who disagree with him with a self-conscious tenderness unprecedented in public affairs." No other president having been so immune to criticism, Kent concluded that it was "an interesting problem in public and political psychology."[35]

In large part the contrast stemmed from a widely held belief that Roosevelt was a man of "good intentions" who was occasionally led astray by the bad advice of those around him. While Roosevelt was sometimes faulted for lacking a consistent economic philosophy or program to guide the New Deal, there were only a few in the first years who recognized the extent to which its inspiration derived, instead, from Roosevelt's prejudices and political acumen. Arthur Schlesinger has pointed out that Roosevelt rationalized his presidential role as not dissimilar to that of the quarterback of a football team. According to his view, policies must unfold as conditions develop, in the same way that the plays called by a quarterback depend on what happened as the result of preceding plays.[36] James McGregor Burns has described Roosevelt's leadership in terms of his function as a "broker" between various interest groups.[37] The result, in either case, was a hodgepodge of unrelated, even contradictory and sometimes scatterbrained programs that offered no clues to the future for businessmen, bankers, or investors, and that frequently posed obstacles to business recovery. Labor Secretary Frances Perkins likened Roosevelt to the artist "who begins his picture without a clear idea of what he intends to paint or how it shall be laid out upon the canvas, but begins anyhow, and then, as he paints, his plan evolves out of the material he is painting."[38] While perhaps appropriate for an artist, such a procedure was hardly reassuring to businessmen seeking some predictability and consistency in the actions of their government. As the prominent progressive Amos Pinchot put it, Roosevelt was "worse than an Egyptian flea for no one can guess which way he is going to jump, thus leaving the country in a fog of doubt."[39] Moreover, as one critic observed, Roosevelt painted "pictures that look beautiful from a distance but which will not bear close inspection.''[40]

And then there were the Roosevelt trips. In mid–1937 columnist Franklyn Waltman wrote:

The New York Times last November 15 reported that since he entered the White House Mr. Roosevelt has traveled 82,910 miles by railroad. . . . This is exclusive of five sea cruises, taken solely for pleasure, two long ocean voyages and many thousands of miles by automobile. Since that tabulation was made, the President has added many thousands of miles to this railroad travel record, made a 13,000 mile ocean voyage and another sea cruise to fish. Indeed, there have been periods when Mr. Roosevelt has been so seldom in the White House that some of the newspaper correspondents assigned to him commenced referring to Washington as ''a whistle stop.''[41]

Not only the frequency, but also the timing of Roosevelt's trips came in for criticism. As the economy collapsed late in 1937, Roosevelt responded by taking a fishing trip. The New York *Herald-Tribune* wrote: ''No one begrudges the President his many vacations. . . . But it is most regrettable that he feels it important to go on a nine-day fishing trip at this precise moment of the nation's economic crisis.''[42] A critic noted that if Hoover had done the same thing ''he probably would have been impeached for being absent from his command during battle.''[43] But Roosevelt's absences from Washington were not without their positive side. Congressman Bruce Barton computed that during Roosevelt's 47 trips from Washington over a six-year period, a sampling of stocks had risen an average of 33.3 points, thus realizing for American investors ''a net gain of $11,322,000,000 by having the President away from Washington.''[44]

THE BRAIN TRUST

From the beginning of his campaign for the presidency, Roosevelt was surrounded by a corps of advisers—loosely referred to as the ''brain trust''—that was quite unlike any such group of advisers in the history of the presidency. The first brain trust was assembled in New York City by Judge Samuel Rosenman to assist in the 1932 campaign. It was Rosenman who ''suggested to Roosevelt that we ought to go to the universities for advice rather than to industrialists and/or financiers or politicians.''[45] Rosenman selected the brain trust from the faculty at Columbia University because ''we could include only men living in the city who could come to the many conferences I anticipated on a five-cent subway fare.''[46] With names like Rexford Tugwell, Raymond Moley, and Adolf Berle, they shared an academic knowledge of American life and the workings of the economy unsullied by actual experience outside the walls of academia. St. Louis *Post-Dispatch* columnist Marquis Childs wrote some years later of these early Roosevelt advisers:

In their company you had the heady sense of a rarer, higher altitude. They were as bright and fresh as paint. Writers, economists, artists, sociologists, they were something brand new in government. It was still a little strange to Washington then and I remember being exhilarated and at the same time disturbed after a dinner or a lunch with these pioneers of a brave new world. I felt that somehow they didn't know the Middle West that I knew and the people in the Middle West. The whole process seemed far removed from the deeper currents of American life and no one was working to relate these exciting experiments to main currents. It was happening in Shangri-La, a classic Shangri-La that was growing at a startling rate.[47]

Others found the brain trust possessed ''not so much of a youthful spontaneity, as of a rather precocious juvenility,'' or wondered why, if the brain trusters were so able, were not businesses scrambling for their services?[48]

For a nation mired in depression, Roosevelt's cabinet choices, too, seemed strangely inappropriate. The Chicago *Tribune* surveyed their qualifications in *Who's Who* and found that Roosevelt had ''surrounded himself with men who resemble him in their inexperience of business.'' They were of a type that was likely to fall ''readily for schemes upon which no one of experience would waste five minutes.''[49] The *Magazine of Wall Street* was charitable in describing them as ''men who look forward, instead of backward, to fame.''[50] The two key economic posts in the cabinet—Commerce and Treasury—were given, respectively, to Daniel Roper and William Woodin. Roper was a former commissioner of internal revenue and a Roosevelt floor leader at the convention that nominated him. Woodin was an able industrialist with no banking experience beyond his service as a director of the Federal Reserve Bank in his district. He was, at heart, a musician. Labor Secretary Frances Perkins, and the ''czar'' of relief, Harry Hopkins, were both social workers. Interior Secretary Harold Ickes was an undistinguished Chicago lawyer who had married wealth, while Agriculture Secretary Henry A. Wallace had inherited a farm journal that was being sued for violation of the antitrust laws. They were not a group likely to inspire confidence. H. L. Mencken described them in his inimitable prose:

In the whole outfit at Washington there is scarcely a man who, in secular life, would stand out more conspicuously than a police sergeant. They are all, with a few lonely exceptions, complete nonentities—professional uplifters, third-rate lawyers, chronic job-holders, decayed chautauquans, and the like. The one criterion that seems to have been applied to them is the criterion of *in*competence.''

''No administration in recent history,'' Mencken concluded, ''not even Harding's, has brought together a more forbidding gang of quacks and shysters.''[51]

The lack of business experience on the part of Roosevelt, his cabinet, and his brain trust, did not make for confidence within the business community, particularly when the Roosevelt administration began to gather to itself more and more authority over business, banking, and financial operations. Industrialist Pierre DuPont found it ''astounding that those who cannot pretend to any experience whatever on certain subjects are willing to undertake the complete making over of finance, industry or anything else offered.''[52] A *Magazine of Wall Street* writer added: ''At personal ease and elated with authority and power, they buzz around with equal indifference to the value of money, the principles of economics, the burden of taxation and the mounting problems of business management.''[53] The *Wall Street Journal* found it remarkable that ''men who never before have maneuvered dollars except in single file have been lifted from the economic ranks and invited to direct a charge of drafted billions.''[54] Willard Kiplinger observed that ''repairs of fine watches are entrusted to young apprentices who know how watches OUGHT to run, but don't know how watches ACTUALLY run.'' Roosevelt's advisers, he said, exhibited ''a plain case of psychological drunkenness—too much power, taken too fast, without accompanying doses of responsibility and experience.'' The result: ''arrogance, and conviction by those afflicted that ONLY THEY are honest, long-visioned.''[55] His remarks might have been applied, with equal validity, to the president himself.

Adding to the difficulty was the inability of Roosevelt's advisers to work together as a team. Kiplinger described the conflict among the New Dealers:

They work at cross-purposes. One set pushes one way, another set pushes another direction. Their objectives are different. They don't agree among themselves, and there's no one who dares *make* them work together, or to fire those who don't fit into the general program—whatever the general program is. If the internal affairs of any corporations were as messy as the affairs of the United States Government, the corporations would automatically go busted.[56]

Columnist Frank Kent found them ''the most amazing conglomeration ever gathered together under a government tent.'' There would, he said, ''be confusion'' even ''if they all knew where they were going. But, under an Administration which proceeds simultaneously in all directions and changes its strategy with every plan, the condition is such almost to justify the 'Economic Bedlam' phrase recently used by a friendly critic.''[57] The problem for observers then (and historians since) was to somehow organize the conflicting voices among Roosevelt's advisers into categories that would make the babble understandable.

In the early New Deal there were at least three discernible groups harboring different points of view on economic matters.[58] The first of these, and the shortest lived in terms of influence at the White House, might be described as the monetarists or inflationists. Within the administration their strongest early advocate was Roosevelt's Hyde Park neighbor, Henry Morgenthau, and the gurus of the group were Dr. George Warren, an agricultural economist at Cornell University, and Professor James Harvey Rogers of Yale. Their remedies for the depression were supported by a number of western progressive senators, including Key Pittman and Burton K. Wheeler. Outside the government, they could count on the vociferous assistance of a lobbying group known as The Committee for the Nation, headed by industrialist James Rand, which included a large number of businessmen (principally retailers) and progressives like Amos Pinchot. Their solution to the depression was simple: remove the United States from the constricting gold standard and inflate the money supply by one device or many. The results, they insisted, would all be positive—the reduction of the debt load and the restoration of purchasing power.

A second group of Roosevelt's advisers consisted of disciples of the early twentieth-century progressive philosophy represented by Supreme Court justice Louis Brandeis. Tactically, the group was led by Harvard law professor Felix Frankfurter, and its members were referred to variously as the "legalists," the "atomizers," or "Frankfurter's Red Hots." The group exerted its influence largely through Frankfurter's former law students who were placed at strategic points within the White House and in the various agencies of the New Deal. These included people like Thomas Corcoran, Benjamin Cohen, and James Landis. They derived much of their standing in the New Deal from Frankfurter's influence on Roosevelt, and they were supported in Congress by like-minded progressives like Senators Robert LaFollette and William Borah. The Brandeisians were little interested in economic recovery, preferring to use the depression as an opportunity to make radical transformations in the role of business, banking, and finance in American life. Obsessed with the "curse of bigness," the Brandeisians sought to encourage small business units by penalizing large ones— through taxation, regulation, and the enforcement of antitrust laws. Their radical atavism was nostalgic for an earlier era when Americans had not been dwarfed by giant corporations and other large institutions. While many of the monetarists were economists and derived some support from business and finance, the Brandeisians were almost entirely lawyers, ignorant of the operations of the economy, and they commanded little support from business, even from small business.

The third group possessed a good deal less unity than the first two. In general, this group could be said to accept the existence of large corporate units, and to seek remedies to the problems they posed by government regulation that went beyond telling business what they could *not* do, to telling them what they *must* do. The same applied to agriculture. Within the group there was considerable disagreement, however, over the extent of the role that the federal government should play in directing business and for how long. Conservatives, who were primarily interested in recovery from the depression, visualized the government's role as moderate and temporary. The more radical wing, sometimes referred to as the "collectivists," coalesced around brain truster Rexford Tugwell, Columbia University economics professor. Lacking the unity of the Brandeisians, the policies and programs produced by this third group, sometimes referred to as the "planners," tended to be compromises that reflected such diverse views as those of Raymond Moley, Adolf Berle, General Hugh Johnson, and others, in addition to Tugwell. They were the driving force behind the National Industrial Recovery Act and the Agricultural Adjustment Act. In the early New Deal, the drive toward increased federal regulation of business and agriculture was supported by important elements in both areas—the U.S. Chamber of Commerce and by farm organizations.

Although they possessed more initial influence with Roosevelt than did the Brandeisians, because of their dominance of the early brain trust, the planners were at a disadvantage in competing with the Brandeisians because they lacked the unity and discipline of the latter. The Tugwell group among the planners, however, agreed with the Brandeisians on one fundamental point. As journalists Ernest Lindley and Jay Franklin Carter pointed out, both groups felt "a determination to wrest the major control of [the] American economy from the big financiers."[59] This was oversimplifying the case, but it did indicate that both the Tugwellians and the Brandeisians viewed the depression less as a problem to be solved than as an opportunity to be exploited for radical surgery on U.S. business and finance.

Each of the three groups could lay at least some claim to being fundamentally "conservative." The Brandeisians were, after all, only seeking to restore the competition and individual opportunity that had supposedly existed in a happier time of small business units in the past. The planners were conservative in the sense that they accepted, at least, the trend toward bigness in American life, and rather than "atomize" it sought instead to direct it toward what they regarded as more socially useful goals. Yet of the three it was the monetarists who were the most conservative of all. Although the specter of inflation frightened many businessmen and bankers, the monetarists were seeking a solution to the depression that would require the least alteration of existing economic practices and institutions. Indeed, much of their support derived from businessmen and bankers who, however fearful of inflation, regarded it as preferable to such alternatives as the regimentation of business under the National Industrial Recovery Act (NIRA). Conversely, memories of the German experience with inflation in the 1920s drove some businessmen, who were otherwise chary about government regulation, to support the NIRA as the least objectionable of the alternatives. This must be kept in mind in order to grasp the shallowness of much of the business support behind either the monetarists or the planners.

In the early New Deal it was Rexford Tugwell who emerged as the principal administration "bogey-man" of U.S. businessmen. His appearance on the scene as a prominent brain truster led businessmen, journalists, and other observers to consult his writings in order to learn his views and to find out what advice he might be expected to give Roosevelt. Many were understandably shocked by what they found. Although Tugwell's good looks had won him such nicknames as the "Braintrust Barrymore" and "Mr. America," his writings and speeches gave him a less complimentary description: "Rexford the Red."[60] Other historians of the New Deal have summarized Tugwell's views in very diluted form, but to understand business apprehensions about his presence near Roosevelt it is better to read the professor's words themselves.

In a paper published as a supplement to the *American Economic Review* in

March 1932, for example, Tugwell suggested that the quest for profit no longer motivated business. It did, however, inject "into industry many of those elements of uncertainty which we as economists unanimously deplored." Set aside as surplus reserves, such profits produced "insecurity," because they were "optimistically used for creating overcapacity in every profitable line; they are injected into money market operations in such ways as to contribute to inflation; they are used, most absurdly of all, as investments in the securities of other industries." If profit was no longer a motivation for business and was, in fact, a malign influence, why did Americans "protect and argue for it with a violence and persistence out of all proportion to the gains we may expect?"

Because . . . we are not genuinely interested in security, order, or rationality. . . . Industry is thought of rather as a field for adventure, in which the creation of goods is a minor matter. Who among our millions of Wall Street amateurs hopes merely for dividends on his investment? Or who thinks of the securities he buys and sells as having anything to do with an economic function? The truth is profits persuade us to speculate.

Henry I. Harriman of the U.S. Chamber of Commerce and Gerard Swope of General Electric had already advocated voluntary planning of the nation's economic life. Tugwell wrote:

Strange as it may seem—directly antithetical to the interests of business and unlikely to be allowed freedom of speech, or say nothing of action—it seems altogether likely that we shall set up, and soon, such a consultative body. . . . It seems to me quite possible to argue that, in spite of its innocuous nature, the day on which it comes into existence will be a dangerous one for business; just as the founding day of the League of Nations was a dangerous one for nationalism. There may be a long and lingering death, but it must be regarded as inevitable.

For from such experiments with planning would come "a clear recognition, one that can never be undone, that order and reason are superior to dangerous competition. It will demonstrate these day by day and year by year in the personnel of a civil service devoted to disinterested thinking rather than romantic hopes of individual gain." Business would "logically be required to disappear. This is not an overstatement for the sake of emphasis; it is literally meant."[61]

   In October 1932 Tugwell formulated a six-point program for dealing with the depression, with the emphasis on increasing consumer purchasing power. Tugwell opposed reductions in wages, insisted on reductions in retail prices, favored organized federal relief, "drastic income and inheritance taxes," "avoidance of budgetary deficits and monetary inflation." Since it was admittedly unlikely that businesses could simultaneously maintain wage rates, reduce prices, and still pay increased taxes, Tugwell also advocated "the taking over by the government of any necessary enterprises which refuse to function when their profits are absorbed by taxation." Put another way, the federal government should first make it impossible for private business to function, and should then bring it under some form of national socialism. Referring to his paper in the *American Economic Review*, Tugwell added: "So long as prices, profits and individual production programs are at the disposal of independent business executives, our system will continue to show much the same faults it displays at present." Recovery from the depression, then, was not enough: "We shall not have become very civilized until we have really done something toward the insuring of stability on a higher level, even, than our brief periods of prosperity have provided."[62]

Quite naturally, given his point of view, Tugwell gravitated toward the League for Industrial Democracy, the object of which was "education for a new social order based on production for use and not for profit." Socialist Party leader Norman Thomas was co-executive director of the group, and Tugwell spoke to the League in late January 1932.[63] In April the League asked Tugwell for suggestions on its proposed farm planks. Tugwell's views on agriculture were not as widely known as his well-published observations concerning business, but in his diary for January 23, 1935, Tugwell wrote:

I personally have long been convinced that the outright ownership of farms ought greatly to be restricted. My observation has been that where a farm is held on a long term lease it belongs to the user of the land much more than if he actually owns it because if he owns it there is constant temptation to build up mortgage responsibilities and quite a likelihood that in the first depression of farm prices that comes along he will lose his land. I also feel that for such of the farm population as is represented, for instance, in the South by the negro tenants or even by the poor whites, the bettering of farm practices and the raising of living standards requires some supervision of farm practices.[64]

Thus, if Tugwell's ideas had prevailed in agriculture, farm ownership would have been "greatly restricted," with sizable numbers of American farmers leasing their farmland, presumably from the federal government, which would then also undertake to supervise their farming activities. So much for the "yeoman farmer" so valued by Jefferson.

Fortunately, Tugwell had less influence on Roosevelt's policies than the public thought, but not because Roosevelt was unreceptive to his ideas. Bernerd Baruch recalled: "Roosevelt told me on many occasions, 'You know Rex wants me to do over night what it is going to take years for me to do.' "[65] What the public saw, however, was a highly visible and apparently influential adviser to the president making speeches (Americans "want production which they can use and are not particularly worried whether or not there are profits," January 1935) and publishing articles ("The New Order is . . . a beginning, not an end. . . . If this be Socialism, let our enemies make the most of it!" April 1934), which apparently expressed views in harmony with those of the president.[66] It was enough to paralyze any businessman when he contemplated the future.

In the tug of war with the Brandeisians over Roosevelt, Tugwell felt that the planners were at a distinct disadvantage because of a psychological dimension to the president's relations with Brandeis. Tugwell wrote in a later introduction to his diary: "What I did not know in 1932, and never gave enough weight to when I did know, was that there was one old man in the shadows to whom the awe and reverence of sonship went without reserve. This, of course, was Brandeis. And Frankfurter was his prophet." Tugwell and the other "planners" could not take the views of the radical atavists seriously, since clearly the time had passed when such "horse and buggy" ideas were appropriate. "All of this liberal atomism," Tugwell wrote, "seemed so completely inconsistent with the reality of our high-energy, large-scale economy that we could not take it seriously. That was our mistake. It was to have another run" under Roosevelt.[67] Thus, after what Tugwell regarded as a promising start, at least in potential, with the NIRA and AAA (Agriculture Adjustment Act) the direction of the New Deal shifted away from planning, in large part, Tugwell believed, because of the disapproval voiced by Brandeis.[68]

Brandeis, too, should be allowed to speak for himself in outlining the philosophy that guided his disciples in the New Deal. To a caller in December 1933, Brandeis explained that "the object is to make men free. The Government is to impose limitations in order to achieve that object." As for the details:

First, I would take the Government out of the hands of the bankers. I would do that by opening the postal savings departments to all depositors without limitation of amount. I would establish in the post offices also a checking department, so that the post office could be used for commercial accounts. I should also make the postal department the agency for the issuance of securities. By appropriate federal taxation, I would split up the banking business into its separate parts and prohibit any bank from doing any more than one kind of banking business. . . . This would avoid the evil of great concentration of financial power in the hands of bankers. Secondly, by appropriate federal taxation I would limit the amount of property which any person could acquire or pass down upon death. . . . Thirdly, by appropriate federal excise taxes I would limit the size of corporations. I would do it not only with respect to corporations to be formed in the future, but also for existing corporations.

Brandeis was opposed to federal incorporation of businesses, because "the federal government must not become too big just as corporations should not be permitted to become too big." He continued:

Fourthly, I would establish a system of unemployment compensation similar to that adopted in Wisconsin. The system should be operated by the states but the federal government by appropriate taxation and exemption from taxation should furnish the force which would compel the establishment of such systems.

These were, he said, the main points in his program. When his caller interjected that some of his program seemed to be an attempt to "turn the clock back," Brandeis' response was "immediate and spirited: Why shouldn't we turn the clock back? We just turned the clock back on a 'noble experiment' [prohibition] which was unanimously adopted in the country and was being tried for some time."[69]

Since Frankfurter, even more than Brandeis, furnished the leadership of the radical atavists, he deserves study for the attitude that guided their actions. In an April 1932 letter to columnist Walter Lippmann, Frankfurter wrote:

The general history of the last twenty or twenty-five years is an experience that we ought not to forget. When I first came out of Law School and found myself at once pitched into work with [Henry L.] Stimson on prosecutions for rebates by railroads and big shippers, on the sugar fraud cases, the bank manipulations, and commodity cornerings revealed in the panic of 1907, I was still innocent and assumed that those manifestations were merely the pathology of big business. But in the years that followed I naturally began to wonder to what extent what I had theretofore regarded as aberrations and incidents were really organic. The resistance to, even more than the disclosures of, Brandeis regarding waste and exploitation in railroad management, the relation of the bankers to these abuses, the far-reaching implication of banker control and big business as analyzed by Brandeis in his *Other People's Money* in 1914, the passionate intensity of the opposition to his appointment [to the Supreme Court] in 1916 on the part of finance and big business and their retainers, the accentuation of motives of greed after the War, the subversion of even the most established banking traditions to recklessness and gambling parading under the new devices of pyramiding and affiliates—all this and more took me out of my age of innocence.

What Frankfurter feared, he told Lippmann, was that attention might be so concentrated on the problem of recovery from the depression that "as a result of the depression our social situation will have been worsened, not merely because of the impoverishment of vast numbers of our fellow beings, but even more so because when the tide will have turned, a greater percentage of the wealth of the country will be found to have come into the control of even a smaller percentage of the population than was the case before the depression." He told Lippmann:

And if that be so, those of us who, by temperament or habit or conviction, believe that we do not have to make a sudden and drastic break with the past, but by gradual successive, although large, modifications may slowly evolve out of this profit-mad society, may find all our hopes and strivings indeed reduced to a house of cards.

Thus, reform of the economic system must proceed hand-in-hand with any recovery measures, and the "advice" of business must be distrusted because business and financial leaders lacked "the capacity for disinterested insight."[70]

Frankfurter began his cultivation of Roosevelt during the latter's days as governor of New York through fawning letters that puffed Roosevelt's ego—a favorite Frankfurter device.[71] After Roosevelt's nomination by the Democrats in 1932, the campaign was broadened to take in the brain trusters, particularly Raymond Moley. Although Frankfurter privately expressed contempt of Moley for being a "third rater" who was "unfit for the society of scholars," he set out to develop a close working relationship with the brain truster because of

Moley's closeness to Roosevelt.[72] The planners—Tugwell, Moley, Berle et al.—
constituted the early brain trust and seemed to have all of the advantages. The
NIRA and AAA represented partial achievement of their goals. But Frankfurter
busied himself with planting proteges wherever he could within the burgeoning
bureaucracy of the New Deal, situating them where they could interpret and
administer the statutes that originated with the brain trusters. Moreover, Frankfurter was frequently called upon to assist in the drafting of legislation, for which
purpose he furnished other proteges who could make sure that the wording of
the bills sent to Congress advanced the goals of their group.[73]

In addition, by letters and personal contacts, Frankfurter worked to plant the
Brandeis-Frankfurter attitude and programs in Roosevelt's mind. Thus, in October 1933 Frankfurter wrote Roosevelt of reports he had received of a rising
tide of business opposition to the New Deal, then added:

None of which . . . will be news to you, and all of which and more will, I am sure, only
whet your appetite for the joy of battle [with business], and still more stiffen your purpose.
That the greater body of the nation will rally to your side, as the fight stiffens and the
lines will be drawn, I have not a shadow of doubt.[74]

Thus did Frankfurter work to create a view in Roosevelt's mind that distorted
the issue before the nation from a war on depression to a war against business.
Given Roosevelt's natural prejudices, Frankfurter's efforts found fertile ground,
particularly when the failure of the New Deal led him to search for scapegoats.

As the original brain trusters left the administration, or saw their influence
reduced, the Brandeis-Frankfurter group moved up to greater influence. Washington journalists Joseph Alsop and Robert Kintner wrote in their book, *Men
Around the President* (1939), that Frankfurter's disciples "worked harder, and
stayed longer, and went farther, and stuck together better than the others." They
were continually at odds with others in the administration, "but they do not fall
out among themselves." As a result, they gradually replaced the early brain
trusters as Roosevelt's most intimate advisers.[75] As Tugwell described it later,
if Roosevelt

wanted to ask—or even if he did not want to ask—it was made known to him what the
Brandeis judgment was about everything he intended to do or be. The influence was all
around him, giving comfort and certainty as well as daily advice. The comfort came from
remote Olympus as a kind of emanation which could turn baleful if the god was displeased.
. . . The time came when everyone else, even those who had been loyal and sacrificing,
could be ruthlessly excluded. I was one of those.[76]

Of course, Tugwell's difficulties were in considerable part of his own making,
but in the struggle of ideas the omnipresence of the Brandeisian influence was
doubtless critical.

Frankfurter spent the winter of 1933–1934 in England where he encouraged
John Maynard Keynes to turn his analytical skills to the U.S. depression and

Roosevelt's policies. Thereafter the Brandeis-Frankfurter group supported the deficit spending that Keynes advocated, but without yielding to Keynes' insistence on priority for recovery over reform. In August 1934 Frankfurter counseled Roosevelt in five hours of discussions at the White House. Although he recommended a bold spending program, Frankfurter counseled a continued war against big business. According to historian Michael Parrish, in one fundamental sense, he [Frankfurter] agreed with Tugwell and the radicals: the New Deal, he told the president, faced an "irrepressible conflict" with big business that would have to be faced sooner or later. The president did not need to declare war verbally, Frankfurter added, but he should "recognize that there is war and act on that assumption." Roosevelt agreed with the Frankfurter view of the "irrepressible conflict," but was chary of deficit spending on the scale that Keynes had recommended.[77]

Frankfurter could not spend enough of his time in Washington, nor could Brandeis meet with Roosevelt often. It remained for the Brandeis-Frankfurter group to plant one of their most trusted members at the hand of the president. In March 1935 Frankfurter addressed another in his series of ego-puffing letters to Roosevelt. Frankfurter was, he told Roosevelt, "outraged" at the conditions under which the president was forced to work in the White House, denied even "a fraction of the facilities available at 10 Downing Street," forced to read "fat reports" submitted to him "without any precis, without any intellectual traffic directions. Equally intolerable is it that you should not have at your disposal the kind of preliminary sifting of legislative proposals and bills that you had when you were Governor of New York." Frankfurter knew of Roosevelt's "generosity," of his "readiness to carry the burdens of all sorts of people," of his "incredible resources of strength and spirit," but the president of the United States "ought not to be made to do the work of understudies." Roosevelt needed an assistant possessed of "an unusual combination of qualities," all of which, happily, Frankfurter's disciple Thomas Corcoran possessed. And then the infusion of rarified atmosphere: "Against the judgment of all the wise ones, I sent [Corcoran] as secretary of [Oliver Wendell] Holmes, and Brandeis is my authority for saying that of all his secretaries Tom was dearest to Holmes."[78] Within a week Corcoran was installed at the president's hand, sifting, sorting, interpreting, providing Roosevelt with the right "intellectual traffic signals."[79] For the remainder of the New Deal years, the Brandeis-Frankfurter group would exert the greatest influence in the White House.

THE CABINET

Of the others around Roosevelt little need be said. Harry Hopkins, relief administrator and later Commerce secretary, moved among the combatants with a minimum of discord. Concerned primarily with relieving the destitute and with little interest in the questions that divided the ideological rivals, Hopkins shared their antipathy for business until he faced the responsibilities of Commerce secretary. Eventually, Hopkins would war with the Brandeis-Frankfurter group and supplant Corcoran in the White House inner circle, but not until the New Deal had ended and war clouds had gathered over the horizon.[80] The cabinet exerted little influence over Roosevelt's policies, with the exception of Treasury Secretary Henry Morgenthau, whose growing conservatism brought him into opposition with the Brandeisians, too, by 1938. Commerce Secretary Daniel Roper was ignored and an object of derision in the White House. Postmaster General James Farley carried out the president's orders and busied himself with political matters. Agriculture Secretary Henry A. Wallace presided over one of the principal battlegrounds in the early New Deal years—the AAA—and managed to grow in stature during the New Deal years, eventually gaining the vice presidency in 1941. Secretary of State Cordell Hull saw his own agenda for recovery—increased foreign trade—undercut by Roosevelt's insistence on nationalistic monetary and economic policies, and found himself the object of ridicule by the Brandeis-Frankfurter group. Labor Secretary Frances Perkins was a social worker who would have been woefully out of place in any cabinet but Roosevelt's. Attorney General Homer Cummings was at his best in providing bad advice—the worst being his plan for packing the Supreme Court in 1937. As for Interior Secretary Harold Ickes, he was, as the New York *Times* described him, "the Fat Boy of the Administration who wants always to make your flesh creep."[81] Scrupulously honest and close to the Brandeis-Frankfurter group, Ickes exhibited the loyalty and jealousy of one who had nowhere else to go. And, finally, there was Jesse Jones, head of the Reconstruction Finance Corporation, pink-cheeked, soft-voiced, and as near to a conservative as anybody in Roosevelt's administration, who contributed a quote that summed up the degree of expertise of most of Roosevelt's advisers: "The brain trust thinks you can populate the country by masturbation."[82]

CHAPTER 2

New Faces and New Fears

THE ELECTION

When voters went to the polls in November 1932, the dominant issue was the depression that had dogged the nation for three bleak and bitter years. Economic indices had fallen relentlessly downward until the summer of 1932, while indices of unemployment and human misery had climbed steadily upward. The ability of state and local governments and of private agencies to care for the indigent had been strained to the breaking point and often beyond. Nothing that President Herbert Hoover or Congress did seemed to bring any improvement. The mood was somber. Clearly it was time for a change.

There seemed only minor differences between the candidates except for their personalities. In that respect it was an uneven contest. Roosevelt would have been a formidable opponent for Hoover in the best of times. The New York governor exuded confidence, good humor, and possessed an enticing radio voice—qualities that would not be found in another presidential candidate in such abundance until John F. Kennedy nearly three decades later. If the voters took the trouble to look for issues that separated the two candidates, they found few. In some ways Roosevelt's campaign seemed the more conservative of the two, tied as it was to a Democratic platform that promised sound money and economy in government. Roosevelt lambasted Hoover for his spending and unbalanced budgets, and criticized his "trickle down" recovery policies. Everywhere the placards made it clear that there was a third item on the Democratic ballot: "Roosevelt, Garner, and Beer!"

All over the world the depression touched bottom in the summer of 1932, and a gradual recovery began. It happened in the United States no less than elsewhere, when the Federal Reserve Board's index of industrial production fell to 58 percent of the 1923–1925 average in July, then began to rise. By September it had climbed to 66 percent. Factory employment also rose, although at a slower rate than production.[1] Business journals reflected a more optimistic attitude and so did the letters and comments of businessmen themselves.[2] As one economist noted later,

it became evident in July of 1932 that a sweeping change was taking place in the prevailing attitude of mind of the people of this country. Gloom and doubt and apprehension were being displaced by hope and by feelings akin to confidence. These alterations in mental attitude accompanied changes in the prices of goods and securities. The wholesale quotations of commodities, and especially those of farm and food products, advanced strongly. Bond prices steadily strengthened, and so consistently that on every trading in July the number of bond quotations that advanced on the New York Stock Exchange exceeded those that declined. Between the Fourth of July and Labor Day in early September the average prices of industrial stocks doubled, those of railroads increased by 200 percent, and the average prices of high-grade bonds increased by about 30 per cent. In the second half of the year industrial production increased by nearly 10 per cent and bank credit showed the first sustained expansion of the long depression.

The advance in industrial production between August and September 1932 was, he noted, "the greatest percentage improvement from one month to the next that had ever occurred in the history of American business."[3]

What happened to abort this promising recovery in the United States that left it wallowing in depression while the rest of the world proceeded with its gradual recovery? On September 12, 1932, Maine held its state elections and the results seemed to augur a Democratic sweep of the nation in November. Referring to the Maine result, a businessman wrote: "Since that time, the stocks listed on the New York Stock Exchange have lost substantially one-half of all the advances which they made during the upward movement beginning in July." If the Democrats won in November, he feared "a long period of depression."[4] A week before the presidential election a newspaper publisher who supported Roosevelt opined that it was "very sure" he would be elected, but he added:

Already we have a business uneasiness which reflects the inability to accommodate itself to the idea of anything other than a Republican high tariff administration. I am afraid that this state of mind is going to continue for some six months at least after the election, and that, while we will have no new money panic, we will have a continuation of the present hopelessly reduced volumes of business. That will be very, very hard.[5]

A few days after the election an industrialist observed, in a letter: "Since the election I have somewhat lost my enthusiasm for added sales effort; for it seems to me that the return of prosperity cannot help but be delayed by the coming of a Democratic administration."[6]

From the foregoing it would seem futile to deny, as those around Roosevelt did, that recovery had begun in the summer of 1932, and that the prospect and then the reality of Roosevelt's election aborted it. Adrift in a sea of uncertainty after the election, businessmen, investors, bankers, and others awaited the policies of the new president and Congress. The downward march of the economic indices continued and quickened with the convening of the lame duck Congress in December, particularly as a result of the apparent loss of any control by Hoover over Congress, and the confusion, chaos, and paralysis in that body.[7] By early February the nation's banks had begun to falter as a result of panic withdrawals and currency and gold hoarding by depositors.

THE BANKING CRISIS

That Americans were seized with panic in February and early March 1933 cannot be doubted. The question is: What were they afraid of? As the Federal Reserve Board (FRB) described the panic, currency demand increased in every Federal Reserve district after a banking holiday was declared in Michigan on February 14, and the demand increased as similar holidays had to be declared in Maryland and other states later in the month. According to the FRB: ''Between February 15 and March 4 these demands amounted altogether to $1,630,000,000, including demands for gold coin and gold certificates of $300,000,000. Three fourths of these demands occurred during the week beginning February 27, and more than half was concentrated in the first 3 days of March.''[8] The fourth day of March was the date of Roosevelt's inauguration as President of the United States.

What happened, then, was a run on the banks of 17 days' duration, during which three-fourths of the withdrawals occurred within the five days before Roosevelt's inauguration, and over half just in the final three days before he entered the White House. That the frenzy of withdrawals and gold hoarding increased as Roosevelt's presidency approached can hardly be ignored.

Over three years of depression had produced no panic comparable to the one that accompanied Roosevelt's inauguration. Why then did it occur at precisely that time? The banks were certainly in no weaker condition than they had been a year earlier, but even the strongest and most liquid of banks would have found difficulty in standing up to the assault by depositors that took place in the week before Roosevelt's inauguration. Other factors have been cited: the publicity given by the House of Representatives (under the vice-president-elect, Speaker John Nance Garner) to loans to banks by the Reconstruction Finance Corporation, and the sensational exposures of bank malpractices by a Senate committee that, under the leadership of Ferdinand Pecora, had wandered far afield from its mandate simply to investigate the New York Stock Exchange. These influences supposedly contributed to erosion of confidence in the banks.[9]

The charge that most disturbed the New Dealers, however, and of which friendly historians have ever since sought to acquit Roosevelt, was the accusation that the panic was largely stimulated by fears of inflationary policies by the incoming administration. This was the interpretation that Hoover put on the banking crisis, and it was echoed by many others. Certainly, Roosevelt and his advisers had, by their words and by the type of people with whom they took visible counsel, given ample grounds for such fears. During January rumors circulated that Roosevelt intended to devalue the dollar. He held numerous conferences with those who favored tinkering with the value of the currency. On January 31, Henry A. Wallace, an intimate of Roosevelt who would soon be tapped as Agriculture secretary, publicly advocated "going off the gold standard a little farther than England has." Roosevelt refused to disavow any of these rumors, thus further stimulating fear of inflation. The fears of inflation also extended to concern over the obvious inflationist sentiment in Congress, and to Roosevelt's ability to control Congress even if he did not, himself, favor inflation.[10] In sum, it was a potent combination that wrenched confidence as February began.

Historians friendly to the New Deal have suggested that because only $300 million of the $1.6 billion withdrawn from the banks during the panic was taken in gold, the "fear of inflation was not as important in creating runs on banks as fear that the banks were unsound."[11] Such an argument assumes that if the withdrawals were triggered by fears of the future value of the dollar, a higher percentage of withdrawals would have been taken in gold—supposedly inflation-proof. It ignores, however, the fact that there were, and are, other hedges against inflation besides gold (which, under the New Deal, turned out not to be a hedge at all). During the winter of 1932–1933 businessmen and others were obviously seeking methods to protect themselves against inflation by converting money into goods and property. The *Magazine of Wall Street*, responding to numerous requests for advice on what methods to follow, recommended in its February 18 issue the acquisition of "lasting" property—real estate, durable household goods, personal possessions, or stocks.[12] Only inflationary concerns can account for the fact that even in the midst of the bank panic and the downturn in most economic indices that accompanied it, both stock purchases and stock prices were showing gains. It is indicative, also, of inflationary concerns that there was a marked rise in the purchase of diamonds—another historic hedge against inflation—in the days just preceding Roosevelt's inauguration.[13]

For Roosevelt and his followers, the panic of February and early March represented the final, ignominious collapse of the "old order," and historians friendly to the New Deal have echoed their interpretation. A recent study observes: "The spectacle of commercial America with all its banks shut down symbolized the demonstrated failure of the old order not only to restore the nation's business prosperity but even to preserve its own vital institutions."[14] In fairness, however, an alternate theory must be considered: that lack of confidence in the future value of the dollar under Roosevelt was an important, perhaps the primary, cause of the panic that accompanied the approach of his inauguration. George Harrison, governor of the Federal Reserve Bank of New

York, for example, described the panic in late February: "This represents something more than a hoarding of currency, which reflects a distrust of banks. It represents in itself a distrust of the currency and is inspired by talk of the devaluation of the dollar and inflation. . . . The only way to stop it . . . is to revive the conviction that the currency was not going to be inflated or devalued."[15] James Warburg, financial adviser in the early New Deal, observed later that Roosevelt's order prohibiting banks from paying out gold without special permission was "dictated by necessity, because distrust of the currency had gone so far that the minute the banks would be allowed to open, people would again begin to withdraw gold."[16]

For those, like President Hoover, who were convinced that the assault on the banks was largely owing to distrust of the future value of the dollar, the solution to the panic seemed obvious: Roosevelt should give the panicky public assurances that he did not intend to abandon the gold standard or tinker with the value of the dollar. For whatever reasons, Roosevelt refused, and the panic rushed on to its tragic climax. It is true, as many historians have pointed out, that to have made such a pledge would have required that Roosevelt rule out many of the policies and programs that would later form the New Deal. It is equally true, however, that in asking Roosevelt to make such a promise Hoover was asking nothing of Roosevelt that the president-elect was not already pledged to do by the Democratic platform on which he had been elected and by campaign speeches.

New Dealers would insist that conditions had so changed between election day and inauguration day that such earlier pledges were obsolete. Banking authority H. Parker Willis found such reasoning "untenable," however, observing:

The changes said to have occurred during the months in question were deteriorations of public confidence, fear for the future, and general inability to get anything done. If such fears existed they must have been equivalent to fears that the incoming administration would not live up to its pledges or would adopt a policy that was new, or different from what had been expected.

So far as there was foundation for such fears the deterioration that occurred must be ascribed to the incoming administration itself. It would, indeed, be strange sophistry if we were to find an excuse for the violation of pledges in the fact that a man or party had itself deliberately made the fulfillment of these pledges impossible.[17]

A New York University economics professor later opined: "Had the incoming Administration cooperated properly, and had fears of its monetary policies not been allowed to spread, it would seem that the closing of the banks could have been avoided."[18] But, according to Rexford Tugwell, when Roosevelt was approached late in February to cooperate in alleviating the banking situation, "he took it all smiling and could see no reason why he should save these bankers."[19] That it was the millions of depositors in the banks whose deposits needed to be saved seems not to have occurred to Roosevelt.

The banking crisis that coincided with Roosevelt's inauguration can be viewed then, with considerable justification, as a further expression of lack of confidence in the New Deal that would come to power on March 4, rather than a symptom of the final failure of the "old order." It can also be viewed as an early indication of Roosevelt's inability to see beyond the range of his own prejudices, beyond the "interests" that he sought to punish and to the people who would suffer as a result. The bank panic, therefore, would seem to be much more revealing of the future than of the past. It was, moreover, an artificial occurrence, one that almost certainly would not have occurred but for the imminent change of administration in Washington.

It is important to understand the causes of the bank panic, because without such an understanding it is easy to be misled about subsequent developments under the Roosevelt administration. In the early months of the Roosevelt presidency, after the closing and reopening of the banks, there was a marked upturn in many economic indices. From this it is easy to assume that there was a revival of confidence in business and financial circles under the new administration. In fact, however, at least part of the improvement appears to have been only a continuation of the panic in other forms. The *Annalist* observed, late in April 1933, that the

basis on which the present advance rests is largely speculative. In part, indeed, it represents nothing more than a continuation of the recent hoarding movement. Hoarding can take many different forms, depending upon individual opinion as to what at any given moment constitutes the safest form in which to store wealth. . . . Now that the private holding of gold has been prohibited, and paper money has been allowed to depreciate, people have bought silver, wheat, rubber and a considerable variety of other tangible goods merely because commodities are at the moment considered safer stores of value than either bank deposits or paper money.[20]

Manufacturers strove to acquire raw materials before inflation drove the prices up any higher, and wholesalers and retailers bought in anticipation of the same prospect. *American Salesman* wrote:

How this works out is seen in a report from a flour salesman traveling in east Texas. For some time he had been lucky to sell three to five cars of flour weekly. One week in March he sold thirteen cars of flour, simply because merchants wanted to protect themselves against price advances thought sure to result from whatever inflation program this country eventually decides to try.[21]

THE NEW DEAL BEGINS

In the midst of the banking crisis, Franklin Delano Roosevelt was inaugurated as president. The policies and the legislation of the New Deal would not begin for days or weeks, but the attitude that was to guide the administration was expressed in Roosevelt's inaugural speech. In it he told the American people:

Plenty is at our doorstep, but a generous use of it languishes in the very sight of the supply. Primarily this is because rulers of the exchange of mankind's goods have failed through their own stubbornness and their own incompetence, have admitted their failure, and have abdicated. Practices of the unscrupulous money changers stand indicted in the court of public opinion, rejected by the hearts and minds of men.

True, they have tried, but their efforts have been cast in the pattern of an outworn tradition. Faced by failure of credit they have proposed only the lending of more money. Stripped of the lure of profit by which to induce our people to follow their false leadership, they have resorted to exhortations, pleading tearfully for restored confidence. They know only the rules of a generation of self-seekers. They have no vision, and where there is no vision the people perish.

The money changers have fled from their high seats in the temple of our civilization. We may now restore that temple to the ancient truths. The measure of the restoration lies in the extent to which we apply social values more noble than mere monetary profit.

Happiness lies not in the mere possession of money; it lies in the joy of achievement, in the thrill of creative effort. The joy and moral stimulation of work no longer must be forgotten in the mad chase of evanescent profits.[22]

Here was a remarkable speech for a new President of the United States to make—remarkable both in its attempt to pit class against class, rather than appeal for unity, and for its frank attack upon the basis of the American free enterprise system, the pursuit of profit. Yet these aspects of the speech attracted little adverse comment, perhaps because the day was dominated by the banking crisis and by the actions that Roosevelt quickly took to extend the bank closings and then gradually to reopen those banks judged solvent. But here was preached, at the very outset of the New Deal, the attitude that would dominate the words and actions of the Roosevelt administration for over seven years—until the gravity of the world crisis would cause Roosevelt finally and gradually to abandon his crusade. It was an attitude of bitterness, even of open hostility, toward American business and finance, and against the mainspring of the economic system in which they operated.

Historians have given more prominence to Roosevelt's attacks on business in his 1936 campaign speeches, excusing them as a natural reaction by the president to the growing opposition to the New Deal on the part of business and finance, which they date from 1935. Yet, as Washington journalist and Roosevelt biographer Ernest Lindley later observed, there was no essential difference between the mood of the 1933 inaugural speech and that of the 1936 speeches.[23] The state of war between the New Deal and business did not begin in 1935 or 1936, but dated from March 4, 1933, and the opening shot in that war was issued by the new occupant of the White House.

Despite the inflammatory rhetoric of the inaugural speech, however, the Roosevelt administration began in a "honeymoon" atmosphere. Although many businessmen and investors feared the prospect of inflation and were seeking hedges against it, a review of most banking and business periodicals in the month following the inauguration indicates that most of them found hopeful signs in a part of the inaugural speech that put a priority on finding jobs for the millions who were unemployed. Yet, if they read the speech carefully, they found no prescription for the business recovery that was required to provide the needed jobs; indeed, there was in the speech no explicit recognition of the necessity for business recovery at all.

Nevertheless, the frantic pace of legislation in the Hundred Days that followed the inauguration, almost all of it hailed as recovery measures, seemed to leave little doubt that the new president was determined to break the back of the depression and quickly. This was especially true during the first weeks, since the initial legislation of the New Deal was precisely of the nature that attracted the plaudits of business and finance. After extending the bank holiday and calling Congress into special session, Roosevelt rushed past the dazed legislators an emergency banking bill and an economy bill. The former gave the president control over gold movements, made "hoarding" of the metal illegal, and empowered him to open solvent banks while reorganizing the rest; the latter gave Roosevelt authority to slash $500 million from federal expenditures on veterans' payments and federal salaries, thus redeeming a part of the Democratic platform while also seeming to signal business that the long-sought economies in government spending were at last at hand. A few days later yet another platform pledge was redeemed when Roosevelt signed into law legislation permitting the sale of beer and wine.

A nation that had almost abandoned hope that its legislators were capable of anything but quarreling and temporizing was invigorated by Roosevelt's ability to lash both houses of Congress into rapid action. The applause for his early leadership was well-nigh universal, and it is doubtful whether even in time of war a president has commanded the unanimity of support that was Roosevelt's in the first week of his presidency. If he had adjourned Congress at this point, as was his original intention, and waited to observe the effects these first initiatives would have on the economy, the course of recovery during the next seven years might have been happier. Encouraged by the docility of Congress, however, Roosevelt chose to press on with additional legislation produced by his brain trust.

The economy bill had already prompted Arthur Krock to warn in the New York *Times* that Roosevelt now had "more arbitrary authority than any American statesman has had since the Constitution was framed," and that no other head of a democratic nation had "even a goodly percentage of this authority."[24] The introduction of the Agricultural Adjustment Act (AAA) in Congress caused a perceptible growth of concern regarding the "dictatorial" powers sought by the Roosevelt administration. The Washington *Post*, until now friendly toward the administration, warned that passage of the bill would bring farming "completely under the Federal Government," and would "produce the most far-reaching social and economic revolution that the country has ever experienced."[25] The AAA sought to restrict agricultural production (thereby raising prices of agricultural products) by rewarding farmers who agreed to reduce their acreage in certain basic crops with government payments derived from taxes paid by processors of agricultural products. On the reasonable assumption that these processing taxes would be passed on to consumers, they amounted to the equivalent of a sales tax on food and clothing (since one of the basic crops was cotton).

The consumers thus faced the prospect of finding their pocketbooks pinched in two ways: by the increased price they must pay due to lessened supply, and by the addition to the price caused by the processing tax. Less emphasized by most historians, however, is the fact that the AAA was more than simply a device for relieving farmers. Of particular concern for those interested in business recovery was the intrusion under the AAA of the federal government's hand into industries processing agricultural products. As one critic wrote, it put "at the personal discretion of the Secretary of Agriculture the very existence of many industries, their employees and their invested capital."[26] The AAA, then, represented an extension of government control over business orchestrated by some, like Tugwell, who represented the antibusiness viewpoint within the administration. The AAA would, in fact, soon become a battleground between those primarily interested in relief for the farmers and those who represented the Tugwellian emphasis on controlling the processing industries. The final bill also included the Thomas amendment, which authorized the president, at his discretion, to utilize any or all of a variety of devices to inflate the nation's currency, from the use of printing press money to devaluation of the dollar.

When the AAA was signed into law, with the Thomas amendment attached, it injected a new cloud of uncertainty into an already muddled business outlook. Many felt that it would have been better for Congress to legislate a specific plan for inflation than to give Roosevelt such broad, discretionary powers, for the latter only created further uncertainty. The Baltimore *Sun* warned: "It is doubtful that ever in any Constitutional government was such power given to one man to manipulate and even to destroy private property in the name of the common weal." It wondered "how much healthy, permanent business will be done if a man must plant his own or borrowed dollars today in the full knowledge that . . . Mr. Roosevelt, by a stroke of his pen, can cut in half the value of the dollars that he will collect three months hence or six months hence?"[27] The old Wall Streeter, Bernard Baruch, agreed that few people would risk dollars that the government had the power to devalue. "Business moves on faith in promises," he noted, "and money itself is a promise."[28]

Roosevelt also obtained from Congress legislation that authorized $500 million in direct federal grants to the states for relief—the same sum he had earlier sliced from government spending under the economy act—and the establishment of the Civilian Conservation Corps. On March 29 he asked Congress to pass legislation to regulate the sale of new security offerings in order to protect investors. As March turned into April, Roosevelt's popularity remained high and there was as yet little dissent from the New Deal program. In April, Roosevelt moved to save farms and homes from foreclosure through the Emergency Farm Mortgage Act (passed in May) and the Home Owners Loan Corporation (passed in June).

Both items found wide support and met little opposition, despite the intrusion of the federal government into mortgage financing, an activity heretofore regarded exclusively as the province of private enterprise.

Other legislation introduced during the Hundred Days was, however, more controversial. On April 10, Roosevelt asked Congress for the establishment of a Tennessee Valley Authority (TVA) to end "the continued idleness of a great national investment in the Tennessee Valley"—the Muscle Shoals development, which dated back to World War I.[29] The program was a logical extension of Roosevelt's bias in favor of public-owned electric power while governor of New York, and it also solidified the support for the New Deal of Senator George W. Norris, of Nebraska, who had long advocated the use of the facilities there for the generation by the government of cheap electrical power. Predictably, however, the entry of the federal government into competition with investor-owned utilities was not welcomed by business. In retrospect it can be seen that the call for the TVA was but the opening gun in what was to be a prolonged war by Roosevelt upon the investor-owned utilities of the nation.

Far more disturbing for businessmen, however, was the reappearance in Congress of a bill that did not bear the New Deal imprint. This was the so-called Thirty Hour Bill of Senator Hugo Black of Alabama. Black's bill represented an attempt to force plants producing goods for interstate commerce to spread the available work among a larger number of employees, thus relieving unemployment, by setting the maximum work week at 30 hours. While "work-sharing" of this type had already found some acceptance in industry during the depression, there was a vast difference between its voluntary adoption on a limited scale by industries that found it appropriate, and the type of mandatory "straitjacket" into which Black's bill would force all large industries and many smaller ones. Critics charged that the Black bill was not a recovery device, but would instead "give business such a shock as to endanger recovery."[30] When Labor Secretary Frances Perkins suggested amendments to the bill, businessmen assumed that the amendments had the support of the president. They were appalled to find that the proposed changes went even "far beyond the Black bill" to the point where they would establish "federal control over industry, lodging dictatorial powers as to wages and hours and production in the Secretary of Labor," thus making her every bit the dictator over industry that the Agriculture secretary had become over farming.[31] Others, however, refused to believe that such "a product of hysteria" and "wild dream" was really a serious New Deal proposal, and concluded that it had been floated, instead, "as a warning to industry with a view to encouraging voluntary adoption of shorter hours, equitable wages and stable production."[32]

Scarcely had Perkins' bombshell exploded among jittery businessmen than Roosevelt dropped one of his own. By an executive order of April 20, embargoing the export of gold and gold certificates, the president effectively removed the United States from the hitherto sacred gold standard. While opinion was divided over Roosevelt's action, there was a surprising degree of support for it—the

Washington *Post*, for example, applauding the president's "refusal to allow Europe to drain away the American gold supply."[33] Some, however, warned that the short-term appearance of economic improvement, fueled by inflationary speculation, might work to the detriment of genuine recovery over the long term. Indeed, it almost seemed as if, having given the economy one inflationary "fix" to stimulate a speculative revival in the form of the *threat* of inflation, Roosevelt now found it necessary to administer a "fix" of the real thing in order to keep it going.[34]

Confronted not only with inflation, but also with the antibusiness provisions of the AAA and the specter of the Black-Perkins proposal, businessmen could not but regard the prospects of genuine business recovery with increasing pessimism. Given their concern over the Black-Perkins proposal, businessmen were ready to clutch at almost any alternative. On May 4, Roosevelt spoke before a friendly convention of the U.S. Chamber of Commerce and reported that his administration was seeking to "increase the volume of trade, to give employment to the unemployed and to effect a broad elevation of commodity prices." He called upon the assembled employers to increase their wage scales to keep pace with the rise in commodity prices, and to cooperate in eliminating unfair methods of competition and cutthroat pricing. Although Roosevelt did not mention it in his speech, the chamber's president, Henry I. Harriman, was working actively with the administration in putting together the New Deal's industrial bill.[35]

That bill, the National Industrial Recovery Act, was submitted to Congress on May 17, when Roosevelt asked the legislators to provide machinery that would make possible "a great cooperative movement throughout all industry in order to obtain wide reemployment, to shorten the working week, to pay a decent wage for the shorter week, and to prevent unfair competition and disastrous overproduction." The president's message also asked for an appropriation of $3.3 billion "to start a large program of direct employment" through public works. That amount would be added to the national debt.[36]

When business leaders later moved into open and bitter opposition to Roosevelt and the New Deal it became a favorite theme of the president that those same businessmen had rushed to him begging for assistance during the early months of his administration, but once "saved" they had turned on their benefactor. Yet a perusal of business periodicals and of the correspondence of businessmen reveals a business attitude considerably at variance with this Rooseveltian interpretation of events. It is true that businessmen were greatly disturbed during the first months of the New Deal (and even before), but their principal concerns were those created by the administration and by Congress. Except for the inflationists among businessmen, who viewed inflation as a preferred alternative to regimentation, most businessmen were unsettled by the prospect of inflation. At the same time, inflationists and antiinflationists alike among businessmen were disturbed by the Black-Perkins proposal. If businessmen consented to the NIRA, and in some cases welcomed it enthusiastically, they did so in large part because they regarded it as the least objectionable of the alternatives. On the surface, at least, the NIRA seemed to offer the prospect of industrial self-government, as an alternative to the rigid governmental control contemplated in the Black-Perkins proposal, and thus appeared to embody the type of program that had been sought even during the Hoover years by such industrial leaders as General Electric's Gerard Swope. The support of Swope and of Henry I. Harriman also tended to soothe concerns and win acquiescence or approval.[37]

Even such conditional acceptance of the NIRA was, however, far from unanimous. While Harriman's position at the head of the Chamber of Commerce enabled him to rally that organization behind the NIRA, the other major industrial group, the National Association of Manufacturers (NAM), opposed its passage by Congress, arguing even now that it would "tend to retard rather than promote business recovery. It will in fact nip in the bud the business recovery already manifesting itself. It will hurt rather than help." The NAM dismissed as "illusory and ill-founded" the "assertion widely disseminated that this legislation primarily gives to business and industry the power and authority to regulate itself." On the contrary, it found that "anything may be ordered or may be forbidden by Presidential edict."[38] In short, the idea that it represented industrial self-government was a sham. The Washington *Post* also penetrated the facade of "industrial self-regulation" and found that Roosevelt was empowered to impose codes on those industries that refused voluntarily to enter into them, could punish those who failed to comply with the codes, and could arbitrarily prescribe maximum hours of labor and minimum wages as well as other working conditions. This, it pointed out, was "a prerogative very different from the power [simply] of approving agreements voluntarily entered into by industrial groups." The NIRA, it concluded, might very well "kill enterprise and create more unemployment than now exists."[39] The attitude of many businessmen was probably summed up by the *Commercial and Financial Chronicle* when it looked past the enactment of the NIRA into law to the day when its legality would be tested in the courts.[40]

It appears that those few businessmen who genuinely supported the NIRA saw in it only what they wished to see. Conditioned by a few of their most prominent leaders, like Harriman and Swope, to believe that recovery could be achieved by the relaxation of antitrust regulations and through business cooperation in trade associations, they thought they saw in the NIRA both the opportunity to *escape* governmental authority and to engage in self-regulation. They were blind to, or ignored, the extension of further governmental authority over them in the bill. Moreover, few of them apparently perceived that the real purpose of the bill was not business recovery but increased employment—and that the latter was to come about not as a result of, but at the expense of, the former.

The NIRA, including its public works component, was a further reflection of the theory revealed in the AAA—the theory that some referred to as the "bubble-up" theory of recovery. In opposition to the "trickle-down" theory, which Roosevelt had denounced in his acceptance speech, the "bubble-up" approach held that recovery could best be achieved by increasing the purchasing power of consumers, thus providing a market for the products of industry and stimulating their manufacture. By raising agricultural income, by forcing industry to pay higher wages to more workers, and by employing the jobless on public works projects, the "bubble-up" theorists expected to generate recovery from the bottom up. If the theory was valid, then the New Deal vision of recovery required no concessions to business and finance, no moves to foster confidence, no compromises on the issue of profits. The New Deal could proceed with its reforms, confident that business would improve despite any blows to business confidence caused by reforms, as increased consumer spending "forced" a recovery. The interests of business were distinctly considered subordinate in the NIRA to the objective of increased employment and purchasing power, and it should have been reasonably clear that in any conflict between the objectives of business and those of the NIRA, the profitability of business was likely to be subordinated.

The deficiencies of both the general theory and its specific application through the NIRA should have been obvious. The "bubble-up" theory directed the primary stimulation at those industries that needed it the least, and largely ignored those that needed it most. Increased consumer spending would largely assist the consumer goods industries, where the volume of business showed the least decline from predepression levels; it did little or nothing for the heavy industries that had been most affected by the depression and where the bulk of unemployment was concentrated. As for the NIRA, it imposed higher wage costs on industry in advance of recovery, thereby forcing businesses to accept reduced profits (or greater losses) or to raise their prices. Neither alternative was likely to promote recovery.

Meanwhile, early business and financial support for the objectives of the proposed bill to regulate the sale of new securities had turned to opposition as the details of the legislation were revealed.[41] After an early draft of a bill proved unsatisfactory, the task of writing the legislation was entrusted to two Frankfurter proteges, James Landis and Benjamin Cohen, under his supervision. Landis joked that Frankfurter had made him "overnight, an authority on finance."[42] There was little, if any, input from those with practical experience in the field. Raymond Moley later recalled that the Frankfurter bill illustrated "the fact that in the zeal for reform in those days, there was altogether too little consultation with men who might have thrown some light on how a bill would operate in practice." It also showed that "men who were familiar with business practice were looked upon with such grave and unnecessary suspicion that they were not permitted to share . . . in the consultations that attended the drafting of such legislation."[43]

Supposedly modeled after the British Companies Act, the bill was a good deal more punitive in its provisions, reflecting what Moley called "a deep suspicion of bankers, of Wall Street lawyers, and of corporation lawyers in general."[44] James Warburg likewise observed later in the year that the bill had set up "a series of liabilities and penalties, which are neither well-defined nor reasonable, and which certainly bear no similarity to the British Companies act.'' The bill, he concluded, had been "pushed through with unnecessary haste and with unnecessary fanaticism. An atmosphere of emotion surrounded the whole question from the start, and anyone who dared to criticize was instantly accused of ignorance or self-interest.''[45]

The bill aroused a storm of protest from those who saw in the measure not an attempt to regulate new securities but to eliminate them altogether. Critics objected that the amount of information required of corporations by the bill would impose too great a burden upon established companies to comply with— both in time and money. But the principal objection was with the liability provisions of the bill, for which Landis was chiefly responsible. Liability was extended even to directors of firms, not only for willful misstatements, but even for the accidental omission of a "material fact." Yet the bill was so vaguely worded that it gave no clear definition of such terms as "material fact." Thus, the bill seemed to grant a license to sue to every investor who suffered a loss for whatever reason. Since the bill was drafted under the supervision of a man touted to have one of the leading legal minds in the nation, such vagueness could hardly have been accidental, and Frankfurter must surely have known that the effect of such clumsy draftsmanship (whether intended or not) would be paralysis in the securities markets.

The White House mailbags bulged with letters reflecting the concern of businessmen, financiers, and economists, and containing detailed suggestions for modification of the bill.[46] In response to one such letter, Roosevelt wrote: "The difficulty about the opposition to the Securities Bill is that no one seems to be in the least specific in regard to what section or sections will hurt legitimate business.''[47] Either the president was not reading or could not understand the detailed criticism and suggestions arriving at his door.

Criticism of the bill did not come only from businessmen and financiers. Dean Wallace B. Donham of the Harvard University School of Business wired the White House in mid-May that a faculty group studying the pending bill had advised him "that in its present form it will produce economic and business results different from those intended including serious disturbances of flow of credit and capital from financial centers to small businesses and to areas most needing aid and great increase in strain on government as source of new business capital.'' Since few securities were then being issued, there seemed no emergency requiring immediate passage of a securities bill, and Donham suggested further study of the bill's "business and economic as well as legal implications.'' To Donham went a letter similar to that quoted above.[48] When Donham wired again that his faculty group was prepared to make a detailed study of the bill if the president desired, the telegram was filed without a reply.[49] Clearly Roosevelt was uninterested in hearing about the negative impact the bill was likely to have, even when it was from academic experts in the field. On matters of critical importance for business and finance, the president was taking his advice from

Harvard Law School (Frankfurter) and not from the experts in the Harvard Business School.

A year later, Dean Donham coauthored with a colleague a study of the recovery efforts of the Roosevelt administration in which they wrote:

The Securities Act gives too little attention to business realities and to human behavior. . . . With much idle equipment and inadequate returns on existing investment, great activity in expanding our factories was not to be expected, but even a small amount of additional employment in capital goods industries would have been a great aid to recovery and to the Administration. By increasing the risk of business men, the Act checks recovery.

In an obvious reference to Frankfurter's influence on the administration, they observed:

The merits of the proposal and the credentials of its sponsors need searching examination. Being professors ourselves, we believe that sound analysis and balanced judgment may be found in academic circles, but the mere fact that the sponsor of a proposal to sustain recovery holds an advanced degree or a professorship is not sufficient evidence that the measure in question will really work as its promoter expects.

They found "the philosophy, sometimes dominant in Washington, that we must get wholesale reform without regard to costs in human misery . . . a most dangerous factor in our social situation."[50] But it was Frankfurter who had Roosevelt's ear.

In the midst of the debate over the securities bill, the Glass-Steagall banking bill was also making its way through Congress. This was not a New Deal measure and, in fact, it contained at least one provision of which Roosevelt initially disapproved—the federal guarantee of bank deposits. In general, the measure was supported by businessmen and bankers, many of whom regarded it as tragic that the bill had not been passed by the previous Congress before which it had been pending. One aspect of the bill deserves note, however, for its relation to the Securities Act and the problem of securities flotations. This provision of the bill required that banks engaged in the securities business make a choice between commercial banking or investment banking. Commercial banks, in short, were no longer to assist in the flotation of securities. In view of the abuses that had recently been revealed in such operations by a Senate committee, this "divorce" of commercial banking from investment banking was widely hailed as overdue.

Viewed in connection with the Securities Act, however, this provision of the Glass-Steagall bill closed off what had been one of the most active sources of investment capital to business at the same time that the Securities Act threatened to create further impediments. As one economist pointed out: "The Banking Act of 1933 introduces needed reforms in our banking system but destroys most of our financial machinery for creating and distributing new securities just at the same time when our recovery effort is in large measure dependent for success on the origination and sale of new capital issues.''[51] Basil O'Connor, Roosevelt's former law partner, was sufficiently alarmed to write the president:

I may be wrong, but in view of the amendments to the Glass Bill set forth in this morning's papers, that if one made an analysis of that bill and of the Securities Bill it would be found that the sale of any securities has been effectively eliminated. If this is not the desired result, probably this matter should be resurveyed.[52]

Not even such counsel from his former law partner, however, caused Roosevelt to reassess the contents of the two bills.

IMPLICATIONS OF THE HUNDRED DAYS

By the time Congress adjourned on June 16, the implications of the legislation it had passed had become increasingly apparent to journalists, businessmen, bankers, economists, and business academicians. The AAA, critics found, was only partly an effort to aid farmers and partly an attempt to regiment agriculture-related industries. It increased the purchasing power of the agricultural sector even while it reduced that of other consumers because of the higher prices it produced. The NIRA was less a device for industrial cooperation and self-regulation than one that offered the prospect of broad federal control over business, and less a device for promoting industrial recovery than one for raising wages, increasing employment, and promoting collective bargaining. If businessmen raised their prices, as seemed likely, to meet the added costs of operation under the NIRA, then this bit of legislation, too, would reduce the purchasing power of consumers even while it added to that of workers.

Both of these initiatives reflected the influence of the Tugwellian wing on the early New Deal, though neither went nearly as far as Tugwell would have liked. Except for provisions in the NIRA regulating minimum wages, maximum hours, and child labor, the two acts were at odds with the aims of the Brandeisians. Their philosophy was more clearly represented in the Securities Act of 1933, which, far from fulfilling Roosevelt's promise that it would hinder honest business as little as possible, seemed bent, instead, on making it impossible for industry to raise capital through the securities market. Such a paralysis in private financing was, however, a prospect that could as easily be welcomed by the Tugwell group as the Brandeisians. If, as critics charged, an inevitable result would be a growing dependence by business upon the federal government for capital, that dependence could provide either group with the opportunity to advance their programs. Either increased government control over business, or the "atomizing" of big business, could be accomplished by decisions on where and under what conditions government capital would be furnished to an economy dependent on that financing.

The picture, in sum, was of the establishment of very nearly a dictatorship in the White House over the nation's economic life. This was especially the case because Congress, which until now had generally written into statutory law the provisions under which laws were to operate, abdicated that responsibility during the Hundred Days. Instead, by blanket grants of power to the executive branch, Congress gave to Roosevelt and his delegated officials the responsibility and authority to, in essence, legislate in its behalf through the decrees, rules, regulations, interpretations, and other pronouncements that would carry the force of law. As commonly criticized, the result was the rule "of men, not of laws," since such pronouncements bearing the force of law would not hereafter be based on congressional debate and vote, but rather on the whims of the president and of those empowered to act in his name. In addition, much of the legislation was so vaguely worded and clumsily written that it offered little guidance to the businessmen or bankers who sought to adapt their practices to the law, or even to the legal experts from whom they sought counsel. It offered, therefore, the prospect of increased work for the courts and enrichment for members of the legal profession, as a result of the efforts to test and clarify the provisions of the laws and the interpretations put on them by the bureaucrats.

The legislation of the Hundred Days provided many more questions than answers for those in business and finance. Could an economic system heretofore fueled by the prospect of profit as an encouragement to enterprise be expected to recover with the substitution of what the *Dry Goods Economist* described as the "sociological viewpoint" for its motive?[53] Could businessmen be expected, even in the best of circumstances, to enter into long-term commitments with the prospect of inflation ever present? What was likely to be the result for businessmen of either the success or failure of the NIRA experiment? If it succeeded in restoring a measure of prosperity would it mean that this two-year "emergency" experiment would be fastened upon them permanently? If it failed, would failure invite even more radical experiments from the Roosevelt administration? It is small wonder that by the middle of 1933 some had already begun to view the Supreme Court as the only possible source of relief from the myriad of new obstacles that the New Deal had erected to business confidence and recovery.

CHAPTER 3

Rising Criticism

THE DECISION FOR ISOLATIONISM

That the United States would pursue its economic policies largely in isolation from the rest of the world was clear from Roosevelt's first venture into international economic relations. During the Hoover presidency, a World Economic Conference had been scheduled for the summer of 1933 in London at which the United States was to be a participant. The conference represented President Hoover's conviction that the depression, being international in scope, could be solved only by international cooperation. Inheriting the conference from his predecessor, Roosevelt met in preliminary conferences at the White House with assorted heads of state and financial ministers from the other participating nations. The statements that followed these preliminary meetings invariably encouraged the nation and the world in the belief that Roosevelt was committed to international cooperation for world economic recovery. A joint statement following a meeting between Roosevelt and the Canadian prime minister late in April was typical:

No one of these problems can be profitably dealt with in isolation from the others, nor can any single country accomplish a satisfactory solution. We therefore recognize the vital importance to mankind of the World Economic Conference, and the necessity of reaching, in the weeks which remain before it is convened, as great a measure of mutual understanding as possible.[1]

However, Roosevelt had already demonstrated that his words were not always are reliable guide to his actions. At the same time that he seemed to be committing the United States to international cooperation for world economic recovery, the implications of the legislation of the Hundred Days were clearly isolationist. Any meaningful international monetary agreement, for example, must collide with Roosevelt's ability to utilize the threat or the actual implementation of changes in the value of the dollar. A recovery program based on increasing prices and wages could clearly not countenance a reduction of tariff barriers that would result in an influx into the country of cheaper goods from abroad and the loss of American jobs. The AAA and NIRA, on the contrary, offered the prospect that higher rather than lower tariff rates might be required on imports. It was precisely for this reason that the Baltimore *Sun*, a Democratic newspaper, had opposed both the AAA and the NIRA, noting, in the latter case, that tariff protection would have to be extended to industrial products else "the effect of the law will be to transfer orders abroad at the expense of American labor, which the law is ostensibly designed to protect."[2]

In the midst of the deliberations in London, Roosevelt torpedoed the conference by rejecting U.S. participation in any monetary agreement. His final message to the conference, dispatched while he was sailing and away from his key advisers, read like a lecture to the conference. A European finance minister complained: "We are not children and we do not see why we should be talked to in such language."[3] The London *Daily Herald* observed that Roosevelt had "treated the World Economic Conference a little too contemptuously"; while British Prime Minister Ramsay MacDonald found in Roosevelt's behavior "a complete misunderstanding of how an international conference, representative as this is of sixty-six different nations who are here in the persons of Prime Ministers, Foreign Secretaries, Finance Ministers, has to be conducted if any good results are to be had from it."[4] Clearly Roosevelt had won few friends and little respect for himself in the world arena.

In June, John Maynard Keynes had published an article in the *Yale Review* in which the economist supported economic nationalism as necessary in a world where "private competitive capitalism" could not compete with "political economies" like those of the USSR, Germany, and Italy in free trade situations. Free nations must adopt the techniques of totalitarian nations or they must turn to national self-sufficiency so that their ideals could be "safely and conveniently pursued."[5] This was enough for Frankfurter, who applauded Roosevelt's action, but his mentor, Supreme Court justice Louis Brandeis, was less enthusiastic. He wrote Frankfurter that "Keynes notwithstanding [the] tone and circumstances" of Roosevelt's message to the conference had been "very disquieting." Brandeis wondered if "this may be a manifestation of the disintegrating effect of absolute power on mind and character."[6]

Perhaps the most incredible aspect of the entire episode was Roosevelt's satisfaction with his performance. In early 1937, as a world of economic nationalism moved ever closer to war, Roosevelt told columnist Arthur Krock that of everything he had done he was proudest of the message that had smashed the

London Economic Conference in 1933 and crushed the possibilities of international economic cooperation.[7]

THE NEW DEAL IS IMPLEMENTED

Domestically, the implementation of the legislation passed during the Hundred Days was proceeding. Despite their early opposition to passage of the NIRA, the NAM called on its members to cooperate wholeheartedly in trying to make the law work. But as businessmen came face to face with the provisions of the NIRA, many liked what they saw even less than when the bill had been before Congress. As a consequence of such feelings, *Business Week* reported that trade groups were showing little eagerness about submitting codes to the National Recovery Administration (NRA) for approval, and the NRA had begun to phrase its "invitations" to industry to cooperate in words that sounded increasingly like commands.[8]

Frustrated at the slowness with which business was responding, NRA administrator Hugh Johnson formulated a blanket code to cover all businesses until their trade codes had been worked out and approved. The Washington *Post* revealed the blanket code prospect on July 15. It doubted that Congress had anticipated such an action in approving the NIRA, but admitted that the statute was "couched in general terms, conferring wide powers upon the President."[9] The provisions of the blanket code were well known by July 18, the United Press having calculated by that date that the expense of compliance with its provisions would increase its own costs of operation by $180,000 per year.[10] It has been suggested by historian William Leuchtenburg that one of the factors leading to the formulation of the blanket code was a break in the stock market that occurred on July 19, but quite obviously the movement for a blanket code was already well under way by that time and hardly secret, and that the motive was the slowness of business in embracing the NIRA.[11] Indeed, it seems more likely that it was the prospect of the blanket code that contributed to the stock market break than vice versa.

The blanket code, or President's Reemployment Agreement, revealed clearly the iron fist of the government within the velvet glove which the more naive among businessmen had believed the NIRA to be. It dashed for all time the conception of the NRA as a method for voluntary self-regulation. For those businessmen who adopted a code, committing themselves to the wage, hour, and other requirements therein, there was the Blue Eagle insignia that signified compliance and that could be prominently displayed as evidence that the business was cooperating with the NRA. The Blue Eagle could, of course, be withdrawn upon evidence that the business was not complying. For those businesses that could not, or would not, sign the blanket or industry code, or who had their Blue Eagle withdrawn for noncompliance, there was the implied threat of consumer boycotts against "chiselers." As columnist Frank Kent put it, there would be no legal sanctions, but the Roosevelt administration could "manufacture a public sentiment that will stamp the recalcitrants as unworthy and unpatriotic, and ruin their businesses far more effectively than it could by legal steps."[12]

The results were rapid. *Business Week* reported in mid-August that "there were signs of delay a month ago, holding back, lawyers advising the waiting game, rumors of revolt against the original industry control plan, protests against 'the regimentation of American industry,' " but now "the real regimentation" of the blanket code had "definitely cured that."[13] The *Wall Street Journal* explained the reason for the blanket code campaign as indicating that the Roosevelt administration now understood "that the business community must be either terrorized or chloroformed into submission. . . . So, the suggested resort to tidal waves of synthetic oratory to wash away the honest and informed criticism of men who know their business."[14]

The Federal Reserve Board's index of industrial production climbed from 60 to 98 percent of the 1923–1925 average between the months of March and July, and the stock market rose at a similar rate.[15] In part, Roosevelt's decision against currency stabilization at the World Economic Conference was apparently motivated by his concern that such an agreement would undermine the speculative rise in stock and other prices.[16] On July 19, however, the market broke and other business indices began an abrupt decline. For inflationists, the break was indicative that the effects of the *threat* of inflation had worn off, and that it was time now for genuine inflationary action.[17] Others drew a different lesson. The drop in economic indices (the FRB index declined to 73 by November), they pointed out, coincided with the implementations of the NRA and the AAA.[18]

Criticism of the NRA, especially, began to increase. The *Wall Street Journal* noted that in past recoveries wages had increased as a *result* of recovery; by its insistence that businesses increase wages *before* recovery, the NRA was attempting "to transform what has been an *effect* of recovery into a *cause* of recovery."[19] This smacked of a confusion of cause with effect in the Roosevelt administration, of treating symptoms rather than the disease itself. Walter Lippmann was appalled by the punitive potential of the NRA, particularly for small businesses.

All over this country today there are men with little stores who in the face of incredible difficulties have just managed to stay in business. . . . It is intolerable to my mind that the federal government should now reach into these towns, and without an investigation of the facts, without any knowledge of each man's circumstances, presume to make public judgment as to whether this man or that is a slacker or a patriot. Where, I should like to know, does it derive the right to do that kind of thing? In what statute is there such a grant of power? In what principle of American government is there the authority for such an inquisition? . . . To foment discord and discrimination, boycotts and bitterness in the neighbors of cities and in the towns is no way to revive business.[20]

Businessmen were also growing concerned over the evidence that labor unions intended to capitalize on the guarantee of collective bargaining contained in article 7a of the NIRA to force the unionization of U.S. industry. *Iron Age* found labor disturbances erupting in every branch of industry, stimulated by the NIRA, despite "the almost universal granting of shorter hours and higher wages" under the NRA codes.[21] In the midst of the great effort, however misguided, of the New Deal to improve conditions, and amid the declining economic indicators of the fall months, the willingness of labor unions to further disrupt the economy and retard recovery was disheartening. By the end of November, the NAM estimated that there had been, since July, "more than 1,100 strikes, involving directly almost 700,000 workers who have lost a total of over 9,500,000 working days, with a loss in wages of more than $33,500,000." If workers supplying raw and partly manufactured materials were included, the total climbed to over 1 million workers and $50 million in lost wages.[22]

As for the National Labor Board, established under the NRA to deal with labor disputes, business found its record far from satisfactory. The decisions of the board, one critic observed, were "all one-sided, and . . . the underlying purpose always is to carry out the demands of labor, and especially of organized labor." The NLB had "been invested with the attributes" of a judicial tribunal, but had shown that it could not be depended upon to act with the impartiality of one. The prospect for businessmen was "a complete loss of private initiative in the direction of their own business," with "Government bureaus the supreme master."[23]

Labor difficulties were only one of the many problems that shattered the few remaining business illusions concerning the NRA. The hearings for the first of the NRA codes, that of the cotton textile industry, was a revelation for those businessmen who had assumed that free cooperation would be permitted between those companies that embraced the NRA codes. On the contrary, administrator Hugh Johnson told them, since the primary purpose of the NRA was to put people to work, it was not possible to allow the more efficient companies to drive less productive competitors to the wall. Thus, many of the codes would contain restrictions on the maximum hours that machinery could be worked, prohibitions against adding new and more efficient machinery (which meant less business for the durable goods industries), and regulations making it difficult or impossible for new enterprises to enter into competition with established firms.[24] Yet another source of concern for businessmen was the growing evidence that the NRA was not intended solely as a temporary, emergency measure, but as a permanent fixture for economic planning by the government. Such concerns were fueled by public statements from New Deal figures like Rexford Tugwell and Hugh Johnson.[25]

THE FAILURE OF THE AAA AND NRA

As businessmen scanned their journals and newspapers in the fall they found convincing statistical evidence that the NRA and AAA were not producing recovery, and also authoritative voices insisting that they could not do so. The immediate prospect, which appeared unlikely to aid recovery, was for substantial price increases to meet the added costs of doing business that were a result of the NRA and union activity. Retailers, however, worried that consumer resistance was already rising.[26] Others warned that if there was no increase in sales volume, industry would be unable to pay the increased wages.[27] *The Economist* noted that "the wage-raising policy has already begun, by raising costs, to check the original speculative revival." The Roosevelt administration would now "have to find some way of increasing consumers' incomes without increasing costs, and it will have to find it soon."[28]

The Economist, from its perspective in London, studied the New Deal with amused skepticism. In early September it found confirmation of "the doubts that we have expressed from the beginning with regard to the success of Mr. Roosevelt's great experiment." And yet it found that "Mr. Roosevelt still insists that he has converted a 'downward drift' into an 'upward surge,' " despite all of the evidence to the contrary.[29] When the Roosevelt administration tried to stimulate lending by banks to industry to help it meet the higher costs caused by the NRA, *The Economist* found it natural that bankers were chary, given the reduced likelihood of business profits under the higher costs of the NRA, and especially after they had "for three years been repeatedly and publicly berated for the alleged recklessness of their operations."[30] As for the administration's claim that the NRA was, at least, achieving its primary goal of increasing employment, *The Economist* was skeptical. While it conceded that unemployment had dropped to below 11 million from an estimated 13.75 million in early March, it pointed out the obvious fact that the March figure had been artificially high due to the bank closing, "the gradual easing of which could be expected to lead to rapid improvement" even without the NRA. The NRA, in fact, "had a surprisingly small effect upon the unemployment problem."[31]

By early October *The Economist* found farmers needing twice as many bushels of wheat or pounds of cotton to buy a pair of overalls as had been required three months earlier, partly because of lower farm prices and partly because the price of finished textiles had been driven up by 50–100 percent by the NRA codes. It found Roosevelt in a cruel dilemma caused by the obvious failure of both the NRA and the AAA, and likely to "exercise the inflationary powers placed in his hands by Congress and already more than once . . . brandished by him."[32] The New York *Herald-Tribune* agreed, but warned that such action would only undermine business confidence rather than aid it.[33]

By mid-October Walter Lippmann, too, was running out of positive things to say about the NRA. Obviously disappointed with its failure, he now recognized that it was an ill-timed reform that was working to the detriment of recovery because it stimulated only the consumer goods industries and did nothing for the durable goods industries where the depression had hit the hardest.[34] The durable goods industries could recover only if credit expanded. The reservoirs of credit were "full to overflowing," but industry was not making use of it, and the reason, for Lippmann and other critics of the New Deal, was obvious: they lacked confidence that they could earn a profit. While the New Deal was doing everything possible to expand credit, it was at the same time "threatening those who use credit and direct its flow with dire penalties not only for misbehavior but for negligence, with drastic taxation of potential profits, with severe regulation of all kinds of corporate enterprise. It has been encouraging the expansion of capital and discouraging the enterprise that would use that capital." Lippmann, then, had joined the ranks of those who recognized that Roosevelt was not only wrong in emphasizing consumer purchasing power, but that he was compounding the error by seriously hampering recovery where it was needed most—in the durable goods industries.[35]

BOTTLING UP CAPITAL

One reason for the trickle of capital to industry seemed obvious to critics of the Securities Act of 1933. Harvard University's *Review of Economic Statistics* maintained that the law had "carried regulation to an extreme that meant strangulation."[36] The Brandeisians who were responsible for drafting it continued to deny that this was the case, and further insisted that such a result was not to be deplored even if it were true. As Brandeis wrote, early in August:

I do not believe that 2 billion or any appreciable amount of securities are needed or are held back by the Securities Act. My own guess is that nothing can be more wholesome in finance than not issuing securities for private enterprise now. What we need is that banks shall lend to business men of ability and trustworthiness.[37]

Frankfurter agreed that the "Wall Street sheep and their stupid lawyers" were "talking so much nonsense these days about the effect of the Securities Act on capital investment."[38] Two such displays of economic ignorance and indifference to recovery would not be remarkable except for the influence that their views exerted on the president.

Despite criticism of the act from such authorities as Henry L. Stimson, who concluded that it did not seem "to be at all well adapted towards stimulating the recovery of a sick world," Roosevelt continued to follow the Brandeis-Frankfurter line.[39] At a press conference in mid-October he insisted that there was excess capacity in the steel and cement industries, and he cited these as examples of the waste of investors' money. The flow of such money, he told reporters, must be planned and controlled. This suggested that Roosevelt contemplated ultimately dictating to investors the industries in which they could invest and the amounts those industries could receive. Roosevelt also continued to maintain the Brandeis-Frankfurter position that the Securities Act was modeled after the British law, taking the incredible position that the U.S. law was not nearly as stringent. Nobody, Roosevelt insisted, would suffer if they conformed to the law and used reasonable care in making accurate statements.[40] No more than the law itself did Roosevelt define "reasonable care." Finally, the president ruled out any possibility that the law might be amended. Except for the latter statement, none of the president's remarks could be taken seriously.

At the annual convention of the Investment Bankers Association, the incoming president attacked the Securities Act, asking the assembled investment bankers how they were expected to know what a "material fact" was, or a "willful omission," under the language of the law. He added: "What information is necessary when a security is sold? Who among us has sufficient wisdom and foresight to be willing to take a chance, not only affecting his property, but affecting his liberty as well, in the determination of these questions for the sake of making an underwriting commission?" The convention adopted a resolution calling for amendment of the law.[41] When the advisory council to the Federal Reserve Board added its authoritative judgment on the side of the contention that the law was an obstacle to the financing of legitimate enterprise, the *Wall Street Journal* hoped that the Roosevelt administration's response to critics of the act would now be addressed to the facts, instead of consisting of "standardized prejudices and imputations of sordid motive."[42]

Late in October, Henry L. Stimson met with Roosevelt in the White House and, in his words, "told him very seriously and emphatically the result of my observations on the working of the Securities Act." After describing the implications of the law, Stimson told the president that he had been called upon to advise some businessmen on the law and had felt it necessary to advise them "that I would not dream if I were in their place of taking the risk" of floating securities. Roosevelt still insisted that his advisers (presumably Frankfurter and his disciples) had told him that the act was the same as the British law, so that there was no reason why the American act should not work. Stimson promised him a memorandum detailing the differences.[43] As a result of this and other pressures, Roosevelt announced in December that he was considering amendments to the law.

Meanwhile, in the absence of normal operation of the securities markets, the administration had tried to stimulate loans to industry by banks to make it possible for businesses to meet the increased expenses caused by NRA without raising their prices. To this end, bankers were exhorted by the NRA, the Federal Reserve Board, the Reconstruction Finance Corporation (RFC), and even by Roosevelt himself "to loosen up" their requirements for granting loans. When Jesse Jones, head of the RFC, intimated to the American Bankers Association (ABA) convention that bankers were not very bright for not supporting the recovery program more avidly through loans to business, the president of the ABA, Francis H. Sisson, suggested that Jones was trying to provide an "alibi" for the failure of the NRA by blaming bankers.[44] The economic policy commission of the ABA insisted that bankers should not jeopardize the funds of depositors by making bad loans simply to support the recovery program.[45]

The apparent willingness of the Roosevelt administration to countenance "gambling" by bankers with the money of their depositors on questionable loans furnishes a striking and curious contrast with its zealous concern for the protection of investors in the purchase of securities. Perhaps Roosevelt was still as confused as he had apparently been at the time of the bank panic over whose money was at risk—that it was the money of the "bankers" and not of depositors. But the rhetoric of the administration was also far removed from its actual policies, for at the same time that bankers were being exhorted to lend liberally to businesses, Roosevelt's comptroller of the currency was, as one observer noted, criticizing the banks "for nearly every liberal credit extension which they make."[46] As a matter of fact, after the banking crisis of February and March, the requirements of the government's bank examiners were stricter than ever. When the issue was taken up with Comptroller of the Currency J.F.T. O'Connor, his answer was a question: "How are you going to frame a set of instructions for the examiners which will do what you want to do and at the same time not open the door to all sorts of lax practices?"[47] Clearly no relief was to be received from the rigid requirements of the bank examiners, even if that were desirable.

Roosevelt, however, preferred to believe that the failure of the bankers to respond to his pleas for more liberal lending practices was evidence of a conspiracy on the part of bankers to block the New Deal's recovery efforts. In this he was, of course, encouraged by the hostility toward business and finance in the Brandeis-Frankfurter wing of his advisers. According to Interior Secretary Ickes' account of a cabinet meeting in mid-October, Roosevelt told his cabinet

that the bankers of the country were in a conspiracy to block the Administration program. He said the banks were not lending any money even on good security and that they were seriously hampering the business recovery. Rumors have come to him from a number of sources as evidence of the unwillingness of the bankers to help out in this situation. He was quite clear in his own mind that a conspiracy existed, and he spoke of the possibility of extending Federal credit to business men who could not secure loans on good security at the banks.[48]

The Roosevelt administration would find, when it did attempt to provide federal credit directly to businesses, that the problem was less an unwillingness on the part of bankers to lend than the absence of demand for loans on the part of creditworthy businesses. In large part this went back to the issue raised earlier by Lippmann—the uncertain prospect of profits with which to repay loans. And in this it was the NRA that was largely to blame, for its insistence on higher costs to business before improved earnings.

To the extent that the Roosevelt administration addressed the problem of recovery in the heavy or durable goods industries, its vehicle was to have been the $3.3 billion public works spending program that was part of the NIRA. In theory the spending of this amount on public works would provide direct employment on the projects, "prime the pump" of economic recovery by injecting this amount of spending into the economy, and also provide orders for goods supplied by the durable goods industries thereby providing "secondary" employment in these industries. In practice, however, three factors reduced the effectiveness of the Public Works Administration program. In the first place, the amount was inadequate to serve the purpose. Secondly, so much of the money was drained off from the public works program to be used for other purposes—in part to replace funds that the Roosevelt administration had cut from its ordinary operations—that the initial inadequate amount was reduced even further. And third, the public works program proceeded much too slowly to furnish any measurable assistance to the economy for months after its inception. Entrusted to Interior Secretary Ickes, as public works administrator, the dwindling funds were dribbled out in the fall of 1933 since Ickes was concerned that the money entrusted to his stewardship should be spent wisely and without taint of inefficiency or graft. While this scrupulousness of "Honest Harold" would, in most circumstances, have been laudable, it prevented this element of the New Deal from being applied with full force in unison with the other elements, especially with the NRA. In November, Ickes suffered for his failure in getting the PWA under way the indignity of having another $400 million of his dwindling funds stripped from him to be used by Harry Hopkins' Civil Works Administration (CWA) to succor the destitute through the winter.[49]

Established by Roosevelt's executive order in early November 1933, the CWA was intended to put 4 million of the unemployed on work relief for 30 hours per week at the prevailing wage rates of their communities. In fact, the CWA wage rates turned out to be so generous that they actually exceeded the minimum rates provided in the NRA codes for every major industry, thus, as one critic observed, providing "a higher standard of living than our regular employees enjoy."[50] Indeed, of all the silliness that passed for serious policy under Roosevelt, the wage rate of the CWA was certainly one of the least defensible. Yale economics professor James Harvey Rogers, sometime financial adviser to Roosevelt, explained the obvious to Hopkins when he told him, "you are going to increase unemployment faster than you can relieve it."[51] Typical of the news stories that would bear out Rogers' prediction was one in December that reported workers in Toledo were quitting factory jobs in order to go on the rolls of the CWA. In the factories they were receiving 35 to 40 cents an hour, while the CWA was paying 50 cents.[52]

A NEW RABBIT FROM FDR'S HAT

The Roosevelt administration was incensed when the FRB monthly bulletin for October took note of the declines that industry had experienced during the previous months and pointed out that the decline had "been marked in industries in which [AAA] processing taxes or [NRA] codes have become effective recently."[53] While not explicitly blaming the AAA or the NRA for the declines, the statement certainly implied a causal relationship. Immediately both NRA administrator Johnson and Agriculture Secretary Wallace challenged the FRB's figures, insisting that *their* figures did not agree with the FRB's.[54] But the failure of the NRA, especially, was already too obvious to be ignored. Wags had already begun to refer to it as "Nuts Running America," "Never Revive Again," and, most telling of all, "No Recovery After All."[55] Reporting on depressed conditions in his part of the South, publisher George Fort Milton observed that businessmen there felt that "the N.R.A. has been tried, that it has not been up to expectations, that so far as giving us the needed stimulus for recovery is concerned, it is now as definitely out of the picture as a last year's birdnest."[56] After comparing the FRB index of department store sales in October 1933 with the same month in 1932, and adjusting the figures for the increase in retail prices reported by the Bureau of Labor Statistics, *United States News* concluded that unit volume of retail sales was actually lower in October 1933 than a year earlier.[57]

Already, by early November 1933 a Washington observer found "confusion, turmoil, disagreement and bad feeling within the government." Nothing about the New Deal seemed popular but the president himself.[58] *Business Week* found the Roosevelt administration "on the defensive for the first time. A rising tide of criticism slaps against all parts of the government's program, but the waves pound hardest and the spray dashes highest where NRA and AAA have been so boldly built."[59] Harvard's *Review of Economic Statistics* concluded that an important factor in the loss of confidence in Roosevelt's policies during the third quarter of 1933 was

the growing recognition by business and other leaders in the community that the formulation of Washington economic policy was in important respects under the influence of radical and unsound advisers, who not only proclaimed that sound economists and practical business leaders were out of date, but also disregarded the teachings of economic science and the facts of business experience.[60]

Unaffected by the criticism, Roosevelt told Ickes "that what we are doing in this country were some of the things that were being done in Russia and even some things that were being done under Hitler in Germany. But we are doing them in an orderly way."[61]

Roosevelt could ignore businessmen's complaints about the failure of the NRA, but he could not as easily disregard a growing revolt in the Farm Belt over the failure of the AAA. Plowing up crops and destroying pigs had proved no answer, and a besieged Roosevelt cast about for a device by which he might give the economy a shot in the arm that would make unnecessary a confession of failure or a retreat at any point in the New Deal program. Inflationists pressed forward their solutions. Even for those who were otherwise cool toward inflation, some inflationary action by the president was preferable to continued suspense over what he might do under the powers granted him by the Thomas amendment.[62]

In a fireside chat on October 22, Roosevelt outlined a new policy to the nation. He was

going to establish a Government market for gold in the United States. Therefore, under the clearly defined authority of existing law, I am authorizing the Reconstruction Finance

Corporation to buy gold newly mined in the United States at prices to be determined from time to time after consultation with the Secretary of the Treasury and the President. Whenever necessary to the end in view, we shall also buy or sell gold in the world market.

My aim in taking this step is to establish and maintain continuous control.

It was "a policy and not an expedient," Roosevelt told the nation, another step in the "move toward a managed currency."[63] By this vague message the Roosevelt administration launched one of the strangest and least defensible of its economic adventures.

The father of the gold-buying scheme, Cornell University agricultural economics professor George Warren, maintained that complex problems were susceptible to simple solutions. For the problem of raising commodity prices the simple solution stemmed from an apparent relationship between the prices of commodities and the value (price) of gold. Since the two had historically risen and fallen together, according to the professor's charts, Warren assumed a cause and effect relationship. The key to raising commodity prices was to increase the value (price) of gold.

It was a rare economist who agreed with Warren's insistence on a cause and effect relationship; to most it seemed apparent, instead, that the underlying economic conditions that pushed up commodity prices simultaneously pushed up the price of gold, and that raising the price of gold would have no more effect on commodity prices than, for example, raising the price of alfalfa. It seemed manifestly another instance of Roosevelt's confusion of cause with effect and his preoccupation with treating the symptoms of the depression as if they were causes.[64] While lighting a fire in the furnace produced a warm room and a rising temperature, it seemed apparent to critics that altering the numbers on the thermometer would neither light the fire nor warm the room. Yet many of those who advocated the Warren plan did so not from any confidence that it would work, but from a desire to see Roosevelt move in the direction of a flexible, commodity-based dollar, and they viewed the gold-buying program as a step in that direction.[65]

Roosevelt's gold-buying program only increased the criticism of his policies. *The Economist* found that "for the first time since March the President finds the Press of the country virtually unanimous in opposition to his policies," and it shared their misgivings over the Warren plan.[66] Of particular concern to some observers was the impression that Roosevelt had adopted the policy solely to calm the agrarian discontent that had blossomed in the Farm Belt, that he seemed to be allowing the tail (the farmers) to wag the dog (the rest of the country) in questions of value of the dollar.[67] Largely ignored in all of the comment was the apparent reversal of priorities that it seemed to signify in part of the New Deal program. The devaluation of the dollar, if effective, would surely raise all prices—not merely those of farm products. Any increase in industrial prices without, or in advance of, corresponding wage increases for workers, would be a reversal of the priorities of the NRA.

Critics of the gold-buying plan watched commodity figures as avidly as did Roosevelt and proponents of the plan for signs of its effect. Four days after it began, critics had already pronounced it a failure and Roosevelt expanded it to include purchases of gold in foreign markets.[68] Walter Lippmann found that the episode had created a "turn in underlying sentiment toward the whole question of concentrating such immense authority in the hands of the President."[69] *Business Week* found that the scheme had led to the release of "all the pent-up criticism that had been accumulating—against financial policy, against the bank program, against NRA, the progress of the farm program and the public works program, the Securities Act."[70] Economists, too, now began to organize in opposition to Roosevelt's monetary policies.[71]

In mid-November, amid evidence that the gold-buying program was causing weakness in the government bond market and a flight of capital from the United States to Europe, the standing of the Roosevelt administration was further shaken by important departures from the Treasury Department over the Warren program. One was Treasury Undersecretary Dean Acheson, who believed that the gold-buying program was illegal, a view shared by the Brandeisians. But, as Thomas Corcoran put it, "F.D.R. was stubbornly arbitrary, didn't give a damn for the law."[72] Acheson left quietly, but Dr. O.M.W. Sprague, financial adviser to the Treasury, departed with a blast at Roosevelt's monetary policies for threatening "a complete breakdown of the credit of the Government," and his announcement that he intended to play an active role in arousing public opinion for a battle against inflation.[73] Since Sprague was highly regarded among businessmen, bankers, and economists as one of the foremost experts in the world on financial and monetary matters (he had formerly served as an adviser to the Bank of England), his resignation exerted a profound effect in stimulating further opposition to Roosevelt's monetary policies and was, in fact, the signal for mobilization of an antiinflationary movement that was thereafter able to nullify the efforts of inflationists.[74]

In mid-December the prestigious Brookings Institution added its assessment of the gold-buying program, concluding that "no definite predictable rise in the commodity price level can be assumed to follow a given depreciation of the currency," nor could commodity price levels "be automatically controlled by altering the price of gold." Moreover, it warned that the program harbored great potential for damage to foreign trade, long-term investment and the government's credit.[75] *The Economist* likewise found no effect of the program on commodity prices and concluded that "the most conspicuous consequence of the programme has been its weakening effect upon Government securities."[76]

By the time of the Brookings study, however, reports of the failure of this amazing program had ceased to be news and so had the program itself. By late December, rumors of a possible stabilization of the dollar, the abandonment of the gold-buying program, and the apparent disposition of the Roosevelt admin-

istration to propose revisions to the Securities Act, combined to reduce somewhat
the anxiety that businessmen had felt in October and November.

There was some consolation, too, in developments within the AAA. Scarcely
had the turmoil in the Treasury settled down before dissension surfaced in the
agricultural program between those who, like AAA administrator George Peek,
put the recovery of the farmers first, and the Tugwellians, who seemed bent
primarily on campaigning against profit in agriculture-related industries. The
New York *Times* described the conflict:

The Right, represented by Mr. Peek, is described as favoring a minimum of regulation,
particularly with respect to profits. It believes the millers, packers and other processors
should be permitted to earn what they can, so long as the farmer himself receives a fair
price. The Left, with the university economists in the van, favors regulation all along
the line, with a strict curb on profits.[77]

As one AAA official later recalled,

there was a type of person that didn't know anything about farming and that came from
the city, who thought that we were pretty much on the verge of a revolution and that the
whole Roosevelt regime was going to be almost revolutionary or radical. They thought
it was going to do a number of very radical and very drastic things, moving in the direction
of socialism.[78]

Peek's successor as head of the AAA likewise recalled that it was filled with
people uninterested in its objectives, but who ''were interested in rearranging
the social, political and economic pattern to suit their own ideas. It wasn't
necessary that the Triple-A should have all the crackpots in Washington. There
weren't any in other places to match the number that we had in the Triple-A.''[79]

As a result of the conflict within the AAA, Peek was induced to resign as
administrator to take another position in the New Deal. His replacement, Chester
Davis, was, however, closer to the Peek faction than to the Tugwellians. Moreover, supervision of many agriculture-related industries was shifted from the
AAA to the NRA where, *Business Week* observed, they would be happier than
under the AAA left-wingers.[80] The outcome was regarded by most observers as
a victory for the Peek policies over the Tugwellians.[81]

ROOSEVELT AND HIS CRITICS

If businessmen could have been privy to the state of mind of Roosevelt and
of the most influential of his advisers, they would have been less sanguine about
the prospects as 1933 ended. Frankfurter wrote Roosevelt in December that the
''lines were fast being drawn between those to whom Recovery meant Return—
return to the good old days—and those for whom Recovery was Reform—
transformation by gradual process, but radical transformation no less, of our

social and economic arrangements." After Roosevelt had saved business they had "returned to their old gods," and now "the lines are being formed along true alignments of interests. . . . But no one, I am sure, has been more fully alive than you from the very beginning that the lines would be formed along interests."[82] Roosevelt responded to this candid advocacy of class warfare by writing a few days later: "You are right about the lines becoming more closely drawn. . . . The true alignment will, of course, become clearer as the winter progresses, and I welcome it."[83] Thus did Frankfurter counsel a willing president to wage war against business rather than against the depression.

Frankfurter's emphasis on reform over recovery was not, however, echoed in a letter he forwarded to Roosevelt on December 16.[84] This was an "open letter to President Roosevelt" that John Maynard Keynes had written at the request of the New York *Times*. The letter was published in the final issue of that newspaper for 1933. In the letter Keynes applauded Roosevelt's activism in confronting the depression, but criticized the premises and priorities on which much of the New Deal was based, and the policies that had resulted. Echoing the points made by American critics of Roosevelt's policies, Keynes pointed out that the administration had erred in giving priority to reform over recovery and in sometimes confusing the former with the latter. Roosevelt had also confused the symptoms of recovery with recovery itself, Keynes noted, with the result that his policies had sought to treat symptoms rather than the disease. While rising prices, for example, were to be welcomed when they resulted from increased output and employment, it was impossible, Keynes pointed out, to reverse the process and seek to stimulate either output or employment by raising prices. Such a policy only reduced both demand and output and resulted in less, rather than more, employment. The NRA was "essentially reform and probably impedes recovery," while the gold-buying program had been "foolish" because there was no "mathematical relation between the price of gold and the prices of other things." It was but another example of Roosevelt's attempt "to put on flesh by letting out the belt"—the New Deal's confusion of cause and effect.

Keynes suggested that Roosevelt introduce some stability into the situation by announcing that he would control the dollar exchange at a definite figure. The administration must also increase its deficit spending in the economy and speed up the distribution of funds. Keynes suggested "the rehabilitation of the physical condition of the railroads" as a project that would mature quickly and be on a sufficiently large scale. Keynes also recommended a reduction in the interest rate on federal long-term bonds to bring down interest rates generally, thus making it more appealing for industry to borrow for expansion.[85] In counseling larger deficit spending for projects like the railroads, Keynes was recommending spending that would not only provide employment but also stimulate the vital durable goods industries that had been ignored by the New Deal. Yet in his advocacy of more spending, Keynes also recognized that other policies of the New Deal, notably its emphasis on reform over recovery, were making economic recovery difficult, with or without the requisite level of deficit spending. This was the dilemma that Roosevelt would create for the nation throughout the remainder of the 1930s.

The Baltimore *Sun* concluded from Keynes' letter that he seemed "to admire Mr. Roosevelt because of his willingness to do something. . . . On the other hand, Mr. Keynes seems to question the propriety of almost every important feature of the Roosevelt policy except the Public Works program."[86] As for Keynes' observation that Roosevelt's reforms were blocking recovery by upsetting the confidence of business, the *Wall Street Journal* remarked that "Mr. Keynes here joins the majority for once in his life."[87]

Keynes' letter was followed a few days later by the publication of *The Economics of the Recovery Program*, an appraisal of Roosevelt's policies by seven Harvard University economists. Professor Seymour Harris found Roosevelt's monetary policies a "threat of inflation," "unfriendly toward capital," and "tinkering with the monetary machine," the net result of which was to undermine confidence among businessmen. Professor Joseph Schumpeter found that Roosevelt's attempts to generate an artificial recovery were making it impossible for capitalism to function. Professor Edward Mason viewed certain provisions of the NRA codes as a menace not only to recovery but also to reform, while Professor Douglas Brown faulted the added costs to business involved in the work-sharing aspects of the NRA. Professor Overton Taylor concluded that "the recklessness of ignorant emotional effort at reform must be held in check in order to minimize the risks that discourage honest business while reforms are in the making."[88] In sum, Roosevelt's policies had not made a passing grade.

The Economist agreed that Roosevelt's polices were retarding rather than aiding recovery, and it concluded that "the world is less advanced on the road to prosperity than it would have been if a less ambitious and more consistent programme had been pursued in Washington."[89] Similar criticism was voiced by a growing number of American economists.[90] Although Roosevelt had drawn many of his early advisers from Columbia University, 37 of the 50 faculty members of the business, economics, political science, and social science departments there signed a letter opposing the economic policies of the New Deal.[91]

The fundamental issue in the situation seemed to many to be the one revealed in Roosevelt's inaugural speech—his prejudice against profits. Roosevelt and his Brandeis-Frankfurter advisers might decry the "selfishness" of businessmen and investors in their emphasis on profit, but, Tugwell to the contrary notwithstanding, most recognized that in a free economy it is precisely the pursuit of profit that fuels the economic machine. If the economic system were not to be made over into something radically different from a capitalistic one, then to attack the profit motive and seek to restrict or reduce profits through governmental policies was destructive of the incentive for economic recovery. When Harold J. Laski, the noted British political scientist and socialist, surveyed the "Roosevelt Experiment" for *Atlantic* magazine in February 1934, he wrote with obvious sympathy for Roosevelt as the first leader of a capitalist nation to seek ''deliberately and systematically to use the power of the state to subordinate the primary assumptions of that society to certain vital social purposes,'' the first ''to experiment on a wholesale scale with the limitation of the profit motive.'' But Laski also recognized the dilemma which Roosevelt faced in seeking to generate economic recovery while pursuing such policies:

Business men and financiers will not seriously be won to Mr. Roosevelt's programme until its success is proved by the return of prosperity; and prosperity is unlikely to return unless he can win the support of the financiers and business men. This is the dilemma the administration confronts; and only as it is to be met can we measure the implications of the time.[92]

Another British economist, Sir Josiah Stamp, writing from a very different perspective, noted:

What appalls me about the American new order is not merely the speed at which things are being done, but the fact that men are being encouraged to suppose you can revive industry while you are still sitting on the mainspring. After all, the mainspring of all individualistic enterprise of any kind, outside Russia, is the making of profit. Unless you are getting people to make money, you will never get re-employment. Yet this is the last thing that seems to have been thought of in America.[93]

Dr. Joseph Willits, dean of the Wharton School of Finance and Commerce of the University of Pennsylvania, agreed that Roosevelt seemed to have lost sight of the importance of the profit motive. He wrote of the Roosevelt administration:

They seem to me to have adopted somewhat the social worker's complex towards all profit motive which seems to justify any ''picking'' at industry. It is the prevalence of such unwise sniping at legitimate industry which seems to me to contain something of the threat that recovery may be prevented or greatly retarded.[94]

Would the attitude and policies of the Roosevelt administration change in 1934?

CHAPTER 4

Delaying Recovery

REGULATION OF SECURITIES

As 1934 began, many critics of Roosevelt's policies continued to regard the Securities Act of 1933 as the most serious of the obstacles to recovery created by the New Deal. Economist C. J. Bullock observed in Harvard's *Review of Economic Statistics* that the obstacles which the act erected to the flow of capital into industry suggested that, indeed, "one of its purposes was to hamper the growth of private and to stimulate the expansion of public enterprise," to "further socialization of industry and not to protect investors." While he conceded that such was probably not the intent of the New Dealers in writing the act, the point was made: if the Roosevelt administration *had* purposefully set out with the goal of destroying private enterprise and promoting government operation of an increasing share of the economy, the Securities Act of 1933 could hardly have been better designed to attain that result.[1] Like Bullock, most intelligent critics of Roosevelt's economic policies were still less concerned about the purposes behind those policies than their likely result. The charges of the more extreme critics that the Roosevelt administration was intent on transforming the United States into a communist or national socialist state still seemed hysterical to most, but they did worry that the apparent lack of deliberation behind many of Roosevelt's actions and, above all, the lighthearted, even flippant way in which policies and programs of major implication for the economy were adopted, might lead to that result by accident. They were concerned that a cycle ultimately destructive of a free economy and society had been unleashed. Roosevelt's policies were retarding the ability of business to recover and furnish needed employment; impatience with the absence or slowness of recovery would inevitably bring new governmental intervention in the economy that would weaken and retard business enterprise even more. If the trend were not reversed, it could result ultimately in the destruction of both the free economy and a free society.

American liberals found embodied in many of Roosevelt's programs reforms for which they had long struggled, and large numbers of them supported Roosevelt in both his goals and methods. But, as Otis Graham has pointed out, more of the liberals of the earlier progressive era seem to have opposed the New Deal than supported it.[2] For the opponents among them the quarrel was less over goals than methods. Many were enthusiastic about the early months of the New Deal, but, while some would not move into opposition until 1936 and 1937, many defected as early as 1934 and 1935. Their motives in opposing or defecting from Roosevelt varied, but if the example of two prominent defectors—Amos Pinchot and Walter Lippmann—may be taken as typical, a prominent reason was dissatisfaction with Roosevelt's recovery efforts. No matter how unsympathetic they might feel toward business, they joined other New Deal critics in faulting Roosevelt's antibusiness policies for retarding recovery.

Walter Lippmann is a case in point. Despite a derogatory appraisal of Roosevelt's qualifications for the presidency that he published in 1932, Lippmann's response to the early New Deal ranged from mildly critical to enthusiastically supportive. But Lippmann did not lose sight of the primary problem before the United States—recovery from the depression—and by early 1934 he had begun to recognize, as had Keynes, that Roosevelt's preoccupation with reform was retarding recovery. Pump priming by the federal government could admittedly keep the economy afloat for some time, and perhaps bring about some improvement, but it could do so only as long as the federal credit held up, and it was imperative to stimulate private enterprise to bring about genuine recovery before the money ran out. The success of the Roosevelt administration in bringing about recovery, then, depended "upon the clear-headedness and decision with which it does those things that have to be done to stimulate private enterprise and private investment," Lippmann wrote early in January 1934.[3]

By March, Lippmann was openly condemning both the NRA and AAA for raising costs ahead of profits, thus discouraging enterprise and causing the "real net income of the community" to fall. Such policies could not work and were "a menace to recovery."[4] By April, Lippmann was counseling Roosevelt to give business a "breathing spell" free of new reform burdens so that it might be possible at last to "concentrate attention and effort on making the existing reforms workable and above all stimulating the forces of recovery." It was time, he insisted, for the Roosevelt administration "to release enterprise by abandoning some of the measures that constrict it and revising others." He concluded that much of the New Deal, "from A. A. A. to the Stock Market Bill," in fact retarded enterprise "at a time when the relief of unemployment and of insolvency depends primarily upon the revival of enterprise."[5]

Lippmann, however, found little evidence that Roosevelt and his advisers even understood the problem. In May 1934 he wrote:

In the process of a managed recovery like the one we are having, the transition from government spending to private investment is the critical point. It is not clear as to how that transition is to be made. Yet on the making of it everything depends. Moreover, it is not clear that the Administration and Congress are fully aware that this is the critical problem or that they are sufficiently impressed with its importance to be willing to deal with it effectively.[6]

Indeed, such concerns were, in fact, far from the minds of those pressing further reforms upon Roosevelt. Felix Frankfurter, for one, found it "amusing how much idle chatter still goes on about 'recovery' vs. 'reform.' "[7] But Frankfurter was employed. Well over 11 million Americans were not. And in 1937 the administration would wish that it had paid heed to the advice of critics like Lippmann.

Particularly dear to Frankfurter and the other Brandeisians was the securities exchange bill introduced in the 1934 session of Congress and written by two Frankfurter proteges, Benjamin Cohen and Thomas Corcoran. More than simply a proposal for regulating the stock exchanges, just as the Securities Act of 1933 was more than a bill for protecting investors, the Cohen-Corcoran product cloaked the Federal Trade Commission with such powers that, in the words of one critic, it would be able "completely to interrupt the currents of finance, and thus paralyze the industry and commerce of the entire country."[8] *Nation's Business* found the bill "one more instance of the tendency of the reforming mind to see only the evil and to desire to rectify that evil without inquiring what the effect might be on the others." It was like "a policeman who charges down the street shooting wildly at a fleeing thief and . . . wounds or kills harmless citizens."[9] After careful study of the bill, *Barron's* questioned "whether its 'young liberal' framers are more interested in their own theories of a planned and centrally-controlled economy than in recovery."[10] In a front page editorial, the *Wall Street Journal* warned:

The immediately essential thing is that the country recognize the bill for what it is, the cornerstone of a completely socialized economy. If that is what the country wants it will have it. But it must be under no delusion that this bill is only a measure of stock exchange protection.[11]

Even the veteran crusader against Wall Street, reformer Samuel Untermeyer, warned that the proposed bill went "too far and is likely to defeat its own purposes." It was, moreover, an "unworkable law."[12] The Business Advisory Council of the Commerce Department warned that passage of the bill in the Cohen-Corcoran version would be "a national disaster."[13] After comparing the Roosevelt messages at the time the Securities Act of 1933 and the securities

58   *Pride, Prejudice, and Politics*

exchange bill of 1934 were introduced in Congress, with the actual bills that were produced by the Brandeisian draftsmen, Fred Kent, prominent banker and regular Roosevelt correspondent, wrote the president:

Often I wonder whether you have any realization of one important question that is going through the minds of the people in relation to legislative acts and proposed legislation. Your messages, for instance, on the Security Bill and the Stock Exchange Control Bill met with universal approval and are thoroughly sound. The legislation, however, that has resulted in a law in one case and a proposed law in the other, has led to the belief in the minds of a growing part of the public that certain forces in Washington are unfairly taking advantage of your fine statements to accomplish something not at all asked for by you, and for purposes other than reconstruction, that are apparently intentionally aimed to make it impossible for business to function.

Having thus suggested that Roosevelt was at best dimly aware of the contents and real motives of the legislation being sent to Congress in his name, and that he was being used by his more radical advisers, Kent went on to describe the securities exchange bill as "apparently deliberately aimed to effect such rigidity in business operations that the production required by the people would be impossible." He warned Roosevelt that "when the urge for punishment exceeds that for sound regulation it means a very real setback to progress."[14]

Roosevelt was at a disadvantage in replying to Kent, for he had only recently admitted to the press that he had not even read the securities exchange bill, despite all of the controversy surrounding it.[15] Ignoring, therefore, the main point of Kent's letter, Roosevelt responded angrily that he was "sick and tired of all the complaint against the Stock Exchange and Securities Bills." He admitted that the Securities Act of 1933 needed "clarification and slight amendment," and he told Kent that the securities exchange bill had already been "amended to take care of certain phraseology which went beyond the purpose."[16]

Indeed, the securities exchange bill had by this time experienced important revisions by Congress. Those amendments, the New York *Herald-Tribune* observed, could "not be acclaimed as a perfect solution of the problem of exchange regulation," but they would at least dispose "of the suspicion, harbored seriously in some quarters, that its sponsors were bent on the destruction of rather than the regulation of the machinery of Wall Street."[17] In this and other cases, however, it is to the original bills submitted to Congress that students of the Roosevelt administration must look for the intentions of Roosevelt and/or his advisers, not to the final bills that were modified as the result of opposition.

Roosevelt was also moving toward the revision of the Securities Act of 1933, which he had promised late in 1933. By this point the Brandeisian motives behind the original law had become more apparent, or at least the likely effect of the law in that direction, whether intended or not. In criticizing it, William O. Douglas observed that its Brandeisian sponsors reflected a "nineteenth century" philosophy in their attempt to " 'turn back the clock' to simpler days." It was based on the assumption that the United States must return to a simpler economy, "that our large units of production should be pulverized." Such a view was no longer appropriate, he pointed out, and as an instrument for such "pulverization" the securities law was "antithetical" to such other New Deal measures as the NRA and AAA, which envisioned "a coalescence of present forms of organization into even more stable forms."[18] Roosevelt turned the writing of amendments to the securities law over to James Landis and others of the Brandeis-Frankfurter group who were responsible for the problems they were now called upon to correct. This time, however, Landis consulted with bankers and brokers to obtain their recommendations.[19]

Scarcely two weeks had passed since Keynes' "open letter" to him was published before Roosevelt moved to provide the monetary stability that the British economist had recommended. The Gold Reserve Act gave him the authority to devalue the dollar to a point between 50 and 60 cents in gold, and Roosevelt set the value of the dollar at 59.06 cents of its previous value by establishing $35 as the price of gold. The action was hailed as, at the least, "a further element of certainty," where previously there had been "entirely too much fluctuation for comfort."[20]

FDR UNDER SIEGE

Roosevelt had hardly moved constructively on the monetary front, however, before he blundered badly on another. Early in February he summarily canceled all domestic airmail contracts, charging that there had been collusion in the granting of contracts by the Hoover administration.[21] When Roosevelt's action was not followed by action against the airlines in the courts, which would have furnished the airlines with an opportunity to defend themselves, his action was criticized for having "tarred" an entire industry when only a few, if any, of the companies were guilty.[22] *Business Week* decried the "impetuosity" that Roosevelt had shown in the episode, while a businessman wondered if any contracts with the federal government could hereafter be considered safe. "In time," he wrote, "no corporation nor business could afford to have any dealings with a Government who has no respect for contracts entered into."[23] The *Magazine of Wall Street* agreed that "if private industry is to be thus summarily punished without even a fair hearing, what industry can confidently enter into contracts with its Government?"[24] The Roosevelt administration's case was not strengthened when First Assistant Postmaster General William Howes admitted before a Senate committee that the same methods of negotiating contracts had prevailed during the first ten months of the Roosevelt administration, that he considered it perfectly legal, and that it seemed, indeed, the only "intelligent" way of dealing with airmail affairs.[25]

Meanwhile, U. S. Army pilots were losing their lives in the attempt to fly the mail in place of the airlines whose contracts had been cancelled. The whole affair had revealed Roosevelt's "feet of clay," Arthur Krock wrote, and now "a degree of distrust of his methods and judgment pervades groups where it did not exist before."[26]

The NRA came under new attacks early in 1934 from an unexpected direction when Senators William Borah and Gerald Nye charged that it was fostering "monopoly" at the expense of smaller businesses. Their attacks led to numerous letters from small businesses complaining of their plight under the NRA codes.[27] Typical was the situation of the small textile mills in New England, distant from markets and raw materials, who had thus far been able to exist as the principal employers in their areas—and as the major source of wages for their communities—by paying lower wages that larger companies more advantageously situated. Forced by the NRA codes now to pay the same wages as those larger competitors, these mills found it impossible to compete.[28] The NRA codes failed to recognize or to permit many of the adjustments necessary in a free market. The suit presser on a low-traffic side street was forced to charge the same price and pay the same wages as his competitor on the main street and was not allowed to offer any inducements to overcome his poor location. The maladjustments that such rigidity must create were obvious, as were the difficulties of enforcement.

The confusion and inconsistency in the NRA, combined with the obvious favoritism shown toward organized labor by its National Labor Board, led increasing numbers of businessmen in early 1934 to oppose it.[29] Banker Fred Kent could find no enthusiasm for the NRA anywhere. Even consumers, he noted, no longer cared "whether the store they enter has the Blue Eagle in its window." They didn't even stop to look. In the end, he predicted, the codes would be ignored even as prohibition had been ignored.[30]

At a meeting of NRA code executives early in March, Roosevelt called for further increases in wages and further cuts in hours. "The Government cannot forever continue to absorb the whole burden of unemployment," Roosevelt told them. "The thing to do now is to get more people to work." But "to get more people to work" in the manner Roosevelt suggested, offered only the prospect of further delay in recovery and a continued burden on the government.[31] One critic remarked of Roosevelt's request: "It is to suggest that we arise into the air and yet remain on the ground, that we advance at break-neck speed but slowly, that we expand purchasing power at once but without its costing anybody money."[32] In short, Roosevelt's proposal was nonsensical. But there was little likelihood that the code authorities would follow Roosevelt's lead, one journalist observed, because "business has started to revolt. . . . five thousand business men [the code executives] assembled in Washington simply told Johnson and Roosevelt that they would not do it."[33] Instead, the code executives called for revision of the Securities Act of 1933 and modification of the securities exchange bill in order to release the flow of private capital to the durable goods industries.[34]

Late in the month, Roosevelt revealed the siege mentality that prevailed in the White House, writing Frankfurter:

The scattered forces of the opposition seized on the loss of life among the Army fliers to come together and make a concerted drive. For the last three weeks we have been under heavy bombardment. The steel crowd have shown their teeth, the aviation companies have been shrieking to high heaven, using the Chambers of Commerce and every small community with a flying field to demand the return of their contracts, the automobile companies are, at this writing, still trying to flaunt the provisions for collective bargaining, the bigger bankers are still withholding credits at every possible opportunity, the Republican politicians . . . are denouncing me as a murderer and the old line press harps increasingly on state socialism and demands the return to the good old days.

Roosevelt, however, predicted that Congress would enact his package of legislation and "that this major offensive on the part of the enemy will fail just as the one last Autumn failed."[35]

THE LEGISLATION OF 1934

When businessmen surveyed the legislation pending before Congress in 1934, they found much to disturb them. The amendments to the securities exchange bill made that piece of legislation more palatable, but there remained the Wagner labor bill, which seemed to concede everything to the labor unions that might have been overlooked by the NRA and its National Labor Board, the Bankhead cotton control bill, and the reciprocal tariff bill. The New York *Times* observed of the Wagner labor bill that, while it proclaimed as its object the ending of "unfair practices," it did not forbid or condemn "a single unfair practice by a labor union—such as intimidation, coercion or violence," so that it hardly represented an attempt to create "even-handed justice" in employer-employee relations.[36] Bankhead's bill acknowledged the failure of the AAA's voluntary controls and sought now to penalize those cotton farmers who produced in excess of a quota allotted them by the administration.[37] The Chamber of Commerce denounced it as subordinating "the free American citizen to the dictation and tyranny of the government." If allowed in cotton, what was to stop such tyranny from being extended to other crops, to business and to labor?[38]

Opposition to the reciprocal tariff bill was primarily motivated by fear and distrust of Roosevelt, and of concern over granting him such powers as the bill contained to negotiate lower tariffs with other countries. With the recent example of the airmail episode obviously in mind, the New York *Herald-Tribune* wondered: "What is to prevent the Executive from using his tariff-bargaining powers so as to ruin industries which some of his advisers wish to see broken for any one of a number of possible reasons, either political or theoretical."[39] *The Economist* was almost alone in pointing out the continued incompatability between reduced tariffs and the NRA/AAA, particularly when Roosevelt continued to call for shorter hours and higher wages for industrial workers.[40] Nevertheless, Roosevelt's request for passage of the bill, with its explicit recognition that domestic policies alone could not produce recovery, was greeted by some as a sign that common sense was at last intruding into the White House.[41]

GROWING UNEASINESS

For a short time late in March the front pages of the nation's newspapers were captured by the sensational charges of Dr. William Wirt, a distinguished Indiana educator, that "brain trusters" had disclosed to him a secret plot to hold back recovery from the depression in order to stimulate popular demand for a far-reaching "revolution" of the economic and social order.[42] Wirt's account of the conversation was quickly contradicted and his credibility in the matter destroyed. Historians who have dismissed Wirt and his charges as ludicrous have, however, missed the important point of the episode—the fact that Wirt's charges received the attention they did revealed the uneasiness that was widely felt over the course and objectives of Roosevelt's policies. The principal issue was not what Wirt had heard or not heard, but whether the charge he made possessed any validity. And if those around Roosevelt were not purposefully obstructing recovery in order to create the conditions for a revolution, was their incompetence leading to the same eventuality?[43] The end result would be the same in either case.

The Washington *Post* wrote of the Wirt affair:

when the national situation is as serious as is the case today; when . . . economic recovery is being held back by legislation with obviously ulterior objectives, such assertions [as Wirt's] become cause for reflection. They arouse widespread attention not because they are intrinsically startling but because candid analysis of the situation reveals that the assertion, whatever its source, is based on certain substantial premises.[44]

Walter Lippmann agreed that "the conviction that recovery is being held back is the basis of the outcry against the Brain Trust, and the reason why, in spite of the collapse of Dr. Wirt's charges, the Brain Trust is increasingly unpopular." Lippmann agreed with business critics that "the common character of all this legislation—from A. A. A. to the Stock Market Bill, is that it constricts enterprise." Some of Roosevelt's legislation, he observed, was "not unlike laws to prevent railroad accidents by stopping the trains."[45]

FRB and other statistics did not indicate that consumers were any better off in the early months of 1934 than they had been a year earlier. *Barron's* found in the statistics of the Federal Reserve Bank of New York evidence that department store sales were no larger in dollar volume in January 1934 than a year earlier, while grocery sales had actually declined, and wondered "is not the implication clear that perhaps we are getting nowhere, in fact, that the country is actually consuming fewer things."[46] *Dry Goods Economist* and the Chicago *Tribune* made similar analyses and reached the same conclusions.[47] Instead of the "more abundant life" that Roosevelt had promised, it appeared that the American standard of living was slipping. Such results were clearly not what the purchasing power theorists, Roosevelt included, had anticipated. A writer in *Magazine of Wall Street* suggested the obvious solution: if Roosevelt genuinely believed that purchasing power was increased by a 10 percent rise in wages and reduced working hours, "why not swell purchasing still more by establishing a 10-hour week and quadrupling wages?"[48]

Such criticism appears to have had little effect on the administration, but in April a ripple went through the White House when Brandeis passed the word to Roosevelt via three of the brain trust that he was opposed to the whole concept of the NRA. Adolf Berle described the conversation with Brandeis:

His idea was that we were steadily creating organisms of big business which were growing in power, wiping out the middle class, eliminating small business and putting themselves in a place in which they rather than the government were controlling the nation's destinies. He added that he had gone along with the legislation up to now; but that unless he could see some reversal of the big business trend, he was disposed to hold the . . . legislation unconstitutional from now on.[49]

Tugwell confided to his diary that Brandeis had, in effect, declared war on the NRA. Frankfurter, he thought, shared Brandeis' prejudices but did not "feel so strongly about it." Even Tugwell, however, recognized that the NRA had failed, when he noted that "price disparities have been made worse by N. R. A. and consumer purchasing power dried up by that much." Tugwell blamed the failure on Johnson's poor qualities as an administrator and his error in attempting to cover all industries with the codes instead of just the largest ones.[50]

If "price disparities" had been worsened by the NRA, no doubt the collective bargaining provisions in the act bore at least part of the blame because of the incitement they furnished to labor union activity in the midst of a depression. Largely as a result of that incentive, strikes in 1933 had involved more workers (1,170,000) in that single year than in the four Hoover years combined. In 1933, 6.3 percent of those employed participated in strikes, compared with 1.8 percent in 1932, the highest of the preceding four years. But in 1934 labor disturbances spread, embracing nearly 1.5 million workers and 7.2 percent of the work force.[51] Economist Leonard Ayres noted in April that wage increases had been granted in the iron and steel, coal, and automobile industries to settle labor disputes. These were on top of the increases under the NRA, and inevitably each settlement had been followed by higher prices to pay the increased wages. The same thing was now happening in smaller industry, and Ayres warned that the effect was likely to "check demand and production" and disrupt the price parities between agricultural and industrial goods.[52] Fred Kent warned Roosevelt that the labor offensive was destroying "the opportunity for recovery in the lines in which they occur."[53] An industrialist who had supported Roosevelt in 1932 wrote Raymond Moley that "we see businesses all around us being destroyed by the government's [pro-labor] attitude and we, of course, cannot tell when our turn will come." He found businessmen "scared to death" because they did not know when "some bunch of radicals will descend on their plant and forcefully take possession and drive out the good, loyal employees and even the owners of the plant and in many cases wreck the institution almost beyond repair." The result was that businessmen he knew were "trying to get their business in as liquid a shape as possible, because they don't know what day they will have to close and liquidate. Can business expansion go on? Will private capital seek any investment when this is the feeling in general of industry in the United States ...?"[54] Noting the downturn in business indices in July, the *Guaranty Survey* concluded that of all the factors impairing confidence and retarding recovery, the labor situation was the most serious.[55]

When Roosevelt sent the customary message to the annual convention of the U. S. Chamber of Commerce in May 1934, he warned that the American people were impatient with those who complained and held out "false fears" concerning the government's recovery efforts. It was time, he told businessmen, "to stop crying 'wolf,' " and to cooperate with the administration in working for recovery and "for the continued elimination of evil conditions of the past."[56] Henry I. Harriman, reelected to a third term as head of the organization, continued his efforts to moderate the chamber's criticism of the New Deal. *Business Week* found the businessmen at the convention divided into three categories. One, which seemed totally opposed to the New Deal, was not large, but contained important and influential figures like former chamber president Silas Strawn. A second, which supported most of the New Deal, was about the same size as the anti-New Deal group. The third, constituting a majority of the convention, took its lead from Harriman in giving the New Deal credit for any economic improvement that existed. It favored, however, a pause now in the forward movement of the New Deal.[57] Enclosing a copy of the resolutions the convention had adopted, Harriman wrote Roosevelt that business "earnestly desires to cooperate with the government to the end that permanent and lasting prosperity can be restored at any early date."[58]

In May the amended Securities Exchange Act was passed by Congress and there was a new surge of labor strife. After five months of moderate improvement in business indices that began in December 1933, the New York *Times* and other business indexes tended downward in early May.[59] Amid signs that another decline had begun in the economy, columnist David Lawrence wrote:

The causes may be the multitude of uncertainties produced by the legislative situation, but any such analysis ignores the fundamental weakness of our economic set-up which have been there ever since our vision was blurred by the CWA money and every other artificial stimulus to recovery. We are now beginning to see what a false prosperity can do when it starts to collapse.[60]

Iron Age found the principal cause of the downturn to be the renewed labor strife that had broken out in the automobile, steel, textile, and other industries.[61] *The Annalist* agreed that, while there were many factors contributing to the weakness of the business situation, "chief among them is the labor situation," which was now "as bad if not worse . . . than at any time since the New Deal got under way."[62]

On June 8, Roosevelt sent to Congress a message "reviewing the broad objectives and accomplishments of the administration." Clearly designed to assist Democrats in the congressional elections that were only five months away, Roosevelt's message put the best face possible on the New Deal's record to date, but more importantly outlined a vision for the future. Roosevelt told Congress that he was "looking for a sound means which I can recommend to provide at once security against several of the great disturbing factors in life—especially those that relate to unemployment and old age." As for recovery, Roosevelt remarked that he was

greatly hoping that repeated promises of private investment and private initiative to relieve the Government in the immediate future of much of the burden it has assumed, will be fulfilled. We have not imposed undue restrictions upon business. We have not opposed the incentive of reasonable and legitimate private profit. We have sought rather to enable certain aspects of business to regain the confidence of the public. We have sought to put forward the rule of fair play in finance and industry.[63]

Most press comment dismissed Roosevelt's message as a campaign document. The Baltimore *Sun*, however, pointed out that the real issue was not whether Roosevelt believed in private profits or not, but the fact that he had "followed certain policies that have interfered seriously with the play of private initiative and which have made it difficult for private enterprise to relieve the Government of the burdens to which in his message he refers."[64]

During that same month John Maynard Keynes journeyed to the United States, accepted an honorary degree from Columbia University, published a syndicated essay on the New Deal, and, through the good offices of Frankfurter, conferred with the president in the White House. In his essay, Keynes summarized the problem facing recovery in the United States: "How soon will normal business enterprise come to the rescue? What measures can be taken to hasten the return of normal enterprise? On what scale, by which expedients and for how long is abnormal Government expenditure advisable in the meantime?" Keynes foresaw no likelihood that business would invest in durable goods on an adequate basis for many months, because he found "the important but intangible state of mind which we call business confidence, is signally lacking." A major cause of this, he concluded, was "the menace of possible labor troubles," but more important was "the perplexity and discomfort which the business world feels from being driven so far from its accustomed moorings into unknown and uncharted waters" by the New Deal. While business would likely adjust in time to the altered conditions already created by the New Deal, it must be assured now by Roosevelt that the worst of his program had already been enacted, and that it would now be allowed to "settle down to adjust . . . to a known situation." It was, in other words, time to call a halt to reform and concentrate on recovery.

Keynes called for an increase in deficit spending to $400 million per month, at which figure he was "quite confident that a strong business revival would set in by the autumn." To ensure that result, "active preparations should be on foot to make sure that normal enterprise will take the place of the emergency [spending] program as soon as possible." One vital element in this process was "sincere efforts on both sides to establish cooperative and friendly relations between the commission which works the [securities and stock exchange] acts and the leading financial interests," since such cooperation was "vital to reopen the capital market." Interest rates should be reduced, building costs brought down, and Roosevelt should promise that there would be no further experiments with monetary policy—that "henceforth a wise spending policy and a gradual but obstinate attack on high interest rates . . . will occupy the foreground of the economic program."[65]

From this it will be seen that Keynes' advice to Roosevelt suffered from a fatal flaw: the assumption that Roosevelt was sincerely interested in recovery and was willing to sacrifice or postpone his reform measures to obtain it. Far more than simply advocating "a wise spending policy," Keynes continued to echo American critics of the New Deal in finding serious errors in the Roosevelt policies toward business. Like those critics, Keynes recognized that recovery was impossible until business confidence was no longer assaulted by a stream of unsettling New Deal reforms; that the principal problem of recovery lay in the ignored durable goods industries where it was "vital to reopen the capital market" that had been hampered by the New Deal; that a genuine recovery could take place only if "active preparations" were made to ensure that "normal enterprise" could take the place of the artificial stimulation furnished by government spending. Keynes knew that spending could not promote recovery in the presence of government policies that simultaneously retarded such recovery. When the New Deal embarked in 1935 on a spending program such as Keynes had suggested, it did not do so in unison with Keynes' other recommendations, but rather used the spending as a substitute for the retreat or cessation that he had called for in the New Deal.

The 1933 New Deal emerged from the 1934 session of Congress largely intact, except for some important revisions in the Securities Act of 1933 to make it more workable. Important new legislation was added, including the Securities Exchange Act, which had, however, been much modified by Congress in response to business and financial criticism. Much would depend on the character of the new Securities and Exchange Commission that would administer it and the Securities Act. Congress also enacted the Communications Act, which placed regulation of the radio, telegraph, and cable industries under the Federal Communications Commission; the Railroad Retirement Act, which would soon be found unconstitutional; the Frazier-Lemke Farm Mortgage Moratorium Act, which was not a part of the New Deal program and which would also be found unconstitutional; the Bankhead Cotton Control Act, which would soon arouse such protests that even Senator Bankhead would lead a movement to repeal it;

the Jones-Connally Farm Relief Act; the National Housing Act; the Air Mail Act, which sought to retrieve the Roosevelt administration from the embarrassment of its earlier impetuous action; and further relief appropriations. One of the major sources of business apprehension during the session—the Wagner labor bill—was not passed. Vigorously opposed by businessmen, and lacking support at this time from the Roosevelt administration, it was held over for further consideration.

A MIXED SUMMER

Business breathed a sigh of relief with the adjournment of Congress, but business writer Ralph West Robey pointed out that they should not breathe too deeply just yet. Under the Roosevelt administration, the uncertainties over government policies that might alter business and banking conditions were not limited to the periods when Congress was in session. With the broad powers that were delegated to executive agencies, the process of "legislating" went on even when Congress was not in session.[66] One New Deal agency that would be of critical importance to business and finance was the Securities and Exchange Commission (SEC) established under the Securities Exchange Act of 1934. As the Washington *Post* pointed out, if the appointees to that commission were primarily interested in stimulating recovery, then "neither business nor the organized stock exchanges need fear the restrictive and punitive provisions of the law." But if they mirrored Roosevelt's insistence on reform over recovery, then they possessed powers under the new law "to work irreparable damage to the community as a whole."[67] Late in July, Roosevelt surprised the business and financial community by naming entrepreneur Joseph Kennedy to head the SEC. A cautious initial response to Kennedy's appointment turned to widespread approval when the new chairman's first public statements did much to remove fears over the attitude the new agency would harbor. Kennedy's words were quickly followed by actions equally reassuring to business when the SEC moved gradually and moderately into operation.[68]

In other respects, however, it was not a summer that inspired business confidence. One issue of the Chicago *Tribune* in mid-July spoke reams about the difficulties businessmen and their employees were experiencing in their relations with the NRA. Three news stories in that issue described: (1) the plight of over 600 employees of the Harriman Hosiery Mills in Harriman, Tennessee, who had been thrown out of work when the NRA took away the company's Blue Eagle, thus forcing the shutdown of the only major industry in the town; (2) the closing of the G&H Clothing Company in Fredricksburg, Virginia, with 500 workers thrown out of work, owing to a dispute with the NRA; (3) the planned closing of a manufacturer of lumber and lumber products in Mobile, Alabama, owing to its inability to meet the requirements of the NRA code.[69] In August the Roosevelt administration injected further uncertainty when the NRA arbitrarily imposed a 36-hour week on the cotton garment industry, thereby raising the specter that other industries might be subjected to similar arbitrariness.[70]

Those who scanned the earnings statements of business for the first quarter of 1934 found them disappointing. Most had shown "a sharp decrease in profit margins," one economist observed, even in those cases where they had done a larger dollar volume of business than the previous summer. In some cases a larger volume of business had even resulted in profits turning to losses. Moreover, it was the smaller companies that had been hardest hit.[71] Other business statistics were equally disappointing. The economy lurched through May and June, and then began a decided plummet downward in the first week of July. The decline in that week was exceeded in the New York *Times* weekly business index only by those that had accompanied the stock market crash in 1929, the banking crisis in early 1933, and the decline in the summer of 1933 upon the implementation of the NRA and AAA.[72] By the end of the month, the AFL estimated that 10.3 million workers were still unemployed.[73]

While Roosevelt vacationed by fishing on the high seas and taking in the sights of Hawaii, the nation spent an uneasy July of falling economic indices, widespread strikes, and other evidence of his failure to produce either economic recovery or industrial peace. As Roosevelt made his leisurely way across the western United States on his return from Hawaii, businessmen awaited his scheduled August 9 speech in Green Bay, Wisconsin, for some indication that he now understood the difficulties that he had placed in the way of recovery and that his administration was now ready to cooperate in a recovery effort. In a radio speech earlier in the month, Tugwell had lashed out at New Deal critics, calling them "Tories" and "reactionary obscurantists," and labeling their criticism "wicked," "infantile," "obscene," and "indecent."[74] Did Joseph Kennedy's constructive approach, or Tugwell's abusive epithets, represent Roosevelt's attitude? An uneasy business and financial community awaited the answer.

CHAPTER 5

The First Roosevelt Depression, 1934

THE COLLAPSE

Roosevelt's speech at Green Bay was a shocking performance. In a scornful reference to the pleas that he do something to restore business confidence, Roosevelt claimed that he had answered one such request by asking the unidentified "important" man what he should do. The response, Roosevelt said, had been that "the way to restore confidence was for me to tell the people of the United States that all supervision by all forms of Government, Federal and State, over all forms of human activity called business should be forthwith abolished." Roosevelt's interpretation of this recommendation, obviously manufactured for him by one of his speechwriters for the occasion, was that it meant the repeal of all laws that regulated business, including those dating back to the turn of the century that dealt with railroad rates and pure food and drugs. "In fact, my friends, if we were to listen to him and his type, the old law of the tooth and the claw would reign in our Nation once more," Roosevelt insisted, and the American people would "not restore that ancient order." Such palpable nonsense and scornful indifference to the legitimate need for action to restore business confidence, recognized by New Deal critics as disparate as John Maynard Keynes and the Chicago *Tribune*, was not mitigated by Roosevelt's statement later in the speech that his administration intended "no injury to honest business."[1] Business had heard that when the Securities Act was introduced into Congress in 1933. With over 10 million unemployed and their number increasing, and with economic indices falling, the nation had a right to expect better from the president of the United States.

The shock waves quickly radiated out from Green Bay. The reaction of the *Wall Street Journal* was typical of press response in deploring Roosevelt's demagoguery when it wrote: "Not one business man in a hundred, if he had it within his own power, would do what the President gives us to understand is the typical aspiration of business men who have asked that the Administration define more intelligibly its purposes and its intended course of action." Roosevelt had set up "a man of straw, malevolently reactionary in his thoughts and feelings," and had then proceeded to crush it "by vociferating his unnecessary and wholly irrelevant refusal to reinstate 'the old law of the tooth and claw.' "[2] The Washington *Post* took up Roosevelt's reference to the "old law of tooth and claw," and told the president that it was time to put aside such "obsessions" and "squarely confront the question of how the New Deal is to be made workable." It concluded that the "ceaseless reiteration of that soapbox theme can only lead to suspicion that it is put forward to distract attention from more humdrum realities."[3] Kiplinger reported that the more conservative of Roosevelt's advisers were "disappointed and shocked" by the speech, but from Frankfurter came "warm congratulations" to the president for it.[4]

Hurriedly, other administration figures, most notably Treasury Secretary Morgenthau and Commerce Secretary Roper, tried to repair the damage done by Roosevelt in the Green Bay speech. While appreciated, the efforts met skepticism. *The Annalist*, especially, linked the sudden conciliation campaign of Roper and Morgenthau in August with the fact that the Treasury contemplated a new government bond issue in September that would need investors.[5] Clearly, the number of New Deal critics who could be taken in by such transparent devices was shrinking rapidly.

As the economic indices continued to worsen in August, the tone of the letters addressed to Roosevelt grew more pessimistic and negative about his policies— not only the letters from business and banking leaders, but also the poorly spelled and ungrammatical efforts of those more modestly situated. Typical was a letter from Detroit in September:

Industry does not know where it is at because of the uncertainty as to where you are at and the present condition will continue to grow worse until industry is assured of a sound constructive policy on the part of the administration. We have had a year and a half of uncertainty with a spurt in business at the beginning because of faith in your New Deal; then, there being nothing to sustain it, business lagged. Get rid of the Communists, Reds, and Socialists and let industry take care of itself; it can, and will.[6]

In mid-August, Roosevelt's secretary Stephen Early sent him a survey of newspaper editorials on the New Deal that showed that month by month the trend had switched from favorable to unfavorable. NRA had attracted the most criticism, with the AAA second. In summary, though, the survey pointed out an aspect of the criticism that had also aroused the comments of newspaper columnists—the fact that "the criticism continues to be directed toward the *Admin-*

istration rather than the President, personally.'' The newspapers seemed ''to have lost faith in his experiments, but to keep faith in him. And what they are beginning to demand more and more is that he keep his word to scrap such emergency measures as have been proven failures and to do it as quickly as possible.''[7]

Business indexes continued to show a downward trend. The New York *Herald-Tribune* index had dropped below 50 only twice during the depression—to near 48 in July 1932, at the depth of the depression, and to 43 during the bank holiday in March 1933. On September 28, 1934, it fell to 49.[8] The New York *Times* noted later in the month that its own index had fallen ''back approximately to the level of January, 1933, a few weeks before the bank closings,'' and found the U. S. level of business in sharp contrast with that of Canada, where ''business indexes point to activity well over 50 percent greater than that in January of 1933.'' What the United States was experiencing, it observed, was a decline both in business activity and business confidence.[9] Yale University economics professor Irving Fisher wrote Roosevelt that the NRA had ''*retarded* recovery and especially retarded re-employment.'' But for business and investor fear of the New Deal, he wrote, ''we could, I think, have been practically out of the depression many months ago.''[10]

Early in September, Donald Richberg of the NRA estimated that some 5 million families would require federal relief during the coming winter. The New York *Herald-Tribune* was quick to point out that this figure, if true, would represent approximately one-fifth to one-sixth of the population of the United States, and would be ''nearly double the number on relief last winter and something like one-third more than the previous maximum, reached in May.''[11] The *Wall Street Journal* wondered if Roosevelt realized that the growing numbers on relief were ''the measure of the New Deal's failure to launch lasting or continuing recovery.'' Stunned by the apparent complacency with which Roosevelt appeared to regard the problem of unemployment, it added:

We need to attack unemployment at its root by eliminating purposeless and vindictive hostility to those who can make jobs from the councils of state. . . . But first of all we must rid ourselves of the dangerous fallacy that relief appropriations of public funds, if only they are large enough, will tide us over present misfortunes until better times in some unknowable fashion are brought in.[12]

Typically, however, Roosevelt was preoccupied with a symptom of the depression rather than the depression itself—with relieving the unemployed instead of relieving unemployment. When Irving Fisher traveled to Hyde Park early in September at Roosevelt's request, he found the president had computed ''that it would cost about five billion dollars to provide for the five million men for one year. He was thinking in terms of employment by the Government rather than reemployment in private industry.'' Fisher suggested that, on the contrary, Roosevelt ought to pursue policies that would ensure the reemployment of the idle by private industry as soon as possible.[13]

Nearly a year after attacking bankers for not cooperating in the recovery effort by increasing their loans to businesses, some in the Roosevelt administration finally began in September to confront realities. RFC head Jesse Jones, who had been one of those most critical of the bankers earlier, now admitted that the problem was not unwillingness to lend but with reluctance to borrow. Granted authority by Congress to lend up to $300 million to businesses, the RFC had been able to find borrowers for only $10 million in three months, and of that total only $400,000 had actually been disbursed. The problem, Jones now conceded, was "uncertainty on the part of both bankers and industrialists that markets could be found for the manufactured products to finance which the loans were intended to be made."[14] In that same month, Treasury Secretary Morgenthau convened a gathering of field agents of the Federal Reserve System, the Federal Deposit Insurance Corporation, the RFC, and the national bank system in order to work out a more liberal set of guidelines for bank examiners.[15] The Roosevelt myth of a banking conspiracy against his administration seemed to have taken a back seat to reality—at least among his subordinates.

Meanwhile, the American Bar Association had brought another aspect of the New Deal wider attention. At its annual convention late in August, an ABA committee charged that the "judicial branch of the federal government is being rapidly and seriously undermined" by the NRA, AAA, and other New Deal agencies. These agencies, to which Congress had delegated judicial and legislative powers, had removed large areas of legal controversy from the jurisdiction of the courts, the ABA report charged, and had "substituted a labyrinth in which the rights of individuals, while preserved in form, can easily be nullified in practice." The committee admitted that even lawyers could not "ascertain the law applicable to a given state of facts" from the thousands of pages of interpretations, edicts, and regulations that flowed from the agencies.[16]

As the economic situation continued to deteriorate in the fall, criticism of the New Deal increased. In mid-September approximately one hundred executives from the durable goods industries gathered at Hot Springs, Virginia, and reaffirmed their opposition to many of the Roosevelt policies.[17] A few days later, Henry I. Harriman sent to Roosevelt a statement by the board of directors of the U. S. Chamber of Commerce in which they expressed their belief that Roosevelt could contribute much to business confidence if he would make a definite statement as to his future plans in a number of matters of concern to businessmen, including international monetary stabilization and balancing the budget.[18] A reply was prepared for Roosevelt's signature but was not sent.[19] Instead, Roosevelt ridiculed the request at a press conference.[20] This was the president's response to an inquiry from the most conciliatory of the business organizations.

Meanwhile, a meeting of over 100 financial experts and industrial executives had been held on Long Island under the auspices of the American Management Association. This meeting adopted, with only two negative votes, a statement for presentation to Roosevelt through Treasury Secretary Morgenthau, which argued that the continuance of a heavily unbalanced budget, combined with "the inconvertibility of our money,'' represented the major factor in creating business uncertainty, and that the government could neither spend nor tax the country back to prosperity.[21] The board of directors of the Chamber of Commerce also criticized Roosevelt's fiscal policies in a statement issued on September 21, warning: ''There are definite indications that uncertainties concerning the fiscal situation likely to result from the Government's borrowing and spending activities, with consequent effects upon monetary and revenue policies, are retarding reemployment and recovery.''[22]

Later in the month Commerce Secretary Roper forwarded to Roosevelt the results of an inquiry made of its members by the Illinois Manufacturers' Association, which included the statement:

Our inquiry . . . indicates that in the opinion of the great majority of the business executives with whom we have contact, that the principal obstacle to business revival, with accompanying increase in unemployment, is the almost universal attitude of uncertainty and apprehension on the part of business executives regarding the future policies of the federal government on issues directly affecting the welfare of private enterprise.

The report also went into specific criticisms of New Deal policies and attitudes, expressing objections similar to those made by other critics.[23] Two days later the New England Council sent to the White House a canvass of business sentiment in that part of the country. As the author of the report put it, ''not to keep a secret any longer, New England business does not like the New Deal. There seems to be no room for doubt on that score. To be statistical about it, 94 percent of all returns reported lack of confidence in the general business situation.''[24]

Sharp criticism of Roosevelt's policies was also expressed by the Boston Conference on Distribution, which included some of the leading retail executives in the nation. Dr. Paul Nystrom, professor of marketing at Columbia University and president of the Limited Price Variety Stores Association, attacked the NRA and ''those queer documents that emanate from the code-making bodies of hundreds of the manufacturing industries'' as ''unsocial and unsound,'' and largely responsible for the slowness of recovery. Lessing J. Rosenwald, chairman of the board of Sears, Roebuck, pointed out that the negative attitude toward the New Deal expressed at the conference reflected ''not only the sense of the meeting but of the national business world as well.''[25] Dean Wallace B. Donham of the Harvard School of Business joined the ranks of those urging Roosevelt to dispel the uncertainties among businessmen over his future policies, saying: ''If managers are not so encouraged, I expect business to decline in the next twelve months and unemployment to increase.'' Government, he pointed out, could not be relieved of the burden of caring for millions of unemployed until business was allowed to recover.[26]

Business Week summarized the amazing developments of September:

Under leaders of the U. S. Chamber of Commerce, the National Association of Manufacturers, the New England Council, and the Durable Goods Industries Committee, business men of the United States are seeking to compile and then present the concrete, specific evidence that the owners and managers of business enterprises, big and little, are seriously worried over the trend of government policy.... Unless, or until, the apprehensions of such representative men are removed, there can be little hope of recovery to normal business levels. The Administration may not know this, but it is so. Fear and discouragement among the men who are at once the country's employers and its principal consumers of durable goods are a dead weight that no recovery program can carry up the hill.

It found, however, in the Green Bay speech and other utterances from the Roosevelt administration, little evidence that the New Dealers were aware of the uneasiness, and, if such an awareness did exist, a disposition on Roosevelt's part to brush it aside as unimportant.[27]

A fireside chat by Roosevelt on September 30 revealed how little he had grasped the situation. In the midst of crippling labor strife, rising unemployment, and business indices that were flirting with the lowest levels of the depression, Roosevelt told the nation that he was "happy to report that after years of uncertainty, culminating in the collapse of the spring of 1933, we are bringing order out of the old chaos with a greater certainty of employment of labor at a reasonable wage and of more business at a fair profit." Roosevelt then listed the steps he had taken to promote recovery, ignoring the evidence that many of them had, on the contrary, retarded rather than promoted recovery. The picture that Roosevelt drew for his listeners of the accomplishments of his administration was very likely a true representation of his understanding of the situation, but it was far removed from reality. He insisted, for example, "that the extent and severity of labor disputes during this period have been far less than in any previous comparable period," but the figures told a very different story.

For those who had believed that the NRA was an emergency and temporary device, Roosevelt's talk contained the disquieting news that he intended it to be permanent. On the positive side, Roosevelt promised "to confer within the coming month with small groups of those truly representative of large employers of labor and of large groups of organized labor, in order to seek their cooperation in . . . a trial period of industrial peace." He expressed commitment to the "national principle that we will not tolerate a large army of unemployed and that we will arrange our national economy to end our present unemployment as soon as we can and then to take wise measures against its return," but he offered no concrete steps.[28]

Critics of the New Deal busied themselves with filling in the omissions from the speech. If the Roosevelt administration had reduced unemployment, the Baltimore *Sun* wondered, why was it "making preparations to feed more people this winter than have been fed by public or private charity at any time in the country's history. Indeed, he did not discuss relief at all."[29] Frank Kent noticed the same omission, and concluded: "Who can help feel that this was a defensive speech from a man anxious to avoid the ugly realities?"[30] Mark Sullivan found it typical of Roosevelt that, instead of addressing himself to the reasons for lack of business confidence, he had expressed his irritation at the businessmen who lacked confidence.[31]

In the two weeks following Roosevelt's fireside chat, the New York *Herald-Tribune* business index dropped to 49.1 and then to 48.3, rivaling the low point that had been reached in the summer of 1932.[32] Even measured against the artificially low mark during the bank holiday, 19 months of Roosevelt's presidency had brought almost no improvement in the economy. Comparing the state of the economy in the midst of what it called the "Roosevelt depression," with that at the peak of the Roosevelt "recovery" in June 1933, the *Herald-Tribune* observed:

We have just passed through a contraction in industrial activity that has amounted to more than 22 percent and that has been roughly comparable, statistically, with the major depression experienced in 1920–21. In other words, the hundreds of millions in government funds that have been spent have not primed the pump at all; they have maintained retail business at a fairly good level, but they have, so far as priming heavy industries is concerned, been like so much water spilled on the ground.

The lesson should be clear, even for Roosevelt, "that there is no legislative legerdemain, whether it be monetary manipulation, price fixing or regulation, that is a sound substitute for business confidence."[33] By October 25 its business index had fallen to 48.[34]

Reviewing the third quarter of 1934 for the *Review of Economic Statistics*, economist Joseph Hubbard concluded that "government measures to stimulate business had failed to bring about a sustained and substantial recovery," as demonstrated by the recession during the quarter. He found a major cause in "the failure to maintain the confidence of business in the whole gamut of governmental measures undertaken by the Administration."[35]

In the White House, Roosevelt played with figures, seeking a way to put 5 million unemployed to work on federal projects. According to Morgenthau's diary, Roosevelt "thought we might start as an objective the employing of five million people, and then gradually decrease it to, say, three million for the second year, one million for the third year, and the fourth year it would disappear."[36] Disappear? If Roosevelt would not allow business to recover and reemploy them, where would they go? The president apparently still could not grasp the connection between business recovery and reemployment, between waging war on business and increasing the number of casualties of that war—the unemployed.

The war was still very much in Roosevelt's mind in early November, as revealed by Ickes' diary. He wrote of Roosevelt's siege mentality:

He seems to feel, as a result of information that has come to him, that big business is bent on a deliberate policy of sabotaging the Administration. There is an impression in some quarters that big business is carefully planting its own people wherever it can in various Government agencies and these people not only keep big business advised of what is going on but block the program whenever they can. He has some very definite information along this line.[37]

Certainly ex-brain truster Raymond Moley found influential figures in the administration encouraging him in such paranoia, and it is not difficult to guess who they were.[38] It was characteristic of Roosevelt and many of those around him to seek scapegoats for the failure of his policies rather than to admit error.

BUSINESS SEEKS A BASIS FOR COOPERATION

The last two months of 1934 were notable for the efforts of businessmen and bankers to find a basis for cooperation with the New Deal in bringing about recovery. The first initiative came from the American Bankers Association, whose president, Francis M. Law, had throughout 1934 endeavored to impress Roosevelt with the desire of bankers to cooperate in every way with the administration. At the ABA convention in October, the leading bankers of the nation gathered to join in the effort at cooperation and to hear Roosevelt address the group.[39] Raymond Moley overcame the hostility of Roosevelt's advisers toward bankers and produced a conciliatory speech for the president to deliver.[40] In that speech, Roosevelt stirred the bankers with a call to action:

The time is ripe for an alliance of all forces intent upon the business of recovery. In such an alliance will be found business and banking, agriculture and industry, and labor and capital. What an all-American team that is! The possibilities of such a team kindle the imagination—they encourage our determination—they make easier the tasks of those in your Government who are leading.[41]

Newspapers, businessmen, and bankers hailed the speech as leaving no doubt of Roosevelt's determination to work cooperatively with business and banking in bringing about economic recovery at last.[42] The New Haven *Journal-Courier* was convinced that "the President now understands he is working with real men in a real world toward a real recovery," and not the theoretical world of his advisers.[43]

Frequently, however, even the most enthusiastic comments were hedged with a nagging pessimism. Would the words be followed by actions? Certainly Roosevelt had left the bankers just as uninformed and confused as before about his intentions, nor had he given any indication that he was prepared to make any concessions to critics of his policies.[44] But what is most striking about the press and other comments about the speech, is the fact that this president of the United States was regarded as so hostile to the banking and business interests of the nation that he was praised for not delivering a hostile speech to the ABA convention.

But, as would so often tragically be the case in the New Deal years, it was the views of the skeptics and cynics concerning Roosevelt that would be validated by subsequent events. The speech that Roosevelt delivered to the bankers represented the moderate views of the writer of the speech, Raymond Moley, not the mood of Roosevelt or of the advisers around him. As Moley recalled, Roosevelt's own draft of the ABA speech had been "more like a thistle than an olive branch."[45] With Moley now editor of *Today* magazine in New York City, except when called to Washington by the president, Roosevelt was surrounded by advisers who encouraged the "thistle" disposition rather than the "olive branch." Late in November, Roosevelt asked Frankfurter, the chief among the "thistle" men, to visit the White House to help him draft some speeches that he expected to give "the liberals . . . more comfort . . . than the Tories."[46]

Scarcely had the ABA convention adjourned before the 1934 congressional elections were held in November. The Democratic campaign was widely hailed in the press as an attempt to "Tammanyize" the entire nation, a reference to the highly successful Democratic machine in New York City frequently cited for corrupt practices.[47] Since the Maine elections were held first, in September, the Roosevelt administration concentrated its attention there first. PWA head Harold Ickes was hustled off to the state to discuss a possible hydroelectric project that the administration knew could not be built because the PWA did not have the money for it. The people of Maine did not know that, however, and Louis Howe, Roosevelt's political adviser, thought that discussion of it would help politically.[48] Meanwhile, the money had been pouring into Maine. The Baltimore *Sun* compared the gubernatorial vote of 1932 in the small town of Eastport with that in 1934. In the former year, the GOP had won by 785–502. But then, under Roosevelt, an outdoor basketball court had been constructed at the high school, the streets had been ditched, a bridge rebuilt, some tennis courts completed, a seawall constructed, the fire station remodeled, and the New Deal had also taken over the canning factories—the main industry of the town—put up 40,000 cases of canned fish for free distribution, and spent about $350,000, most of which went to the factory employees and fishermen. It also paid higher than the local minimum wages for relief work. Not surprisingly, the 1934 gubernatorial vote went 906–502 for the Democratic candidate.[49] Santa Claus should not go unappreciated. With the Democratic victories in Maine in September it was apparent that the 1934 elections were going to be a landslide nationally for the Democrats. But to make sure, the Roosevelt administration in the final week before election day poured $135 million of relief money into every state in the nation—except Maine.[50]

Even Raymond Clapper, one of the few political columnists who remained supportive of the New Deal by late 1934, deplored Roosevelt's use of PWA "surveys" to win votes for Democrats. The announcement that the PWA was planning a "survey" in a state implied that large sums of federal money would be spent there later on. Clapper noted that the offering of these surveys was going on almost daily in the weeks before the November election, and he wrote that even friends of Roosevelt were disturbed by his use of the tactic. He wrote:

"One souring former New Dealer . . . shook his head sadly as he viewed the scene and observed 'They've got a whole lot of money to spend and they're running around looking for gigolos.' "[51] Humorist H. I. Phillips, however, summed up the election best: "It look$ like one of the mo$t one-$ided election$ in the hi$tory of the United $tate$." The battle cry of the Democrats, he added, was "Never change Santa Clauses in mid-chimney."[52]

Despite the enormous disbursement of AAA, PWA, relief, and other funds, the GOP gained slightly on the Democrats, percentagewise in 1934, even while they lost additional seats in Congress. No one denied that the election constituted an endorsement of Roosevelt, but that it meant an endorsement of the New Deal was less certain. The only aspect of the New Deal that seemed roundly approved by the majority of the electorate was its spending habits, and this offered ominous possibilities where the conduct of Roosevelt and the 74th Congress were concerned. If spending were the key to political success, there was certainly no incentive to reduce it.[53]

The Democratic victories in the 1934 elections provided further impetus to the movement of businessmen and bankers toward a cooperative relationship with the Roosevelt administration. In mid-November the U. S. Chamber of Commerce moved to cooperate with other business groups in drafting a recovery plan as a basis for cooperation with the administration.[54] Donald Richberg, described now as "Roosevelt's right-hand recovery aid," congratulated the Chamber of Commerce on its cooperative attitude and acclaimed the prospective new partnership between government and business.[55] The day after the Chamber of Commerce action, the NAM called upon all manufacturers to attend a "national industrial congress" to draft "constructive recommendations for presentation to President Roosevelt."[56]

A financial writer for the New York *Herald-Tribune* gushed: "At no time since business and the Administration were drawn together during the banking moratorium, as against a common foe, has there been anything approaching the efforts of the last few weeks on both sides to effect something like a genuine entente cordiale."[57] The *Commercial and Financial Chronicle*, however, warned that there had been "no fundamental alteration of the general course of the New Deal policies," but, on the contrary, there were indications that Roosevelt had in mind even more "drastic action of the sort constituting the warp and woof of the New Deal." Any cooperation of business with the Roosevelt administration would have to be on the president's terms, rather than "a bona fide cooperative effort to modify these programs into some semblance of workability and reason."[58]

One whose speeches were stimulating optimism in the business community in November was Donald Richberg, chief coordinator of the NRA after Johnson's departure. Even the New York *Herald-Tribune* hailed a Richberg speech late in the month as "so full of sound sense and orthodox economics that it might well have been written by a critic of the New Deal a year ago."[59] Other newspapers and business periodicals echoed the pleased surprise of the *Herald-Tribune*.

Charles Hook, president of the American Rolling Mill Company, wrote Richberg that he appreciated the "constructive position" Richberg was taking "with respect to the relation between government and business."[60] Obviously, Richberg had become too sensible to last for very long in the Roosevelt administration.

While critical observers could still detect disturbing words and deeds emanating from the administration during November, most refused to allow them to undermine their sense of optimism that Roosevelt was at last emphasizing recovery and would welcome cooperation with business and banking in seeking that goal. The ABA journal concluded late in the year that the six weeks prior to December 1, 1934, had seen more "accomplished in laying a foundation for business recovery by securing genuine and effective cooperation among the Government, the banks and the nation's private business interests than in any six months in the last five years." It found what it thought were encouraging signs that Roosevelt was altering his policies to meet the needs of business in recent modifications of the NRA, the removal of restrictions on the legitimate international movement of funds, and a tacit promise to limit further social reforms to what was practicable without interfering with recovery.[61] Even the Chicago *Tribune* detected hopeful signs that Roosevelt now recognized that reform must give way to recovery efforts. If Roosevelt now demonstrated that recent promising moves in that direction were part of a general policy, "a brilliant business recovery may soon be under way."[62] A reader wrote to the *Magazine of Wall Street*:

We who own a few shares of this and that ought to feel sort of cheered up, now that Franklin D. is offering his pipe of peace to the business chiefs. . . . I do feel cheered up— some; but does Roosevelt really mean it or did he have his fingers crossed? And if he's smart enough to fix everything for us why did it take him eighteen months to find out that the profit system can't run without business confidence any better than my Ford can run without gas and oil?[63]

A pending problem between the Roosevelt administration and business was the future status of the NRA, which was due to expire the following spring but which Roosevelt had already indicated he wanted to retain. Columnist Raymond Clapper, no opponent of the New Deal, found businessmen justly concerned about the "wholesale delegation of combined legislation, executive and judicial functions to the Recovery Administration." The result had been to create in NRA "a quasi law-making organization in which hundreds of subordinate officials write the laws and enforce them." Clapper estimated conservatively that between 4,000 and 5,000 business practices were prohibited by NRA orders that carried the force of law. These were contained in some 3,000 administrative orders covering, he said, more than 10,000 pages, and supplemented by "innumerable opinions and directions from national, regional and code boards interpreting and enforcing provisions of the act." There were also "the rules of the code authorities, themselves, each having the force of law and affecting the lives and conduct of millions of persons.'' Clapper concluded: ''It requires no imagination to appreciate the difficulty the business man has in keeping informed of these codes, supplemental codes, code amendments, executive orders, administrative orders, office orders, interpretations, rules, regulations and obiter dicta.''[64] Indeed, even had business confidence not been lacking, it is difficult to see how the average businessman could have found time to spend on business affairs away from the mass of regulations with which he must now familiarize himself.

What was perhaps worse was the demonstrated inability even of those responsible for enforcing this kaleidoscope of ''laws'' to keep abreast of them. The confusion of the NRA officials, themselves, was brought to public attention when four Texas oil producers were arrested and imprisoned for violating an NRA ''law'' which, upon investigation, was found not to exist. Subsequent investigation revealed that there was nowhere available a codified publication of all of the executive orders, rules, and other regulations handed down by New Deal agencies with the force of law. As the *Magazine of Wall Street* explained the problem, ''the only way a violator of this multitude of executive laws could find out where he stood would be to make a tour of all the offices from which executive orders pour in an endless stream. Moreover, no man has any assurance that these edicts are authorized by any basic statute of Congress.''[65]

Some business indexes showed slight improvement late in October, others began to reveal gradual upward movement in November. By late November the New York *Herald-Tribune* index had climbed slightly above 50 once again.[66] Most observers were, however, more heartened by the improvement in business sentiment caused by the apparent movement toward cooperation than by the slight improvement in business statistics.[67] Early in December the NAM produced a tentative draft of a business program for the proposed meeting of the National Industrial Conference.[68] A committee of the NAM, headed by Lewis H. Brown, president of Johns Manville Corporation, then merged with the Silas Strawn committee of the Chamber of Commerce. The joint committee was to consult with the nation's businessmen and industrialists in order to shape a final set of recommendations that could serve as the basis for government-business cooperation in generating economic recovery.[69] Meanwhile, at the close of their joint annual convention, the NAM and Congress of American Industry added to the original draft new recommendations for an extension of a modified NRA for one year, and the appointment of a commission by Roosevelt to plan a comprehensive national program of unemployment insurance, old age pensions, and other measures for social security.[70]

The *Wall Street Journal* saw in these additions to the original draft a ''sincere offer to cooperate with the Administration in its efforts to bring about better living conditions for all the people.''[71] And it came, as *Newsweek* pointed out, from delegates who represented 70,000 manufacturers and employers across the nation.[72] Commerce Secretary Roper addressed the joint convention and promised that their suggestions would receive careful consideration from the Roosevelt administration. A meeting of approximately 100 leaders of commerce, industry, and finance was scheduled for White Sulphur Springs, West Virginia, to hammer out the final program in mid-December.[73]

The meeting at White Sulphur Springs received wide media attention. The problem the conferees faced was to agree upon a program that would provide the basis for a sound business recovery, even at the risk of opposing some New Deal policies that were deemed detrimental to recovery, but a program that would also be sufficiently "liberal" to appeal to Roosevelt. The task was complicated by divisions among the conferees, with the NAM delegates a good deal less conciliatory than those from the Chamber of Commerce, and it was only because of the mediation of Owen Young, respected industrialist and veteran Democrat, that a program was produced that seemed conciliatory enough yet firm in its insistence upon the essentials for recovery. Since most businessmen and economists agreed on what those essentials were, any number of such meetings as that at White Sulphur Springs must inevitably produce essentially the same recovery program. What set the program of this Joint Conference on Business Recovery apart from all earlier efforts was that it had been produced by the first cooperative effort of the NAM and the Chamber of Commerce, put together by a virtual "who's who" of the U.S. business and industrial community, who represented virtually every employer in the United States.[74] If the unemployed were to find jobs, these men and those they represented were the ones who would have to hire them.

Outside the Roosevelt administration, the program of the Joint Conference was generally regarded as moderate. Kiplinger noted that while "between two-thirds and three-fourths of these business leaders privately doubt the wisdom of New Deal economics," they had nevertheless acquiesced in "a majority of administration plans," opposing "only a few, and these in [a] qualified way." There was, he concluded, "more economic statesmanship among these business men than has ever been displayed at similar conferences previously."[75] Turner Catledge observed in the New York *Times*:

This program was marked throughout by a conciliatory attitude of business toward the administration. Nevertheless, private enterprise spoke frankly of the difficulties it has encountered in efforts toward recovery. The specific suggestions were infiltrated throughout with an inventory of these difficulties, but these were offered to the administration and the public with a plea for "patience and tolerance" in the reconciliation of any divergent views that may now, or hereafter, exist between various elements over recovery measures.[76]

John J. Raskob, industrialist and former national chairman of the Democratic Party, presided over the Joint Conference and wrote at its conclusion:

Personally, I think we accomplished a great deal of good, because in my opinion, no man, not even the President of the United States, even though he be a Roosevelt, can laugh off the serious efforts of ninety reputable business men sincerely working to be helpful for three consecutive days, because the American people will not stand for it.[77]

Logic was certainly on Raskob's side. For a nation still mired deep in depression after nearly five years, the business effort to forge a program for cooperation with the administration should have been welcome, if only as a basis for discussion. If, as even the Roosevelt administration belatedly appeared to recognize, the crying need was for private enterprise to revive and supply permanent jobs in place of costly and temporary work relief, then a concrete program from employers, outlining the ways by which they believed business confidence could be restored and roadblocks to recovery eliminated, was exactly what was called for. But, as Arthur Krock once observed, "pettiness and unwillingness to recognize the good faith of critics have smirched the New Deal."[78]

THE RESPONSE FROM THE WHITE HOUSE

Roosevelt's response to the Joint Conference would be a test of his sincerity in uttering the words he had addressed to the ABA convention. Would the moderate approach of the writer of that speech, Raymond Moley, prevail now, or would the natural "thistle" disposition of Roosevelt and his closest advisers govern his reaction? The question had in reality already been answered at a cabinet meeting a few days before the Joint Conference concluded its deliberations. When Commerce Secretary Roper told Roosevelt that business was prepared to cooperate with the administration in working for economic recovery, Roosevelt's reply was: "Well, Dan, all I can say is that business will have only until January 3 to make up its mind whether it is going to co-operate or not." He then added: "I believe it is the custom in hospitals, when a patient is to be operated on, to try to build him up, and we ought to build up our patient as much as we can before January 3."[79] January 3 would see the convening of the 74th Congress. Clearly, Roosevelt was looking not to cooperating with business, but to "operating" on it with a new barrage of reform legislation in disregard of the continuing depression, the millions of unemployed, and the millions on relief rolls. The president who hoped that the 5 million who needed to be cared for in 1935 would decline to 3 million the following year, and gradually "disappear," still could not see that it was his war on business that was preventing the unemployed from "disappearing."

Roosevelt's response to the program of the Joint Conference, then, was predictable, even though shocking. As Arthur Krock described it,

all that the Joint Conference on Business Recovery has . . . received from the government . . . is a series of slaps in the face. Its emissary, a dignified Texan and Mississippi Democrat of long standing, Judge Ames of the Texas Company, was asked to leave the document with a Presidential secretary and told that if he wanted to wait around, the President "might" find time to see him for a few minutes the next day. Two of the closest insiders in the New Deal—Administrators Hopkins and Ickes—satirized and denounced the resolutions. From the President came only the remark, to a press conference, that he had received five or six similar documents and was planning to take Sunday off to read them.

"The result," Krock wrote, "was, when Judge Ames came to the executive offices, he found he was bringing just one more bundle of papers, as far as the receiving officers were concerned. This, notwithstanding the fact that the White Sulphur Springs conference represented perhaps 90 percent of the industrial employers in this country."[80] The Baltimore *Sun* found Roosevelt's treatment of Ames "just a trifle childish," while the Washington *Post* was shocked at Roosevelt's response.[81]

The *Commercial and Financial Chronicle* pointed out that in almost any other country a program put together by leaders of the two major business and industrial organizations would receive serious attention from the government. Such, however, was not to be expected from the Roosevelt administration, where "the ideology of the New Deal is ill-attuned to the voice of experience, and a vested interest in dictated 'recovery' has been built up which stubbornly resists encroachment."[82] Judging from the attitude of the Roosevelt administration, the business and industrial leaders of the nation were, at best, outcasts to be shunned, or, at worst, enemies to be subjected to unrelenting warfare by their own government. Recovery could not be achieved under such conditions, whichever was the case.

As 1934 ended, Roosevelt prepared for his 1935 "operation" on business and banking, unaware that the New Deal had an operation of its own in store for it, at the hands of the Supreme Court.

CHAPTER 6

The Supreme Court Rules

AN INDIFFERENCE TO RECOVERY

Despite Roosevelt's statement to his cabinet that he intended to "operate" on business once the new congressional session opened, there was nothing particularly disturbing for businessmen and bankers in his first two messages to Congress. In asking for $4 billion in work relief funds, and a budget unbalanced by approximately that amount, in place of the "definitely balanced budget" by 1935–36 which he had earlier set as his goal, Roosevelt acknowledged the failure of his policies to bring about business recovery and the employment of the idle by private industry. While these first two messages contained nothing to indicate that he had taken any note of the program of the Joint Conference, they were sufficiently vague as to contain nothing particularly disturbing to business confidence.[1] Despite his attempts to gloss over the fact that his first two years in the White House had ended in failure, that failure was obvious enough. As *The Economist* pointed out: "Neither the easy-money programme, nor the N. R. A., nor the Public Works Programme has made any perceptible impression on the Relief Rolls; nor on the unemployment statistics except in comparison with the few worst weeks of the depression."[2] It found "a single fact" dominating all other considerations before the new Congress: "This is the fact of unemployment (now estimated at 11,459,000 by the American Federation of Labor) and its corollary, the undiminished number on relief rolls."[3] Frank Kent found it "impossible to reconcile Mr. Roosevelt's report of 'progress' during the year with the conceded fact that there are more unemployed and more on relief than when he as hopefully addressed Congress one year ago." The relief rolls, he pointed out, had grown by nearly 20 percent in that time, the number of unemployed by a half-million.[4]

Economists, foreign and domestic, remained baffled by Roosevelt's apparent indifference to recovery. Lionel Robbins, of the London School of Economics, viewed the prospects for recovery in the United States as largely a function of the "intentions of the administration." "Hitherto, at a distance, it has been almost impossible to resist the conclusion that many of the measures adopted by the [Roosevelt] administration have had the effect of making recovery by way of spontaneous revival of business enterprise not easier, but rather more difficult." Robbins wondered:

Will the difficulties which have been imposed on business in the last few years be eased so as to produce revival? Or will the relative stagnation of business continue, accompanied by even more grandiose attempts to produce by government spending the results which the frustration of private enterprise have prevented?[5]

Economist C. J. Bullock recalled, in Harvard's *Review of Economic Statistics*, the "striking" effect upon business morale and government credit furnished by Roosevelt's few cooperative gestures late in 1934 and observed that it "might well have encouraged other moves calculated to increase confidence and thus improve the economic outlook." Instead, Roosevelt had spurned cooperation and it was "now evident that economic recovery is not to have the right of way." Comparing the economic statistics of the United States with those of other countries, Bullock found it significant that "the comparison results so unfavorably for the country [the United States] which went further than almost any other in its efforts to end the depression."[6]

Late in January the "operation" that Roosevelt had promised began at last with the introduction of the Wheeler-Rayburn public utilities holding bill in Congress. The bill was designed to break up the large holding companies that dominated a good part of the public utilities in the United States, but many regarded it as only the opening shot in a general Brandeisian attack on bigness of all kinds in industry.[7] *Business Week* found a measure of spite in the legislation, as well, for utility executives had opposed Roosevelt's nomination in 1932. Roosevelt, it observed, had not forgotten, nor had his closest political adviser, Louis McHenry Howe.[8] Certainly such a basis for Roosevelt's animosity and action would have been consistent with other aspects of his behavior toward those who had opposed him, or had failed at least to support him at the convention. As Raymond Clapper observed, "this Administration bears its grudges to a degree not often seen in politics."[9]

Dr. Hugh Magill, president of the American Federation of Utility Investors, called attention to the people beyond the "interests" who would be hurt—some 10 million Americans who had investments directly or indirectly in the investor-owned utilities. That Roosevelt could not see beyond the "interests" to the people who would be hurt had already, however, been demonstrated during the bank panic. Magill also uttered a widely harbored view when he charged that the New Deal was "openly out to socialize business and they are using the false and misleading public utilities arguments as an opening wedge."[10] *Business Week* found the bill "fairly representative of the ethics and intelligence of the political forces that dominate Washington today. These bills cannot even pretend to be regulatory in character. They are purely punitive and destructive. They are intended to be so."[11] The Washington *Post* warned that passage of the bill could only lead to further business uncertainty, depress the capital market, and "thereby again set reform ahead of urgent recovery needs."[12] Indifferent to the effects that passage of the bill would have on recovery, Roosevelt called in mid-March for its speedy approval.

The Brandeisians were exhilarated over the bill, which two of their number, Corcoran and Cohen, had written. Brandeis wrote that "if [Roosevelt] carries through the Holding Company bill we shall have achieved considerable toward curbing Bigness—in addition to recent advances."[13] But when Frankfurter defended the bill against what he claimed were unjustified fears, Frank Buxton, editor of the Boston *Herald*, replied:

If the provisions of the Rayburn-Wheeler bill are as beneficent as you say, wherefore the general apprehension? . . . If men are to go back to work in large numbers, a measure which antagonizes them, especially a measure which is not of urgent necessity, might very well be postponed for later consideration. . . . Maybe the New England utility men "have nothing whatever to fear from the holding company bill." I wish that you would try to prove that to them. I wish you'd try to prove it, also, to the holders of utility stocks.[14]

An investment banker asked a Congressional committee studying the bill:

Is it the wish of the Government in Washington to advance recovery; to ease those who are seeing their income and their savings shrinking, to quiet fears that retard all progress, to do the utmost possible to help us out of this depression? Or is is the desire to increase confusion and difficulties; to take advantage of opportunities to press its social theories and to distort the whole concept of American business? If the former, this Bill seems a mistake; if the latter—and all the indications of this Bill suggest it—then it is a success.[15]

In early May, the Business Advisory Council of the Commerce Department, after reviewing the many positive contributions made by public utility holding companies to the expansion of low-cost electric power in the United States, recommended that the "drastic" Wheeler-Rayburn bill be amended.[16]

Damaging as the Wheeler-Rayburn bill was to business confidence, the Eccles banking bill appeared to many critics to threaten even more revolutionary changes in the nation's political and economic life. It seemed nothing less than an attempt to centralize the entire Federal Reserve System under the direct control of the president, thereby making it an instrument of politics rather than of banking. H. Parker Willis, former secretary to the FRB and technical adviser to Senator

Carter Glass when the original Federal Reserve Act was written, called the Eccles bill "a barefaced usurpation of the control over the entire banking assets of the nation. It provides for opening the door to political favoritism and control of the worst kind."[17] The *Commercial and Financial Chronicle* agreed that the bill would place the Federal Reserve System "under the thumb of the President of the United States," making it possible for him to use the banking system for political purposes.[18]

Curiously, bankers did not in the beginning express the opposition that one might expect. Vilified by the Roosevelt administration during its first two years, bankers had taken the first steps in the attempt to forge business and banking cooperation with the New Deal late in 1934. Now, even in the face of the evidence that Roosevelt had spurned cooperation, they continued to entertain the hope that by a cooperative attitude they could bring about a sensible compromise on the banking bill.[19] Frank Vanderlip was the only prominent banker who attacked the bill in the early weeks. He explained the reluctance of other bankers to do so by further pointing out that the RFC owned stock in some 6,000 banks, in many of which it was the predominant stockholder.[20] Inside the Treasury Department, however, where officials were directly in contact with leading bankers, it had become clear by mid-March that bankers would oppose the controversial section of the bill—Title II.[21]

While bankers remained publicly silent about the bill, others took up the fight against it. Early in March, Title II was attacked in a statement issued by 76 economists.[22] Warren Spahr, professor of economics at New York University, warned a congressional committee that the bill was "a dangerous attempt of political minded planners to increase their destructive and devastating hold on business enterprise."[23] Yale economist James Harvey Rogers warned "that one of the great dangers with which we are now threatened is that our banking system may be subjected to a thoroughly vicious political control."[24]

The moderate tactics of the American Bankers Association having apparently had no effect in achieving modification of the bill by late April, the Chamber of Commerce now moved toward what the New York *Times* called an "open break" with Roosevelt over it.[25] A few days later the three top officers of the ABA visited the White House to inform Roosevelt that the bankers intended to lobby Congress in order to assure that the Federal Reserve System would remain free of political control.[26] Clearly their policy of moderation and cooperation toward the New Deal had failed to bear fruit, and the ABA was acknowledging its failure. As the New York *Times* explained it, "bankers here and in other sections of the country feel that the conciliatory attitude originally taken by the American Bankers Association and the withholding of criticism practiced by bankers in general have failed to achieve any success."[27]

The Wagner labor bill, unpassed by Congress in 1934, was again in 1935 perceived as a further threat to harmonious industrial relations if passed into law. The American Newspaper Publishers' Association found it "nothing more or less than an incitement to agitate and keep industry and business in a turmoil until the unions have achieved their objective."[28] The Business Advisory Council (BAC) of the Commerce Department warned:

It is not an impartial bill. It establishes a code of unfair practices for the employer, but not for the employee. It makes the decisions of the proposed National Labor Relations Board binding upon the employer, one party to a dispute, but in no way binding upon organized labor. . . . This would seem unfair in a judicial body.[29]

The bill, however, passed the Senate in mid-May, and a few days later Roosevelt, ignoring the views of the BAC, threw his support behind passage of the bill by the House.[30] It was apparent that the bill would pass in 1935.

Late in December 1934, Henry I. Harriman had sent to Roosevelt the results of a survey by the Chamber of Commerce, which showed that 87 percent of the commercial and trade organizations that had responded to a poll favored termination of the NRA in June as scheduled, with 78 percent favoring new legislation in its place. Eighty percent of these latter favored limitation of the new legislation to interstate commerce and 96 percent favored voluntary formulation of codes. Overwhelmingly (95 percent) they felt that the role of the government should be limited to approving or vetoing the voluntary codes.[31] Almost coincidental with the Chamber's report, economists of the Brookings Institution told the American Economic Association that the NRA had failed. One of them, George Terborgh, asserted that not only would "the NRA have retarded recovery if it had worked out as planned, but that it retarded recovery as it actually did not work."[32]

The Business Advisory Council of the Commerce Department recommended that the NRA be continued in force for two more years, but with amendments to incorporate many of the recommendations of the Chamber of Commerce. Industries would have the right to withdraw from any code provision it might voluntarily have accepted, and the president should have the right to cancel outright an entire code, but not to modify existing codes without the consent of the industry.[33] Meanwhile the criticism of the NRA for retarding recovery continued. As one newspaper pointed out, the issue was now "clear cut." The NRA had, on the evidence of leading economic authorities, retarded recovery, and if the NIRA was continued beyond its expiration date in the present form it would be "manifest that the present administration is sabotaging economic recovery.[34]

If the Roosevelt administration did not see the issue this clearly, judging from its criticism of the Brookings report, Congress apparently did.[35] By early May, Frank Kent concluded that except for Senator Robert Wagner of New York there was not a convinced NIRA supporter in the Senate.[36] Walter Lippmann agreed: "If any one knows just how to let go gracefully and safely when you have a bear by the tail, he should proceed promptly to Washington and tell Congress what to do about N. R. A." The feeling of Congress was, he said, very clear: "The idea of a planned economy, which swept the country like a fad in 1933, is discredited."[37]

PART WAY WITH KEYNES

In assuming that Roosevelt was interested in recovery from the depression, John Maynard Keynes had advised him to halt the reform initiatives that were destroying business confidence, and to launch a public works program on the scale of $400 million in deficit spending per month. Clearly Roosevelt had ignored the first aspect of Keynes' advice, but he appeared to follow the second closely. In sending to Congress a "public works program" pegged at $4.8 billion for the fiscal year, with a deficit of nearly that amount, Roosevelt was clearly influenced by Keynes. That the New Deal had "gone Keynesian" in its deficit spending policies was apparent, at least, to observers in London. The *Investor's Review* of that city tried to warn Roosevelt against following Keynes, but admitted that since Roosevelt had "no knowledge of the principles of economics" he was "not unnaturally eager to accept any schemes which coincide with his ignorance."[38]

Sir Ernest Benns, in an article on "Maynard Keynes and America," published in *The Independent* (London), pointed out that "the rehabilitation of the United States is of vital importance not only to the Americans but to the world as a whole." But, under the New Deal,

anti-trust laws have been replaced by trusts of disordered brains, and almost every obsession that ever entered the economic madhouse has been installed in a building of its own at Washington and forced upon a bewildered and distracted nation. For two years past American economic life has only survived in so far as it has been able to evade these imbecilities or cheat its way through them. That is the position today.

Now came the news from the United States that Keynes had captivated Roosevelt and that the administration was going to try to "buy back prosperity" with a $4.8 billion public works expenditure. This being the case, Benns felt it his "duty" to warn Americans about "the latest of the professorial dangers which Mr. Roosevelt is so fond of inflicting upon them." He pointed out that Keynes' advice had been rejected even by the government of his own country.[39]

Given the attention that Roosevelt's conversion to Keynesianism attracted in Great Britain, it is curious how few American observers were aware of it. *The Annalist* was one of the few to note that with the spending program of 1935, one would "almost suspect that John Maynard Keynes were the real occupant of the White House."[40]

It soon developed, however, that while the spending program approximated the amount that Keynes had suggested, it did not follow his advice in other important respects. Rather than a program of public works as Keynes had suggested, and Roosevelt at first promised, the plan quickly degenerated into another work-relief program as Roosevelt and his advisers calculated the maximum number of unemployed who could be put to work immediately with the spending, rather than taking into consideration the benefits to recovery that might be obtained from secondary employment and stimulus to the durable goods industries through a genuine public works project.[41] When the bill was passed by Congress in April, critics found in it only appropriations of $800 million for roads and grade crossings and $900 million for nonfederal works as holding genuine recovery aspects—far too little to have any real impact.[42] Once again most of the money would go to stimulate the consumer goods industries that needed stimulation the least.[43] A businessman wrote Amos Pinchot: "While the spending of this vast sum of money may be a temporary stimulant to business its eventual effects will be bad. The whole thing will prove to be just another experiment and when the money is gone there will be very little of value to show for it."[44]

Business indexes continued early in 1935 the moderate improvement that had begun late in 1934. The New York *Herald-Tribune* index rose to 62.4 by mid-January, then began to decline as the full Roosevelt legislative program was revealed, thereafter fluctuating around 60 and standing at 59 in mid-May.[45] The New York *Times* index likewise showed a general decline from the beginning of the congressional session.[46] Clearly the improvement that had begun late in 1934 in the midst of the supposed "cooperation" between government and business had been checked and in part erased as a result of the renewed assault on business and banking by the Roosevelt administration. Business was drifting and the prospects of a renewed upturn were not rosy.

A small army of observers, including economists as detached as John Maynard Keynes, had called Roosevelt's attention to the destructive effects on recovery caused by any continued legislative assaults against business and had called for a halt. At a time when Roosevelt was preparing to pour nearly $5 billion into the economy to care for the unemployed because of the failure of his policies, there was certainly nothing to be gained and much to be lost by continuing that legislative onslaught. The repeated counsels that spending could have no lasting effect on recovery if business confidence was simultaneously being destroyed by other policies seemed to have no effect on Roosevelt and the claque of advisers with whom he had surrounded himself. Even the friendly Raymond Clapper found, in late February, that for "some around the ringside at Washington it begins to appear as if President Roosevelt is facing exactly the same task that confronted him two years ago almost to the day." Clapper wrote of the two New Deal years that had passed:

Money was poured out by the billion. The public debt was kited to unprecedented heights. This was all right for a while. But the number of unemployed remains as large as ever. Relief rolls are just as long. . . . New proposals, such as the Rayburn-Wheeler bill to abolish utility holding companies, have stirred up new apprehension in business quarters.[47]

Clapper admitted that "Roosevelt hasn't found the answers."[48]

For *The Annalist* it looked like a repetition of 1934, when "a promising revival was cut short by the passage by Congress of legislation unfavorable to business. . . . it is obvious that business recovery cannot be promoted by the discussion by Congress of legislation which is generally regarded with alarm by businessmen and investors."[49] The *Saturday Evening Post* wrote: "If anyone started out with malice aforethought to destroy the immediate prospects of further business revival, he could hardly do it more effectively than by the introduction of some of the reform bills that are being considered by Congress."[50] Felix Frankfurter, who was perhaps more responsible for the situation than anyone except Roosevelt, remarked flippantly: "So that's the trouble with business—that it's a psychopathic problem," to which Eugene Meyer, former RFC head and now publisher of the Washington *Post*, responded: "The states of mind of large groups of people constitute facts of economic importance whether you like it or not."[51]

BUSINESS FIGHTS BACK

Late in April both the NAM and the U. S. Chamber of Commerce appealed for the postponement of further legislative experiments until 1936 in order to give business a chance to recover from the depression. The New York *Times* foresaw little likelihood that the appeals would receive sympathetic consideration from Roosevelt, but thought "at some point, discovery of the fact that Washington is itself standing in the way of normal business recovery is bound to influence even the political point of view."[52] Roosevelt's response to the appeal from the NAM and Chamber of Commerce came in a fireside chat later in the month, in which he expressed his determination to push on with the program before Congress.[53]

The day after the fireside chat, the annual convention of the U. S. Chamber of Commerce was the scene of what Ernest Lindley called "scorching criticism of the New Deal" by business speakers. Lindley observed that "if there has been a 'truce' between the New Deal and big business there were few evidences of it today."[54] The Washington *Post* observed that the speakers appeared "to have forgotten that a truce between business and Government was once informally declared," the businessmen having apparently decided "that the policy of cooperation is not yielding results that warrant moderation of comment."[55] The mood of the 1935 convention was in sharp contrast with the cooperative attitude that Harriman had encouraged in 1934 and that had resulted only in a new Roosevelt onslaught against business and banking. As outgoing president, Harriman and others worked to avoid an open break with the administration, but Roosevelt's refusal even to send the customary message of greeting to the convention appeared to demonstrate his total lack of interest in cooperation, thus undercutting the efforts of the moderates at the convention.[56] The balance within the 1934 convention that had made it possible for Harriman to steer moderate resolutions through it had been destroyed by Roosevelt's actions. As Kiplinger pointed out, "business men who were enthusiastic New Dealers a year ago are now lukewarm. Men who were on the fence a year ago are now on the hostile side. Men who were hostile a year ago are now bitter."[57]

The result was that within a week after Roosevelt had thrown down the gauntlet before business by demanding the passage of his program of antibusiness legislation despite the pleas of the NAM and the Chamber of Commerce for a year of relief, and after he had shown his disdain for the assembled businessmen by refusing to send a greeting to them, the Chamber of Commerce moved to respond with resolutions denouncing Roosevelt's policies.[58] There was some criticism of the Chamber's response, the Washington *Post* admonishing them for resorting to "scolding and jeremiads," but critics could offer no better course of action.[59] Responding to critics of the Chamber's actions, the *Commercial and Financial Chronicle* wrote:

These doubtless sincere commentators seem to us to be crying peace, peace, when there is no peace. If they suppose that American business can escape the darts of the New Deal by making genuflections before the White House, let them run over the list of enactments now on the statute book. . . . Then let them inspect the Congressional calendar and note the measures now pending with Administration approval. . . . If they are still in need of convincing, they might reread the recent radio address of the President.[60]

The *Wall Street Journal*, generally on the side of moderation, agreed that businessmen had learned that their "supplication of Washington" had been in vain and that Roosevelt obviously did not intend to assist in bringing about recovery.[61] Kiplinger pointed out that the Chamber's resolutions were, in fact, representative of most business feeling about Roosevelt's policies, despite the president's reluctance to believe it, and concluded that the breach between Roosevelt and business had not really been widened by the resolutions. "It had existed previously," Kiplinger wrote, "It is now merely made a matter of record."[62]

Roosevelt brushed aside the Chamber of Commerce resolutions as not representative of business feeling in general, and in support of this view he received a large number of letters from businessmen and local chambers of commerce dissenting from the resolutions. He also, however, received a large number that agreed with those resolutions.[63] Roosevelt's response to the convention was to call the Business Advisory Council of the Commerce Department to the White House for a highly visible visit, thereby to give the impression that he was supported by the business leaders in that body.[64] The quandary into which the BAC was thrown by Roosevelt's obvious political use of them as a smokescreen against the denunciations coming from the Chamber of Commerce led some in the council to advocate an *en masse* resignation. Although there was no mass resignation, many of the members did leave the BAC in May and others soon followed them.[65]

Such actions by the president led publisher and columnist David Lawrence to examine Roosevelt in a lengthy essay in the *United States News* in mid-May. Lawrence, who had known Roosevelt since the latter had served as assistant secretary of the Navy under Wilson, began by noting a change in the mail he was receiving—from "tolerant and understanding sympathy" toward Roosevelt, to "bitter and intolerant criticism." Lawrence would, he said, "be among the first to applaud," if Roosevelt's policies produced recovery, but he had concluded that the president was "being misled, if not betrayed, by men lacking in scruple, lacking in patriotism, and imbued only with the idea that government is an instrumentality for the attainment of their individual and personal ambitions." He wrote:

To one set of Administration officials the New Deal signifies plainly that the end justifies the means, that justice was not intended to be applied to the possessors of property or the management of our large or small businesses, and that a punitive spirit is not only desired but is the basic purpose of the New Deal itself. . . . It is regrettable that the tendency of most Administration officials is not to consider themselves responsible to the American people as a whole, but merely as zealots in behalf of a complex and experimental philosophy of government, popularly called the New Deal, but representing, as each official views it, anything from state socialism and government ownership to the tyrannical use of governmental power for the benefit of class interests.

The "rank and file" of the Roosevelt administration, Lawrence observed, were "to no small extent political, class-conscious, and addicted to the idea that two wrongs make a right and that most anything is pro-New Deal which removes from our economic system its various profit-making elements." He concluded that "recovery cannot be achieved in such an atmosphere."[66]

THE SUPREME COURT AND THE NRA

If Roosevelt and Congress would not provide an "atmosphere" for recovery, perhaps the Supreme Court would. In January 1935 that body handed down its first decision on the New Deal in a case that challenged the exercise of presidential authority through the NIRA in the oil industry. By an 8–1 verdict the court decided against the administration.[67] David Lawrence thought the decision might "have furnished the largest single stimulus to business recovery that 1935 may see."[68] The next test of Roosevelt's policies was to be over the abrogation of gold clauses in contracts. If those who credited (and those who still credit) Roosevelt with "good intentions," despite their criticism of his policies, had been privy to his state of mind as that decision approached, they might have questioned their appraisal of him. On January 14, Roosevelt huddled with Attorney General Homer Cummings and Treasury Secretary Morgenthau to outline the "strategy" in preparing for the gold clause decision. It was, Morgenthau recorded in his diary, "one of the most unpleasant hours I have had since I have been in Washington."[69] According to Morgenthau's diary:

The President argued with me that he wanted to keep things on an unsettled basis until the Supreme Court handed down its decision. He said that he wanted this for judicial and political reasons. He said that the only way the man in a taxicab can become interested in the gold case is if we keep the story on the front page. He said I want bonds to move up and down and Foreign Exchange. He said if we keep things in a constant turmoil if the case should go against us the man on the street will say for God's sake Mr. President, do something about it, and he said, if I do everybody in the country will heave a sigh of relief and say thank God.

Morgenthau argued, he said, "harder and more intensely than I have ever before in my life." It was a heated exchange, with Morgenthau prepared to resign as Treasury secretary if Roosevelt insisted on going through with his plan. Eventually, Morgenthau won the argument, and Roosevelt backed off from his design to throw the government bond market and foreign exchange into turmoil for its "judicial and political" effect.[70]

Certainly there was enough uncertainty in the financial world over the imminent Supreme Court decision without any added turmoil induced by the president of the United States. The investment world was "at sea" awaiting the decision— any decision was better than the continued uncertainty.[71] The decision, when it came, upheld the right of the government to abrogate the gold clauses in private contracts, though not in government bonds, but in the latter case it denied any recourse to bondholders claiming damage. Thus, those who had bought bonds on the assumption that the gold clause guaranteed them repayment in money of the same value (as measured in gold) that they had invested, found now that they would only be repaid in currency depreciated in value. Though the decision was widely criticized, most observers probably agreed with Walter Lippmann that "any other decision by the Supreme Court would have created an almost impossible situation."[72]

The gold clause decision was, however, but one victory in a sea of judicial defeats for Roosevelt. Frank Kent observed early in March: "The consistent frequency with which the lower federal courts have been rendering decisions against the government makes clear a situation inevitable from the start. The day of judgment for the New Deal has almost arrived and its fate hangs by a hair."[73] But despite the adverse decisions against the NIRA, the Supreme Court was not called upon to render a verdict on that act. Roosevelt was clearly chary about permitting any case to go before the Supreme Court that tested the constitutionality of the NIRA. Criticism of that reluctance, however, led the administration to look about for a test case in which they would occupy a strong position.[74] On Donald Richberg's advice, Roosevelt consented on April 4 to allow the Schechter case to go to the Supreme Court.[75] On that same day, Felix Frankfurter called the White House to warn against the action.[76] His advice was wired to Roosevelt too late. The president was at sea fishing. The decision to take the case to the Supreme Court had already been announced.

According to Arthur Schlesinger, the Schechter brothers had been convicted of "violating the [NRA] code not only by filing false sales and price reports but by selling diseased poultry, unfit for human consumption."[77] William Leuchtenburg has it that they were "convicted of violating the NRA's Live Poultry Code on several counts, including selling diseased chickens and violating the code's wage and hour stipulations."[78] All of this conjures up images of brothers who were lying, sweating their workers, and regularly dispensing diseased poultry to unwitting customers. In fact, however, of the 18 counts of the indictment upon which the Schechters were convicted, only *one* dealt with the sale of a *single* "unfit chicken," and that to a butcher. Only *two* counts charged violation of the minimum wage and maximum hours provision of the code, and only *two* charged "the making of false reports or the failure to make reports relating to the range of daily prices and volumes of sales for certain periods." Curiously, both historians mentioned only three of the counts against the Schechters, while neglecting their major "crime"—the subject of *ten* of the 18 counts against them—the charge that they had violated the NRA code requiring "straight killing."[79]

"Straight killing" was defined in the NRA code under which the Schechters operated as "the practice of requiring persons purchasing poultry for resale to accept the run of any half coop, coop, or coops, as purchased by slaughterhouse operators, except for culls."[80] The principal charge against the Schechters, then, was that in violation of that provision they had engaged in the selective killing of chickens for their customers. In other words, if a customer objected to one or more of the chickens in a batch, the seller was not allowed to make substitutions. The buyer must take the "run" or go elsewhere. The Schechters, however, had allegedly replaced objectionable chickens for their customers. That such an action should be considered worthy of pursuit to the highest court in the land is illustrative of New Deal thinking and methods.

Early in May the case against the Schechters was presented "amid hilarity seldom seen in the Supreme Court." If the Roosevelt administration (and New Deal historians) failed to see the absurdity of the case, it obviously was not lost on the judges. After a description of "straight killing," the New York *Times* reported, "even the usually solemn justices were provoked to gales of laughter."[81] A few days later the Supreme Court found the Railroad Retirement Act unconstitutional by a vote of 5–4. When he discussed that decision with Roosevelt, Tugwell found him convinced that the decision boded ill for the NIRA.[82] Businessmen agreed.[83]

On May 27, 1935, Attorney General Cummings recorded in his diary: "Today was a bad day for the Government in the Supreme Court." Three cases had been decided by the justices and all three had gone against the government. In the first, the court ruled that Roosevelt had exceeded his authority in removing William E. Humphrey from the Federal Trade Commission in 1933. In the second, the justices found the Frazier-Lemke Farm Mortgage Act unconstitutional. Since that act had not been a part of the New Deal program, the decision did not strike directly at Roosevelt, although he had signed it into law. In the Schechter case, a sweeping decision by the court found that not only had Congress unconstitutionally delegated powers to the executive, but that the powers had not even belonged to Congress in the first place under the Constitution. In each of the cases the vote was unanimous, 9–0 against the government.[84] Raymond

Clapper reported that after the decision was handed down a spectator burst from the courtroom shouting, "The revolution is over!"[85]

The Schechter decision, especially, Cummings found, "shifts the whole situation and introduces strange and unexpected elements."[86] How right he was. Supreme Court Justice Brandeis summoned Ben Cohen and Thomas Corcoran immediately after the decision was rendered. "Visibly excited and deeply agitated," Brandeis lectured his two followers on the changed situation created by the decision. They must bring Frankfurter down from Harvard to explain the implications for Roosevelt and those around him, Brandeis told them. "They must understand that these three decisions change everything. The President has been living in a fools' paradise."[87]

Two days later Frankfurter met in the White House with Roosevelt and Cummings.[88] The gist of Frankfurter's advice to the president can be gathered from his letters to Roosevelt of May 29 and 30. Frankfurter suggested that Roosevelt avoid a battle with the Supreme Court at that time, but not foreclose the possibility of a fight later on when the prospects for success were more favorable. He also suggested various legislative initiatives to carry on some of the work of the NIRA, including passage of the Wagner labor bill. Frankfurter also suggested that Roosevelt vigorously push *all* the New Deal legislation then before Congress as a challenge to the Supreme Court. As Frankfurter put it: "Put *them* up to the Supreme Court. Let the Court strike down any or all of them next winter or spring, especially by a divided Court." Then Roosevelt could propose a Constitutional amendment broadening the powers of the federal government, Frankfurter advised, and he would be assured of greater support than at present. By vigorously pushing his legislative program now, Roosevelt would also serve notice to the public "that the momentum of your purposes and your leadership is unabated."[89] Thus, Frankfurter furnished Roosevelt with yet another reason to push his antibusiness legislation through the 1935 session of Congress.

Rexford Tugwell was convinced that there would be chaos from the invalidation of the NRA. The nation, he believed, realized soon after the decision that "something terrible has been done to the economic system," although their initial reaction to the decision had been one of jubilation. He recorded in his diary, probably on information from the president, that Roosevelt was "being besieged by all the people who were fighting the NRA before to save them from industrial chaos."[90] Such a greater misreading of the situation and of the mood of business could hardly have been made. It was, of course, wishful thinking, for, as Interior Secretary Ickes observed in his diary,

if business holds or takes an upturn, then the court will be vindicated along with those conservative gentlemen who have been saying that the NRA has retarded business. If, on the other hand, business takes another nose dive, in my judgment the Supreme Court will be placed distinctly on the defensive and will be made a political issue.[91]

The Roosevelt administration could certainly derive no satisfaction from the press response to the Supreme Court decision. The Washington *Post* welcomed the decisions as serving "warning that the era of administrative law-making under loose legislative grants of power, and the effort to invade the field of law-making reserved under the Constitution to the several States has come to an end."[92] The New York *Herald-Tribune* wondered about the blow to Roosevelt's pride: "He is shown after two years, by the unanimous opinion of the Supreme Court, including all its most liberal and progressive members, to have been leading the country down a blind alley. No great leader was ever so completely mistaken. No great country was ever so completely misled."[93] Frank Kent wrote that the American people were now "confronted by the cold, hard facts that this engaging, sincere, well-meaning man they have been following, and who waved and shouted, 'We are on our way,' did not know where he was going, what he was doing, nor where he was coming out."[94]

Business periodicals also hailed the demise of the NRA. *Foundry* spoke for iron and steel foundrymen with an editorial approving the court decision headed: "NRA IS DEAD, LONG LIVE INDUSTRY."[95] The *Bulletin of the National Retail Dry Goods Association* considered the Schechter decision the most important Supreme Court action since the Dred Scot decision.[96] *Manufacturer's Record* hailed it as promising a "New Day," and wrote: "America has been in a maze of uncertainty and apprehension" over "the attempted chiseling of the Constitution," and the "advantages to industry in the abolishment of NRA will outweigh the disadvantages." It hoped that the decision would cause Congress to pause before enacting into law the New Deal legislative program then pending.[97] *Motor* spoke for the automobile industry in concluding that "the automobile industry has lost little of practical value through the Supreme Court's decision."[98] The *Commercial and Financial Chronicle* regarded the decisions as "the outstanding and the most encouraging event since March 4, 1933."[99] *Editor and Publisher* spoke for the newspaper industry in observing that there was no doubt "that majority publisher sentiment rejoices in the elimination of NRA."[100] The *Guaranty Survey* found businessmen, in general, more hopeful regarding the future course of industry and trade" with the NRA out of the picture.[101] Such comments did not support the delusion within the New Deal that business was "besieging" Roosevelt to "save them from industrial chaos," as Tugwell had recorded in his diary, nor did it support hopeful predictions within the administration that there would be a drastic downturn in business as a result of the demise of the NRA.

ROOSEVELT'S REACTION

Roosevelt could not conceal his anger toward the court when he faced reporters at a press conference on May 31. He told them that the Schechter decision had relegated the nation back to "the horse-and-buggy definition of interstate commerce," and direly predicted an economic collapse. Frank Kent found Roosevelt's outburst "remarkable" for what it left out. The president had not admitted that, "as everyone knows, before the court decision the NRA was a discredited agency, which had ceased to function and was in a state of demoralization and confusion." Nor had he admitted that he could have had a decision from the Supreme Court on the NIRA 18 months earlier if he had chosen not to delay it for that length of time. Roosevelt had also failed to admit "that the tragic situation in which he finds himself is due not to the court but to the lack of logic, experience and judgment upon the part of his advisers, and upon the part of himself in taking such advice." Kent wrote: "On the contrary, the impression Mr. Roosevelt sought to create was that he and his New Deal advisers were wise, right, farsighted and enlightened, the Supreme Court bad, blind, and benighted. If mistakes were made, it was the court which made them, not he."[102] The New York *Times* considered Roosevelt's remarks pervaded with "resentment and despondency."[103]

Four days after his press conference outburst, Roosevelt announced that the skeleton of the NRA would be retained as a statistical bureau until April 1936. The Washington *Post* noted that Roosevelt was taking a more drastic interpretation of the court's decision than was warranted, and concluded that "for purposes best known to himself, it seems to be Mr. Roosevelt's desire to tear down the whole structure because a part of it, as at first hastily designed, has been inferentially condemned."[104] Willard Kiplinger speculated about Roosevelt's motive: "The worse the effects of having no NRA, the bigger the later push for its reestablishment, and perhaps for constitutional amendment. Therefore do little to salvage NRA."[105] Raymond Clapper agreed that Roosevelt obviously expected that business would decline without the NRA, and that the need for it would appear obvious, but he wondered "what if business recovery goes forward, wages remain good and get better and the country continues its steady climb?"[106] Only the business statistics for the remainder of 1935 would tell if Roosevelt's strategy was wise.

CHAPTER 7

An Air of Unreality

BUSINESS WITHOUT THE NRA

It was normal for business to slump during the summer months and then to stage an upturn in the fall. Even those who viewed the demise of the NRA as beneficial to business expected that the summer slump would take place as usual and that any upward movement would not reveal itself until the fall. However, the normal slump did not take place in the summer of 1935. Instead, business indices rose slightly during the month of June, following the NRA decision, and then maintained their level through the summer. In late July, *Business Week* reported that business had shown "more vitality this summer than even the most sanguine expected."[1] On September 15 the New York *Times* reported that its business index had reached 88.5, which it described as "the highest level since the week ended August 19, 1933, during the pre-code boom period."[2] The implication was obvious: the two highest levels in its business index had been reached before the NRA codes went into effect and after they had been invalidated.

The business statistics were only bearing out the optimistic predictions of economists. In mid-June, Professor Malcolm McNair, director of business research at Harvard, predicted a substantial amount of business recovery over the next 18 months.[3] Economist Leonard Ayres issued a similar prediction a few days later. Observing that in the two years during which it had operated under the New Deal the U.S. economy had made "almost the worst record of the nations of the world insofar as recovery is concerned," Ayres regarded the demise of the NRA as now giving businessmen confidence and improved business conditions.[4] As for Ayres' criticism of U.S. recovery in relation to the rest of the world, Dr. Leverett S. Lyons, of the Brookings Institution, confirmed that on a scale for comparing industrial recovery that had been worked out by League of Nations experts, the United States stood at -9, while Canada rated $+17$, Sweden $+41$, the United Kingdom $+20$, Russia $+19$, and Germany $+26$.[5]

THE 1935 NEW DEAL

The package of New Deal legislation before Congress continued to attract business and banking opposition. Owen D. Young repeated the familiar arguments against the Eccles banking bill in testimony before the Senate committee, and then told the senators that what the country needed was less action from the federal government, not more.[6] While Eccles at first resisted any weakening of the provisions of Title II, congressional resistance to it led him at last to compromise and the amended bill passed in July.[7] Late in the month Arthur Krock observed that "the easy passage" of the bill should not obscure the fact that the Senate had "rejected noiselessly" a major "New Deal tenet."[8] *Business Week* found that the bill, as passed, had been "so greatly modified that the good in it possibly outweighs the bad."[9] A University of Iowa economist found, in fact, that, contrary to Eccles' purpose, the Banking Act of 1935 had made "the Federal Reserve Board, in effect the whole banking system, less responsible to, and less under the influence of the administration than it was before the passage of the act."[10]

One reason that the dimensions of this major defeat for the administration were so little noted at the time was that most attention was focused on the battle over the public utility holding bill and the series of temporary setbacks it was suffering in the House of Representatives. This is the bill of which the 1924 Democratic nominee for the presidency, John W. Davis, wrote: "I have just spent four days analyzing the Public Utility Bill. If that Bill is constitutional, then, in the language of Mr. Shakespeare, 'I am soused gurnet.' "[11] The bill was pushed by Roosevelt over the opposition of the Business Advisory Council, despite his intimation early in the year that he would consult with them on business legislation.[12]

While the Senate passed the bill, retaining under fierce pressure from the White House the so-called death sentence for holding companies, by one vote, the House surprisingly showed more independence. A vote against the "death sentence" in the House led Arthur Krock to write that Roosevelt had "made such an issue of this one point, and has used his influence to such an extent in an effort to have his viewpoint upheld, that today's vote . . . must go down against him as a political defeat of the first magnitude."[13]

For Roosevelt, whose economic views were based on prejudices, a major one being his distaste for investor-owned utilities, the defeat in the House was unacceptable. The full power of his administration and of his supporters in Congress was thrown into the battle to retain the "death sentence." Even pro-New Deal columnist Raymond Clapper was appalled by the spectacle of the administration's "arm-twisting" of congressmen to get the death sentence approved:

Why all of this? The Administration has lost its sense of proportion for one thing. Second, Mr. Roosevelt has long nursed deep hostility to holding companies and refuses to let them have even a empty victory if he can prevent it. Third, it has been a political axiom that an attack on the power trust is good popular politics. Fourth, holding company abuses have been inexcusable and the disposition is to use any stick to beat a dog.[14]

But of course a major reason was that this was legislation dear to the Brandeisians. Walter Lippmann attacked the death sentence as "a bad method of promoting reform," and observed that Roosevelt's recent behavior looked "altogether too much like what Mr. Santayana used to say of a fanatic, that he redoubled his efforts when he had forgotten his aim."[15]

Under the whip of the Roosevelt administration, the New Deal leadership in Congress launched an investigation into the lobbying efforts against the bill in order to take some of the steam from the opposition. Without at the same time publicizing the Roosevelt administration's lobbying efforts in behalf of the bill, House and Senate committees exposed many of the telegrams and letters addressed to Congress in opposition to the bill as bogus, and revealed that the utility companies had spent over a million dollars in fighting the bill. That this amount was puny in comparison with the millions that Roosevelt was prepared to use to "bribe" those same congressmen and senators to support the bill was not lost on critics. Late in August the House and Senate fashioned a compromise that preserved, in form, much of what Roosevelt had sought. Not all holding companies were to be destroyed—only those more than twice removed from the operating companies, and the SEC was granted a good deal of discretion in applying the law.[16] As with the Securities Act of 1933 and the Securities Exchange Act of 1934, business must once again hope that the SEC would exhibit the wisdom that Roosevelt, the House, and the Senate had not displayed.

Late in June the House joined the Senate in approving the Wagner labor bill and sending it to the White House for Roosevelt's waiting signature. While businessmen had opposed passage of the bill, for reasons already given, they derived some consolation from a belief that the Supreme Court decision on the NIRA boded ill for both the Public Utility Holding Company Act and the Wagner Labor Act, since both seemed based on the same premises that had been struck down in the Schechter case.

THE BRANDEIS/FRANKFURTER INFLUENCE

The growing influence of the Brandeisian philosophy was obvious in Roosevelt's 1935 legislative program. It was even more obvious to Morgenthau, who found Frankfurter constantly at the White House. After a meeting with Roosevelt in mid-June, at which Frankfurter was also present, Morgenthau recorded in his diary:

The President's attitude was most peculiar all thru the meeting. . . . He constantly turned to Felix Frankfurter for admiration and approval on everything that he said. He was constantly showing off and doing it in a rather unpleasant manner seemingly for the benefit of Felix Frankfurter. After seeing Felix Frankfurter at several meetings I find he always uses the President, and constantly plays up to him in a rather bootlicking . . . manner.[17]

With Thomas Corcoran placed at Roosevelt's right hand since March, and Frankfurter's direct influence over Roosevelt, combined with the extensive network of Brandeis-Frankfurter agents that Corcoran had successfully placed in every strategic point within the New Deal, it would be a rare piece of New Deal legislation hereafter that would not bear the imprint of the Brandeisian philosophy, be written by its adherents, and then administered, after it became law, by members of the same group.

Typically Brandeisian was Roosevelt's tax bill, sprung on a surprised Congress and nation late in the session on June 19. The bill proposed a simultaneous attack on wealth, through increased inheritance taxes, gift taxes, and higher income taxes for the wealthy, and on big business, through a graduated scale of corporate income taxes. Frankfurter's influence was present both in the philosophy of the bill and in the decision to introduce it in June.[18] The tax bill was a shock to businessmen and to the press since Roosevelt had given the distinct impression in January that he would seek no additional taxes during the 1935 session.

For some, Roosevelt's move smacked of an attempt to "cut into the political forces behind Huey Long and Dr. Townsend," in their demands to "share the wealth."[19] For others, however, the bill was only a further exposition of Roosevelt's own prejudices, as previously revealed in his other policies. Roosevelt, as one critic observed, was "against bigness, both in personal fortunes and in the corporate units of industry," and he proposed now to use the taxing power of the federal government not alone for government revenue but also for redistribution of wealth. The tax bill, then, was simply an extension of the philosophy behind the public utility holding company bill but in this case was striking at other large industries as well.[20]

The *Annalist* was representative of most press reaction to the bill when it found it remarkable that Roosevelt would introduce such a far-reaching proposal when, "for the purpose of achieving recovery from the depression, nothing could be worse." Moreover, it concluded that new taxes could not hope to produce the revenue forecast by its proponents.[21] This being a Brandeisian bill, however, the amount of revenue to be derived from the taxes was irrelevant, as was the extent to which it would retard recovery. In dealing with zealots, such objections were of no weight. One New Dealer reported, after a conversation with Brandeis:

For fifteen minutes he "held forth" philosophically on the horrors of bigness and the sanctity of littleness in *all* fields of human activity. These views of his are well known; what seemed significant to me was the fervor with which he made these sweeping statements. . . . Here is a grand old man who really feels that he is helping people. His mind widens when he talks about a greater happiness for the average man. It begins to narrow when he considers just what constitutes well-being for ordinary people. But when he turns to the *means* to bring it about, strong emotions surge through him, and his reason seems to abdicate in favor of his feelings. I cannot imagine a person less open to change on the subject of his pet conviction.[22]

And with the Brandeisian influence all-pervasive in the White House, this "abdication of reason" was the rule in government policy.

Identifying the Brandeisian philosophy behind the bill does not, however, account for the timing in springing it on Congress late in the session. The motive most commonly given by historians is a desire on Roosevelt's part to steal a march on Huey Long and the other "share the wealth" demagogues well in advance of the 1936 election. A different motive, however, was more commonly seen behind Roosevelt's action at the time—a desire to punish big business for its opposition to him, and especially from spite over the Schechter decision by the Supreme Court. The Chicago *Tribune* went further in suggesting that, having predicted an economic crisis after the demise of the NRA, Roosevelt was now determined to bring it about.[23] But Roosevelt had already made the decision to propose new taxes even before the Supreme Court decisions of late May. Although the exact contents of the tax bill were not finally settled until shortly before he sent the message to Congress, its general Brandeisian outlines and the decision to send it to Congress during the 1935 session had been established by mid-May.[24] Thus, if the bill and its timing were intended, at least in part, to "punish" big business for its opposition to the New Deal, as critics charged, that desire must have been kindled not by the Schechter decision but by the wave of business opposition to his early legislative program that included the denunciations of the New Deal by the Chamber of Commerce convention.

Shortly after Roosevelt's tax message he conferred with Democratic congressional leaders and pressed for immediate passage of the bill, causing yet another storm of protest. Walter Lippmann wondered what emergency existed that required such a frantic course of action.[25] The House Ways and Means Committee, however, insisted that the procedure advocated by Roosevelt—passage of the bill as a "rider" to an unrelated Senate bill—was unacceptable, and that the legislation must originate in the House of Representatives as provided under the Constitution.[26] Raymond Clapper applauded the return to constitutional processes, noting that "we had what could almost be called a foray in dictatorship, which, after being sharply rebuffed by public opinion, has retreated and given way to regular democratic procedure." Clapper found that "the chief damage has been to undermine confidence in Mr. Roosevelt's judgment."[27]

As for the bill itself, critics searched for any logic to its provisions. *Forbes* concluded that "a fundamental motive of the New Deal is to wage war against bigness in business, to enact legislation and enact taxes calculated to harass and dismember our most successful employment-giving enterprises."[28] Noting that the bill imposed higher taxes on large corporations than on small ones, the New

York *Herald-Tribune* wondered why small investors in large corporations should be penalized more than large investors in small corporations.[29] Walter Lippmann agreed that the bill made no sense unless its primary purpose was to penalize and discourage investors in large corporations. Having failed to find any *rational* motives behind the bill, Lippmann concluded that it looked ''like the absence of any plan and the lack of intellectual effort, the work of tired brains, relying on their wishes and their prejudices and throwing out casual suggestions which they are too hot and bothered to think about.''[30]

As for the ''soak the rich'' taxes on the wealthy, Attorney General Homer Cummings summed up its philosophy eloquently before a Senate committee when he blurted out: ''I cannot understand why it is immoral to stop people from becoming rich.'' The New York *Herald-Tribune* found in this ''the quintessence of the Roosevelt ideal and accomplishment. Stop the creation of wealth, limit the production of income and keep everybody poor. What better summary of the New Deal program could there be?''[31] A Brooklynite wrote the *Magazine of Wall Street*:

Sirs: Do you think Mr. Roosevelt is on the level about this share-the-wealth stuff? If he means it don't you think he ought to divide up his Hyde Park estate? I would like to make early application for five acres on the river. Of course, I'd accept one acre on the river. In fact, just to show I'm not greedy, I'd compromise for half an acre not on the river.[32]

Not even the gold-purchase program of late 1933 had aroused the intense opposition that the tax bill met in 1935. *Forbes* wrote of the business reaction:

Many employers and executives who heretofore have cooperated with the President and urged other men of affairs to do so, now confess that he has deliberately slapped them in the face; and they agree that the only course to follow is to oppose openly every recommendation made by the Administration calculated to injure recovery.[33]

Previously pro-Roosevelt newspapers, newspapermen, businessmen, and progressives abandoned him in large numbers over the tax bill, many of them not to return to the New Deal fold again. In large part the defection resulted because, as with the Supreme Court plan that would follow in 1937, the arguments put forth in defense of the bill were so quickly and easily discredited, and that when these layers of argument were peeled away nothing remained to justify the bill but prejudice, vindictiveness, and spite. No rational argument was put forth to justify the attack on big corporations, the revenue projections of the Treasury were not sufficient to justify the bill as a revenue measure, the impact of the bill for any redistribution of wealth was revealed as insignificant. None of these arguments justified the impact the bill was likely to have in retarding recovery. Even the liberal *New Republic* agreed that ''the whole conception behind [the tax bill] overlooks the fundamental fact that there is little point in trying to redistribute wealth as long as nothing is done to produce more than a fraction of the wealth we are equipped to create.''[34]

Again, Congress did not give Roosevelt all that he had sought when it passed the tax bill. The tax on higher incomes was raised, and a graduated corporate income tax was added, but it was less drastic than Roosevelt had requested. The confiscatory tax on inheritances was dropped and the tax on estates was raised instead. The gift tax was raised as Roosevelt had asked. The modifications made by Congress were not, however, enough to satisfy critics of the bill. If there was any validity to the objections raised to the original bill, then the modified version would continue to be a deterrent to economic recovery.

In other respects, the first session of the 74th Congress presented a mixed picture where the prospects for recovery were concerned. Congress severely modified amendments proposed by the administration to the AAA, amendments that one newspaper observed "would have made Secretary Wallace the czar of every growing thing from 'egg to earth.' "[35] The same Congress, however, passed the Guffey Coal Act, an attempt to restore NRA-like controls over the coal industry, despite the fact that even the attorney general doubted its constitutionality.[36] The bill was hardly a major piece of legislation, but it possessed great symbolic value as one of the bills that Roosevelt regarded as a challenge to the Supreme Court. When Roosevelt told Congress that they should not allow doubts as to the bill's constitutionality to block its passage, his words aroused widespread criticism.[37] This, Roosevelt told Breckinridge Long, would give the Supreme Court an opportunity to back away from the strict interpretation it had put on the interstate commerce clause of the Constitution in the Schechter case, and if they failed to take advantage of the "opportunity" he would be forced to consider seeking an amendment to the Constitution that would remove the Supreme Court as an obstacle.[38]

What would have to be regarded in retrospect as one of the major accomplishments of the New Deal in 1935— the enactment of the Social Security Act—aroused comparatively little comment from businessmen or bankers. Preoccupied with the fight against other legislation of more direct concern to them, they apparently gave little attention to the social security bill. One reason, perhaps, was the fact that the tax upon them for employee retirement benefits would not begin until 1937.[39] One action by Roosevelt that was cheered by businessmen and other critics of the New Deal was his veto of the Patman veterans' bonus bill, which would have required payment of $2 billion to veterans. Roosevelt had at first planned a largely *pro forma* veto so that the onus of the inflationary bill would not rest on him; he was prepared to acquiesce in a congressional override of his veto so that the issue could be removed in 1935, not to crop up in the 1936 election year. Largely under the persuasion of Morgenthau, Roosevelt vetoed the bill with vigor.[40]

Surveying the legislation passed by the 1935 session of Congress, the *Guaranty Survey* concluded:

The laws passed at the recently adjourned session of Congress, like those enacted by its immediate predecessors, are mainly unfavorable from the point of view of business. While they contain some constructive features, they are mostly of such a nature as to create uncertainty rather than confidence in the business outlook, either by imposing or threatening higher taxes, by raising the costs of doing business, by further straining public credit, by broadening the fields of regulation and of governmental competition with private business, or by striking at the security of property and the sanctity of contracts.

In general, however, it found the 1935 session "somewhat less unsettling in its effects on business than those of 1933 and 1934," particularly due to the absence of "potentially inflationary monetary measures" such as had been enacted in the previous two years. It added that much of the negative potential influence of the 1935 session had been countered by the evidence that "normal recuperative forces are in the ascendancy in the general economic situation and ... have been powerful enough to overcome serious impediments of a political nature," and also by "the trend of recent court decisions, and particularly by the invalidation of the NRA by the Supreme Court" which was "regarded as casting doubt on the legality of a rather wide range of other Federal legislation enacted in the last two years."[41] Perhaps the much-modified New Deal program of 1935, then, could not undermine the positive support to business confidence that had been furnished by the elimination of the NRA and the entry of the Supreme Court into calculations about other New Deal laws.

WORK RELIEF

The $4.8 billion work relief bill, passed early in the congressional session, soon began to arouse negative comment. In part, this was because of delays in implementing the program, and in part because what had been "sold" to the American people and Congress as a public works program had degenerated into a work relief program. One critic combined the two complaints by suggesting that the program had been delayed because administrator Harry Hopkins was waiting for the autumn leaves to fall so that there would be work for leaf-rakers.[42] *Engineering News-Record* denounced the change in the program as turning it into "a magnified copy of the CWA," that would do nothing to aid recovery and reemployment in the durable goods industries.[43] What such critics overlooked, however, was the highly useful role that the $4.8 billion had played for Roosevelt in staving off greater legislative defeats during the rest of the congressional session. Having delivered the money to the president early in the session, congressmen faced the possibility of having their districts penalized in the spending of the money if they did not vote right.[44] As Raymond Clapper put it: "They want to keep on the good side of Santa Claus in the hope that they can have some direct influence upon his distribution. This does not seem to be good government, but it is right now the lasso which enables Mr. Roosevelt to hold the country in hand."[45]

The New York *Herald Tribune* noted that Roosevelt had launched his first work-relief program in November 1933, at a time when the National Industrial Conference Board (NICB) estimated unemployment at 9,645,000. Now, as the

$4.8 billion was being inaugurated for the same purpose, the NICB estimated unemployment at 9,711,000 nearly two years later.[46] Treasury Secretary Morgenthau was struck by the fact that ''while unemployment figures seem to have levelled off, the amount of money that we are spending on unemployment is constantly increasing.'' This, he noted, was contrary to what ''the President has repeatedly said, that as private industry picked up the unemployed, he would reduce the amount of money that he spent for the unemployed.'' Morgenthau worried that ''the four billion eight is being flitted away with no centralized plan and that this year will fly by before we know it and they will be around asking for another three or four billion.''[47] The Washington *Post*, however, saw in the apparent planlessness an effort ''to create a feeling of mass contentment, however transient, on the eve of the 1936 election.''[48]

In the White House the same air of unreality continued in Roosevelt's considerations of the unemployment problem. Despite the continued unemployment after more than two years of the New Deal, Roosevelt seemed unable or unwilling to come to grips with the contribution that his attitude and policies were making to the unemployment problem. Instead, a meeting between Roosevelt, Morgenthau, Hopkins, and Ickes late in December 1935 found the president virtually repeating his performance at a similar meeting 14 months earlier. In October 1934 he had talked airily of a program that would begin by employing 5 million on work relief, then gradually reduce until the unemployed had disappeared in the fourth year. Now he envisioned a five-year program totaling $15 billion for work relief, starting with $5 billion in the first year, then dropping by $1 billion a year until it ended in the fifth year with a $1 billion appropriation, after which the unemployed would have disappeared as under his earlier scheme.[49] There was in such calculations no plan for eliminating unemployment, only the expectation that somehow the problem would go away, despite every obstacle that economists and businessmen told him he had erected to make it impossible. Some 14 months of evidence to the contrary had taught Roosevelt nothing.

THE "BREATHING SPELL"

In the meantime, however, Roosevelt had tried to inject a certain amount of reassurance into the business situation. After the adjournment of Congress in August, Roy Howard, friendly head of the Scripps-Howard newspaper chain, addressed a letter to Roosevelt in which he called the president's attention to the fact that businessmen were ''frightened.'' There could, he said, be ''no real recovery until the fears of business have been allayed through the granting of a breathing spell to industry, and a recess from further experimentation until the country can recover its losses.'' Raymond Moley was entrusted with the task of rewriting Howard's letter for publication and of drafting Roosevelt's reply. As revised by Roosevelt, the reply told Howard and the country that the ''basic program'' of the New Deal had ''now reached substantial completion and the 'breathing spell' of which you speak is here—very decidedly so.''[50]

Moley recorded in his memoirs: "The public reaction was so favorable that Roosevelt was astonished. Thousands of letters and telegrams came in congratulating the President. Stock issues hit the highest level since September 1931 and the Gallup poll showed later a spectacular rise in Roosevelt's popularity." Impressed, Roosevelt told Moley that he "wanted to strike a note of peace and unity and harmony again" in the speeches he was planning. For Moley "it seemed for a time that we were back in the old days of the spring of 1933."[51]

But a lot had happened since the spring of 1933 to make businessmen suspicious of any such conciliatory words from Roosevelt. While many businessmen greeted the statement with relief, that relief was mixed with large quantities of skepticism and cynicism. Cynics saw in the "breathing spell" a bid for business support in the 1936 election. Skeptics pointed out that the "breathing spell" did nothing to relieve business operations from the load of New Deal burdens already imposed, nor from those likely to be produced in the future under the new powers granted by the most recent session of Congress. Moreover, Roosevelt had said that his program was "substantially" completed; and that qualifier left the door ajar for future legislative surprises.[52] David Lawrence pointed out that the very term "breathing spell" implied "not only that there has been strangulation but that after a brief interval the process of strangulation will be resumed."[53] The *Magazine of Wall Street* found it suggesting only "a lull in a storm," while *Business Week* reported the warning by one New Dealer that the breathing spell would "develop into asthma" once business found out what it was all about.[54] *Newsweek* found many on Wall Street likening the breathing spell to a story about a Missouri farmer:

"Wait till I catch the guy that stole my best coon dog," fumed a Missouri farmer. "I'll chain him to my Ford and drag him over the roughest road in Webster County. But I ain't gonna kill the critter right off. I'm gonna drive like hell for a space, then slow down and give the son-of-a-gun a breathing spell, and then drive some more."[55]

But despite the skepticism over the breathing spell, despite the opposition to the legislative program of the 1935 Congress and uncertainties over its application, and despite delays in implementing the $4.8 billion spending program, business activity continued the upward trend that had begun within weeks after the Supreme Court's nullification of the NRA. Further stimulus was no doubt derived from evidence that the appeal of the New Deal had waned with voters. A Rhode Island congressional election in early August saw the Republicans taking a seat from the Democrats by 13,000 votes in a campaign based entirely on the New Deal.[56] In the November off-year elections the GOP made additional gains, winning, for example, control of the New York state legislature. One newspaper noted that the Republican resurgence had been followed by a rise in the stock market, with the "broadest trade in 21 months, heaviest in 15," and gains of as many as 9 points in leading stocks.[57]

Businessmen, business writers, and business periodicals hailed the beginnings of the long-delayed recovery.[58] Only a few skeptics warned that despite any boom that might occur, the foundations for a genuine recovery had not yet been laid.[59] Usually the Supreme Court was credited with having created the business confidence that launched the recovery. As one financial writer put it, the "decisions of federal courts holding various provisions of the Agricultural Adjustment Act unconstitutional, coming on the heels of the unshackling of American business from the restrictions of the NRA," had "encouraged industries to forge ahead."[60]

THE WAR ON BUSINESS, HOWEVER, CONTINUES

Meanwhile, Roosevelt's declaration of a breathing spell for business did not halt the defections among businessmen and others from the New Deal that had accelerated during the 1935 congressional session. Friendly columnist Raymond Clapper remained a Roosevelt supporter, but a column in September reflected the growing disillusionment that had begun to seize others like him:

The Roosevelt administration, for all of its personal charm, has been violent in its attacks on the business community. Long and loudly, it has whipped up sentiment, making little effort to single out the malefactors, broadsiding the "money changers," "Tories," "financial racketeers," and "sinister forces"—these being usually anybody opposed to the Administration program.

Until the Roy Howard letter of a few days ago, practically no attempt had been made by the Administration to isolate its targets. If you owned a cash register, you were one of the old tooth-and-claw gang. Administration indictments were allowed to lodge against the whole business community, and the fellow who had no other interest in life except to go ahead getting more business and meeting his pay roll, found himself roped off in the concentration camp reserved for the "sinister forces." Such persons, smarting under the feeling that the Roosevelt Administration was hostile to them, are providing a receptive audience for the most violent critics of Mr. Roosevelt.

It is a violent reaction. Whereas only a few months ago Republicans were privately debating the advisability of attacking Mr. Roosevelt by name or confining their campaign to the Tugwells and the Farleys, they are out now with full artillery pounding at Roosevelt himself. His promises are publicly scoffed at. The public is told that his word cannot be relied upon. Practically anybody, we are told, would be better in the White House than Mr. Roosevelt. The violence of the New Deal crackdown has bounced back in the President's face.[61]

Here is the answer to those historians who insist that Roosevelt's violent attacks on business in 1936 were inspired by attacks *from* business.

The 1935 program of New Deal "must" legislation had finally demonstrated conclusively to most members of the Business Advisory Council that they were exerting no influence on Roosevelt's policies.[62] Noting in early July that five members had resigned within the previous two weeks, the New York *Herald-Tribune* wrote that "for two years these men have stood by, believing and hoping that they could be of some genuine usefulness to the Administration and to the country,'' but the events of the preceding two months had "served to disabuse them completely of that belief."[63] A writer usually friendly to the New Deal described in mid-October the growing anti-Roosevelt sentiment in the East. As an example, he wrote: "In a moving picture house recently a picture of the President drew but one lonely handclap and the comment from a man in the audience, 'He must be on relief.' ''[64] A Gallup poll in October found Roosevelt beating a nameless GOP candidate by 58–47 percent, down from the 59–41 percent by which he had beaten Hoover in 1932, and weaker in all sections of the country except for the mountain states.[65] Another Gallup poll a week later showed that 53 percent were opposed to curbing the powers of the Supreme Court while only 31 percent favored it.[66]

The breathing spell did not silence business and banking criticism of the New Deal. Of particular note are the issues raised at the convention of the American Bankers Association in November 1935. Orval W. Adams, vice-president of the Utah State National Bank in Salt Lake City, warned that a substantial business recovery could cause grave problems for the nation's banks. Recovery, he pointed out, would drive up interest rates and make the low-interest government bonds that the banks held in large amounts unattractive. Warned Adams:

It is clear that a drop of 10 points in the market value of federal obligations—and this would be the inevitable consequence of revived business activity—would wipe out approximately 40 percent of the total invested capital of our national banks. A business revival, with its expanding need for credit, would at once reduce the market value of all lower interest bearing obligations, including those of the federal government.[67]

In short, according to Adams the Roosevelt administration had created a situation in which the nation's banks would be threatened in the event of an economic recovery. Both to safeguard the banks, and to force the federal government to adopt sounder fiscal policies, Adams advocated that banks thereafter refuse to make further purchases of federal bonds—an action that would make it extremely difficult, if not impossible, for the federal government to continue with its deficit spending. The response of bankers was indicated when they rejected the choice of their nominating committee for the office of second vice-president (and eventual president) of the ABA for the first time in their history and chose Adams instead.[68]

Apparently incensed by ABA and other criticism of the growing federal debt of his administration, Roosevelt lashed out at bankers in a speech later in November, charging that it was bankers, themselves, who had suggested to him early in his administration that he vastly increase the debt of the federal government as a means of producing recovery. Certain bankers had, he said, assured him that a national debt of $55 to $70 billion could be safely handled by the government's credit. Immediately newspapers and bankers sought the name of any bankers who might have given such advice to Roosevelt. No banker would admit to having made such a recommendation, one observing that no responsible banker would say such a thing "drunk or sober."[69] A search of speeches made by bankers revealed none that could be used as the basis for Roosevelt's assertion. A leading banker suggested that the culprit in this case might be the same imaginary "influential man" who had popped up in Roosevelt's Green Bay speech in 1934.[70] To repeated requests for the names of the bankers Roosevelt claimed had given him the advice, the president responded evasively by saying that he had letters from bankers, and that newspapermen could consult financial periodicals from the period and find the same kind of assertions.[71] None could be found. Mark Sullivan explained Roosevelt's statement away as the result of a quirk in the president's mental processes in which imagination easily triumphed over fact.[72]

Looking at business conditions late in 1935, the *Guaranty Survey* found "some tangible betterment in business" had occurred as a result of a "considerable revival of confidence" following the Supreme Court decisions, but it warned that Roosevelt had not "succeeded in producing a sound, normal, and sustained recovery." It pointed to the continued high level of unemployment, the inability of banks to find commercial outlets for their surplus funds, and the absence of a demand for corporate capital in the securities markets. What was needed, it concluded, was not a breathing spell from reform measures, but a complete cessation of such measures and a concentration by Roosevelt on producing recovery.[73] The National Industrial Council agreed at its meeting early in December that "what is needed is not a temporary cessation of regulatory legislation," but "a 'cease and desist' order, and a removal of strait-jacket legislation."[74] Alfred P. Sloan, Jr., head of General Motors, pointed out that the major problem was that of finding jobs for the unemployed, and that could not be solved "by edict, prejudice or threat, or by government spending."[75]

In a perceptive essay in mid-December, Walter Lippmann explored the contrasts between Roosevelt's policies toward agriculture and business:

The President's attitude toward the farmers has been one of complete sympathy; towards industry and finance it has been one of distrust. Thus, for example, when he set out to regulate agricultural production, he devised a system to pay the farmer if he complied. But when he has tried to regulate industry and finance, he has resorted to coercive laws, to threats, to punishment, to "death sentences." There can be no doubt that there has been a profound difference of temper and of fundamental attitude. He has done everything he could to help the farmer. He has tried to compel and overawe the business man. . . . [I]n the case of agriculture the temper of the laws and their administration has been friendly, and in the case of industry the temper has been coercive, unfriendly, and often hostile. . . . It has, for example, done little if anything about the wretched labor conditions among many migratory farm workers or about the abuses to which some tenant farmers are subject. . . . But when they have dealt with industry, they have been so much concerned with abuses, so overzealous about fixing this and that, here, there and everywhere, that they never have wholeheartedly devoted themselves to the main thing—which was to stimulate an industrial recovery.

For the main problems that the country faced in promoting economic recovery, Lippmann concluded that "the worst advisers are those who like fighting for its own sake, who have confused their own views with the certain and absolute truth, the cocksure, self-satisfied, and suspicious men who are suffering from the awful delusion that not only are they right in their views but that they alone are righteous in their hearts."[76] It was an apt description of the Brandeisians, who, under Frankfurter's leadership, had begun to dominate the White House.

Exactly such attitudes as Lippmann had denounced pervaded Roosevelt's first speech of 1936, his extraordinary State of the Union address. The speech was unprecedented in being delivered to Congress at 9 P.M.—in "prime time" for radio listeners across the country—and it was remarkable in its contents. Instead of reporting on the state of the nation, Roosevelt launched again into the theme of class warfare that had saturated his 1933 inaugural speech, and revealed further the siege mentality in the White House. He told his audience: "In these latter years we have witnessed the domination of government by financial and industrial groups, numerically small but politically dominant in the twelve years that succeeded the World War." His administration had, however, sought "to restore power to those to whom it rightfully belonged," to establish "a new relationship between Government and people" based on "the ideal of the public interest." He added:

To be sure, in so doing we have invited battle. We have earned the hatred of entrenched greed. The very nature of the problem that we faced made it necessary to drive some people from power and strictly to regulate others. I made that plain when I took the oath of office in March 1933. I spoke of the practices of the unscrupulous money-changers who stood indicted in the court of public opinion. I spoke of the rulers of the exchanges of mankind's goods, who failed through their own stubbornness and their own incompetence.

Now those "interests" were seeking "the restoration of their selfish power." Their weapon was "fear" but it was not "a natural fear, a normal fear; it is a synthetic, manufactured, poisonous fear that is being spread, subtly, expensively and cleverly by the same people who cried in those other days, 'Save us, save us, lest we perish.' "[77]

Both Roosevelt's method and message were widely denounced. The method was attacked for "tying Congress to the tail of the radio kite" in an effort to "salvage" his administration "from the tide of unpopularity which is overwhelming."[78] Walter Lippmann charged that "never before has the radio been used in America with such calculated purpose to establish any one man's domination of public opinion."[79] It was the message, however, that attracted the most criticism, with demagogic the term most often used to describe it. *Banker's Magazine* found Roosevelt's speech less revealing of the state of the Union than of the "state of his own mind." The president, it noted, still seemed to regard "those who oppose his policies as public enemies."[80] Others found it simply a further example of Roosevelt's demagogic appeals for class hatred.[81] The Minneapolis *Tribune* wrote that it was "less a report on the state of the union than it was a bitter and vindictive attack on those who challenge the New Deal." No president, it observed, had "ever packed fewer pertinent facts or more quivering emotionalism into an opening message to Congress."[82]

Most observers agreed that Roosevelt's demagogic haranque was exactly what the country did not need while still mired in a depression with 10 million unemployed.[83] David Lawrence wrote that it was "the very opposite of that which the nation needs at the moment. The healing of the wounds of class warfare rather than their reopening is the paramount duty of him who would lead the American people to a sound economic recovery."[84] The brother of a New Dealer wrote Roosevelt:

I was thoroughly disappointed in the political "show" which was staged in our Capitol, under the guise of a constitutional duty. It seems to me that the dignity of the Office of President . . . demands certain things of the occupant of that office. The bitter feeling, the attempt to stir up class hatred, the lack of any definite message to the Congress, and the denunciation of others in your address all call for condemnation, and can only result in alienating from your program all those who are not to be misled by appeals to the lowest feelings of man. You had an opportunity to make a great move toward binding the Country together in its present progress, and I, and many like me, can only deplore the undignified procedure which was resorted to.[85]

Roosevelt replied rather lamely to this verbal spanking, saying in part:

There is today, I believe. no duty more important than the task of awakening the people of the United States to awareness of the fact that the men who produced the collapse of 1929 have learned nothing from that disaster and are now endeavoring to lead the country back to a road which will end in a greater and more dangerous collapse.[86]

Most critics would doubtless have argued that a more important duty for Roosevelt was the responsibility to stimulate economic recovery so that the 10 million unemployed could find productive jobs, and that "the men who produced the collapse" of 1934 (Roosevelt and his advisers) had "learned nothing from that disaster" and were "now endeavoring to lead the country back to a road which will end in a greater and more dangerous crash," to use Roosevelt's words. What Roosevelt's reply seemed to imply was that one way to head off future depressions was to delay recovery from the present one. That Roosevelt's "performance" before Congress was not highly regarded by the public is suggested by an Associated Press story, which reported that "during the hour President Roosevelt spoke over the radio," the New York City utility company showed a comparative drop in electric usage from the night before. An official of the company said that it was "possible to assume" that the decline of 20,000 kilowatts of usage from the same hour the night before "was caused by people turning off their radios when the President started to speak."[87]

CHAPTER 8

Fueling a Boom

THE AAA DECISION

Scarcely had the words of Roosevelt's State of the Union address ceased to reverberate through the press when the New Deal suffered yet another blow from the Supreme Court. On January 5, 1936, newspapers carried the results of a Gallup poll that found 59 percent of Americans opposed to the AAA.[1] The following day the same newspapers carried news of the AAA's demise. The Supreme Court had found it unconstitutional by a 6–3 vote. At a meeting with Roosevelt and others concerned with the matter soon after the decision, Attorney General Homer Cummings found Agriculture Secretary Henry Wallace "inclined to believe that his prediction of more than a year ago would be justified; namely, that prices would be maintained for quite a long period." The attorney general found this presenting "some interesting political consequences. If prices should be maintained, it would probably be charged that the A.A.A. had nothing to do with the creation thereof."[2] Would the AAA now be shown to have been as useless, or even harmful, to recovery as the NRA had been demonstrated to be?

The AAA decision was greeted almost as happily as that invalidating the NRA. *Business Week* found the "whole New Deal house of laws" shaken and trembling now that another of its main "pillars" had been "blown to pieces by the Supreme Court," and with others sure to fall.[3] *The Economist* saw the blow to the AAA signifying "Death to the New Deal," and wrote: "Mr. Roosevelt is obviously in a position of the most excruciating embarrassment. Nothing in America could be more damaging to a President that the belief that he had deliberately pursued unconstitutional policies."[4] Frank Kent agreed, but also pointed out that Roosevelt really had good reason to be thankful to the court, for it had freed him from two "tremendous political liabilities" in his campaign for reelection—the NRA and AAA—both of which had been demonstrated by polls to be unpopular with the voters. Moreover, he had the advantage of the evident business improvement that had begun after the invalidation of the NRA.[5] Business journals found the demise of the AAA furnishing even further encouragement to commerce and industry.[6]

While some worried that the demise of the AAA might be detrimental to farmers unless it was followed by new farm legislation, the Bureau of Agricultural Economics in the Department of Agriculture suggested that, where cotton at least was concerned, farm income would probably have been as large without the AAA and might even have been higher.[7] In the February issue of *Atlantic* magazine, moreover, James E. Boyle of the Cornell University agricultural experiment station charged that among its other adverse effects, the AAA had added at least 2 million men to the unemployment rolls.[8] Early in that same month, Roosevelt called upon Congress to repeal three other elements in the New Deal farm program—the Bankhead Cotton Act of 1934, the Kerr-Smith Tobacco Act of 1934, and the Potato Act of 1935.[9] All three were patently unconstitutional according to the decision rendered in the AAA case.

A NEW ATTACK ON BUSINESS

Despite the new spanking by the Supreme Court, Roosevelt returned to the class warfare theme when he spoke at the Jackson Day dinner in Washington a few days later. He told the assembled diners: "We are at peace with the world; but the fight goes on. Our frontiers of today are economic, not geographic. Our enemies of today are the forces of privilege and greed within our own borders."[10] Certainly, when business contemplated the legislation before Congress in the 1936 session they found ample confirmation that Washington was intent on "waging war" to the detriment of recovery. The NAM found five bills, especially, being debated in Congress that boded ill for business recovery. There was the Walsh-Healy bill, which would require companies doing business with the government to observe the old NRA wage and labor provisions; the O'Mahoney bill, which would require government licenses for all industries involved in interstate commerce; the Ellenbogen bill, which would set up a "little NRA" in the textile industry; the perennial Black-Connery 30-hour-week-bill; and the Robinson-Patman antichain-store bill. Given Roosevelt's unpredictability and hostility toward business, businessmen could not be certain that he would not put all or some of these bills on his "must" list at some time during the session.[11]

These bills were, however, of little moment when compared to the business reaction to Roosevelt's new tax bill introduced in March. Even granting that Roosevelt was forced to find additional revenue to replace that which was lost due to the invalidation of the AAA's processing taxes, and to pay the veterans' bonus (passed by Congress late in January), it is difficult to conceive of a worse tax, from the standpoint of recovery, than that which Roosevelt asked Congress to approve. After weeks of debate within the Treasury Department, the minds there united in advocating a tax that had first been proposed by the brain trust in 1932, particularly by Tugwell. This was a tax on undistributed corporate profits, or, as it was sometimes called, a tax on surplus profits. Given Roosevelt's disposition to follow the advice of lawyers and other amateurs in preference to that of economists, businessmen, and bankers on policies vital to the economy, there was nothing extraordinary in the fact that this tax was now largely the result of the urgings of a lawyer, Herman Oliphant. Oliphant was convinced that the tax would force corporations to distribute these profits to stockholders, thereby increasing consumer purchasing power and making it possible for the government to collect taxes on the additional income that the investors received. Morgenthau was searching desperately for a "political" source of revenue— one that would increase taxes without alienating voters in a presidential election year. Morgenthau and Oliphant even managed to convince themselves that it would have the further beneficent (from a Brandeisian point of view) result of forcing large corporations to compete with smaller ones in securities markets for capital, since they would not now be able to rely on retained surpluses for capital expansion.[12]

How that could possibly benefit smaller industries was not made quite clear, nor does it seem to have occurred to the minds in the Treasury that the tax might, instead, simply halt capital expansion altogether at a time when there was already not enough going on to produce recovery. Intent only on finding a way to raise revenue in a "politic" way, they omitted from their considerations the myriad of possible negative effects of the tax, including the handicaps it would pose for industries if they lacked reserves with which to face another downturn, and the contribution it would then make to further unemployment.

Critics quickly found other weaknesses in the bill. The New York *Times* pointed out that the effect of the tax would be to deflect spending away from durable goods, which desperately needed stimulation, and toward consumer goods, which did not. The bill, then, was the opposite of "what sound policy calls for under present conditions."[13] As for its revenue aspects, stockholders in upper tax brackets, who were intended to be "soaked" by the tax man if dividends were forced on them, could be expected to turn to other forms of investment, such as tax-free bonds, with the net effect being a drop in tax revenue rather than an increase, and discouragement of investors from furnishing funds to industry.[14] A more telling criticism for the Brandeisians around the president was the argument that, as the First National Bank of Boston pointed out, the tax favored "strong corporations" while penalizing the young and weak concerns.[15] The reasons were obvious: small and medium-sized concerns, especially newer ones, generally financed their early expansion largely from profits retained for that purpose. The proposed tax, therefore, would tend to perpetuate the existing stratification of business by keeping the large large and the small small.

Brandeis, himself, saw "dangers in the tax bill," and wondered if it couldn't "be gently shelved for further study & as a 'compromise' get [an] increase of corporation rates in the higher brackets & high estate taxes—'temporarily?' "[16]

Within the Treasury, Morgenthau was already, by May 1, beginning to express serious reservations about the bill his department had produced. At a meeting with advisers he wondered if the bill wasn't beneficial to large companies and detrimental to small ones as critics had charged. Oliphant offered a typical New Deal solution to any such problem that might be created by the bill, telling Morgenthau that "if the tax bill does not permit a small concern to continue in business . . . the Government could subsidize it." Morgenthau reacted heatedly: "That is just what we don't want to do." If it did appear that small and medium-sized businesses were going to be hurt by the bill, Morgenthau wanted to be "big enough to correct this thing and throw it out." Again, on May 4, Morgenthau sought assurances from his advisers that the bill would not harm small and medium businesses, but did not receive a satisfactory answer.[17] He was also growing concerned that the new tax would not increase the revenue of the government as much as planned.[18]

Testimony against the bill before the Senate finance committee ranged from the plaintive pleas of small businessmen to the expert testimony of former Treasury Undersecretary Arthur A. Ballantine, who told the committee that the tax would not only weaken industrial and commercial enterprise, but would also work at odds with Roosevelt's goal of social security. Under the new tax, he pointed out, businesses would not have the reserves with which they could pay wages and furnish security for the bulk of the nation's workers in the event of another collapse.[19] Similarly authoritative testimony against the bill from George O. May, senior partner in the accounting firm of Price, Waterhouse and Company, a wartime adviser to the Treasury, led support for the bill within the Treasury to crumble even further. As Morgenthau's administrative assistant, an opponent of the bill, put it: "It cannot be that the whole world is wrong. Not all of us have ulterior motives to protect the rich. Isn't it possible that the people with social justice looming so big in their minds are prejudiced in their attitude?"[20]

The bill, having passed the House, was now an embarrassing and unwanted child for the Treasury that had fathered it. The confusion there betrayed the accuracy of the observation by the *Magazine of Wall Street* that "as hitherto has often been the case with New Deal legislative proposals, the thought and study which should have preceded recommendation have to be made long afterward.[21] It might have added that the "thought and study" generally had to be made by critics outside the administration. From Wall Street came the further disquieting news to Morgenthau that uncertainties over the tax bill were "at least a slight deterrent" in the government bond market.[22] By early June the Senate Democratic leadership had formulated a compromise that the Treasury supported and the House was induced to accept. The compromise retained the corporate income tax, originally slated to be replaced by the new tax, and added to it a graduated, but smaller, undistributed profits tax. Roosevelt approved the compromise.[23]

Although it was an improvement over the original bill, the compromise did not quiet opposition to the undistributed profits tax. Publisher-columnist David Lawrence observed that the bill still had been condemned by newspapers heretofore friendly to the New Deal, by "independent-minded publications from one end of the country to the other, and by many Senators heretofore supportive of the New Deal, as well as by businessmen and the best accountants." Instead of heeding them, Roosevelt had "accepted the advice of a small group of reformers and nobody else." As for the "breathing spell" that Roosevelt had promised business a few months earlier, Lawrence concluded:

Clearly we have come to a fateful hour in American history when solemn pledges issued from the White House cannot be taken at face value.

It is plain that President Roosevelt either does not know how to cooperate with business or does not care to cooperate.

It is plain also that either Mr. Roosevelt has become a convert to Hitler and Mussolini fascism and is planning a government by the State of all business or else that the President is drifting in a kind of emergency opportunism and does not know how much his inability to adjust himself to economic evolution in America is retarding recovery today.[24]

Ex-New Dealer Raymond Moley found in the final bill "every vicious principle contained in the first raw draft submitted to the House by a Treasury Department infatuated with the novelty of an untried and demonstrably unsound social theory."[25]

The 1936 session of Congress also considered a number of bills designed to interfere with various forms of distribution, the most notable being the Robinson-Patman antichain-store bill. The *Bulletin of the National Retail Dry Goods Association* assailed it as "one of the most vicious measures which has confronted retailers—small and large," and "equally objectionable to the great mass of American consumers because its enactment will result in unwarranted increases in retail prices."[26] Designed to shore up small retail units by destroying many of the advantages that large-scale buying had heretofore provided for consumers and for large retail units, the bill was opposed by farm organizations like the American Farm Bureau Federation and the National Grange for intruding into the field of legitimate business and forcing higher retail prices upon farmers and other consumers.[27] Denounced by Professor Malcolm McNair, of the Harvard Graduate School of Business, as an attempt to force retailing back to the days of the horse and buggy, the legislation was passed, shorn of some of its worst features, but still in a form objectionable to most retailers.[28]

WORK RELIEF AGAIN

In March, Roosevelt sent his request for relief appropriations to Congress. He was determined that the annual deficit should show signs of a decline each year, even if only by small amounts, and this was especially desirable in the election year of 1936. Informed by Morgenthau that $1.75 billion remained from previous appropriations, Roosevelt decided to ask for an additional $1.5 billion.[29] What was striking about Roosevelt's message to Congress was the tacit admission, again, that he had made no progress in solving the relief program. Fourteen months earlier, Roosevelt had described 5 million unemployed on the relief rolls; now he found 5.3 million families and unattached persons in need of government assistance. As one writer put it, "the alarming fact is that in this battle for relief of the unemployed, the Nation has not gained a foot—if anything, it has lost."[30] David Lawrence concluded that with nearly one-sixth of the population on relief after three years of Roosevelt in the White House, it was time to start blaming Roosevelt instead of Hoover for the situation. It was Roosevelt's policies that had made reemployment by industry impossible, he wrote, and it was time for the president "either to recommend complete government control of all industry and business under dictatorial powers or else to withdraw his 'controlled economy' together with the harassments which he is constantly offering to economic progress." Roosevelt's attitude toward the economic system was "the basic misfortune of our tragic era."[31]

Roosevelt, however, was still more interested in using threats and coercion than cooperation in trying to stimulate reemployment of the idle. He told Raymond Moley, the day after his relief message, that increases in employment

ought to be done by individual industry working within themselves, and that a spread of hours ought to be attempted. He told me that he was thinking in terms of next year and the year after, and that if it were impossible to achieve the purposes that he hoped should be achieved by private industry, the government would have to step in and coerce industry in the way that NRA originally planned. If this would be impossible under the rulings of the Supreme Court, an issue would be created.[32]

One can only marvel at Roosevelt's reasoning. Having created conditions that businessmen, economists, and other critics had demonstrated conclusively to be retarding economic recovery and reemployment of idle workers, Roosevelt's solution lay not in altering his policies in order to aid recovery, but in supplementing those policies with new measures that would make recovery even more impossible. Roosevelt proposed now to compel industry to mask the failure of his policies by adding workers to its labor force that it could not afford. Thus Roosevelt was intent on pursuing his vicious circle of restraining recovery, rather than breaking it and allowing recovery to proceed as it was elsewhere in the world.

THE BLACK COMMITTEE

More sensational than the legislation of the 1936 session were the actions of the investigative committee of Senator Hugo Black, Democrat of Alabama.

Black's committee was for the 1930s the equivalent of that of Senator Joseph McCarthy in the 1950s, with one important distinction. While both men ran roughshod over civil liberties, the McCarthy committee at least focused on alleged enemies of the United States, while the Black committee concentrated, instead, on opponents of the New Deal under the guise of an investigation of lobbyists. Walter Lippmann wrote of Black that "the Senator is an enthusiast for investigations but in the realm of justice he is an obvious illiterate." This was all the more frightening, Lippmann said, because Black was "one of the chief investigators of the Senate." Black was "the judge before whom many men are being tried on charges which, whether they are proved or not, will ruin them if the charges are believed," but there was "no suggestion that he even realizes that his function is judicial."[33]

When Black's agents seized thousands of private telegrams as part of his committee's "fishing" expedition, the outrage over this violation of constitutional guarantees of freedom from "unreasonable searches and seizures" was instantaneous in the nation's press.[34] Since the victim of the high-handed action was a newspaper chain, the added issue of freedom of the press seemed to be at stake. *Editor and Publisher* charged that the action had been "so obviously defiant of constitutional free press rights, that one would think at first blush some stupid zealot employee had blundered into a situation that would immediately be repudiated by the responsible federal officials." But that had not happened. Instead, Black had brazenly made a seized private message public, even though it had nothing to do with the lobby investigation, and in disregard of "injunction proceedings and protests of the American Newspaper Publishers' Association." It meant, the journal concluded, "that politicians have devised a means of intimidating editorial expression."[35] The American Society of Newspaper Editors charged that "if such practice is not checked, the threat to liberty of individual action and particularly of the freedom of the press is immediate and menacing."[36]

Criticized from every side, except, conspicuously, the White House, Black responded that the opposition to his actions was coming from "those who want to work in darkness and who dread the condemnation of the honest, patriotic people of this nation for their pernicious practices and sinister activities." Frank Kent responded:

This ridiculous slush is not peculiar to Senator Black, though undoubtedly he has a congenital taste for it. It is symbolic of the New Deal spirit and it strikes the note that will be played upon throughout the campaign. Regardless of the unsoundness, insincerity or unjustifiable nature of the New Deal policies or activities, all critics and opponents are "sinister" and "pernicious," "greedy reactionaries" or "chiselers." In other words, the New Deal policy is—don't argue, abuse.[37]

Senator Homer Bone, Democrat of Washington, urged a Senate investigation of the Black committee, calling it a "nascent and budding OGPU," a reference to the Soviet secret police.[38] That Black's actions and methods were approved by

Roosevelt, however, was made clear the following year when the president shocked the nation by appointing Black to the Supreme Court of the United States.

Black's activities probably did nothing to help Roosevelt's popularity in early 1936. Emil Hurja, pollster for the Democratic National Committee, concluded from his surveys that if the presidential election were held in early February, Roosevelt would lose against Governor Alf Landon of Kansas.[39] Hurja found Roosevelt losing most of the East and large slices of the Midwest. Concluding that the country was in the midst of a conservative swing, Hurja warned Morgenthau that "it was a bad thing to antagonize business by calling names," and that investigations should be stopped since "the people are fed up with them."[40] An Ohio Democrat who intended to support Roosevelt in 1936 was nevertheless candid in his friendly criticism of the situation in Washington. He wrote a New Dealer:

In common with many Democrats who are admirers of and believers in F. D. R., I am apprehensive that many Americans (especially in Ohio) are becoming concerned that the New Deal involves fundamental changes in our form of government and institutions by a manner other than constitutional amendment. . . . There is prevalent in Ohio (and I assume in other states) a general distrust of the advanced views attributed to Professor Frankfurter and his brilliant group of young followers. . . . The danger is that the concept of F. D. R. as a humble American discharging his great responsibility . . . , with a devotion to American institutions and regard for constitutional limitations, may become lost; that the substitute will be a concept of a "peerless leader" of a fight of one group against other groups of Americans. . . . In my very humble judgment, his latest speeches have been too clarion, too offensive in the broad sense, and do not inspire the affection that his earlier attitude invoked.[41]

Walter Lippmann perceived "a kind of loss of balance" in Roosevelt that raised "serious doubts as to whether he can remain master of the situation which he is creating."[42]

A MIXED "RECOVERY"

Business continued the improvement it had begun in 1935, but unemployment remained high. Professor Garfield V. Cox, of the University of Chicago, surveyed the economic situation in the March *American Economic Review* and pointed out that U.S. recovery was not only lagging behind that of other industrial countries, but it had been "more erratic" than those elsewhere and even than past recoveries in the United States. The 10 million unemployed could find jobs in private industry only if there was "a broad and extensive recovery in the production of durable goods," but this had been hampered by New Deal policies. A "disturbing feature of the limited American recovery" he found in "the extent to which business as it is now operating is dependent upon the emergency spending of government." Recovery would require a transition from government to private spending, but there was as yet no indication of how that was to occur in the presence of so many factors that discouraged business spending on durable goods. Until industry began to borrow and spend in large amounts, the transfer from government to private spending could not occur, nor could substantial reemployment.[43]

In 1935 the dollar volume of securities registered with the SEC rose to nearly $2.7 billion by comparison with only $630 million in 1934, a seemingly hopeful sign that this critical economic indicator was at last moving toward normality. But the *Wall Street Journal* found the situation far less hopeful than it appeared. Deducting from both the 1934 and 1935 figures the amounts designed solely for debt refunding, investment trusts, and other purposes than the supply of new money to industry, it found the actual amount of new money flowing into industry through the securities market totaled less than $50 million in 1935, only a slight improvement over the $31.5 million in 1934. "Real reopening" of the capital market, it concluded, had not yet taken place. Confidence was still lacking.[44]

Meanwhile, the government's own figures showed that government relief spending had increased substantially as compared with 1934 and that the average number of people on relief had increased. The failure of the New Deal was written in the increase of the average number of relief cases from 3,566,842 in 1933, to 4,324,953 in 1934, and to 4,681,828 in 1935. Including state and local aid, approximately 24 million persons were found to be dependent on relief early in 1936, compared to about 21 million in January 1934.[45]

The Treasury Department tried to put a better face on the situation by pointing to estimates of over $8 billion in net earnings for corporations in 1936, compared with less than $3 billion in 1933 and about $5.5 billion in 1935.[46] This posed a problem for those in industry who recognized that the increased profits did not indicate the recovery that many outsiders assumed them to mean. As Alfred P. Sloan, Jr., head of General Motors, wrote to a fellow industrialist,

there is one point on which I am very much concerned . . . and that is, with business getting better . . . one is very much on the defensive because of the almost impossibility of getting before the public at large, the fact that notwithstanding profits have come back, notwithstanding profits have increased fundamentally, the situation is just as bad, or worse, than ever. Of course you and I know that, and all thinking people know it, but the general public takes the position: what are you kicking about? Why do you complain about this thing or that thing—look how much money you are making.[47]

Dry Goods Economist agreed. Noting the criticism of business for seeming to ignore the signs of "recovery" all around, it observed: "We see the outward signs of prosperity, but we know they come from borrowed money."[48]

MR. ROOSEVELT'S ATTITUDE

At its annual convention late in April 1936, the Chamber of Commerce moderated slightly its militant tone of a year earlier, but remained critical of much of the New Deal. When Raymond Moley told Roosevelt a few days later that he had "every reason to believe that many reasonable business men were anxious to cooperate in some way in the restoration of the NRA idea, if not in its detail," he was exposed to the real Roosevelt prejudice against business, finance, and the press. As Moley described the conversation in his journal, Roosevelt

launched into a violent attack upon business men generally saying that he had talked with a great many business men, in fact to more business men than had any other President, and that they were generally stupid. He said that the trouble with them . . . was that they had no moral indignation for the sins of other business men. . . . He then turned from that to a violent attack on the newspapers, saying that the newspapers had no moral indignation. . . . He said nothing would help him more [in the election] than to have it known that the newspapers were all against him. . . . He then launched into a denunciation of bankers and businessmen and said that every time they made an attack on him, . . . he gained votes and that the result of carrying on this sort of warfare was to bring the people to his support. I said that was quite true, and that he clearly had the election in hand, but that inasmuch as our system involved the newspapers on the one hand, and business on the other, I did not see how ultimately the welfare of the country would be served by totally discrediting business to the people, unless we planned to go into a different form of economic life. He made no particular comment on this, and the inference can clearly be drawn that he was thinking merely in terms of the political advantage to him in creating the impression through the country that he was being unjustly attacked by business men.

Moley came away from his discussion with Roosevelt deeply disturbed. He wrote in his journal:

I was impressed as never before by the utter lack of logic of the man, the scantiness of his precise knowledge of things that he was talking about, by the gross inaccuracies in his statements, by the almost pathological lack of sequence in his discussion, by the complete rectitude that he felt as to his own conduct, by the immense and growing egotism that came from his office, by his willingness to continue the excoriation of the press and business in order to get votes for himself, by his indifference to what effect the long-continued pursuit of these ends would have upon the civilization in which he was playing a part. In other words, the political habits of his mind were working full steam with the added influence of a swollen ego. My deliberate impression is that he is dangerous in the extreme, and I view the next four years with no inconsiderable apprehension.

Given Roosevelt's mind set, Moley saw no way in which he could gain enough influence with the president "to protect him against his erratic tendencies," and he concluded that his own course should be "to continue somewhat sharp criticism" of Roosevelt's policies in the hope that it might have some effect. He concluded: "If ever a change has taken place, it is in the Washington scene. The rather gay spirit of adventure that permeated that scene in 1933 has degenerated into a mean, almost pathological atmosphere of intolerance and vindictiveness."[49] While the full break between Moley and Roosevelt did not become apparent until after the latter's speech accepting the 1936 nomination, the basis for Moley's opposition had clearly been laid by his exposure to the dominant dark side of Roosevelt's pride, prejudice, and politics in early May.

Moley's conversation with Roosevelt was confirmation that the worst fears of the press and business were valid, that the president had lost whatever limited grasp he might once have possessed of the situation in the economy, that his key motivation was now spite and vindictiveness, and that he was more intent on gaining and keeping the enmity of the press and business for political advantage than he was on bringing about recovery from the depression.[50] For Frank Kent, the most disturbing aspect was Roosevelt's "open appeal to the emotions of the people rather than their reason."[51] Mark Sullivan wrote of Roosevelt's erratic behavior:

That Mr. Roosevelt has a temperament which needs checks from outside himself is clear. And it is a detriment to Mr. Roosevelt and to the country, that for a long time since [Louis McHenry] Howe became ill, there is no one within the President's circle of familiar intimates who supplies the restraint he needs. In the lack of critics or checks within the President's circle, it is perhaps fortunate that there is a newspaper press and also the Supreme Court.[52]

Ernest Lindley, perhaps the most pro-Roosevelt among Washington's press corps, coauthored an article for Moley's *Today* magazine in early May that observed:

it has become almost a commonplace to blame Howe's illness for Mr. Roosevelt's blunders during the past year or so. Now that Howe has gone to the shadows, many observers are wondering—some of them with ill-concealed hope—if Mr. Roosevelt will not begin to crack. For the legend held that Howe, a wise, shrewd, cautious and outspoken man, was the one force which held an "impulsive," "erratic" President in check.[53]

When Moley was called to the White House in late May to assist in writing a Roosevelt speech, he found a draft dictated by the president to Stanley High to be "a conglomeration of vague and scattered ideas," with "attacks on the Chamber of Commerce of the United States, and several very nasty expressions." Moley "frankly told High that I felt he ought, in dealing with the President, to try to protect him against himself."[54] Increasingly, then, the impression spread among Roosevelt observers, including those friendly to the president, that Roosevelt was, as Raymond Clapper put it, an "impulsive adolescent" who must somehow be protected from himself.[55]

THE NEW DEAL AND THE ECONOMY

As businessmen, lawyers, and accountants faced the imposition of the undistributed profits tax beginning in 1937, they found in its provisions cause for utter confusion. *The Controller*, in its issues between August and October 1936, ran articles and symposia through which corporate controllers attempted to understand the tax. All were confused as to how it should be handled by accountants and controllers.[56] The president of the American Institute of Accountants complained that "we are perplexed by its complications, outraged by its inequities, confounded by its conflicts with sound business management. . . . The undistributed profits tax has nothing to recommend it."[57]

In addition to the existing tax burden, and the impending undistributed profits tax, businessmen faced the prospect of the social security payroll taxes that must be collected beginning with 1937. The impending additions in the tax load had caused retailers to request of clothing manufacturers that they reduce their prices so that retailers would be able to hold the line on their prices and at the same time have slightly increased margins with which to pay the additional taxes. The alternative was to increase retail prices still further and risk buyer resistance that would reduce sales in 1937.[58] That the manufacturers, too, were subject to the same increased taxes and would probably have to increase, rather than decrease their prices, to pay them seems not to have occurred to the retailers. Indeed, the likelihood that the taxes would lead to increases in prices at every step in the movement of goods seems not to have occurred to those in the Roosevelt administration who produced the bill. For those intent on creating "the abundant life," the problems of recovery from the depression were distinctly secondary.

In mid-May the American Federation of Labor counted 12,184,000 still unemployed.[59] In that same month the Supreme Court gave further evidence that it would act as a barrier against attempts by the Roosevelt administration to regiment the economy when it found the Guffey coal bill unconstitutional, taking up the challenge that Roosevelt had issued when the bill had been in Congress. Business journals exulted, the *Dry Goods Economist* writing that "unrelated as a ton of coal is to half a dozen stockings," the decision might "prove extremely effective to all fields related to merchandising," for

it is another hint that business, for more than three years bemused by wonderment at what next would crop up to handcuff it, is being gradually released from fear of what has amounted to oppression and which promised, if unchecked, to close with a vise-like grip on the orderly management of enterprise.[60]

In June the payment of the veterans' bonus began, injecting some $2 billion into the economy in the months before the 1936 elections. The New York *Herald-Tribune* observed that "never before in the history of this or any other country . . . has such a torrent of purchasing power been released upon a national economy."[61] *The Economist* found that the cashing of the bonus bonds, combined with agricultural payments and WPA expenditures, had certainly primed the pump, but it wondered "whether this particular pump is one that requires perpetual priming."[62] The *American Banker* warned, however, that the cashing of the bonus checks would result in a rapid increase in the excess reserves of banks.[63]

In April, Roosevelt had already talked to FRB chairman Eccles about raising the reserve requirements of banks ''to show the country that we have the guts to use the new powers given to us to stop inflation and excess speculation in the stock market.''[64] The threat of an uncontrollable boom touched off by the massive spending of election year 1936 was already working its way into the minds of Roosevelt and his advisers. In mid-July the FRB did increase reserve requirements by 50 percent. But Eccles was convinced that the FRB did not have enough power to stop inflation, and that it could only be prevented if the government stopped piling up deficits every year. He counseled balancing the budget by 1938, and Morgenthau agreed with him.[65]

Meanwhile, the increase in reserve requirements caused little comment since, as one newspaper pointed out, there was no demand for bank credit anyway.[66] The point was illustrated by the liquidation of a Colorado bank late in the summer. With $2 million in deposits, it had only $90,000 outstanding in loans compared with $1,250,000 in cash and government securities. Unable to earn an adequate return on the low-interest government bonds and such a low volume of lending, the bank chose to liquidate. The heavy dependence on investment in government bonds also revealed just how vulnerable this and other banks were if faced with a decline in the value of those bonds.[67]

CHAPTER 9

The Election and Boom of 1936

CAMPAIGN AND DEFECTIONS

By the summer of 1936 the campaign for Roosevelt's reelection dominated all other considerations within the administration. Preparing for the convention, Morgenthau found Roosevelt "far more interested in the number of words than ... the subject matter" of the monetary plank in the platform. Morgenthau thought it "more important to get the right thoughts in the platform than it is to keep it down to 200 words," but he had obviously not learned a lesson from 1932 that the content of such a document meant little to Roosevelt.[1] Indeed, some noted that there was little credence given to whatever Roosevelt said. Interior Secretary Ickes confided to his diary:

It is distressing to hear from so many quarters expressions that the President's word cannot be relied upon. The number of people in the country who believe this seems to be growing. Unfortunately, based on my own experience, I regret to say that there are occasions when he does seem to regard his word lightly. I regret to say this about my Chief, the President of the United States, but unfortunately it is true.[2]

Called to Washington to work on Roosevelt's acceptance speech, Raymond Moley found the draft written by Thomas Corcoran "altogether too long and not appropriate," since it was "written from the standpoint of the Brandeis philosophy." Roosevelt told Corcoran and Moley that he wanted a "speech full of quiet philosophy, a solemn speech, not a fighting speech." But in the end Moley found that Corcoran had managed to make it a Brandeisian speech, nevertheless.[3] The result was that, instead of delivering a speech of "quiet philosophy," Roosevelt accepted the 1936 nomination of his party with an address that was described by the Washington *Post* as "a formal declaration of war" against the free enterprise system, replacing what had "heretofore been guerrilla fighting." It wrote of the speech:

It ... opened all the emotional outlets, which unloosed mob psychology and then stimulated it with a master hand. It was the speech of a popular leader who does not know where he is leading. President Roosevelt's assurances to the contrary notwithstanding, it was the sort of speech which paves the way for fascism.[4]

A leading midwestern Democratic newspaper, the Omaha *World-Telegram*, reacted to the speech by declaring its opposition to Roosevelt's reelection:

Mr. Roosevelt, as earnestly and passionately as Hitler once did, assails our own capitalist system. . . . From this "economic tyranny" from "the palace of privilege" he proposes to rescue us by a bold declaration of war upon the existing economic order, just as did leaders in other lands.

By his sweeping onslaught Mr. Roosevelt has precipitated uncompromising war between the government he heads and private enterprise. It will be bitter throughout the campaign. In event of his reelection it will grow increasingly bitter through four long years.

And just as long as that war rages, the billions of credit and money tied up in the banks, idle and unused, will remain idle and unused. The millions of idle workers will remain unused, unless it be on public labor. Enterprise not only will be chilled, as now, but frozen.[5]

Other Democratic newspapers would gradually join the *World-Telegram* in defecting from Roosevelt. The Baltimore *Sun*, which had supported every Democratic candidate except for the 1896 and 1908 campaigns of William Jennings Bryan, announced that it could not support Roosevelt because it continued to advocate the competitive free enterprise system that Roosevelt was apparently out to subvert.[6] The St. Louis *Post-Dispatch*, which had supported the five previous Democratic candidates, also opposed Roosevelt's reelection:

In simplest possible terms, the overshadowing issue in the coming national election is whether or not we shall set up in America, in defiance of the American Tradition and . . . the plain intent of the Constitution as it now stands, a government with vast and centralized authority over the economic life of the Nation. On that issue the Post-Dispatch, believing as it does in an economy of free enterprise, under the political forms of our Federal system of Government, cannot support Mr. Roosevelt for re-election to the Presidency.[7]

On the theory that Governor Alf Landon of Kansas would be the weakest nominee from the field of GOP contenders, Roosevelt had instructed his cabinet not to say anything about him before the convention lest it affect his chances.[8] Landon was, indeed, nominated, and those who had hoped that the Republican candidate and platform would offer a clear-cut alternative to Roosevelt's New Deal were disappointed. *The Economist* surveyed the Republican platform and found little in it that Roosevelt could not run on. The United States, it concluded, was now without a party dedicated to conservative doctrines.[9] Walter Lippmann confessed that he could not belong to either party "without serious misgiving."[10] The *American Mercury* observed:

Citizens recently naive enough to expect from the Republican Party a tangible alternative to the New Deal were rudely jerked back to their senses by the Cleveland Convention's platform, which managed to endorse almost every feature of the More Abundant Life except Franklin Delano Roosevelt himself.[11]

Nevertheless, a Gallup poll in mid-July showed Landon leading Roosevelt in 21 states with 272 electoral votes—enough to win the election—although Roosevelt led in the popular vote.[12] Hurja's poll for the Democrats had shown Landon beating Roosevelt if the election were held in February; the Gallup poll showed the same result in mid-July. For over two years observers had pointed out, and polls had verified, that Roosevelt was more popular than his policies among the public. Would Landon offer the clear alternative to those policies that the Republican platform had not?

If there was any doubt that the American people were uncomfortable with the New Deal, it should have been answered by yet another Gallup poll, released in August, which found an amazing 45 percent of Americans polled answering "yes" to the question: "Do you believe the acts and policies of the Roosevelt administration may lead to dictatorship?"[13] Probably no president in U.S. history had aroused such concern over the possibility of dictatorship in this country. Indeed, it is difficult to imagine the question being asked by a responsible pollster during the administration of any other president but Roosevelt.

A week later, Gallup found Landon leading in yet another state, giving him 276 electoral votes if the election were held then (266 were needed to win). But Roosevelt's share of the popular vote had risen slightly.[14] In New York City the managing editor of the Communist *Daily Worker* resigned from that position and from the Communist Party, and also withdrew as the Communist Party candidate for Congress from the Bronx, charging that while the Communist Party had fielded its own candidates for president and vice-president, its Political Bureau was actually working to "swing the support of its membership and affiliated mass organizations to President Roosevelt."[15]

The initial enthusiasm for Landon soon abated, however, as the Kansan revealed himself as a lackluster campaigner. By late August, friendly columnists were commenting on the lack of force or direction in his campaign. As Franklyn Waltman put it: "If he has not lost ground in the last month . . . at least he has not made any substantial progress. Certainly, a number of persons who wish Gov. Landon well feel let-down, their enthusiasm dampened."[16] Indeed, a day after Waltman's observation, a new Gallup poll showed Roosevelt ahead in electoral votes for the first time.[17] Interior Secretary Ickes, after listening to a Landon speech over the radio, wrote in his diary: "If this is the best that Landon can do, the Democratic Campaign ought to spend all the money it can raise to send him out to make speeches."[18]

Within the administration all stops were being pulled out to make sure that government funds would obtain the maximum number of votes on election day. At a meeting with Agriculture Secretary Wallace in early February, Roosevelt hold him: "Henry, through July, August, September, October and up to the 5th of November I want cotton to sell at 12 cents. I do not care how you do it. That is your problem. It can't go below 12 cents." Morgenthau lamented in his diary that the political use of cotton prices would only cause American cotton growers to lose even more of their foreign markets to cheaper cotton grown elsewhere.[19]

Late in August the decision was made to get Soil Conservation checks out to farmers before election day since, as Morgenthau observed, they could make the difference in carrying four farm states. A month later, when Roosevelt learned that the Works Progress Administration (WPA) was out of money and would have to throw several thousand people off its rolls on October 1, he told his budget director that he wanted money for the WPA, that no one was to be laid off at WPA on the first of October, and, as Morgenthau recalled Roosevelt's words, "he doesn't give a God damn where they get the money."[20]

Two weeks before the election Morgenthau received a memorandum comparing relief expenditures in September of this election year with those for September a year earlier. They were higher in 46 of the 48 states this year, with an average increase for the country of 56 percent. The memorandum reported:

These increases are exclusive of Federal funds spent for relief or welfare by the Resettlement Administration or the Social Security Board. Work relief expenditures increased 268 percent in the United States compared with September a year ago. In 24 States, the increase in September was more than 300 per cent. The largest increases were Pennsylvania with 3,663 percent increase, and Missouri with 3,383 percent increase.[21]

With a Gallup poll showing that 75.1 percent of the relief vote was for Roosevelt and only 17.5 percent for Landon, it was obviously politic to inflate, rather than deflate, the relief rolls.[22]

Late in September, Morgenthau negotiated a tripartite stabilization agreement with Great Britain and France that won international acclaim as a first step toward the likely ultimate stabilization of currencies.[23] George Harrison, governor of the New York Federal Reserve Bank, told Morgenthau that after bankers learned of the agreement, "they said that this move will re-elect Roosevelt; that it is the greatest political move that has been made."[24]

By this time it had become clear that misgivings about Roosevelt did not automatically mean support for Landon. The dilemma posed for opponents of the New Deal became even more acute with Landon's speeches in Des Moines and Minneapolis during the last week of September. Until those speeches, Walter

Lippmann observed, Landon had given the impression that he was opposed to the New Deal practice of inviting "pressure groups to converge on Washington seeking special legislation and cash benefits," but those speeches had left Landon "badly compromised as the champion of the cause which he started so bravely to represent." In the Des Moines speech, especially, Landon had seemed intent, in fact, on "outbidding Mr. Roosevelt" for the farm vote.[25] In addition, as Mark Sullivan pointed out in mid-October, memories of the stalemate between a Republican president and a Democratic congress were still vivid from the final two years of Hoover's administration, so that many Democrats with misgivings about Roosevelt were likely not to vote for Landon lest his election create the same sort of stalemate now.[26]

Others, however, seemed to feel that anything was better than Roosevelt's reelection. Professor Albert O. Keller, who had supported every Democrat except Bryan, now observed that if given the choice he would vote for Bryan over Roosevelt. Although he had supported Roosevelt in 1932, the New Deal had driven him from his party's candidate.

My reason is the sort of misgiving one might feel if he were being chauffeured by a relay of effervescent and talkative drivers, all of the same kind in their habit of grabbing at one gadget after another, their production of lamentable gear-stripping noises, their constant side-swiping, and their hit-and-run complex. . . . My rejection of the New Deal—lock, stock and barrel—rests upon the fact that I cannot discern behind it anything better than noble purposes and intentions. . . . And I perceive little knowledge, together with small respect for knowledge, in the brains-pans of the New Dealers. . . . What has been done has been motivated almost exclusively in an ardent but ignorant emotionalism.[27]

Albert Jay Nock, describing his own opposition to Roosevelt, observed that

my objections to the Administration's behavior rest no more logically on the grounds of either conservatism or radicalism than on those of atheism or homeopathy. They rest on the grounds of common sense and, I regret to say, common honesty. I resent the works and ways of the Administration because of my opinion such of them as are not peculiarly and dangerously silly are peculiarly and dangerously dishonest, and most of them are both.[28]

Professor Arthur Schlesinger, Harvard historian and Roosevelt supporter, concluded in mid-October that the majority of the Harvard faculty would probably support Landon. He had managed to get only 81 faculty signatures (out of a faculty of 1,750) on a statement endorsing Roosevelt.[29] Later in the month, 13 members of the Harvard Law faculty, including Dean Roscoe Pound, declared their support for Landon, adding that the majority of Professor Frankfurter's colleagues agreed with them.[30] On the opposite coast, a vote among University of California at Berkeley faculty endorsed Landon, 302–269.[31] From it all, the *American Mercury* concluded: "It is possible that we may be treated, next November, to a singular spectacle—the re-election of a President who has been repudiated, either openly or covertly, by almost every literate American not actually on the dole or employed by the Post Office Department.''[32]

When both John W. Davis and Al Smith, the Democrats' 1924 and 1928 presidential candidates, deserted Roosevelt and announced their support for the Republican candidate, the New York *Herald-Tribune* observed that

not all the "smears" that professional mud slingers can devise alter the basic fact that two of the three living former candidates for the Presidency on the Democratic ticket have now come out against their own party's candidate. . . . [T]he country at large cannot "laugh off" this defection of two great Democratic leaders.[33]

Indeed, such an event was unprecedented in U.S. history. A few days later, Lewis Douglas, former Democratic congressman and Roosevelt's first director of the budget, also announced that he would support Landon.[34] Despite these prominent defections, however, the Gallup poll showed Roosevelt increasing his lead over Landon in mid-October, with 390 electoral votes against 141 for Landon. Gallup now foresaw a possible "landslide in the Electoral College if the present trend continues unaltered."[35] The final Gallup poll, released in the newspapers on November 1, found only three states sure for Landon—Maine, Vermont, and New Hampshire—with Roosevelt guaranteed at least 315 electoral votes, more than enough to win.[36]

With the election so obviously won, Roosevelt could afford to relax and take a statesmanlike course, but he could not resist the temptation to further escalate his war against business and recovery. Before a chanting crowd in Madison Square Garden in New York City on October 31, Roosevelt returned to the theme of his first inaugural address in 1933, and his State of the Union and acceptance speeches in 1936:

We had to struggle with the old enemies of peace—business and financial monopoly, speculation, reckless banking, class antagonism, sectionalism, war profiteering.

They had begun to consider the Government of the United States as a mere appendage to their own affairs. We know now that Government by organized money is just as dangerous as Government by organized mob.

Never before in all our history have these forces been so united against one candidate as they stand today. They are unanimous in their hate for me—and I welcome their hatred.

I should like to have it said of my first Administration that in it the forces of selfishness and lust for power met their match. I should like to have it said of my second Administration that in it these forces met their master.[37]

Bainbridge Colby, distinguished Democrat and former secretary of state under President Wilson, observed of Roosevelt's speech:

Here was a President not smarting merely under criticism, but writhing under it; swept headlong by hysterical resentment; shaken by the intensity of his hatreds, and so bitter and reckless that he threw reserve to the winds. It was a shocking spectacle for the President to make of himself.

Colby found in this "disclosure of the President's mind, purpose and feelings," startling confirmation of the conclusions of the distinguished Swiss psychiatrist and founder of analytic psychology, Dr. Carl Jung. After meeting Roosevelt, Jung wrote that "he has the most amazing power complex, the Mussolini substance, the stuff of a dictator absolutely."[38] The New York *Herald-Tribune* also recalled the Jung analysis of Roosevelt's dictatorial tendencies, adding that until the Madison Square Garden speech few Americans would have given it much credence, but

Today [Jung's] words can be ignored by no one. By his own speech the President has revealed his mood of bitter scorn for his opponents, his ruthless will to power. . . . Surely no American audience ever before heard such a threat from a President. With equal confidence we set down the prediction that the American people will never call any President "master."[39]

Jung's analysis of Roosevelt's mind would seem even more penetrating as a result of the events of 1937.

On election day, Roosevelt swept to victory over the hapless Landon by a popular margin of 11 million votes and by an electoral vote of 523–8. Landon carried only Maine and Vermont, two of the three "sure" states Gallup had predicted for him. The awesome Democratic majorities in both houses of Congress were further increased. It appeared that there would be no check by Congress on Roosevelt's ambitions during the first half of his second term, at least. In casting about for reasons for the Republican failure, some, like David Lawrence, blamed Landon for failing "to present an affirmative program," but found the principal reason in the fact that the New Deal had "direct financial transactions of one kind or another with at least 10,000,000 citizens."[40] *Business Week* predicted that Roosevelt would now push "for greater political and labor control of industry."[41] *Barron's* was skeptical about the Supreme Court's ability to withstand a new legislative assault since Roosevelt could easily increase the number of judges.[42] A Gallup poll late in November showed what the people wanted of Roosevelt's second administration. Surprisingly, in view of the campaign and the electoral result, 50 percent wanted it to be more conservative, 35 percent about the same as the first, and only 15 percent wanted it to be more liberal.[43]

ANOTHER BUSINESS ATTEMPT AT COOPERATION

Faced with another four years of Roosevelt in the White House, business leaders tried to put the best face on the situation by accepting the verdict of the voters and moving toward yet another attempt at cooperation with the president.

One source of optimism came in mid-November with the departure of Rexford Tugwell from the administration to enter the molasses business.[44] With Tugwell gone, however, the Brandeisians would exert even greater influence, if that were possible. Thomas Corcoran, their field marshal within the administration, confided to Moley in mid-November that they intended to break all investor-owned public utilities and to put all public utilities under government ownership and operation within 20 years.[45]

The Washington *Post*, however, was optimistic in late November, feeling that "widespread re-employment of idle men in private industry seems to be assured by the attitude of organized business as well as by the Administration." It thought it detected "a significant change" in the attitude of the Roosevelt administration now that the election was over.[46] *Bankers' Magazine* agreed that businessmen had not disregarded the voters' apparent approval of Roosevelt's policies and "those heretofore opposing them have made up their minds to go along with the crowd." It wrote: "If the 'New Deal' policies are sound, such cooperation may be justified on the ground that in this way their beneficial results will be hastened. On the other hand, if they are really unsound, the sooner this is demonstrated, the better."[47] At its convention in mid-December, the National Association of Manufacturers declared: "Industry pledges its cooperation with government in the promotion of economic and social progress."[48]

The *Wall Street Journal* applauded the intent of the industrialists, but cautioned that "there is still no real meeting of minds concerning the guiding principles which are to govern legislative and administrative courses of the near future."[49] Frank Kent was even more cautious, if not cynical, concerning the real prospect for business-New Deal cooperation, writing that "there are those who believe that before this session [of Congress] is far advanced there will emanate shrill cries of pain from the trusting business men who at the moment are touchingly confident that the effort to regulate, dominate and direct industry . . . will not again be made." Business might now be fawning over Roosevelt in their desire to "cooperate," Kent wrote, but "the day after they get their full look without blinders at the 'set-up' now being arranged, they are going to leap back with alarmed cries." Kent also warned that 1937 would "start off with more labor trouble and strikes in progress and prospect than any year which now can be recalled."[50] Again it would be the cynics and skeptics whose views would be validated by events.

THE BOOM BEGINS

Curiously, however, the dominant concern within the Roosevelt administration as 1936 drew to a close was not with stimulating recovery and reducing unemployment, but with bringing a potential "boom" under control.[51] The massive spending of 1936, including the bonus, had poured billions of dollars into the hands of consumers. Theoretically, if consumer spending rose sufficiently, factory capacity would at some point become strained, and businessmen would commit capital funds to expand their manufacturing capacity. The result would be the beginnings of recovery, the shift from government spending to private spending. In fact, of course, this need not happen. Faced with consumer demand based only on the temporary stimulus of government spending, and lacking genuine long-term prospects of profit because of Roosevelt's policies, few manufacturers would be foolish enough to commit funds to such expansion. In such a situation, the increased demand by consumers was likely, instead, to result in increased prices for consumer goods.

A variety of other New Deal programs would also contribute to a rise in prices, and the beginnings of an ominous wage-price spiral. The Social Security taxes, due to begin in January 1937, would have that effect. Another New Deal program unexpectedly contributed to the same result. This was the undistributed profits tax. Not all corporations responded to the onset of the tax as predicted by its advocates in the Treasury. In fact, they exercised other options that had apparently not even occurred to the framers of that legislation. Increased dividends were paid, as the Treasury had expected and hoped, but corporate surpluses were also disposed of in a variety of other ways. Late in October, Sears, Roebuck and Company approved three steps in response to the new tax. First was the payment of extra dividends; second, the sale of approximately 625,000 shares of stock to replenish the working capital that it had been forced to pay out; third, the payment of a $1.5 million bonus to employees before Christmas.[52] Other large corporations quickly followed suit. In the days following Sears' action, newspapers carried announcements of more dividend and bonus payments, together with substantial pay increases for employees, all the result of the undistributed profits tax.[53]

Early in November General Motors met the tax problem by presenting its employees with a Christmas bonus of $10 million and a 5 cent per hour wage increase (estimated to cost $21 million per year), and by paying a special year-end dividend of over $65 million. Its action was followed by the granting of bonuses by Chrysler ($4 million) and Standard Oil of Indiana ($4.5 million). Others quickly followed suit.[54] The financial writer for the Chicago *Tribune* observed that "with private industry pouring out a flood of dividends, wage boosts and special bonuses to workers, which eclipses in its effect the meager stimulus provided by government 'pump primers' in previous years, Chicago business men are anticipating the biggest Christmas buying since the boom period of the late '20's.'' The distribution of cash, he noted, had been "forced by the new tax on undistributed corporate earnings." The effect, however, would be to further stimulate consumer goods industries needlessly, as critics of the tax had pointed out, while diverting the money away from the heavy industries where recovery was lagging.[55]

Worse still, the disposal of the undistributed profits in the form of wage increases offered ominous prospects in conjunction with other trends in the economy. Businesses saw in this method the prospect not only of disposing of the surpluses but also, they hoped, of fortifying them against the labor disturbances that most felt were sure to come under the Wagner Labor Act and as a result of labor's support for Roosevelt's reelection. But increased wages led to another product of the tax that its advocates had not foreseen, and that was more serious—increased wages inevitably meant increased prices. By mid-November the press already carried stories of advance buying of steel by automakers, railroads, and other large users in anticipation of increases in steel prices.[56] The undistributed profits tax, then, would exert a dual influence in the direction of inflation: by the added dollars poured into the economy it added further to the boom in consumer spending already induced by election year federal spending, and by the wage increases it exerted an upward pressure on prices in both the consumer and durable goods industries. An administration concerned about a boom watched helplessly as one of its legislative acts added fuel to that boom. On November 23 Carnegie-Illinois Steel raised its prices, and others were expected to follow.[57] *Textile World* found the "wage level in most branches of the textile industry was advanced approximately 10%."[58]

FIGHTING AGAINST RECOVERY

Within the Roosevelt administration, priority continued to be given to heading off a "boom," even though, as some kept reminding them, the nation had not yet recovered from the depression.[59] George Haas, director of Research and Statistics in the Treasury Department, complained that the Federal Reserve Board was worrying about checking a boom when there had still been no recovery from the depression, and recovery was needed if the unemployed were to be put back to work. The FRB, he noted, seemed frightened of the prospect of recovery and intent on throwing "sand in the tracks."[60]

Concern about the effects of a boom had already reached the stage where the New Dealers were casting about for scapegoats. When the Investment Bankers Association held its annual convention early in December, James Landis, now chairman of the SEC, told the assembled bankers that they would have to accept full responsibility for any boom that took place.[61] The *Commercial and Financial Chronicle* found it curious "that business itself must bear the responsibility for a number of the ill-advised policies of the Federal government during the past four years" and for any "unfortunate consequences" that might flow from them, particularly when they had, according to the president in 1933, "abdicated," leaving their "duties to a government glad of the opportunity to take over the task of controlling, guiding and directing the economic activities of the Nation."[62]

When the Treasury Department offered in December long-term bonds at 2 percent and short-term paper at 1 percent, the Baltimore *Sun* noted that these were the lowest interest rates ever paid on government obligations of this type. The Treasury seemed to take pride in its ability to borrow money as cheaply as possible, thereby to save money for the government. But the *Sun* noted that there was another side to the question of interest rates, as explored by Dr. Lionel Edie, head of a New York firm of economic consultants, in a speech before the Investment Bankers Association convention. Edie pointed out that low interest rates had produced an unhealthy speculative boom in the securities markets. Moreover, with the progress of recovery there would be increased demand for working capital and other funds that would drive interest rates up. When that happened, the market for low-interest government bonds would come tumbling down. Holders of those bonds would suffer, and since many banks now had a large part of their funds tied up in the low-interest government bonds, they could find their surplus and even their capital wiped out. The losses might be so great that the Federal Deposit Insurance Corporation (FDIC) would be driven into insolvency. The banks would doubtless be blamed for the result, given their low standing with the public, but it would really be the low interest policies of the administration and its unbalanced budgets that would be at fault.[63]

This, it will be recalled, was the same problem that Orval Adams had warned bankers of at the ABA convention a year earlier. If Edie and Adams were correct, then the Roosevelt administration's policies of the previous four years had created a situation in which the United States could not afford to recover from the depression. It could do so only to the accompaniment of a major banking crisis such as had accompanied the New Deal's arrival in Washington in 1933.

By late December 1936, even the leading Keynesian in the administration, FRB Chairman Marriner Eccles, was insistent that there must be an end to deficit spending, that new relief money for the balance of the fiscal year should be kept at or below $500 million, and that all new expenditures, including relief, should be met hereafter by taxes, not by further borrowing from the banks. He told Morgenthau that "if a program such as this is not adopted" he wanted "to make it clear to the President that he will accept none of the responsibility for controlling credit conditions and preventing a runaway inflation."[64]

With this sense of crisis pervading the Treasury and the FRB as 1937 approached, Roosevelt was preparing the ground for what most Americans would regard as an even greater crisis during the year. Ten days after the election, Roosevelt took up with his cabinet possible courses of action toward the Supreme Court as a result of the mandate he had received from the electorate.[65] The day after Christmas, Attorney General Cummings presented Roosevelt with his plan for "packing" the Supreme Court. Cummings' plan took note of the objections that could normally be expected to any proposal for adding justices to the Supreme Court, by using the argument that it was necessary to add justices to all levels of the federal judiciary in order to dispose of cases more promptly and efficiently. When any federal judge reached 70 years of age and had served for ten years, the president would nominate and, with the consent of the Senate, appoint an additional judge. Roosevelt, Cummings wrote in his diary, "caught the point immediately." Unfortunately, any plan so transparent that Roosevelt could "catch" it could also be seen through by everybody else, and would be when it was launched weeks later. But on this cheery day-after-Christmas, Cummings convinced Roosevelt that his statute could be rushed through Congress quickly, with the whole matter "over within sixty days, and the excitement would subside and the job would be done."[66] It would not, however, be that easy.

CHAPTER 10

Megalomania and Mindlessness

GRAND DREAMS, UNPLEASANT REALITIES

More so even than in the previous four years, 1937 would find serious questions raised concerning Roosevelt's mind and character—particularly his ability to grasp reality, and what an increasing number of observers would perceive as a megalomania that seemed to be pushing him relentlessly in the direction of dictatorship. Treasury Secretary Morgenthau was a ringside observer to these growing tendencies in Roosevelt. On January 4, 1937, he recorded in his diary a conversation with the president, in which Roosevelt discussed his "big idea"—his belief that international cartels should be established in various commodities.

I asked the President whether this had anything to do with the idea he had a couple of years ago where he was going to divide the world up into different production areas. He said, "No, this idea superseded that one." He pictures himself as being called in as a consultant of the various nations of the world. He said, "Maybe I can prescribe for their ailments or, after making a study of their illnesses, I will simply turn up my nose at them and say, 'I am sorry—I cannot treat them.' For example, I would tell England that she had too many people and she should move out ten million of her population. I would take a look at each country and, of course, when we made them disarm we would have to find new work for the munition workers in each country and that is where this international cartel would come in and your job would be to handle the finances.[1]

With such adolescent and megalomaniacal daydreams was the Roosevelt mind preoccupied as 1937 began. In the midst of the concern of those in the Treasury and the FRB, as well as outside the administration, that the nation faced the prospect in 1937 of either a disastrous boom or an equally disastrous collapse, the president of the United States airily contemplated a new role as economic consultant to the nations of the world and the inauguration of an international NRA.

THE ASSAULT ON THE COURT BEGINS

Two days later Roosevelt delivered his State of the Union message to Congress. In it was a hint that he contemplated a revival of the NRA in the United States. As for the barrier that the Supreme Court had raised against the NRA and other New Deal initiatives, Roosevelt insisted that it was not the Constitution that was at fault, but the interpretation placed on it by the present court, which was hamstringing his administration's ability to act. He added the ominous words that "it is not to be assumed that there will be prolonged failure to bring legislative and judicial action into closer harmony."[2]

The next day, Cummings presented Roosevelt with the draft of a bill that incorporated his suggestions of December 26. The attempt to "pack" the Supreme Court was launched, which for months would dominate the newspapers of the country and paralyze action by Congress on other matters, at the same time that it contributed to further erosion of business confidence. Kiplinger viewed the court proposal as "the super-issue of the New Deal to date," since "it bundles all other issues together in a single package." If it passed, "practically all past policies of the New Deal will be ratified, and the way will be cleared for a dozen different brands of legislation on which there is now hesitancy due to doubts about constitutionality."[3] Since Roosevelt already effectively controlled the legislative branch, success with the court packing bill would give him control of all three branches of government. No dictator could ask for more.

Business journals were inclined to view Roosevelt's court proposal as important mainly for what he planned afterward. It seemed obvious that Roosevelt would reinstate the NRA and AAA, or similar forms of control, once he had a pliant court.[4] The *Commercial and Financial Chronicle* found Roosevelt "determined to have the equivalent of this defunct [NIRA] law if he can, and if he succeeds in 'packing' the Supreme Court one of the most formidable of the obstacles heretofore in his path will have been removed."[5] *Business Week* feared that far worse, though, would be in store for the country than the rebirth of the NRA if Roosevelt were successful in establishing his control over the Supreme Court.[6]

Early in March, Roosevelt took an interesting position in a speech at a Democratic victory dinner:

After election day in 1936, some of our supporters were uneasy lest we grasp the excuse of a false era of good feeling to evade our obligations. They were worried by the evil symptom that the propaganda and the epithets of last Summer and Fall had died down. Today, however, those who placed their confidence in us are reassured. For the tumult and the shouting have broken forth anew—and from substantially the same elements of opposition.[7]

Under this remarkable Rooseveltian view of the world, "propaganda," "epithets," "tumult," and "shouting" were desirable, and "good feeling" was apparently undesirable. Under this view the rightness of the Rooseveltian course could best be judged by the cries of pain and opposition that it elicited from his "enemies." Since those "enemies" were business and finance, it followed that the more viciously he struck at the very mechanism of recovery from the depression, the more "right" his policies were. This was Roosevelt's answer to the attempts of business to cooperate with the administration in the final months of 1936 and early 1937.

The Washington *Post* sensibly observed: "To the rational mind it would seem a most healthy sign that the eighteen million voters who cast ballots against Mr. Roosevelt were so generally disposed to accept his sweeping victory in good part. How any responsible person could regard this as an 'evil symptom' is incomprehensible."[8]

In another part of the same speech, Roosevelt tried to defend his court packing plan by arguing that the threat of a future crisis required that he be granted the additional powers that he was seeking. The Washington *Post* observed that the argument "forces one of two conclusions—either that four years of the New Deal have only served to intensify, not eliminate, the problems of 1933, or that the new crisis is primarily of the President's own making."[9] Many observers concluded that the "crisis" referred to by Roosevelt was the specter of inflation.[10]

CONFUSION IN THE ADMINISTRATION

Whether the prospect of inflation was a real factor in Roosevelt's assault on the Supreme Court, or not, it was clear by March that the New Deal was on the verge of giving birth to something far removed from the "abundant life" it had trumpeted. The Treasury, especially, found itself grappling with the results of past Roosevelt policies come home now to roost. Morgenthau saw his carefully constructed budget early placed in jeopardy by the wave of strikes fomented by the new Congress of Industrial Organizations (CIO) headed by John L. Lewis. Morgenthau knew that any hopes of balancing the budget rested not only on reduced spending but also on expanding revenues. Unhappily, the incitement to labor activism furnished by the Wagner Act and the "alliance" of Lewis and Roosevelt in the 1936 presidential campaign encouraged the CIO in its drive for recognition in 1937 and threatened to disrupt recovery further, thus shrinking the revenues upon which the Treasury depended.[11]

Morgenthau was also taking another look at the undistributed profits tax, as evidence mounted of its harmful effects. In January he learned that Deering Milliken and Company, sole creditor of a number of textile corporations, was facing the prospect of foreclosing on loans that the textile concerns were unable to pay because of the tax.[12] Later in the month the Interstate Commerce Commission (ICC) criticized the tax for its harmful effects on the railroads and urged that Congress reconsider its application to that industry. *Business Week* quickly pointed out that what was true of the tax's affect on the railroads was equally pertinent where other industries were concerned.[13]

Although confronted with evidence that the tax was harmful and was failing, even, to generate the predicted revenue for the Treasury, Morgenthau was reluctant to propose any changes, since he feared that they might result in further losses of revenue. His primary concern continued to be with the apparent fiscal crisis that faced the administration in 1937, and the necessity to balance the budget promptly in order to meet it. Marriner Eccles agreed on the necessity to balance the budget, but he also counseled changes in the undistributed profits tax in order to provide relief for at least those corporations that were heavily in debt.[14]

Barron's found early in January that "commodity prices and labor" were the two major concerns businessmen and investors faced in 1937. It warned that if commodity prices continued their upward movement at the present pace, "the resultant increases in the cost of living will be such as to force general, wide advances in wages and in costs of manufactured goods, which, in turn, will force up the cost of living still further." The result could well be more strikes, disruption of markets and of production, and increased unemployment.[15] In that same month, four Brookings Institution economists surveyed "The Recovery Problem in the United States" and warned of "the possibility of a serious breakdown of Government finance." They recommended the balancing of the federal budget, maintenance of a fixed price for gold and the establishment of a system of stable foreign exchange, further extension of reciprocal trade agreements, preservation of the "generally favorable ratio of prices and wage rates," maintenance of prevailing hours of labor, an emphasis on increasing industrial and agricultural production rather than restricting it.[16] Winthrop Aldrich, chairman of Chase National Bank, also warned that brakes must be applied to the expansion of bank credit and the rise in commodity prices to head off a dangerous boom. He also called for a balanced budget, increased bank reserve requirements, a reduction in the holdings of government securities by Federal Reserve banks, and higher interest rates.[17]

In February the FRB announced an increase in bank reserve requirements. When called before the House Banking and Currency Committee to explain the reasons for the action, Eccles reiterated the line that had been taken by other Federal Reserve officials: that the move was necessary in order to forestall a possible speculative boom in stocks and commodities. But Eccles also linked the action to worries about the low-interest government bonds sitting in the portfolios of banks all across the country—the same concern expressed earlier by Orval Adams and Lionel Edie—although Eccles did not confront the problem as directly.[18] To have been more explicit might well have triggered runs on banks by worried depositors.

On March 11, 1937, commodity prices reached new highs.[19] The following day a ripple went through the Roosevelt administration, particularly the Treasury, when government bond prices sagged.[20] Hurriedly, the Treasury began purchasing bonds in order to stabilize the market. Morgenthau spent much of the day on the telephone consulting on the situation in New York City and with Eccles. From New York came word that bondholders had "a case of jitters" over prospects of inflation that would send prices and interest rates up and bond values down. Morgenthau and Eccles argued over the FRB's responsibility to assist in propping up the government bond market.[21]

While the Treasury cast about for solutions to the sag in the government's credit, the liquidation of government bonds continued. March 13, one newspaper noted, was the "worst trading session in point of sales volume . . . in more than sixteen years and their most nervous trading session in more than three years." Over $23 million in government bonds had been exchanged that day, the most since $28 million on December 23, 1920. Prices had not declined significantly, but only because the Treasury was buying heavily in order to support the price. Investors were worried that interest rates might be raised in order to hold inflation in check, which would force the prices of bonds down.[22]

The Washington *Post* was certain, however, that Roosevelt intended to continue his "easy money" policy despite administration concerns about the prospect of inflation, because he apparently saw "no incongruity in clinging to cheap-credit policies that encourage speculative activity after the emergency that justified them has passed." If that avenue for dampening inflation's fires was to be closed off, then there remained only the alternative of "bringing the budget into balance and abandoning the pressure policies that are bound up with deficit financing."[23] Some economists, however, insisted that the Roosevelt administration must do both.[24]

By April 1 it had become apparent that the efforts of the Treasury and the FRB to support the government bond market were not solving the problem.[25] Roosevelt told a press conference the next day that production of durable goods was increasing at a more rapid rate than that of consumer goods, and this was "a danger sign." Ignoring the fact that recovery in the durable goods industries had lagged for seven years and had a good deal of catching-up to do, Roosevelt now announced that the administration would "discourage Government expenditures on durable goods and . . . encourage Government expenditures on consumer goods." The nation, he told reporters, needed "more expenditures at the bottom and less at the top, because . . . expenditures of funds at the bottom go primarily to people, millions of people, who are the consumers of consumer goods rather than consumers of durable goods."[26] Here was Roosevelt's beloved "bubble up" theory once again. Previously advocated as a cure for depression, it was now introduced as a cure for inflation as well. Like snake oil, there was nothing that it could not cure. In the afternoon, Morgenthau went over a plan for selective spending with the president. Of particular emphasis was the deflection of government purchases away from steel as much as possible.[27]

Engineering News-Record reminded the administration that the major source of unemployment was in the durable goods industries, and if the "wasteful and degrading relief system" was ever to be ended, these industries needed every assistance to recovery. On the other hand, the consumer goods industries were already "working to capacity."[28] As for Roosevelt's contention that production in the durable goods industries was nearing the level of the consumer goods industries, *Business Week* noted that such might be the case in the FRB index, which was heavily weighted with iron and steel statistics, but other indexes such as that of the Standard Statistics Company, with a broader cross-section of industry represented, showed a "wide gap between consumer and capital goods" production. Moreover, even if there were an "intersection" between the two, such as so worried Roosevelt, it was no reason to suppose that a recession was imminent. When it had happened in the past, it had been due to overstocks of capital goods, a situation that did not exist in 1937 owing to years of depression-era "under-maintenance and under-replacement."[29] In short, on every count Roosevelt's economic presentation before the press conference seemed to have missed the mark.

Meanwhile, after much heated discussion the Treasury and the FRB had agreed upon a plan to prop up the government bond market. The FRB announced that it would begin to "make open market purchases of government securities for the account of Federal Reserve banks in such amounts and at such times as might be desirable." Critics pointed out the inflationary aspects of such an action, since it was a customary method of stimulating speculative activity and raising price levels by adding to the deposits of the commercial banks of the country. Thus, the action ran directly counter to the FRB policy of reducing excess reserves because it added to those reserves. There seemed, however, no other course of action open to an administration that sought simultaneously to keep government bond prices high and interest rates low.[30]

Morgenthau and Eccles continued to press for a balanced budget in their talks with Roosevelt, with Morgenthau advocating reduced expenditures. At an April 12 meeting with the president, Morgenthau suggested the curtailment of agricultural benefit payments, limiting to $1 billion the amount for relief and resettlement until February 1, 1938, impounding a certain percentage of all but relief funds every month beginning July 1, preparing a new tax bill that would correct existing inequities and increase revenue, and notifying Congress that any appropriation bills in excess of the budget would be "vetoed unless Congress provides additional revenue."[31] Later in the month, Morgenthau rejoiced that Roosevelt's budget message had given him "everything I asked for."[32]

The decision to make spending cuts, then, was not made frivolously, nor from any attachment to the principle of budget balancing, but because of growing evidence that a continuation of deficit spending would court economic disaster. Morgenthau was so determined that the spending cuts be made that he told Vice-President Garner he would resign if Roosevelt did not fulfill his promise to make them.[33]

A major concern for Morgenthau in insisting on the spending cuts was the serious shortfall in government revenue. This was also of concern for individual and institutional investors in their worries about inflation and the value of their government bond portfolios. In March the Treasury was running an estimated $300–$500 million behind schedule in total revenues.[34] The failure of the tax on undistributed profits to produce the anticipated revenue was apparent to all, and with this failure went the last rational justification for continuing it.[35] Despite its failure, however, and the volume of informed and learned denunciation of the tax, Roosevelt made no move to seek its amendment or repeal in the 1937 congressional session.

SEARCHING FOR SCAPEGOATS

Instead, Roosevelt turned to his favorite device of creating scapegoats for the failure of his programs to live up to their billing. Ignoring the impact that labor disturbances had produced on industrial profits—and ignoring also the fact that a large percentage of the profits the Treasury had hoped to tax when paid in dividends to the 4 million taxpayers of the country had gone, instead, in the form of higher wages and bonuses to workers who did not pay income taxes—Roosevelt sought to lay the blame for reduced tax revenues on "tax evaders." In this way public attention could presumably be diverted from the failure of his tax policies.

A survey of 1936 income tax returns was launched that revealed a variety of devices that had been used to avoid tax liability, including personal holding corporations in foreign areas, use of domestic personal holding companies, incorporation of yachts or country homes, creation of multiple trusts, depletion allowances, and purchase of tax-exempt bonds. All of these devices were, of course, perfectly legal under the tax laws in force during the Roosevelt presidency, so the issue was not one of illegality.[36] When Raymond Clapper visited Roosevelt in mid-May he found the president denouncing tax dodgers and referring to them as "Benedict Arnolds." Roosevelt told Clapper that he was thinking of going on the radio to expose their practices to the people. Conveniently, and with a characteristic absence of logic, Roosevelt joined tax evasion with the court packing plan, insisting that "under [the] courts as they are now" it was impossible to strike at such practices.[37] Since the practices he was denouncing were not illegal, it is difficult to see how any court, no matter how constituted, could have dealt with them.

At a meeting with Morgenthau the next day, Roosevelt told him that it was "time to attack." The administration must meet the criticism of its revenue shortfall by fighting back, and this meant naming the names "of these very wealthy individuals who have found means of avoiding their taxes both at home and abroad." In short, the campaign against tax evaders was not so much a campaign against tax evasion as an attack against Roosevelt's critics. And, as Morgenthau observed in his diary, it was also "partly on account of the Court and partly because the Conservative Reactionary members of the Democratic Party are getting the upper hand.''[38]

Morgenthau outlined the ''logic'' behind the ''attack'' to his advisers the next day. ''The question,'' he told them, ''is whether we are going to have a Fascist government in this country or a government of the people, whether rich men are going to be able to defy the government and refuse to bear their burdens.'' The Treasury Department should give Roosevelt what he wanted ''without quibbling as to whether this or that is legal.''[39] On such rambling, incoherent, and illogical premises the Treasury Department fell into line with Roosevelt's search for scapegoats, without suggesting the obvious solution—legislation to close off the methods by which taxes were being avoided. Within a week, however, Morgenthau had lost all enthusiasm for the plan, concluding that it would ''stir up class hatred unnecessarily.''[40] The president, however, pressed on with his ''attack.''[41]

The New York *Herald-Tribune* greeted the assault on ''tax evaders'' by recalling the technique of Roman emperors who had maintained their popularity through bread and circuses. Here was Roosevelt's equivalent of a Roman circus:

> To appease a disappointed and doubting populace there is nothing like a good slaughtering of capitalist martyrs. The sudden discovery that the income tax is being evaded by ''a few bad rich men'' makes neither sense nor justice. If it is the laws that are at fault, they should be amended. If there are some real evaders, they should be punished as the law already amply provides.[42]

Ex-New Dealer Raymond Moley rightly viewed the episode as a smokescreen to cover up the shortfall in government revenues, and concluded that even if all of the loopholes over which Roosevelt was posturing were eliminated, the additional revenue would be insignificant in comparison with the shortfall.[43] Even Raymond Clapper regarded the attack as a clear case of Roosevelt attempting to stir up class hatred.[44] Most telling of all was a *New Republic* article by John Flynn, which revealed that one of the least defensible of the tax loopholes that Roosevelt had pointed to with such ''pious horror'' had, in fact, become law under the New Deal in 1936.[45]

THE COURT BATTLE CONTINUES

Meanwhile, the battle over the court packing bill was continuing amid growing opposition in and outside of Congress. Then, on April 12, a Supreme Court decision upheld the Wagner Labor Act by a 5–4 vote, with Justice Roberts joining the ''liberals'' to form a majority. Supporters of the court packing plan, stymied in their efforts to get it approved by the Senate, tried to find in the Wagner decision evidence that Roosevelt had influenced the court to be more ''reasonable'' through the pressure he was applying in Congress. Roosevelt, though delighted with the decision, recognized that he must push on with his plan, since a 5–4 decision on the Wagner Act did not guarantee the compliant court that could be relied on for approval of other New Deal legislation.[46] The NIRA, after all, had been knocked down by a 9–0 vote.

The limits to which some of those around Roosevelt were willing to go to push the court packing bill through is illustrated by a memorandum from Herman Oliphant to Morgenthau of April 12:

For Your Information. There came to Morris Shafroth from Tom Corcoran, by way of Mr. Morris in the Department of Justice, a request for information concerning the income tax returns of the Justices of the Supreme Court. Morris called me and I advised him to reply that the information could not be disclosed.

Morgenthau concurred in the refusal.[47] Senator Burton K. Wheeler, liberal Democrat from Montana, who was leading the opposition to the court plan in the Senate, also complained of rumors that his tax records were to be used in efforts by the administration to ''get'' him, but Morgenthau assured him that he would not permit it.[48]

Even after Justice Van Devanter announced his intention to retire from the court, thus giving the president the opportunity to appoint a New Dealer to the bench, Roosevelt insisted on pushing on with the court packing bill.[49] This determination to dominate the court convinced business and other critics that Roosevelt had in mind another sweeping program of business control akin to the NRA. Recalling the 9–0 vote against the NRA, which included all of the ''liberals'' on the court, they concluded that Roosevelt was proceeding with the fight for his plan on the assumption that even one or two retirements, plus the switch by Roberts, would not ensure a rubber stamp for everything he had planned. As *Business Week* put it, what Roosevelt apparently realized was ''that the new court must have a majority even more New Dealishly inclined than even Brandeis and Cardozo—if all the White House objectives are to be obtained.''[50]

Roosevelt was to be defeated, however. In mid-June the Senate Judiciary Committee reported out the court packing bill with a report so negative that, Raymond Clapper observed, it read like ''a bill of impeachment except that [it] refers to [the] bill instead of Roosevelt by name.''[51] The New York *Herald-Tribune* agreed that ''it was far more than the disapproval of a bad bill. It was an indictment of the President of the United States by leaders of his own party, for long his supporters and advocates.''[52] Indeed, the committee's report said of the bill: ''It is a measure which should be so emphatically rejected that its parallel will never again be presented to the free representatives of the free people of America.''[53] The *Commercial and Financial Chronicle* found in the ''indictment'' an ''implied challenge'' to Roosevelt's ''fitness to hold office under the Constitution which he is sworn to uphold.''[54]

The response of the Roosevelt administration to the blow was predictable. Vindictive threats were already being uttered by the White House of retaliation against those senators who were opposing Roosevelt over the court bill. Hearing of such threats to Senator Millard Tydings, Democrat of Maryland, Breckinridge Long confided to his diary on June 1 that "if that is an indication of the administration's policy it is a serious sign. It means a definite split—a deep, wide split in our party."[55] But, while the White House tried to salvage something through compromise, the bad news continued to roll in. The death of Senator Joseph Robinson deprived the administration forces of their leader in the Senate battle, and Governor Herbert Lehman, Roosevelt's successor in Albany, issued a public letter opposing the plan.[56] On July 22, the court packing bill was recommitted. Roosevelt had been dealt his most serious defeat by Congress.

Walter Lippmann exulted that in the vote "genuine progressivism had been distinguished from the thoughtless, inexperienced and uneducated, counterfeit progressivism which sees no solution for any problem except to aggrandize the uncontrolled personal power of the Executive."[57] Frank Kent hoped that the defeat had shaken Roosevelt's "belief in his omnipotence, destroyed his idea that he is infallibly right; inculcated in him a little humility, ended once and for all the notion that this can be made a one-man government in which the checks and balances provided in the Constitution are tossed aside or ignored."[58] Few, however, expected that Roosevelt's pride would allow him to abandon the fight even now. The *Commercial and Financial Chronicle* warned that public opinion must remain on the alert, for "there is no reason whatever for thinking that [Roosevelt] has changed his mind, or that the role of dictator has become to him any less dear."[59]

Roosevelt unleashed a tempest when he announced his selection for the vacancy on the Supreme Court created by Justice Van Devanter's retirement. His appointee was Senator Hugo Black, a choice critics found little short of incredible.[60] Raymond Moley headed his comment on the appointment, "An Inquisitor Comes to Glory," and wrote that if Black was an example of the "new blood" Roosevelt wanted to appoint to the court, he was profoundly grateful that "the country escaped six such appointments" under the court packing plan.[61] The Chicago *Tribune* wrote: "If Mr. Roosevelt wanted to degrade the Supreme Court he has made a good effort. If he wanted the worst man he could find he has him."[62] Friendly columnist Raymond Clapper confided to his diary that the Black appointment had "left me cold, the nomination didn't seem to measure up to what it ought under [the] circumstances, with [Roosevelt] making such an issue of court personnel."[63] Donald Richberg later explained the reason for the appointment to him: "Don said Roosevelt was mad and was determined to give [the] Senate the name which would be most disagreeable to it and yet which it could not reject [due to Senatorial courtesy]."[64] Later there would be a renewed furor when Black's connection to the Ku Klux Klan was revealed.

THE REORGANIZATION BILL

Weeks before Roosevelt introduced his court packing plan, he had already launched another legislative initiative that smacked to many of the same type of dictatorial ambitions revealed by the court plan later. In mid-January, Roosevelt sent to Congress his plan for reorganizing the administrative agencies of the federal government, a plan that seemed designed to further increase the power of the White House over those agencies. After reacting positively to the bill after a first reading of it in January, Walter Lippmann came out in strong opposition to it in May. It had by now become clear to the liberal columnist that Roosevelt had no intention of giving up the extraordinary emergency powers granted him by Congress in 1933. On the contrary, Roosevelt was now using these powers "shamelessly to browbeat Congress" in the effort to pack the Supreme Court. "But," Lippmann warned, "that is only a part of a vast program of personal government." The reorganization bill contained "the most extraordinary proposal for the extension of personal government which has ever been seriously proposed in this country."[65]

The plain fact of the matter is that the intoxication of personal power has gone to Mr. Roosevelt's head. He has come to think that the sole function of Congress is to supply him with the means of power and of the courts to justify his use of power. Personally, he wishes to make the laws, either openly and boldly, as in the N.R.A., or indirectly by compelling Congress to ratify what he proposes. Personally, he wishes to fix the powers of all government departments. Personally, he wishes to rule the administrative and quasi-judical commissions. Personally, he wishes to dominate the courts and to interpret the Constitution.

The restraints of a free government were being destroyed, Lippmann concluded, and it was time not only to halt the trend toward personal government, but to begin to diminish it.[66]

A study by the prestigious Brookings Institution likewise opposed Roosevelt's reorganization plan, arguing:

To the contention that large fields of public policy are dominated and controlled by these [independent] commissions, the answer is that they should be. It is not desirable that social policies be the football of politics. These boards and commissions are agents of Congress. . . . They are in no sense agents of the President.[67]

The battle in Congress over this bill, too, promised to be a furious one.

BUSINESS AND TREASURY JITTERS

By late April, the Treasury had found new reasons for concern. On the one hand there was a burgeoning influx of gold into the United States from Europe—"hot money" was the name given to it in the Treasury because of its volatility. The growing gold stock led to speculation that the Roosevelt administration might again alter the price of gold or seek in some other way to discourage its movement to the United States. The alternative was either to increase the excess reserves of banks by the amount of gold accepted by the Treasury, or to increase the government debt by "sterilizing" it. In Europe there was concern that Roosevelt would change the gold price because of the difficulty of issuing paper money to pay for the sterilized gold at the same time that the administration was required to support the price of its bonds by intervening in the securities market.[68] On the other hand, Morgenthau was warned by a prominent Wall Street banker late in the same month that "declining business and a tendency toward growing unemployment" were not remote possibilities, barring action by the Roosevelt administration. While the Treasury had been preoccupied with heading off a boom in the midst of a depression, Morgenthau was now advised that the administration had better act to avoid a worsening of the depression. Specifically, Morgenthau was advised to abandon gold sterilization, since this "would have an immediate and an electric effect on the bond market, both for Government and corporate issues, and would go a long way towards throwing into reverse the feeling of apprehension that has been growing all too rapidly in the last few weeks."[69]

Whether such advice was appropriate or not, the observation concerning the "nervousness and hesitance in the business world" was borne out by other signs that the business upturn was beginning to falter. The Treasury Department's division of research and statistics reported late in April that there had been a decline in first quarter corporate earnings in relation to output, which, it warned, "may indicate a slowing up in business." A decline in stock prices that had occurred could also be expected to "affect business unfavorably, since the stock market influences business sentiment." The report concluded that "the favorable factors in the immediate outlook appear to have less weight than the unfavorable factors."[70]

In May, W. Averell Harriman, chairman of the Business Advisory Council, wrote Commerce Secretary Roper that "the further advance of business and of employment is restrained by the persisting unbalance in the budget." He attached a letter from industrialist Gerard Swope that cautioned: "notwithstanding the encouraging way in which business was going, I had never found people more nervous and jittery around New York than had been true ten days previous, which still continues to some extent." Swope found this feeling rooted in doubts as to Roosevelt's real commitment to balancing the budget.[71]

But if businessmen were concerned about the budget deficit, they were worried about other matters as well. For one, there had been no apparent change in Roosevelt's antibusiness attitude. Late in January, Donald Richberg told Raymond Clapper that Roosevelt was angry over one of Clapper's recent columns on the failure of an "era of good feeling" to develop between Roosevelt and business. Richberg told the columnist that he was wrong in thinking that Roosevelt had ever believed there would be an era of good feeling, that he had known all along that there couldn't be any. It was, in Richberg's words, "just hooey."[72] In the early months of 1937 this antibusiness attitude seemed at its most destructive in the apparent encouragement that it gave to the wave of strikes called by John L. Lewis, and in the reluctance of the Roosevelt administration to act in defense of property rights in the face of the new weapon that the Lewis forces adopted—the "sit-down" strike. As a result, 1937 would see more labor strife than the recession year of 1934.

CHAPTER 11

The Road to the Crash

LABOR DIFFICULTIES

In the labor difficulties of 1937, as with the other crises that his administration confronted during the year, Roosevelt was faced with a situation largely of his own creation. By his administration's support for labor unions, his castigation of business, the class-war nature of much of his 1936 reelection campaign, and his acceptance of John L. Lewis' support in that campaign, Roosevelt had encouraged Lewis in his belief that the administration would be sympathetic to the CIO's efforts to unionize business no matter how extreme its demands and actions might be at the expense of business. At a press conference late in January, Lewis made this attitude clear. Roosevelt should come to the aid of labor against the "economic royalists," just as labor had aided Roosevelt in the election against the same enemy.[1]

The year began with a sit-down strike against General Motors. Strikes were considered bad enough, but the physical possession of their property outraged General Motors, while the prospect of it was equally outrageous to other businessmen. When Secretary of Labor Frances Perkins convened a conference to get labor and management together, General Motors declined to attend since it considered the right of employees to take possession of their employer's property to be nonnegotiable. The *Wall Street Journal* applauded General Motors' refusal, arguing that the issue was larger than just the General Motors affair, since the sit-down strike tactic was spreading to industries of more direct and immediate concern to the people, including electric and gas facilities. Lawlessness, it wrote, could not be negotiated.[2] An even greater blow to business confidence was the refusal of law enforcement agencies and governments to intervene. On the contrary, the *Magazine of Wall Street* found those responsible for upholding the law frequently condoning and even defending the sit-in strikes.[3]

FUELING THE BOOM

If the wave of strikes in early 1937 was the predictable outcome of Roosevelt's attitude and policies, and particularly of his tactics in the 1936 campaign, so were the results of the strikes equally predictable. Confronted by strikes, by pro-labor laws, and by the inability or unwillingness of the authorities to enforce laws against trespass, industry had little option but to seek to buy labor peace by granting further wage increases, which were then passed on to consumers in the form of higher prices. The unwholesome effects of such a result were readily apparent. The purchasing power of workers in the manufacturing industries was already about 8 percent higher than it had been in 1929. Such workers made up only about 25 percent of the gainfully employed. Further increases would raise the purchasing power of this 25 percent even higher, but the increased prices that resulted would cut into the purchasing power of the other 75 percent and of all other consumers. The *Magazine of Wall Street* wondered if the Roosevelt administration, so concerned with heading off a speculative boom, might not better be concerned about the prospect of wage-price inflation.[4]

Early in March, 1937, the *American Banker* wrote:

In the wage raises voted for motor, glass, steel and other workers in the past few days, may well be seen the second stage in the vicious cycle of inflation and also the seeds of eventual deflation. . . . In forcing industry to choose wage increases, rather than increased employment and production, American labor may prove to have been its own worst enemy, for there are no causes more calculated to provoke an anti-labor movement than rising prices and inflation. Can it be possible that industry's policy of giving wage boosts is a sort of surrender that will defeat and destroy the winners? And that the effect of success may result in the downfall of the New Deal "recovery" program far quicker than its success would?[5]

Indeed, the very success of the Roosevelt administration seemed increasingly to be its undoing, because almost all of its successes—the Wagner Labor Act, the Social Security payroll taxes, the surplus profits tax, and others—were fueling the upward spiral of wages and prices.

After United States Steel granted wage increases, the *Kiplinger Washington Letter* found that the "economic consequences of [the] easy labor settlement with U.S. Steel are expected by most Washington authorities to add new impetus to the *upward spiral of inflation*." A further wave of wage increases, it warned, was now inevitable, and the increase in prices and in the cost of living that would follow would be "harmful to the millions who will NOT get higher wages or income."[6] The U.S. correspondent for *The Economist* noted one manifestation of the inflationary psychology that had seized the country by March, when he wrote: "A large part of the emphasis in retail advertising is an appeal to the fear motive, i.e., buy now because prices are about to go up."[7] Dorothy Thompson warned: "The crisis is the serious danger of a price inflation which may sweep everything before it—workers and capital alike." Walter Lippmann agreed, writing that "any one who wishes to believe that an inflationary boom is not under way is in precisely the same position as those who said that prosperity in 1928 was assured."[8]

Three leading indexes of wholesale prices showed rises between October 1936 and late February or early March 1937, of between 5.6 percent (Bureau of Labor Statistics), almost 10 percent (the *Annalist*), and 18 percent (Moody's).[9] *Barron's* warned that consumers had "better buy that car now," since increased labor costs and commodity prices had added about $200 million to the basic costs of automobile production, which would raise the price of the average automobile by about $45.[10]

The Roosevelt administration faced a dilemma. On the one hand, a balanced budget seemed the only way that the administration could put a damper on speculation, preserve the government's shaky credit, and maintain the value of a large proportion of the assets of the nation's banks. On the other hand, if the wage-price spiral was approaching the point where consumers could no longer absorb the higher prices, would not a balanced budget accelerate that process by reducing the government's contribution to purchasing power and trigger a recession? While one set of considerations seemed to demand a balanced budget, another set suggested just as strongly that a balanced budget could be as disastrous to the economy as an unbalanced one. This was the dilemma that Roosevelt's policies and attitudes had produced for his administration and the nation by early 1937. At bottom it existed because after five years of Roosevelt and the New Deal the U.S. economy had still not recovered from the depression, by contrast with the economies of most other nations of the world. Careful observers recognized that the heights to which the economy had risen in 1936 and early 1937 were largely artificial, the result of the flood of bonus, relief, and other spending to aid Roosevelt's reelection in 1936. That artificial "recovery" could only be sustained by further government stimulation.

The difficulty, then, was the one that Keynes and other critics of the New Deal had warned of from 1933 onward: Roosevelt had done nothing to prepare for the transition from government to private spending that must ultimately be required. On the contrary, his every speech and every action seemed calculated to make that transition impossible. His attacks on business, his support of labor in its excessive demands and actions, the implications for business of his assault on the Supreme Court, the impediments to the movement of private capital created by New Deal legislation, the penalizing effects of his tax policies on those who sought to expand through the use of their surpluses and against those who sought to invest in industry, and his continued refusal to jettison radical and incompetent advisers for those committed to recovery and competent to advise him, all combined with Roosevelt's pride and prejudice to discourage and prevent the very transition to private spending and employment that was now so desperately needed.

Reviewing, late in March, the report of securities registered with the SEC during January, the most recent month available, the *Wall Street Journal* found that of $265 million registered that month, only $15 million was earmarked for plant and equipment and $21.4 million to increase working capital. Clearly, business was "still in the refunding phase of private enterprise financing," which meant that

capital is not accepting the hazard of new fortunes to any notable extent. Until it begins to do so we are more than likely to have many unemployed employables on our hands to remain in great uncertainty concerning the probable continuance of that evil condition. As has frequently been remarked, private capital cannot be dragooned into cooperation with government to expand employment, even though it can be taken for government purposes by taxation.[11]

An investment banker wrote Mark Sullivan early in 1937:

There are thousands, yes, tens of thousands, of corporations in this country now whose betterments and improvements have been held back completely for five years and which could usefully spend an enormous amount of capital long term funds, and yet they are afraid to borrow the money.[12]

In the absence of a transition to private spending, the choice, as the *Commercial and Financial Chronicle* put it, was to give up further deficit spending, thus threatening the artificial recovery, or embarking on "a drunken orgy of inflation if it is to be continued at all."[13]

Meanwhile, concern over the wave of labor violence spread beyond the ranks of businessmen. Walter Lippmann observed that "for the first time in their experience the American people are not sure whether the party in control of the government respects the law and means to enforce it." Roosevelt's pro-labor, antibusiness attitude had the "double effect of stimulating the lawlessness and of inhibiting the enforcement of the law."[14] In the textile industry, companies tried to head off sit-down strikes by granting a wave of wage increases in late March that averaged 10 percent, the second such advance in less than six months. In seeking thus to "buy" labor peace, the textile industry added further fuel to the wage-price spiral.[15]

Early in April, *Commerce* magazine surveyed the nation's economy:

Auto wages boosted; steel wages up, hours down; clothing workers win pay boost; rail unions get firemen on oil burning locomotives; packers grant new pay raise following 7 1/2 percent increase four months ago; CIO eyeing textile, oil and electrical industries after victory in steel; unionization in rubber industry being pressed anew; steel prices boosted; copper at new high since 1929; tire prices increased; Washington reported worried about effect of rapidly rising H[igh] C[ost] of L[iving] on white collar voters and farmers . . . .

Thus read just a fragmentary review of the news highlights pertinent to the price level which have been headline material in recent weeks. The trend is so evident that it is idle to discuss for itself. But the implications are another thing.

The question is how far and how fast can the movement progress before bumping us to the point at which business improvement is checked by too rapid cost and price advance?[16]

A writer in *Barron's* found "a good many people are now to be observed talking and thinking about the Next Depression."[17]

PREDICTIONS OF A RECESSION

By early May the term most often used to describe the business situation was "uneasiness." *Business Week* found retailers complaining that sales were below expectations, caused in large part by higher prices. Forecasts of a third-quarter recession were becoming more frequent and strikes were still "rampant," while increased costs of goods had stimulated the building up of inventories against future price increases and had caused too rapid increases in the prices to consumers.[18] *Barron's* found early in the same month that "economists of six government departments and agencies agree that a recession in industrial activity is highly probable before the end of this year."[19]

The problem that manufacturers and retailers faced as a result of the rising costs of labor and materials is well illustrated by two items. The first, a letter from Ralph Flanders, president of a machine tool company, explained the situation that many manufacturers confronted:

The machine tool industry is doing its share in price raising. It would be fair to say that two 10% raises on the average have been put into effect within the last nine months. This is perhaps a 1% or 2% increase over the increased cost of labor and materials, but psychologically the problem is complicated by the fact that present deliveries extend from three to nine months ahead, and there is the fear that labor and material costs will still further advance and that these prices now current but applying to those future months will not be great enough to take care of the future costs. In other words, we are definitely in the grip of inflationist psychology, whether or not there is any factual basis for fearing inflation. Trying to protect oneself on future price rises is both a result and a cause of an inflationary advance.[20]

The second, an editorial in *Dry Goods Economist*, told retailers:

Price increases have been forced upon us through startling tax increases of many kinds and labor conditions. Neither of them can be changed for years to come. Both will show still further advances. The only possible way to slow up either is *to advance* prices in keeping with present day costs. . . . [W]hen prices start marking new all time highs, and people are brought face to face with the necessity of paying—through merchandise purchased—for extravagance in Washington and other places, you'll hear a howl of protest go up which will startle even our most hardened demagogs [sic]. Perhaps the merchants of this country have in their hands the one and only weapon that can force a balancing of budgets. Very often it has been found people can be reached through their pocketbooks when they are deaf to appeals to the mind or heart.[21]

The New York *Herald-Tribune* index of business, which peaked at nearly 100 in December 1936, began a steady decline in 1937 that was only briefly interrupted in mid-February. By the end of April it had dropped to 85, erasing all of the gains of 1936.[22] In 1934, as a serious recession impended, Roosevelt had embarked on a leisurely vacation cruise to Hawaii. Now, as the economic situation again showed evidence of deterioration, Roosevelt departed Washington for a cruise in the Gulf of Mexico. While Roosevelt fished in the gulf, the stock exchange in mid-May staggered under a wave of liquidations despite the absence of any particularly new development in the business situation. While the Commerce Department assured businessmen that everything was on the upswing, the Bureau of Agricultural Economics in the Agriculture Department warned that, on the contrary, the upswing in business that had begun the previous fall was not continuing.[23] Later in the month the reversion to warfare by the CIO in the steel and automobile industries further aggravated business conditions and sentiment.[24] The *Commercial and Financial Chronicle* wrote that "it is seriously to be doubted whether the average man has any conception of the extent to which production and distribution are today being interrupted by strikes and other disputes."[25] A Gallup poll in mid-April, however, showed that 65 percent of those polled favored the use of force by state and local authorities to remove sit-down strikers.[26]

ROOSEVELT RESUMES THE ASSAULT ON BUSINESS

But apparently business confidence and conditions had not been disrupted enough by the events of early 1937 to suit Roosevelt, for late in May he proposed new legislation that struck further at business confidence. The Black-Connery wages and hours bill empowered the federal government to regulate wages and hours in U.S. industry, a goal that, however laudable at other times, seemed calculated to further confuse an already chaotic business situation, and to lead to increased costs of production that could only further fuel the wage-price spiral.[27] Early in June, Roosevelt continued his offensive against recovery by announcing his plan to set up eight regional power agencies under another bill introduced before Congress. Utility executives meeting in convention in Chicago denounced the plan as yet another in "a series of steps to destroy the private electric industry and wipe out billions of dollars of private investments."[28] Looking at the legislation that had been presented to Congress by Roosevelt in the first five months of 1937, columnist Dorothy Thompson found that it added up to "a consistent picture"—one in which there would be "a power and authority vested in the President not far from equal to the power and authority vested in Mussolini or in Stalin.''[29] Frank Kent found the same measures ''linked'' and constituting ''the most amazing and ambitious plan for complete governmental subjugation and economic regulation yet proposed in a free country.''

It seems there must be something fundamentally wrong with men who seriously think, without complete dictatorial power, they can be even measurably successful in achieving the gaudy purpose in mind. Their sense of proportion has been lost. Something has run away with their wits. At least so it seems when the proposals are grouped together and the picture viewed as a whole.[30]

Economist Virgil Jordan, head of the National Industrial Conference Board, thought he saw another consistency in the four-year record in the New Deal:

Governmental mechanism, created and set in motion by the Federal legislation of the past four years, is designed fundamentally to transform the private enterprise organization of production gradually into a system of State capitalism under the ownership or management of an absolute central government. This objective is being attained by persistent application of the following simultaneous processes: (1) Retarding or preventing the accumulation and reinvestment of private, individual and business savings; (2) forcing the division or re-distribution of income from savers to consumers through confiscatory taxation of current savings, borrowing of future savings, and their dissipation by government expenditure; (3) preventing and dissipating existing savings by creating conditions which will compel operation of private enterprise at a loss; (4) destroying the value of present and future private savings by creating conditions which will depreciate the currency; and (5) accumulating and concentrating the liquid savings and credit resources of the whole community in the hands of the government, so as to make the State the ultimate source and absolute allocator of capital funds.[31]

While such charges against the Roosevelt administration might have sounded extreme to many of those who read them, the concerns expressed were shared by responsible political figures. Senator Josiah Bailey, Democrat of North Carolina, wrote Newton Baker that the 1937 New Deal legislative program added up to ''an irretrievable centralization of the Federal Government and an end of representative Government in our land.'' Looking at the growing number of voters dependent upon the federal government, Bailey wondered if it were ''not manifest we are being surrounded and that if we delay efforts to extricate ourselves, it will be hopeless.''[32] In a similar vein, Alf Landon wrote columnist Raymond Clapper:

You laughed at the dictatorship thought. . . . Seriously, I only hope you won't have to reproach yourself that you failed to gauge correctly the relative degree of danger to free election. If you are wrong, it involves far more grave consequences than if I am wrong. Therefore I hope from the bottom of my heart that you are right. But you can hardly dismiss the fears of people like Dorothy Thompson, Walter Lippmann, James Truslow Adams—and even myself, as childish.[33]

Meanwhile, the economy continued to give evidence that a downturn was imminent. Blame for the prospective downturn was laid at the door of rising prices caused by strikes and the added labor costs that resulted. The stock market, too, continued to drift listlessly downward on very little activity, with the blame here likewise placed on the labor troubles and, particularly, the unwillingness of Roosevelt to take a stand on the issue despite the obvious interference of the strikes with recovery.[34] Brookings Institution economist Harold G. Moulton concluded that the economic signs had been reasonably good up to the end of 1936, but

in the past few months this hopeful situation has been changed in one important respect. The prices of both raw materials and finished products have been rapidly rising. The advance of the former is directly related to the military programs of government and the speculative activities that accompany boom conditions in certain lines. The price increases in manufactured goods are the result in part of the increased cost of raw materials, but more largely of the sharp increases in wage rates. The recent abrupt increases in wages ranging from 20 to 30 per cent have not been related to efficiency.

With sharply rising costs all along the line, the natural tendency is to push prices up to maintain profit margins. These recent trends are thus laying the foundations for a rapid spiral of inflation. Rising costs lead to rising prices; higher prices lead to further advances in wages and other costs, and this in turn to still further price advances.

Such price advances frequently provide a temporary stimulus to industrial activity. With prices going up, business men and others hasten to place orders and buy extra quantities in order to be ahead of the price advance. This expansion of orders still further accelerates business activity and stimulates advance in prices.

But developments such as these produce serious maladjustments in the economic system as a whole. Particularly labor groups which receive higher wages may stand to gain for a time. Similarly the industries involved may temporarily pass on the higher costs to consumers. But further extensive expansion appears definitely to be menaced by the inflationary process. . . . Recent trends with respect to wages and prices must clearly be viewed with no little apprehension.[35]

And the strikes continued. As the stock market continued its downward drift, observers found that "strikes in the steel, mining, motor and other major industries continue to sway operations on the stock exchange to the exclusion of almost every other influence."[36]

When the governor of Ohio was so intimidated by threats of violence from the CIO that he sent National Guard troops to prevent steel companies from *reopening* their plants in Youngstown, the Washington *Post* joined the chorus of the incredulous:

If the power of the State is to be used to lock out willing workers from industrial plants every time John L. Lewis threatens to stage a riot, law enforcement will soon be a travesty. Gov. Earle may believe that he is handling a difficult situation in the most expedient manner. But continued surrender to intimidation merely adds fuel to the fire of lawlessness on both sides. If threats of violence are so effective, they may also be used by non-union workers and organized employers. . . . [37]

When Roosevelt likewise appealed to the heads of the two steel companies not to reopen their plants for those workers who wanted to return to work, the *Wall Street Journal* wondered "Who is Governing Us?" From the evidence it was not the administration in Washington, but John L. Lewis, head of the CIO.[38] Raymond Clapper found bitter feeling toward Roosevelt increasing in Washington, with the president denounced daily in Congress and public sentiment turning against him for "letting labor go wild." He judged that this was "the most serious ebb of [Roosevelt] sentiment since he took office." The Macon (Georgia) *Telegram* on June 25 called for Roosevelt's impeachment.[39]

Walter Lippmann, after ticking off the sins of the Roosevelt administration, including "the attempt to seize control of the judiciary," "their use of political terrorism against their opponents," and "their encouragement of class hatred," wrote:

Mr. Roosevelt, intoxicated with personal power, imbued with messianic conception of his capacity to bring salvation to the ill-nourished, ill-clad and ill-housed one-third, has frightened the other two-thirds to the point where they are thinking of lawless devices to re-establish law and order.[40]

Raymond Clapper wrote that "at times Roosevelt disappoints me very much and this is one of those times. It seems to me he has let the labor situation get completely out of hand and has thrown his administration too much to the labor side." He concluded of Roosevelt: "I sometimes think he is his own worst enemy."[41] The only consolation in the situation was the growing evidence that public opinion was reacting negatively toward the CIO.[42]

FEARS OF A DICTATORSHIP

Mixed with concern over the economic situation as of mid-1937 was the remarkable growth of what can only be described as fear of Roosevelt's dictatorial designs. Late in June, Walter Lippmann wrote:

I wish I could recover the belief that the President really is interested in democratic reforms and not in the establishment of irresistible power personally directed. It is not pleasant to have such fears about the Chief Magistrate of the Republic. But for many long months nothing has happened which helps to dispel these fears. Many, many things continue to happen which accentuate them. These fears, I regret to say, are not confined to the uninformed. They are shared in increasing degree by men who have occupied high places in this very Administration and in the confidence of Mr. Roosevelt himself.

Experience shows that the appetite for power grows by what it feeds upon, and my feeling is that if Mr. Roosevelt's attempt to enhance his power by the judiciary bill, the reorganization bill, and the wages and hours bill is not checked here and now, we shall see actions that will astonish us even more than the scheme to pack the court. What will they deal with? They will deal, I should guess, with the last remaining obstacle to the undisputed power of the Administration. They will deal with the independence of the press. . . .

The independence of the press is the last remaining obstacle to the consolidation and perpetuation of this new and vast power, and since eternal vigilance is the price of liberty, we had better be too vigilant than two incredulous.[43]

Columnist Franklyn Waltman saw the assault on the press already under way, with Roosevelt displaying "an increasing contempt for the press." The White House, he observed, was "fretful under restraints—it does not like to be crossed by the press, Congress, the courts, the Comptroller General or anyone else. It is a dangerous state of mind and the sooner such an attitude is abandoned the better it will be for the country and for the White House occupant."[44] Ray Tucker found in Congress a "definite dread of the trend toward dictatorship, supergovernment, personalized policy-making—whatever you chose to call it—at Washington."

Mr. Roosevelt's recent behavior, political and personal, has aggravated these doubts. . . . Back of the smile and winning personality, Congress has reason to believe, there is a Roosevelt whom Washington has suspected but not detected—slightly sardonic, self-centered and vindictive. Adversity has irritated him instead of chastened him. He has publicly ridiculed several distinguished members of the Supreme Court by name. He has closed his ears to contrary advice from well-wishers in his Cabinet and among party leaders. He has exhibited impatience toward all who crossed him, even consigning friendly reporters to the dunce's corner. He has chosen to align himself, in the public mind at least, with labor extremists at a time when the nation's solemn need in the face of expanding production and employment seemed to be industrial peace and progress.[45]

Late in July, Roosevelt told his cabinet that Congress must conclude the work of passing his legislative package before the end of the year, if not in the regular session then at a special session in October. He did not want the wages and hours, reorganization, and agriculture bills held over to 1938, an election year.[46] Yet all the evidence indicated that even if Roosevelt were successful in getting the bills passed by Congress, it would be only after much modification. The wages and hours bill, for example, emerged from the Senate committee in July bearing little resemblance to the bill that his Brandeisian advisors had written.[47] But, while agreeing that many of the worst provisions of Roosevelt's bills had been thrown out, and that the originals could not pass, it was the original bills that the veteran liberal Amos Pinchot found of "immense importance." He wrote Roosevelt:

[The original bills are] important because, only by studying them can the country discover where you proposed to lead it. Finally, they are important because, so far as I know, they are the only authentic written record, and the only accurate description of (a) the kind of government you, and the men who drafted these bills, want to set up in this country, and (b) the degree of control, over industry and labor, you are apparently anxious to impose.

Mr. President, if these bills were placed on the statute books, as they came from the White House, and sustained by a packed Supreme Court, they would throw this country into fascism in a fortnight. They would transform our economic life into a bureaucratic collectivism. In short, they would wholly change the character of government and industry and put both under the personal domination of one man, namely yourself.[48]

The New York *Herald-Tribune*, noting that not even Roosevelt could dismiss Pinchot as an "economic royalist," applauded his letter to the president, but pointed out that others had warned, even in the early months of Roosevelt's administration, that this was his goal.[49]

By August Roosevelt was clearly on the defensive and in a bitter mood. Washington correspondent Ray Tucker recalled in mid-August that Roosevelt had, until a few months previously, retained the support of almost all of the Washington press corps, who "almost worshipped him." Until then "at least 90 percent of Washington newspaperdom thought he could do no wrong." But that was no longer the case:

Of late . . . they have seen another side of Mr. Roosevelt. He has been irritably domineering and scornful—of them. He has suggested that Washington writers consist of two groups—the dumb and the dishonest, journalistically. It is only natural that they should resent such an attitude and reflect their resentment in their "copy." Moreover, reporters have families, a stake in the United States, the same emotions and desires and ambitions as other folks. . . . And a solid majority of the Washington press corps has become deeply concerned over Mr. Roosevelt's post-election attitude and policies. They are looking him over through non-romantic eyes for the first time, and the look-see as reflected in their despatches may be disastrous to the White House.[50]

Late in August the Congress adjourned without passing any of Roosevelt's "must" legislation. Observers marveled at the impotent state to which Roosevelt had been reduced within ten months of his landslide victory at the polls.[51] Others, however, worried that Roosevelt's setback was only temporary, that in election year 1938 he would be able to use the relief money that Congress had given him "as a club to force those same Congressmen and Senators to vote for his legislative program."[52]

THE ECONOMIC DECLINE BEGINS

Meanwhile, retail sales continued higher than for the corresponding months of 1936, but ominously the financial statements of leading corporations showed disappointing profits for the second quarter of 1937 even on higher volume.[53] *Business Week* looked at the increase in prices over the same period in 1936:

wholesale prices up 9 percent, metal prices up 9 percent, raw materials up 14 percent, semimanufactures up 17 percent, finished products up 6 percent, farm products up 18 percent, food up 6 percent, construction costs up 13 percent, department store prices up 7 percent, and the general cost of living up 5 percent. The lumber and steel industries continued to push industrial production indexes up, but insiders noted that they were operating with virtually no backlog of orders in the hope that the fall months would bring renewed demand.[54] One source of optimism was a report from the Bureau of Agricultural Economics, which predicted a cash farm income of about $9 billion for 1937, or about $1 billion more than in 1936.[55]

September began with a sharp decline in the stock market. This was curious timing, since early September usually marked the end of the seasonal summer recession in business and the beginning of the fall upswing. Some observers blamed uneasiness over the increasing costs of operation caused by strikes and the higher costs of materials.[56] Concerned over the effects the jittery market might have on a pending government financing effort, Treasury Secretary Morgenthau wired Roosevelt that "the financial community has one of the worst attacks of the jitters that I have seen in a long time." Aware of rumors that Roosevelt planned to call a special session of Congress in October and recognizing the impact that such rumors were having on business confidence, Morgenthau told Roosevelt: "If you have made up your mind that you are not going to call an extra session of Congress an announcement from you to this effect in Monday's morning newspapers would come psychologically at the right time." Roosevelt wired his reply: "Feel sure financing will go through satisfactorily[.] Domestic situation excellent[.] Sorry[,] no statement possible."[57]

The Treasury, however, recognized that the "domestic situation" was far from "excellent." In early September it groped for a stimulant to the economy.[58] On September 12 the Treasury announced that it was releasing $300 million in gold from its inactive account, thereby placing this amount of funds at the disposal of banks for an increase in their available reserves.[59] Some industries began in September to cut back on their work week because of large inventories accumulated in anticipation of a fall upturn that was not developing.[60] Through the summer, consumer spending remained high, however. Dollar sales in New York City and Brooklyn department stores were 7.8 percent higher than in the same month of 1936, and the 1937 travel season saw more activity than any summer since 1929. The FRB reported that department store sales for the nation as a whole were 4 percent higher in August than a year earlier, while sales for the first eight months of 1937 were 9 percent higher than the same period in 1936.[61]

But businessmen were profoundly worried about the prospect that Roosevelt's legislative package would be passed, either by a special session late in the year, or by the regular session in 1938. The *Kiplinger Washington Letter* told businessmen that Roosevelt seemed "to be adamant in [his] determination to press his major New Deal programs with force and vigor, no compromises."[62] The *Magazine of Wall Street* noted that the "biggest bugaboo of business" was the possibility of a special session, since Roosevelt, it speculated, would only call such a special session if he were absolutely certain that he "can have things his way." [63] In short, if Roosevelt called a special session it would indicate to businessmen that he was certain his program could be passed, since he would not risk another blow to his prestige such as had been delivered by the regular session.

In mid-September the stock market slipped even further. Former brain truster Adolf Berle found Wall Street "scared to death" and "convinced that there will be a real down-turn in business and that the stock market antics are merely an indication of that fact." Berle, however, was convinced that they were only having "a bad attack of nerves." [64] Roosevelt showed no greater sensitivity to the deterioration of the economic situation in 1937 than he had in 1934. In a speech on September 18, he further signaled his intention to push on with new measures of industrial control by the government, and immediately a further sharp break in the stock exchange followed. [65] Adding to the uneasiness of businessmen and investors was the appointment of William O. Douglas as chairman of the SEC. Douglas was viewed as a "radical" and his appointment as "a victory for those who favor a more militantly crusading attitude on the part of the Government agency toward Wall Street and huge corporate units." [66]

On September 24, Commerce Secretary Daniel Roper, until now the perennial optimist, told businessmen they could expect larger tax levies, lower profits, further benefits for small businesses, but enlarged responsibilities for the federal government. "The objective," said Roper, "will be to arrive at a just distribution of economic rewards for bona fide investments; for an economic management surcharged with a high righteous treatment under its trusteeship for the stockholders, for labor and for the public, or consumer." [67] A New Dealer told businessmen that "hereafter corporate issues may be considered on the basis of social desirability in addition to financial soundness." How "social desirability" was to be defined was not explained. "Nor," observed *Nation's Business*, "was it explained how the investor could be coaxed into putting his money into a socially desirable enterprise if he thought it would not pay." [68] Four years of experience had apparently still not demonstrated to the Roosevelt administration that the economy did not operate on sociology but on profits and their prospect. Such statements seemed to confirm the observation of author Bernard De Voto that much of the New Deal "looked like the phantasies one might entertain himself with on a train ride when he didn't have a magazine." [69]

Late in September investment banker Frank Altschul found in the continued stock market decline "an indication of a real smash in business." [70] Bernard Baruch agreed, writing Harry Hopkins that he felt certain increasing unemployment was an immediate prospect. He told Hopkins:

After the pump was primed, there had to be restoration of private business in order to keep the thing moving. We have not restored, but have decreased personal initiative. I am not talking about big corporations only. I refer to the infinite number of business and professional people who would like to go into enterprise and do things and wish to expand their efforts. But they feel doomed to failure (as I can assure you they are) by the stifling effect of what were thought to be effective means of tax collecting, but because unwise, turned out to be punitive revenue provisions.

People feel that if they gain, they have to pay too much. If they lose, they cannot charge it off. Neither can they spread their losses over a period. No one will undertake new, or expand old businesses with that prospect in view. We must not stop enterprises which decrease unemployment and supply jobs which give people self-respect. What we are after is the production of wealth and things that people can enjoy in greater quantity and over a wider area of our population.

No one knows better than you, that if we increase the volume of business, we take people off the W.P.A. and taxes increase and we get it at both ends towards a balanced budget.

If your economic advisers do not agree with me, I wish you would send them to me and let them convince me I am wrong.[71]

The U.S. correspondent for *The Economist* wrote in the same month: "The simple fact is that our economy has neither a functioning money market nor a functioning capital market."[72] By early October the *Kiplinger Washington Letter* found widespread fears that another major business depression was imminent.[73]

Business confidence was further jolted by evidence that Roosevelt's popularity remained high. As the president traveled through the northwest in late September and early October the crowds were large and enthusiastic. Ernest Lindley contrasted this with the fact that at the same time, "even among his friends and supporters there is indifference and in some instances openly expressed hostility to parts of the President's program, especially to the unfinished parts."[74] Roosevelt exhibited all of the old combativeness during his trip, expressing his determination to press on with the legislation he had been denied during the 1937 regular session of Congress, and strongly hinted that he planned to resurrect the "reform" of the Supreme Court.[75] *Barron's* noted of the rumors that a special session of Congress would be called that "there probably never was a more precarious time to call a special session of Congress since Van Buren fumbled in the 1830s."[76] At his press conference of October 6, Roosevelt told reporters that he would make a decision on a special session "within the next week."[77]

THE SPECIAL SESSION

On October 7 both the *Wall Street Journal* and the United Press predicted that Roosevelt would call a special session for mid-November.[78] Lindley agreed that Roosevelt had "all but finally decided" to call the session, and that he would push all of his legislative package including, possibly, judicial "reform."[79] Morgenthau, who was more sensitive to the business situation than any of the others around Roosevelt, opposed a special session. He told Postmaster General James Farley that he thought Roosevelt had not looked carefully at the situation and that his best move would be to, instead, make it clear that he was working to control the budget situation. This, Morgenthau believed, would create business confidence "and God knows we need that." The nation, he said, needed "a breathing spell, to get a chance to tell which way we're going. I haven't seen business men since last November '33 as . . . jittery as they are now. And it's getting steadily worse." Yet Morgenthau was afraid to use this argument with Roosevelt, since "if I do they immediately throw back that I'm just as bad as the rest of them [the conservative critics of the New Deal]."[80]

The *Commercial and Financial Chronicle* of October 9 found businessmen in general concerned by the apparent lack of awareness in the White House of the danger that a serious recession was imminent. It found nothing constructive in Roosevelt's legislative proposals and a great deal in them that would only serve further to destroy the confidence and position of business.[81] Former brain truster Adolf Berle put the problem succinctly: "I wish I could convert anybody in Washington to the theory that you cannot run a government based on business and have a perpetual warfare with business at the same time."[82] Yet when Berle tested Washington sentiment in mid-October he found Roosevelt's awareness of the seriousness of the economic situation reduced to a belief that there was a "concerted action on the part of the New York financial district to discredit the Administration."[83] Even at this critical point, Roosevelt's paranoia would not permit him to view the economic situation as anything other than a battleground between his administration and the "interests" of business and finance.

On October 11 the stock market staggered. Morgenthau was told by a contact on Wall Street that the market had begun "a type of relentless selling, all day long, which you couldn't see the end of," and there was no end in sight. There was a "lack of confidence bordering almost on disorder, or you could use the word panic, . . . but that would be putting it a little strongly. It isn't quite that, it's sort of utter discouragement." Morgenthau was advised that it was important for the administration to show, in its public statements, some appreciation for the difficulties some of the business community was encountering rather than demonstrating antagonism. Morgenthau, however, was not terribly concerned so long as the government bond market remained steady. Reflecting the paranoia of the White House, he regarded the business situation as representing an attempt by businessmen to "stop Roosevelt from going ahead with his reforms."[84]

On that same day, Morgenthau learned that Roosevelt had definitely decided to call a special session of Congress, but he was encouraged by the president's continued commitment to a balanced budget. At the end of a cabinet meeting that day, Agriculture Secretary Henry A. Wallace told Roosevelt:

Mr. President, as we are now approaching a balanced budget, don't you think that you ought to call some of us together and see if we can't think up some suggestions to encourage private business enterprise so that they can go ahead and take up the slack which would be left due to the government ceasing spending?

Morgenthau considered Wallace's remarks "tremendously significant."[85] Indeed, they might have been four years earlier, but it was a little late now, and not a little naive in view of the renewed assault on business confidence that Roosevelt was determined to launch with his call for a special session of Congress.

On October 12, Roosevelt announced his decision to call a special session of Congress for November 25. In the same speech, Roosevelt revealed that he still had no grasp of the economic situation. Despite the abundant evidence that higher wages had driven up prices to the point where a new recession was under way, Roosevelt stubbornly insisted on more in his speech:

A few more dollars a week in wages, a better distribution of jobs with a shorter working day will almost overnight make millions of our lowest-paid workers actual buyers of billions of dollars of industrial and farm products. That increased volume of sales ought to lessen other costs of production so that even a considerable increase in labor costs can be absorbed without imposing higher prices on the consumer.[86]

This sounded like a mandate for further labor union activity and more business concessions to labor, with the inevitable result for the wage-price spiral. Nothing in Roosevelt's speech suggested any grasp of the new crisis into which the attitudes and policies of his administration had plunged the nation by mid-October. As columnist Franklyn Waltman observed, no business could "afford to grant wage increases, institute 40-hour weeks, pay social security taxes and, because of these things, increased prices for his raw materials and then sell his product at the same price. You cannot eat your cake and have it, too." This was exactly the line that Roosevelt had tried to follow with the NRA, without success.[87] Yet Roosevelt had apparently learned nothing from that experience. Yale University economist Irving Fisher told Roosevelt that his insistence on the wages and hours bill would only increase the difficulties that the New Deal had created for production. It threatened "to decrease productivity and to intensify unemployment," and the "unfavorable reaction of the stock market" was due to recognition of that fact.[88] But Roosevelt refused to recognize the inappropriateness of calling a special session for the purposes he had enunciated under the conditions then prevailing in the economy, telling Morgenthau that he had called the session because "the function of the government is to move forward."[89]

Eugene Meyer, former RFC head and now publisher of the Washington *Post*, found no possibility of change in the attitude at the White House: "It is hard to change the mind of a group of people who have been indulging in the pastime of clubbing business with or without excuse. The popular appeal to the masses based on antagonism to the management of industry makes it difficult to shift around and be fair and constructive at this time, even if they want to."[90] Stanley High, former Roosevelt speechwriter, observed that while the president had occasionally talked with businessmen during the first term, his second term had been launched without any such business input.

One of the most portentous facts about the first year of Mr. Roosevelt's second Administration is that he has been almost entirely cut off from conservative counselors. The line which was drawn in 1933 and thereafter between reactionaries and moderate conservatives apparently is drawn no longer. Moderate conservatives, apparently, are now no more welcome than reactionaries. It is not reactionary big business which has become *persona non grata* at the White House. It is big business. A blind spot has appeared which blankets the area in which a major part of the economic activity of the nation is carried on. It would be absurd to contend that the blind spot is a creation of the President's advisers. The inclination had to be there. But it is undoubtedly a fact that the President's Second New Deal advisers have been of a mind, not to curb the tendency, but to encourage it.[91]

Here was the answer to those who insisted that it was not Roosevelt, but his advisers, who were at fault for the attitude and policies of the New Deal.

THE CRASH

Two former brain trusters, not previously noted for their conservatism, were by mid-October sufficiently alarmed by the economic situation that they had begun to sound very much like business critics of the Roosevelt administration. Adolf Berle and Charles Taussig agreed that the situation seemed headed for a "major recession" that must be tackled "on very broad lines." Taussig thought that modification of the undistributed profits tax would be sufficient to improve business conditions, but Berle doubted that would be enough.[92] Such speculations were academic, however, for Roosevelt showed no sign that he understood the unfolding crisis. The *Kiplinger Washington Letter* wrote of Roosevelt's attitude:

Businesswise, his state of mind is not good. He scoffs at fears of decline. He sneers, in public speech, at "sound business judgment." He seems to feel little concern about current business-facts-or-sentiment. He seeks advice more-&-more from chosen handpicked like-minded favorites, less-&-less from responsible officials who don't see eye-to-eye with him.

The calling of [a] special session next month is [the] latest example. The decision is the President's own. He advertised he would seek advice, but he sought none, except from the hand-picked insiders.

Most of his cabinet members were prepared to advise against it. He didn't ask them; he TOLD them.

All of this meant, Kiplinger concluded, that the "President's pressure for new laws will not be checked by any apprehension about business reactions."[93]

It did not sound very much as if Roosevelt was concerned about the deteriorating economic situation. Dorothy Thompson wrote:

It is amazing to read the papers, the comments, and the speeches of Administration leaders, and to observe how studiously the main question before all of us is being avoided. The question is what we are going to do about the new depression that is not merely menacing, but is here. The grandiose program proposed for the [special] session of Congress . . . concerns itself with nearly everything except this all-important question. Optimism officially reigns, but, unfortunately, without convincing basis. Unless the present direction takes a radical turn, we shall soon be confronted with facts apparent to everybody.

The move toward a balanced budget was a "wholly laudable goal, and a necessary one," Thompson wrote, but it would "add and not subtract from catastrophe, unless industry takes up the slack." But, she added,

industry will not be able to take up the slack without revision of the entire New Deal structure, to release capital. This involves not a slight, but a very radical change in the tax system, and a willingness on the part of labor to withhold, for the moment, and until the present tendency is reversed, measures which will add heavily to costs.

The capital gains and undistributed profits tax would, likewise, have to be radically modified.[94]

On October 18 there came a message that even Roosevelt, it seemed, would not be able to ignore. On that day the stock market collapse of 1929 was repeated, and the economy began the plunge that economists, businessmen, and journalists had predicted.

CHAPTER 12

The Second Roosevelt Depression, I, 1937

RESPONSE TO THE CRASH

In the midst of the crash of October 18, 1937, Adolf Berle found Wall Street "most bewildered and frightened." Charles Taussig thought that if Roosevelt would "renounce something; that would open things up," but Berle thought it "possible that the President has lost a good deal of his magic in this particular regard." It was now plain that "business is dropping as well as the market—in other words, we are in for a rather bad winter."[1] Berle warned Roosevelt that the stock market collapse was "beginning to have [a] material adverse effect on business which would reflect itself in unemployment within the next two or three weeks."[2]

The day after the crash, the White House received some 40 telegrams asking Roosevelt to close the stock market, but Morgenthau counseled against it. Sounding very much like Hoover six years earlier, Morgenthau maintained that most business was "as good or better than it has ever been."[3] If his administration's leading financial officer was so out of touch with reality, it is little wonder that Roosevelt was unconcerned. But the figures were staggering. The New York *Herald-Tribune* noted that the plunge in the stock market had produced "a day of broken hearts and pocketbooks," with stock values dropping an estimated $25 billion (a good deal more even than the national debt accumulated by the Roosevelt administration since 1933), as the market reached a new low in over two years. More individual issues had appeared on the ticker tape than ever before in history, and a membership on the New York Stock Exchange sold for the lowest price paid since 1919.[4]

The recriminations began, but contained nothing that had not already been said. Ex-New Dealer Raymond Moley attacked the Roosevelt administration for its ''there-are-villains-lurking-in-the-bushes-ready-to-tear-you-to-pieces-appeal.'' Roosevelt's recent speeches, he charged, ''bespeak an America at war with itself, not an America searching for peace. And their endless repetition, now in one form, now in another, creates the very discord they are intended to portray.''[5] Walter Lippmann pointed out that the world's leading capitalist nation was being governed by an ''administration which disbelieves in the capitalist system.'' Worse yet, it was being ruled by a man who possessed ''decisive personal power over the vital elements of the American economy,'' but who, ''by training, study, experience, and natural endowment,'' was ''not fitted to exercise that much power,'' and who exercised it ''in an entirely haphazard and unaccountable fashion.''[6] Dorothy Thompson agreed that the situation was such that ''no one, today, knows what rules he is playing under, or whether today's rules will be tomorrow's. He is not even clear in his mind what the objective of his government is.'' She added: ''One could adjust oneself to any consistent program, however radical. But not to adventure. Not to sudden shocks. Not to dilettantism, amateurishness, uncertainty.''[7] Frank Kent echoed the others in writing that ''no one can tell anything about the future because everything hinges upon what Mr. Roosevelt does, and no one knows about that—not even Mr. Roosevelt himself, who may have one thing on his mind today and a quite different thing tomorrow.''[8]

Economists, businessmen, business journals, and newspaper commentators scrambled to examine the reasons behind the October collapse of the economy. On October 19, Dr. Melchior Palyi, University of Chicago economist, drew up a study entitled ''The Liquidation of an Induced Prosperity,'' which soon found its way to the White House. Palyi described the recovery, such as it had been, as a ''government credit prosperity.''

The impetus of new money turned out by the government set the wheels of the economic machinery in motion, but failed to create sufficient power to provide the expected automatic acceleration. . . . The assumption was that such indirect methods of financing would lead in due course to the rise of a genuine credit demand on the part of business, which would displace and replace government stimulation. This assumption did not materialize. Whether it was due to the fact that the business situation had not yet sufficiently cleaned up through the previous great depression; or whether it was due to the fear of the impact of political forces, the fact is that government expenditure, price-raising policies, and the stimulus of devaluation did not succeed in setting the machinery of new investment in motion.

That business investment started to develop last year, as the monetary and fiscal management wanted it to, was oddly the beginning of the end. The credit expansion which was the basis of prosperity implied the maintenance of a policy of extremely *cheap money*, supplemented by a number of interest-fixing methods. The hope that cheap money would encourage business was not without foundation, nor the practice without result. But as its results eventuated, cheap money itself became obsolete. How can a banking structure afford to keep 30, 40, and more per cent of its assets in government paper at starvation rates if business upturn offers remunerative investment possibilities for the same funds? The forecast of rising interest rates and therefore of falling prices of first class bonds was the first result which the new phase of the upturn engendered. The first paradox was followed by a second.

With banks holding about half of the national debt in the form of low-interest government bonds, banks became de facto branches of the Treasury, holding cash and government bonds and very little else. But, Palyi pointed out,

the banks' status depends on their liquidity, their liquidity on their earnings, and their earnings largely on the fluctuation of their government bond portfolios. Every rise in the interest rate compels them to take losses and lowers their liquidity; every step in lowering their liquidity must compel them to sell bonds (the only thing they can liquidate). Every such liquidation puts further pressure on bond prices, thus tending to raise the interest rate and compelling, in turn, the banks to more liquidation. And so forth *ad libitum*, adding to the distress by creating concern about the future liquidity of banks.

This mechanism halted the upturn, if it did not start the down trend. It was accelerated by the effect which even a minor fall in government bond prices exerts on the market psychology due to the outstanding volume and importance of bonds as a national investment and due to the surprise which the sheer fact of their price decline has caused.[9]

Thus, Palyi agreed with the analyses contained in the warnings of Orval Adams in 1935 and Lionel Edie in 1936 that Roosevelt's policies had created a situation that made economic recovery impossible without threatening the existence of the banks and the credit of the federal government.

With Palyi's analysis suggesting the inevitability of the downturn that occurred in the second half of 1937, it remains to account for the timing involved in the sudden plummet of the stock market in mid-October that set off the recession that followed. Clearly the upward spiral of wages and prices that had begun in late 1936 was an important factor. The federal spending of 1936, including the bonus payments, the wage increases and bonuses that resulted from the surplus profits tax, the added expense of the Social Security payroll taxes, and particularly the wage increases that resulted from the CIO labor violence of 1937, all fueled the upward spiral of prices and wages. In this respect, the recession of 1937 was very similar to that of 1934. In 1934 wages and prices had been raised by the NRA, AAA, monetary policies, and labor union activity. It is surely no coincidence that the two severest economic declines under Roosevelt occurred in the two years that experienced the largest number of strikes involving the most workers. The inflationary spiral caused businessmen to build inventories in anticipation of further increases in costs, only to find that the goods would not move when the fall upturn of business did not develop because of the high prices. Such a situation contributed to the worsening of the economic situation in September and October 1937, but it does not account for the sudden wave of panic selling on the stock market that began in mid-October.

The timing of this investor panic suggests that it was greatly influenced by Roosevelt's call for a special session of Congress, and by the circumstances in which the call was issued. Business journals had speculated that Roosevelt would call a special session only if he were certain that he could force his legislative package through it. On October 6, Roosevelt told his press conference that he would announce his decision within a week. Rumors were rife that he would call the special session. The panic selling began on October 11, the day before Roosevelt's scheduled announcement, and continued the next day when he announced the calling of the special session. It climaxed in the crash that followed six days after his announcement. In the background was the enthusiasm shown for Roosevelt during his trip through the Northwest, evidence of his continued popularity that brought him back to Washington in a highly combative mood. *Business Week* had cautioned that "if Mr. Roosevelt is still highly approved by the people . . . then he has a good chance of putting over his legislative program in the coming session."[10] Thus, it was not the calling of the special session, alone, that dealt a blow to business and investor confidence, but the prospect that Roosevelt would be successful in ramming his legislative package through it. The combination appears to have converted what might have been a more gradual decline in both the stock market and in business conditions into a plummet unprecedented in U.S. history for its suddenness.

Late in October a Tennessee congressman wired Roosevelt that he must take some action to reinstill confidence in businessmen. If he did not do so, the congressman told him, "I fear the picket lines of a few months past will shortly convert into bread lines."[11] Observers of Roosevelt doubted, however, that his pride would permit him to admit that his policies had failed and needed to be altered.[12] In fact, however, the full impact of Roosevelt's pride on his response to the new collapse was even more blinding than most would have expected. At a press conference on October 29, Roosevelt recited the same stale litany on the need to increase purchasing power, thus indicating that he considered this more important than the revision of the capital gains and undistributed profits taxes being demanded by economists and businessmen. The press conference served to indicate that his mind was closed on the subject, and that he would not entertain any proposals for tax revision that might help business to recover.[13]

Even more illustrative of Roosevelt's retreat from reality to an explanation of events more congenial to his mental processes, is a telephone conversation he had with Morgenthau on November 3. Morgenthau described it in his diary:

I called the President last night at 6:15 and told him that I was now convinced that we were headed into another depression and that I thought he had to do something about it. I said I would like to call in a number of people over Saturday and Sunday and discuss whether we should do something about gold. From then on the President got very excited, very dictatorial and very disagreeable.

He quoted at great length a man whom he described as a "wise old bird" who had told him that there were 2,000 men in this country who had made up their minds that they would hold a pistol to the President's head and make certain demands of him, otherwise they would continue to depress business. He quoted a lot of other generalities.

I said, "A great [deal] depends on who this person is" and like a crack from a whip, he said, "It is not necessary for you to know who that person is,["] which, after thinking it over, led me to believe that the "wise old bird" was himself whom he was quoting.[14]

In fact, the "wise old bird" could as easily have been Brandeis or Frankfurter, since this was characteristic of the nonsense that they fed the president's mind. Whatever the source, however, if this was to be Roosevelt's interpretation of the recession, then he would obviously approach it not as a problem to be solved, but as a test of wills—his against that of the "2,000 men" who were holding "a pistol" to his head. And the American people would suffer for his siege mentality.

At a cabinet meeting the following day, Roosevelt again displayed his impatience with the disagreeable realities that faced him. As Morgenthau described it, Roosevelt lost his temper and told the cabinet that he was "sick and tired of being told by the Cabinet, by Henry [Morgenthau] and by everybody else for the last two weeks what's the matter with the country and nobody suggests what I should do." After a silence, Morgenthau reminded Roosevelt that he could do something about the utilities, about the railroads, and about housing. Morgenthau also told Roosevelt that he must say something positive for business in his speech of November 15. Roosevelt, according to Morgenthau's diary, "sneered at me and he said: 'You want me to turn the old record on.' I said very forcefully, 'If you don't want to hear from me, I don't have to tell you, but you asked me.' " At Farley's urging, Morgenthau continued: "What business wants to know is are we headed towards State socialism or are we going to continue on a capitalistic basis?" Roosevelt insisted that he had "told them that again and again," but Morgenthau insisted that Roosevelt should "tell them for the fifteenth time on November 15th, because . . . that's what they want to know." Farley and Wallace agreed. The difficulty, of course, was that such words meant little when compared with Roosevelt's actions. Morgenthau confided to his diary that the cabinet meeting was the first "in my experience that the Cabinet has ever talked on a man to man basis with the President and that we did not sit back and either talk trivialities or listen to him."[15] If true, this was an incredible comment on more than four years of cabinet meetings under Roosevelt.

At a meeting with Morgenthau and Roswell Magill over proposed changes in the tax laws, Roosevelt further revealed his inability or unwillingness to grasp the problems created by his tax policies, and the continued bias that dictated his actions. While he was willing to allow corporations to retain some surpluses now as insurance against future losses, he was opposed to allowing the productive use of these surpluses to increase productivity and employment, and he still insisted that large corporations should pay heavier taxes than smaller ones, no matter how widely their stock was held. As Magill put the latter point, in a memorandum of the meeting, Roosevelt was "apparently quite willing to discourage the investment by small taxpayers in companies of large units.'' Roosevelt also told them that the next session of Congress would ''be largely devoted to legislation to curb monopoly,'' and that one possible avenue was to lessen the taxes on small corporations as compared to large ones.[16]

From the memoranda of these meetings a number of conclusions can be drawn. Most important, the discussions showed just how absent from Roosevelt's mind the real problems were that faced his administration and the nation late in 1937. In the midst of a rapidly deteriorating economic situation, Roosevelt wanted to play at the game of trust-busting, and continued to be confused over the difference between monopoly and big business. They also showed that even in the modifications he was willing to countenance in the undistributed profits tax, he was unwilling to accept revisions that might promote enterprise and employment. The need to replace government spending by private spending was remote from his mind, or the processes by which it might be stimulated were not understood. He continued to insist on following a policy that, *The Economist* observed, ''might almost have been a concerted programme to discourage capital investment.''[17]

Sensible advice on how to deal with the recession came to Roosevelt from all directions, but the program he demanded from the special session of Congress showed no influence from the advice or, for that matter, any awareness of the economic situation. It was the same legislation he had demanded of the regular session before the recession began. Instead of improving business sentiment, Roosevelt seemed intent on stamping out any confidence that might remain. A North Carolina furniture manufacturer wrote Roosevelt: ''The present economic recession is predicated on FEAR engendered by words spoken by you,'' and added:

We just returned from the mid-season furniture market, the most disastrous of any year, including depression years. Buyers were obsessed with FEAR. No basic economic reasons could be sited [sic] except the FEAR instilled in our people by your last speech, conclusive evidence of further class legislation, another session of Congress from which flows a FEAR of the unknown in new legislation. The foregoing factor has closed the purse strings of the wholesale buyer and the ultimate consumer.

The net result, we must lay off one hundred men. All about us plants are doing likewise. Again a burden is placed upon the government to care for these people who are willing to work.

The wages and hours bill should be abandoned and the undistributed profits tax amended, he wrote, and Roosevelt should ''speak to the American people in a more conciliatory attitude tending to harmonize the now powerful divergent forces[;] a spirit of 'let's all work together' would, I believe, change conditions over night.''[18] A New Jersey stock broker likewise wrote Roosevelt that the consensus of businessmen he talked to was ''virtually unanimous in attributing the poor present situation to fear and to lack of confidence.'' Like the North Carolinan, he asked Roosevelt to tell the people that ''the United States Government will take care of Government affairs and will not heckle, harass and compete unfairly with private American Business." He concluded: "Do not have it said that the Administration is deliberately crushing business with the idea of having the Government take it over lock, stock and barrel."[19]

After a rambling monologue from Roosevelt on November 8, Morgenthau came away with the impression "that he is fighting like a cornered lion; that he does not want to be tamed and still, on the other hand, he does not know where he can put his strength at this particular juncture to bring about recovery."[20] Meanwhile, the letters continued to pour in. One, from a man who claimed to be an "outcaste" among his friends for supporting Roosevelt, told the president that he was "convinced that you must give business a breathing spell, before you resume your campaign for social reform." It was time to "stop setting up the lowest class in the country against the other two thirds." He "beseeched" Roosevelt to "soften up your attitude toward our business men and do something to bring about confidence among investors."[21] A cotton textile mill director wrote that business was so bad his company was laying off 2,500 workers. The situation was due to a "complete lack of confidence on the part of both buyers and sellers," a lack of confidence that originated "entirely from fear of Washington," especially of the "further harassment and handicaps from the Congress which is about to meet." He concluded that Roosevelt could, "if he only wished, change the situation practically over night."[22]

Another letter writer, a small retailer in Battle Creek, Michigan, wrote Roosevelt that there were hundreds of thousands of small businessmen who felt just like him:

These people, Mr. Roosevelt, object to the stirring up of class hatred. It is the last thing we could ever want in this country. . . . To make the people of the country class conscious is to stir up hatred which will defeat . . . progress. No good can possibly be accomplished through hatred, but it will most certainly bring about a very definite harm. . . .

Do all you can to encourage harmony among the people of the country and to stifle hatred. Tell business men that the Government will cooperate with them to bring about a more stable and more prosperous economy under which the living conditions of *all* our people will be raised.[23]

These letter writers would doubtless have agreed with the observation of the *Saturday Evening Post*: "There are times when it is hard to tell from Mr. Roosevelt's tone whether he thinks of himself as the President of a nation or the commander in chief of a civil war."[24] As the New York *Herald-Tribune* put it: "For more than four years President Roosevelt has labored continuously, with all the extraordinary eloquence and political skill of which he is master, to divide the country into two warring sections."[25]

Unwilling as he might be to face the fact, Roosevelt was now faced with a new crisis not unlike that he had confronted in 1933, but without the political capital now that he had possessed on the earlier occasion. In March 1933,

Roosevelt had begun his presidency with the near-unanimous support of the press and of members of both parties in Congress, as well as the backing or acquiescence of most businessmen and bankers. In less than five years hc had managed to squander that political capital even while he had failed to produce recovery. As a writer in *Barron's* observed, by contrast with the enthusiastic support of 1933, there existed,

in quarters where he now needs support, a resentment and suspicion, a 'man from Missouri' put-it-in-writing attitude, sometimes a hope-he-gets-what's-coming-to-him bitterness, that recalls only dimly what he did *for* business then, but with crystal clarity what his tax and labor policies have done *to* business ever since.[26]

All of this meant that Roosevelt's task was a good deal more difficult in 1937 and 1938 due to his record, that it was unlikely the previous trickery of "breathing spells" and "eras of good feeling" and other such deceptions would any longer suffice to disarm business and press suspicion and opposition.

Newsweek reported that "even administration Left-wingers" were pleading with Roosevelt to "stop baiting business, give private enterprise a chance!"[27] The *Wall Street Journal* warned that "the one essential is that business should be convinced that Government is no longer its enemy. It will take action to produce that conviction. Talk will not do it, be it ever so seductively honeyed."[28] Walter Lippmann was skeptical, however, that any such "conversion" was likely on Roosevelt's part. While he expected some "concessions" from Roosevelt in the form of revisions in the tax laws and other minor sops, they would "not serve their purpose if they are granted reluctantly *as concessions*." Lippmann explained:

For the heart of the difficulty is the conviction, now deeply rooted in the minds of industrial managers and capitalists, that the President distrusts them, that he disbelieves in their principles, that he has no real sympathy with their purposes, and that, therefore, he makes concessions only because for the moment he finds it expedient to make them.

Such concessions would "not overcome the main obstacle to the general revival of enterprise; they will not remove the feeling that the system of private enterprise is merely tolerated, that the system is merely allowed to exist under a government which in its heart has condemned it." While not a "full-blown socialist," Roosevelt's mood was "almost invariably anti-capitalistic."[29] Or, as Dorothy Thompson put it, the New Deal was "sadistically anti-capitalist—though dependent on the capitalistic system!"[30] The only way, then, to promote recovery was through the presentation of convincing evidence of a change of heart on Roosevelt's part, or through a shift of the balance of power within the government from the executive branch to Congress.

An exchange with reporters at his November 23 press conference suggested that Roosevelt's nonchalance about the deteriorating economic situation was based in part on ignorance. When asked by a reporter if the government's statistics on the economic situation coincided with the "rather alarming" state of the New York *Times* business index, Roosevelt admitted that he had not seen the government economic statistics for "about three weeks."[31] That it might have been appropriate for the president to review the state of the economy before sending his instructions to the special session of Congress no doubt occurred to some of the newsmen present. Soon after the press conference, in the midst of the recession, and with three weeks remaining in the special session of Congress, Roosevelt departed on yet another of his frequent vacations. Away from Washington and reality, Roosevelt apparently convinced himself that conditions in the economy were not as bad as they were represented to be, and that there was no reason to moderate his attacks on business. On December 8 he told Morgenthau that "after all, we are following the middle of the road program and *if business continues this drive on the Administration* they will simply push the Administration more to the left."[32] Thus, Roosevelt had apparently not abandoned his earlier disposition to view the recession as a test of wills between himself and business. The answer, presumably, was to deal severely with business for creating the recession.

A NEW SEARCH FOR SCAPEGOATS

Early in December a Gallup poll found that 58 percent of Americans believed that the Roosevelt administration was entirely (19 percent) or partially (39 percent) to blame for the recession.[33] Roosevelt, meanwhile, had resumed his search for scapegoats. In November he blamed "monopolies" for raising prices and triggering the recession. The Washington *Post* wondered if it might not be more productive to look at the effects of Roosevelt's policies on the wage-price spiral.[34] In December Roosevelt lashed out at a new scapegoat, now blaming the recession on the "fear" psychology that had been created by newspapers throughout the country.[35] A businessman echoed what others had already told Roosevelt, when he wrote that, on the contrary, "the fear which has fixed upon the country has been caused by these schemes to lodge dictatorial powers in the executive branch of the government."[36] Another letter writer told Roosevelt: "You are the one Mr. President that business is afraid of."[37] A similar Roosevelt charge that excessive inventories were at fault for the recession prompted the obvious response that excessive inventories were a symptom of the business recession, not its cause.[38] Everything, it seemed, was to blame for the recession except Roosevelt's policies. A bank president in Youngstown, Ohio, wrote Roosevelt: "Steel operations in this district are at *fourteen per cent* [of capacity]. . . . Why aren't you honest and big enough to admit that the experiments you tried in all sincerity have failed? Why are you going to such lengths to set up an alibi?"[39]

Late in December, Assistant Attorney General Robert Jackson and Interior Secretary Harold Ickes delivered speeches attacking "monopolies" that further struck at business confidence. This latest search for scapegoats was, the New

York *Herald-Tribune* observed, like throwing business "a millstone in place of a life preserver."[40] Such speeches, however, represented a vacuum in the White House caused by the absence of any real presidential leadership. Former brain trusters Adolf Berle and Charles Taussig met in mid-December after the latter had talked with Roosevelt. Berle recorded in his diary: "The economic situation is getting worse by the minute; the President has no particular ideas as to what to do nor has any of his group."[41] *The Economist* noted that Roosevelt's "leadership has almost lapsed." He had "been caught off his political and economic balance, and in both spheres he is still floundering."[42] The *Commercial and Financial Chronicle* concluded that Roosevelt had not yet even "reached the stage of admitting that there is anything wrong with the state of business."[43] Columnist Franklyn Waltman found Washington in an unusual "state of ennui," with "little enthusiasm for anything," and "virtually everybody . . . bored with everyone else and everything. No one seems to know where we are going. No one seems to care." As a result, "the entire machinery of the Federal Government appears to be stilled." Meanwhile, nothing was being done to turn the recession around.[44] As Adolf Berle put it: "There is no program in Washington and the President has not got any. He is waiting for the logic of circumstances to appear, which in practice means either that the situation becomes acute or that a group emerges whose strength creates logic."[45]

The special session of Congress, the calling of which had been such a blow to business and investor confidence, adjourned just before Christmas. None of Roosevelt's legislation had been passed by the special session, its sole accomplishment being, as Frank Kent noted, "the passage of a bill providing mileage for members and other expenses." It was, Kent observed, "a practically unparalleled performance," which emphasized the fact that "Mr. Roosevelt, with a four-to-one party majority, has lost control of Congress."[46] On the negative side, however, the special session had done nothing to aid business, and the uncertainties of Roosevelt's legislative package now would continue into the regular session of Congress during election year 1938.[47]

A CONFUSED PRESIDENT

Roosevelt's State of the Union message on January 3, 1938, was generally conciliatory. In it the president distinguished between "the overwhelming majority of business men and bankers" who intended "to be good citizens," and the "small minority" who had engaged in "practices which are dishonest or definitely harmful to society." It was the abuses by this minority, he said, that his administration was committed to end.[48] Press reaction was generally favorable, the New York *Times* finding the speech "reasonable in its objectives, praiseworthy in its tone and fair in its treatment of those who disagree with the specific points in the Administration's program."[49] Others, however, found little of substance in the speech. Roosevelt had carefully ignored the subject that was foremost in everyone's mind—the new recession. Instead, he had devoted much of his speech to pleas for all of his 1937 legislative demands.[50] A few days later the New York *Times* business index revealed a sharp drop for the first week of January, bringing it near the low point reached during the 1934 recession.[51]

Soon after his speech, Roosevelt confused businessmen and newsmen alike, with his observations on overproduction. In apparent contradiction of the recent Ickes-Jackson diatribes against monopoly, Roosevelt now proposed that industrial heads should curb overproduction by sitting around a table with government representatives to estimate the needs of the market "for the next six months or a year, so that they won't overproduce." But when asked by a reporter how the "estimated annual production" would then be allocated among the units of the industry, Roosevelt responded: "Don't do that—keep competition."[52] How such conferences could eliminate overproduction if each unit in an industry was free to produce and compete as much as it liked for the estimated market was not apparent to most observers. Roosevelt's ramblings only seemed further evidence of the confusion in his thinking. At his January 14 news conference, the president further revealed the shallowness of his knowledge of business and the economy in a discussion of holding companies.[53]

Noting the ripples that these presidential observations had sent through the business community, Franklyn Waltman wrote: "You cannot properly run a business if you are apprehensive over every press conference the President holds or every speech some subordinate in the Administration makes."[54] David Lawrence agreed that "confidence in the business world cannot be built by such impromptu discussions of vital matters which the President gives in his press conferences."[55] Frank Kent commented on "the extraordinary lack of stability about the President." His actions since the start of the recession had "enhanced confusion, baffled most impartial observers and dismayed the more intelligent of his intimate friends."[56] "So far as broad policies and general intentions go," wrote the New York *Herald-Tribune*, "Roosevelt might be any kitten chasing its tail."[57] Since Roosevelt was inclined to blurt out answers to press questions without thinking, David Lawrence suggested that "all questions be handed in to the White House by correspondents at least three or four hours before . . . the press conference" in order to give the president time to consider his answers more carefully.[58]

Sadly, Roosevelt's diatribe against holding companies torpedoed some promising efforts in the direction of government-business cooperation.[59] One such effort had begun in early December at the suggestion of former brain truster Charles Taussig, and included Adolf Berle, Rexford Tugwell, investment banker Thomas Lamont, labor leader John L. Lewis, industrialist Owen D. Young, and labor leader Philip Murray. The group agreed on a tentative program and were invited to meet with Roosevelt at the White House on January 5.[60] Tugwell, however, learned that Roosevelt had something very different in mind from the cooperation that the group was advocating. Roosevelt had told Tugwell that "he thought we could scare these people into doing something." This revelation of Roosevelt's attitude, combined with the antimonopoly diatribes of Jackson and

Ickes, convinced the group that their efforts were wasted.[61] Taussig, however, was determined to carry through the conference with Roosevelt, and the group met with him in mid-January. Afterward, the group adjourned to Young's hotel room and roughed out the composition of a possible committee to recommend policies to Roosevelt for dealing with the recession.[62]

Meanwhile, another major conference of businessmen with Roosevelt had preceded by one day the labor-business-former New Dealers group's visit to the White House. Alfred P. Sloan, Jr. of General Motors; Ernest T. Weir of National Steel; Lewis H. Brown of Johns-Manville; M. W. Clement of the Pennsylvania Railroad; and Colby M. Chester of General Foods met with Roosevelt at the instigation of Donald Richberg who attended as "unofficial observer." The conferees came away impressed that Roosevelt was interested in cooperation with business. For their part, the businessmen expressed a desire to work with the administration in promoting recovery. But Richberg despaired that any of these efforts would come to fruition, since it was the next day, one hour before Roosevelt met with the Lewis-Lamont group, that the president lashed out at holding companies in his press conference.[63]

Richberg regarded his efforts as "ruined" by Roosevelt's "loose talking" at the press conference. The prospect, he told Raymond Clapper, was for only more and more relief spending to meet the needs of the growing number of unemployed. He lashed out at Corcoran, Cohen, Jackson, Oliphant, and others in the administration as "tadpoles that hadn't lost their tails, yet telling business how to behave," and told Clapper that the "left wing group keep[s] telling [Roosevelt] that [Senators] Norris and LaFollette don't like to see him kissing big business, etc. That scares him and he swings to [the] left to placate them." Richberg wished Roosevelt was as frightened of the economic situation as businessmen were, but he gave Clapper the impression that the forces pushing for business-government cooperation had been defeated, and that the Corcoran-Cohen radical atavists would now "move in." Clapper confided to his diary that Roosevelt's press conference performances had caused him, too, to "practically give up hope" of Roosevelt "being able to pull us out of this hole," and had "caused me practically to lose confidence" in him. Roosevelt, he wrote, seemed unable to "handle himself with any consistency or to concentrate on one line long enough to make it work."[64] Ironically, only a few days earlier Clapper had written one of his typically pro-Roosevelt columns in which he had assured businessmen that they had nothing to fear from Roosevelt.

The Lamont-Lewis group, however, pressed on with its efforts to furnish Roosevelt with an advisory committee, even though they found themselves coming under "heavy fire from many quarters, including, among others, Bob Jackson."[65] Late in January, Taussig told Berle that "there has been no end of a split in Washington over our maneuvers with Lewis and Lamont. Corcoran and Cohen think their position is threatened and have started a row." By early February the whole effort had come to an end.[66] The original New Dealers having grown more realistic about the needs of the economy, they no longer fit into an administration increasingly dominated by the radical atavists of the Brandeis-Frankfurter school.

In the meantime, Roosevelt had turned once again, as in 1935, to the Business Advisory Council, where, Joseph Alsop and Robert Kintner reported, fully 40 of the 50 members were threatening to resign if Roosevelt did not disassociate himself from the speeches of Jackson and Ickes.[67] The group met with Roosevelt on January 19, after which W. Averell Harriman, the chairman, issued a press statement that was full of common-sense criticism of Roosevelt's policies such as had been enunciated by other critics.[68] Like the Richberg and Lewis-Lamont groups, the BAC came away from this meeting with Roosevelt impressed with what they thought was the good will and open-mindedness of the president.[69] Roosevelt's conclusions from the various meetings with businessmen were, however, quite different from theirs. While Roosevelt told Morgenthau that he thought the meetings had been worthwhile, he added that he found "that most of them, as far as their knowledge of Government is concerned, have the intelligence of eighth grade school boys." He also told Morgenthau that he had let the businessmen "understand that if they continue to attack him he is going to attack back and, he said, nothing that the Government has said equals the bitter attacks of business on him.'"[70] What Roosevelt apparently refused to understand was that it was less the words that emanated from the administration that disturbed business, than the legislation harmful to business that accompanied them. And if the businessmen had only an "eighth grade" knowledge of government, surely Roosevelt's understanding of the economy was much lower.

Writing about the "nonchalance" of Roosevelt late in January 1938, Walter Lippmann observed:

So far as I can make out the President not only seeks to give the impression that he does not think the depression is serious; he actually does not think it is serious. If there were not the disconcerting figures and charts, and the very worried look which so many of his important advisers wear, one might suppose that the economists and business men and the labor leaders and bankers are the victims of some kind of mass hallucination and that Mr. Roosevelt alone is too sane to be stampeded.

Lippmann concluded that Roosevelt was so prejudiced against businessmen that "almost by reflex action the President is disposed not to believe anything that he hears from the business community, particularly from the New York business community."[71]

Raymond Moley found Roosevelt's difficulties rooted in his choice of advisers:

Official advisers have been about as effective in assisting the President revive business as were Walt Disney's seven dwarfs in resuscitating Snow White. He has been getting advice on economic problems from young lawyers whose firsthand knowledge of running business has been limited to running the college law review. Then again he has been getting advice from dogmatists who want to make the world-that-is conform to a picture of a world-that-never-was. In between, he has been getting advice from the spokesmen of isolated pressure groups who are moved by no interest excepting their own. Peppering this has been political advice which knows neither law, economics, nor, it would seem of late, common sense.

Out of this witches' brew has arisen a horrendous vapor which, despite the fact that it may be called a moral climate, is actually an atmosphere in which business enterprise can do little but curl up and die. There have been too many lawyers thinking about economics, too many economists thinking about law, and too many politicians thinking about votes.[72]

Breckinridge Long, who had campaigned with Roosevelt in 1936, noted in his diary that the Cohen-Corcoran-Jackson circle of Brandeis-Frankfurter advisers was "a reckless, dangerous aggregation with lots of opportunities for publicity and plenty of influence with the President. They seem to permeate his atmosphere and to suffocate the presence of former advisers and circumscribe the limits of his contacts."[73] *Newsweek* observed that even friendly columnists had "become openly worried over the President's course," Raymond Clapper having written that it was "a good time for President Roosevelt to stop and count ten."[74]

CHAPTER 13

The Second Roosevelt Depression, II, 1938

SEEKING SIMPLE ANSWERS

As the recession continued only Treasury Secretary Henry Morgenthau seemed willing to confront it. He recommended to Roosevelt that he request an additional $250 million from Congress for putting another 650,000 unemployed on work relief and found the president enthusiastic.[1] He was also looking into tax revision and "re-examining everything that the Treasury is doing that affects business." He hoped by mid-February to be able to couple the announcement of an additional $250 million for relief and changes in the gold sterilization policy "with some kind of announcement that we have broken the log jam in the tax field."[2] Outside the administration, most criticism still centered on the undistributed profits tax, and on the "psychological" value for business that repeal or revision of the tax would provide.[3] What critics failed to realize was that, aside from its symbolic value, the repeal or substantial modification of that tax could do little to promote recovery now in a material sense. The tax had already done its damage, and money that might well have been spent on modernization and expansion, during the "boom" of late 1936 and early 1937 to aid in the transition from government to private spending, was not likely to be spent on such things now that the economy was back in the depths of a recession.

Bombarded with criticism from business leaders and unwilling to accept their recommendations, Roosevelt sought a more supportive business forum by calling a conference of supposedly friendly small businessmen to be held in Washington. Not only were the delegates hand-picked by the administration, but the agenda of the conference was also to be directed by the New Dealers.[4] Clearly, the

White House expected that a contrast would be furnished between the critics from "big" business and support of the New Deal by "small" businessmen. Unfortunately, the small businessmen proved to be neither as responsive to administration dictation nor as sympathetic to the New Deal as expected. While the administration tried to "buy" their support through the prospect of government loans, the small businessmen lustily cheered the declaration of a small-town retailer from North Dakota that "the small business man does not need a loan nearly as much as he does to be let alone."[5] The resolutions of the small business conference revealed the same complaints about Roosevelt's policies that had been uttered by other business leaders and economists. Arthur Krock suggested that the result of the conference must "finally persuade [Roosevelt] that at least 90 per cent of American business men are severely critical of the methods of the New Deal."[6] *Business Week* wondered, "if these people are almost solidly against [Roosevelt's] program, who is for it?"[7] When the Commerce Department tried to rewrite the resolutions of the conference to make them less critical of the Roosevelt administration, the action only alienated businessmen even more.[8]

As revealed by the attempt to "bribe" the small businessmen's conference by dangling the prospect of government loans, Roosevelt had begun to view the recession as susceptible to solution through granting federal credit to business. When Donald Richberg met with Roosevelt in mid-March, he found the president had a new scapegoat. Roosevelt was "complaining bitterly that private capital [was] not being put out." The president pointed to a stack of papers and told Richberg they were "proposals by industries for expansion which had come down here because they could not get private capital." Roosevelt told Richberg that they were "good propositions but bankers and capitalists just won't advance money and let things get started." How Roosevelt could tell a sound proposal from an unsound one was not explained, but he told Richberg that he would give the bankers and capitalists more time—"perhaps sixty days"—but that he couldn't wait indefinitely, and "if private finance would not do the job then the government would have to."[9]

But this scapegoat was no better than the others, as Jesse Jones, head of the Reconstruction Finance Corporation, made clear to Morgenthau. Jones noted that in the past two or three years the RFC had received nearly 7,000 applications for business loans, had authorized 2,727, and, after cancellations of one kind or another, had loaned only $104 million to 1,465 borrowers. Moreover, the RFC had received no new applications in the past six months, so obviously they were not the source of the "stack of papers" on Roosevelt's desk.[10] Moreover, William O. Douglas, head of the SEC, told Morgenthau that business needed "junior or equity money, not an increase in debt. Lending more money to industry will not pull us out of the slump." Sounding very much like Roosevelt's business and economist critics, Douglas added that while it was desirable to increase purchasing power, it was impossible to "pull out of the depression by that method." What was needed was "the opening up of the capital markets and getting a regular flow of funds back into industry.'' He found the reasons for the lack of a capital market in "the volume of tax exempt securities,'' which constituted "a huge reservoir of money all dammed up''; the capital gains tax, which was "a psychological dam''; and the paralysis of the "investment bankers' machinery.'' He told Morgenthau that there was "only $60 to $100 million of capital in the investment capital business. This is wholly inadequate. Bank affiliates were properly taken out of the business but have not been replaced.''[11] This latter was a point often made by Thomas Lamont.

THE DIMENSIONS OF THE COLLAPSE

Meanwhile, the economy continued its downward march. The League of Nations' *World Economic Survey* for 1937/38 listed the percentage of 1937 industrial production, compared to 1929, for 23 nations of the world. Of the 23, 19 showed a higher rate of recovery than the United States. Only three trailed the United States: the Netherlands, France (which had flirted with its own "New Deal''), and Poland. And as 1938 began the direction of the U.S. economy was down, not up.[12] On January 10, *Barron's* economic index showed business at 58 percent of normal, the economy having lost 63 percent of the recovery made between March 1933 and December 1936. At 58 percent, the figure was only a couple of points above that in October 1932, before Roosevelt's election.[13] And the business indexes continued to inch downward.[14]

On February 1, John Maynard Keynes addressed yet another letter to Roosevelt. Ascribing the "recovery'' of 1935–1937 to the New Deal's easy credit and pump-priming activities, he told the president:

Unless . . . the above factors were supplemented by others in due course, the present slump could have been predicted with absolute certainty . . . .

Now one had hoped that the needed supplementary factors would be organized in time. It was obvious what these were—namely increased investment in durable goods such as housing, public utilities and transport. One was optimistic about this because in the United States at the present time the opportunities, indeed, the necessity for such developments were unexampled. Can your administration escape criticism for the failure of these factors to mature?

Keynes described Roosevelt's handling of the housing problem as "really wicked,'' and criticized his antiutility policies as "chasing the utilities around the lot every week.'' Like Roosevelt's domestic critics, Keynes emphasized the importance of reviving the capital market, and especially "the revival of sources of demand'' for capital. To soften his criticism, Keynes ended by voicing approval of Roosevelt's agricultural policies, the SEC, collective bargaining, and wage and hour regulation.[15] The principal thrust of Keynes' letter, however, was clear: Roosevelt had failed to provide for the transition to private investment by ignoring steps that might have assisted that transition and following, instead, policies that had discouraged it and had been detrimental to business confidence. *The Economist* described the dimensions of the 1937 collapse:

In the post-war collapse, the index of production fell from its peak of 116 in January, 1920, to its extreme bottom of 74 in July, 1921, in eighteen months, which seemed a violent decline; in 1929, the index of production fell from 123 in August to 99 in December; and this, too, seemed a violent decline. Yet the fall from 117 in August to 84 in December [1937] was larger than that in the autumn of 1929; and in four months was almost as great as in the post-war collapse [which took 18 months].

People refuse to believe it, and the commonest way of expressing such disbelief is to resort to euphemisms in describing it. The word "depression" is absolutely taboo; only such terms as "recession," "reaction," or "slackness" are allowed.[16]

By contrast with the experience of the United States, the *Washington Review* of the Chamber of Commerce pointed out that the index of industrial production had risen in Canada from 99.8 to 104.8 at the same time that the U.S. rate was plummeting.[17]

Economists and others continued to search for explanations for the 1937–1938 downturn. Marriner Eccles faulted the veterans' bonus in 1936 for playing a large part in throwing recovery "out of balance" by creating an "inflationary psychology."[18] Three New Deal economists blamed the upsurge in costs and prices in 1937, which had led to excessive inventory buildup and forward ordering and a reversal of the promising revival in construction. Purchasing power in the hands of consumers had failed to keep pace with the new price levels because of the decline in construction and in government deficit spending. Predictably, they did not fault the taxing or regulatory policies of the Roosevelt administration, but they did recommend revision of the undistributed profits tax.[19] Brookings Institution economist Harold G. Moulton blamed "the aggressive labor movement" for "destroying the existing balance" between wage rates and the prices of manufactured goods, thus "altering the whole course of events."[20] Economist Leonard Ayres summarized the reasons given for the downturn, but as for the stimulus behind the abrupt collapse in October he pinpointed Roosevelt's calling of the special session of Congress.[21]

Others faulted Roosevelt's actions in preventing the transition from government to private spending, particularly his tax policies.[22] Early in March, Walter Lippmann provided a clear exposition of the taxation problem, based on the study, *Economic Consequences of Recent American Tax Policy*, by Gerhard Colm and Fritz Lehman, two members of the so-called University in Exile. Lippmann wrote that according to the Colm-Lehman analysis it was the *combined* effect of high income taxes and the undistributed profits tax that had "throttled" new enterprise and the expansion of business. High income taxes had discouraged the wealthy from risking their money in any investments other than government bonds or other gilt-edged securities. When deprived of capital from such sources in the past, businesses had been able, at least, to plow back their own profits for expansion. But with the undistributed profits tax, that source of business expansion was also penalized by the government. "Thus," Lippmann wrote, "the only two main sources of adventurous capital—the savings of the rich and the savings of corporations—have *both* been closed, or in any event seriously restricted, by the combined effect of the recent tax laws." Far from encouraging the transition from government to private spending, Roosevelt's tax policies had, according to this analysis, made it nearly impossible.[23]

THE INTRACTABLE MR. ROOSEVELT

None of these adverse effects of his tax laws seemed to penetrate Roosevelt's mind, however, In a telephone conversation with Morgenthau early in March, Roosevelt's concern with the tax revision movement then under way in Congress was that: (1) any revision must raise approximately the same revenue as existing taxes; (2) any revision should improve the condition only of "the little fellow"; (3) the "principle of the undistributed or capital gains tax" must be retained; (4) the undistributed profits tax must not be repealed lest it restore "the old tax evasion."[24] Roosevelt's concerns in any tax revision were clearly not the same as those of businessmen, economists, and other critics of the effects of the existing tax laws. Thus, while Adolf Berle found Secretary of State Cordell Hull and Undersecretary Sumner Welles anxious to bring him into the administration as a brain truster to develop a constructive economic program for Roosevelt, Berle told Welles "quite frankly what was needed was not a brain truster, but a priest or a psychiatrist, meaning thereby that what we had to do was to change the habit of mind at Washington which is a singularly unreal place."[25]

In fact, the "unreal place" tended to be wherever Roosevelt happened to be at the moment. Late in March Roosevelt spoke in Georgia where he lashed out against the "feudalistic few" who were thwarting his administration. In that speech he served notice upon members of his own party, as well as the opposition, that he intended to make the New Deal an issue in the 1938 elections. The speech had, one critic noted, "established, in the minds of most operators, brokers and investors, the certainty that the President will go on with all of the ideas, good and bad, which are thought to be fundamental causes of the current business depression; and that New Deal tactics of setting class against class to insure votes will not be altered."[26] The 100 stocks in the New York *Herald-Tribune* index dropped to their lowest point since April 3, 1935, and the composite for 30 rails reached the lowest since the bottom of the depression in July 1932.[27] Raymond Clapper found matters "about as confused as they were in the last two years of Hoover's term," with the entire country "feeling Roosevelt's indecision and floundering."[28] Where taxes were concerned, however, the president showed no indecision. On the contrary, all of Roosevelt's influence was being exerted on Congress to retain most of the destructive features of the undistributed profits and capital gains taxes. The *Wall Street Journal* concluded:

"It all adds up to the fact that the hope of the country for pulling out of this depression lies in Congress, not in the White House."[29]

In April the Senate passed its version of a tax reform bill in a form objectionable to the White House.[30] Clearly the Senate was determined to act in behalf of economic recovery even over the objections of the administration. Roosevelt talked with Democratic members of the House, which had passed a tax reform bill more to his liking, and urged them to "try to trade as best they could with the Senate Committee," and if the Senate would not compromise, he told them, he would think seriously of vetoing the bill.[31] The end product of the House-Senate conference committee was a compromise that retained the principle of the undistributed profits tax but reduced it to inconsequential levels. Roosevelt was torn between signing the bill or allowing it to become law without his signature.[32] In the end, Roosevelt decided to allow the tax bill to become law without his signature and to state his objections to it. His decision, he said, was to allow the bill to become law, and then to press for a new tax bill more to his liking in 1939.[33]

Clearly, the revision of the undistributed profits tax in the 1938 law could have little or no effect on business sentiment so long as businessmen knew that Roosevelt intended to slap them with it again in 1939! The New York *Times* criticized Roosevelt for missing "a great opportunity" when he accepted "only in the most grudging manner the one important measure passed by Congress in this session that would help to make . . . recovery possible."[34] The New York *Herald-Tribune* agreed: "To differ over measures is one thing; to sabotage measures consistently constructed for one purpose because they happen not to agree with one's prestige on other matters is a very different thing."[35]

Meanwhile, the government reorganization bill was again being debated in Congress. That bill had been so emasculated since its introduction in the 1937 session that even critics recognized it "would be a pretty good bill" if in any other hands than Roosevelt's.[36] Much of the opposition to the bill was clearly based on distrust of the president. As Raymond Clapper wrote, the opposition was the result "of a growing lack of confidence in Roosevelt. The protest is, I suspect, not so much a protest against reorganization as against Roosevelt personally."[37] By the end of March, the charge that Roosevelt sought through the reorganization bill to establish a dictatorship had become so compelling that the president of the United States felt obliged to awaken reporters at 1 a.m. so that they could be handed a copy of a letter he had written to an unnamed person disclaiming any intention of becoming a dictator.[38]

Still, Roosevelt remained the principal issue in the debate over the reorganization bill. The *Kiplinger Washington Letter* wrote, early in April: "The main issue is politics—to be FOR or AGAINST the President. That issue determines the vote—vote of confidence or vote of distrust." Kiplinger found the "practical politicians" in the administration trying to restrain Roosevelt:

They say they have him "halfway in hand." They talk among themselves about his "instability," "emotional outbursts," and "lack of judgment." They make no bones about his being "rattled," "dramatic," "vindictive." They say public reaction has set in against the President's growing habit of telling people what to think, how to vote, and writers what to write.[39]

On the eve of the vote, the Democratic Speaker of the House, William Bankhead, told congressmen: "If you vote to recommit the bill . . . you will say 'The House of Representatives by Democratic votes repudiates the President of the United States.' " Roosevelt was "repudiated," with 108 of the 204 votes against his bill cast by Democrats.[40]

The New York *Times* pointed out that the vote had not been against the bill, but against Roosevelt. It was, moreover, an effort to "promote the recovery of business" by rebuking the president.[41] The Hartford *Courant* viewed the defeat as "even more crushing" for Roosevelt than that in the court packing attempt, for this bill had not been "defeated because of its demerits, but because Congress has lost confidence in the leadership of the President."[42]

It was only a few days after this blow to his leadership that Roosevelt took up his proposals for renewed pump priming with Morgenthau. Morgenthau objected because Roosevelt's proposal seemed "so helter-skelter and doesn't seem to be any concrete plan," whereupon the president got in "a very excited mood." Morgenthau confided to his diary:

It seems to me that he has lost all sense of proportion. I stressed the fact very strongly that if we started a spending program now and overlook the difficult things such as railroads and public utilities that we would be right back where we are within six to nine months—only worse off.

Morgenthau found it shocking that Roosevelt had worked out the spending program "without consulting a single person at the Treasury, including his Director of the Budget," and had, therefore, "absolutely no idea how much the thing is going to cost," nor did Roosevelt "seem to worry or care."[43]

The next day, when Roosevelt laid out his program for Hopkins, congressional leaders, and others, Morgenthau dropped a bombshell when he told them it would increase the 1939 budget deficit by $3.5 billion. Afterward, Roosevelt berated him for bringing up the prospective deficit, but Morgenthau defended it as his duty. Morgenthau began to consider resigning in protest against the return of deficit spending.[44] His adviser, Dr. Jacob D. Viner, did resign, in part because of the spending policy, but also because he saw no evidence that Roosevelt intended to "eliminate the factors which made our recovery only a halting and incomplete one, and which now have forced us into a renewal of severe depression."[45] But Morgenthau did not resign, although he continued to entertain the thought in late April.

Meanwhile, the economy continued its downward slide. By early May 1938 the *Barron's* business index had slid to 53.7, lower than in October 1932, and very near the 46.7 of the banking crisis in 1933. The economy had by now "erased all the recovery gains it had made since the late spring of 1933, just following the bank holiday."[46] The New York *Times* index dipped to 75.4 in late April, the lowest figure since the week ended May 6, 1933, lower, even than in the depths of the 1934 recession.[47] Yet, as Walter Lippmann wrote in early April, "incredible as it sounds, the New Deal does not have any program, good, bad, or indifferent, which even pretends to have any relation to the economic crisis. One would scarcely know from the President's utterances that there is a crisis."[48] *Barron's* wrote: "Somehow the Democratic jokes about the Hoover depression and 'prosperity just around the corner' don't seem so funny as they did $18,000,000,000 ago."[49] The New York *Journal of Commerce* reported the amazed chuckles of a group of agricultural editors after they were told by Roosevelt that the farm situation was greatly improved. They had earlier been shown charts that traced the farm index from 86 down to 62, following the trend of the industrial decline.[50] Such a display of ignorance of the real situation in the country hardly bolstered Roosevelt's prestige with those who came into contact with it.

By this point Roosevelt had only one course open to him that was acceptable to his temperament. Incapable of making the concessions necessary to generate genuine recovery, because of his pride and prejudices, Roosevelt could only turn once again to spending in an attempt to stimulate yet another temporary and artificial recovery that, as Morgenthau had told him, would in less than a year leave the country back where it had started with greater debt and none of its problems solved. Rumors of a reversion to the old bankrupt remedies began to spread in April. After Roosevelt explained his new spending program to the nation via a fireside chat, the Washington *Post* wrote: "The proposal is to counter the present depression by the methods which were instrumental in creating it. Here is bankrupt statesmanship."[51] The New York *Herald-Tribune* found the atmosphere of Roosevelt's speech "bedside rather than fireside." It added: "Throughout, Mr. Roosevelt acted like a man who had refused to face the truth until very recently and had still to come to grips with reality. The superficiality of the argument went far to confirm the view that Mr. Roosevelt has never thoroughly mastered any of the fundamental issues over which he has skimmed so blithely."[52]

Barron's concluded from events in Washington that "one thing stands in bold relief: The President will fight it out on the New Deal line if it takes all summer— even if the fight ruins him politically, and the country economically."[53] Walter Lippmann agreed that Roosevelt had shown himself "unwilling to liquidate the commitments and the grudges which are so alarming and so discouraging to investors and business men." Although Roosevelt's subordinates had "recently lapsed into silence," Lippmann found that

the President himself continues to manifest his personal hostility to business men as a class. Thus, enterprise lives in the depressing atmosphere of mere toleration mixed with barely concealed unfriendliness. With all the real difficulties that beset business arising out of wage costs, taxes, and the general confusion of a warlike world, this sense of political hostility at the center of government is a most destructive influence.[54]

By early May, columnist Ray Tucker found that "almost every distinguished Democratic chieftain has now broken with Mr. Roosevelt on major policies. Never before in American history has a Chief Executive been so utterly repudiated by the men who should be serving as his front-line figures, or at least concealing their differences from the gaze of the public." Not only were the Democratic leaders insisting on a "live-and-let-live attitude toward big and little business—toward productive sources of employment," but their position had "caught the imagination of the public." The protests of Democratic leaders, Tucker wrote, reflected "a conviction that the President heads a wrecking rather than a rescuing squad."[55]

A Gallup poll found 79 percent of the people in favor of assistance to business through reduction of taxes, and only 21 percent in favor of renewed spending.[56] Many economists also expressed disapproval of the resumption of deficit spending when it was unaccompanied by positive measures to stimulate enterprise. Professor Neal Carothers of Lehigh University described it as "pouring good money after bad," while Professor Walter Spahr of New York University pointed out that the pump didn't need priming so much as it needed Roosevelt to release the pump handle that he had "tied down by a series of unfortunate governmental policies and acts." Professor E. W. Kemmerer of Princeton argued that reform of Roosevelt's programs "would give the country a quicker, sounder, and more enduring recovery" than would spending. Professor Charles S. Tippetts of the University of Pittsburgh agreed that the spending program was economically unsound, but perhaps "politically unavoidable," since 1938 was an election year and Roosevelt needed to at least create the illusion of improvement before the end of October.[57]

ROOSEVELT REJUVENATED

Early in May Roosevelt's battered prestige was rejuvenated by the results of a Florida primary election. In a campaign fought over the New Deal, the pro-Roosevelt incumbent, Claude Pepper, was elected. In retrospect, it seems incredible that a primary victory by an incumbent should have so influenced the psychology in Washington, but there is no doubt that it did. As Mark Sullivan described it, the victory had "the same effect as a blast of Florida wind on a thermometer."

At once Mr. Roosevelt and the New Dealers determined to force the fighting on both fronts, in the primaries throughout the country, and in Congress. The two lines of attack would reinforce each other. New Deal aggressiveness in the primaries would help New Deal measures in Congress; New Deal aggressiveness in Congress would help New Deal candidates in the primaries.[58]

The New Dealers now resurrected the wages and hours bill in Congress, which only weeks before had seemed to have no prospect of passage. And Democrats in the House and Senate, looking forward to their own primary campaigns in 1938, felt it necessary to heed the Florida result. Nevertheless, the situation in Florida differed greatly from most of the rest of the country, for it was a state that had suffered very little from the Roosevelt depression of 1937–1938. Employment had, in fact, increased there in the face of the decline for the country at large. Voters there, then, could not be expected to be influenced by the same factors as those in other states. But despite this, one journal found "disheartening indications now that the President is more influential in Congress at this moment than he has been for a good while past."[59] By the end of May, Walter Lippmann found in the new receptiveness by Congress for Roosevelt's legislation indications "that the prime objective at the moment is not recovery, not reform, but reelection."[60]

DOES ROOSEVELT WANT RECOVERY?

By mid-June the *Barron's* business index had dropped to 50, only 1.5 above "the historic low-point of six years ago." It was now below the figure for October 1932, and all of the recovery gains since May 1933 had been wiped out.[61] The New York *Times* observed early in the month that cotton was selling at "the lowest level in history in terms of the old gold dollar."[62] The New York *Times* business index remained at 75.1 in mid-June, the lowest point since May 1933.[63]

The new lows to which the economy was falling, combined with Roosevelt's intransigence in the face of criticism of his policies, led more people to begin seriously to question whether the president of the United States was genuinely interested in economic recovery. In May the New York *Herald-Tribune* editorialized: "The longer the Roosevelt depression continues and the more muddled the New Deal policies become, the less confidence any American can feel that a sincere desire for recovery prevails in the high command of the Administration." There was "no serious doubt as to what should be done," it observed, but

the Administration . . . spends its time inventing new ways to harass business and prevent recovery. No one is simple enough to view the spending program as in any serious way related to the revival of business. It is simply an ingenious method of compelling future generations of Americans to purchase next November's election for Mr. Roosevelt.

We return therefore to our original question. Does the New Deal really want recovery?

What does the New Deal really want? A democratic nation, prosperous in its own right, and running itself by its own initiative and enterprise? Or a nation of dependents, living by grace of a bureaucracy at Washington, fit meat for a Duce or a Fuehrer? Before Congress votes any more grants of power to the President, we hope it will consider the answer to these two questions.[64]

Amos Pinchot was convinced that "Roosevelt and his close advisors are not out for real recovery, and that this charge must be made and substantiated."[65]

Forbes found in mid-June that there was "increasing discussion in Washington on the question, 'Does Mr. Roosevelt want recovery, or would he prefer his larger objectives in government, through prolonged depression?' "[66] The secretary of the Illinois Council of Small Business Men wired Roosevelt to call attention to all of the newsletter and newspaper articles that were voicing these suspicions and asked him if it were true.[67] Roosevelt's secretary, Marvin McIntyre, responded that the president was eager for recovery.[68] Only slightly less remarkable than Roosevelt's earlier denial of any dictatorial ambitions was this necessity now to refute charges that he did not want recovery from the depression.

An upward movement began at last in the economic indexes during the second half of June, coinciding almost exactly with the adjournment of Congress. Other factors, however, seem also to have contributed to the revival of confidence. Early in May, a decision of the Supreme Court struck at the work of the National Labor Relations Board, giving evidence that the court had not, in fact, become a rubber stamp for Roosevelt.[69] The rejection by Congress of the reorganization bill also helped to build business confidence, and even the passage of Roosevelt's spending bill and two other bills approved in the closing days of the session—the wages and hours bill and a monopoly investigation bill—did little to undermine business confidence. The former, especially, had been so thoroughly amended since its introduction in 1937 that it bore little resemblance to the bill Roosevelt wanted.[70] Hugh Johnson said of it: "I don't know how it could have been a milder and more flexible measure without being just an empty gesture."[71] In sum, Frank Kent found that in its two regular and one special sessions the 75th Congress had "spent more money, indulged in more talk and passed fewer laws than any . . . in recent years." It had rejected most of what Roosevelt wanted, modified what it did pass, and enacted a tax revision bill over his objections. In all, Congress had begun to show remarkable independence.[72]

There were also other encouraging signs, but none so striking as the evidence that public opinion was rapidly tiring of Roosevelt's attacks on business and the consequences of those attacks for economic recovery and employment. As *Forbes* put it: "The discouraging first half of the year has brought at least one ray of encouragement for responsible citizens: all yardsticks for measuring public sentiment reveal that President Roosevelt's anti-business policies are losing their popularity."[73] The head of the U.S. Chamber of Commerce agreed that "from every quarter one hears that there is a change in public thinking about business. Popular polls and other tests of public sentiment register an unmistakable shift. Extreme pronouncements discrediting business meet with a rising skepticism."[74] By October, Dr. George Gallup could confirm that the pendulum of public sentiment, which had been so strongly antibusiness in the early 1930s, had swung in the other direction. The change had begun, he reported, with the sit-down strikes of early 1937. Gallup now discerned "a growing sentiment for removing many of the restrictions on business" that had been imposed by the Roosevelt administration. Indeed, when polled on what should be done to expedite recovery, the principal response of the public had become: "Let business alone; cut out government interference."[75] If Roosevelt's earlier antibusiness policies had been "politically necessary," as some of his defenders had claimed, then clearly that alibi could no longer be used.

Yet Roosevelt seemed to ignore the change that was taking place in public sentiment. Late in June he delivered another fireside chat in which he left no doubt, in the words of the *Magazine of Wall Street*, that "if we are to have a reconstruction of business and investment confidence, it will be in spite of, rather than because of, the policies and methods of the Administration." Roosevelt had not only made it apparent that he intended to push on with more "social and economic reform, more Government planning, more regulation, indefinite borrowing and spending, more experimentation, more centralization of power in the hands of the President," but had also served "notice that he will use the full power of his position in an effort to defeat opponents in the coming primaries and Congressional elections."[76] The Hartford *Courant* wrote:

The whole tenor of the President's address betokens his belief that he is and ought to be the government, that whatever he proposes is altogether righteous and not to be questioned either in substance or detail. He creates his own standards of liberalism and serves notice on those that do not conform to them that they need expect no quarter from him. . . . He ascribes to his Administration a degree of perfection such as the nation has never before known, and he exhibits little patience toward any one who places a different estimate on it.[77]

Treasury Secretary Harold Ickes noted in his diary that Thomas Corcoran, leader of the administration's Brandeisians, was more conspicuously in attendance on Roosevelt now, and that "the President seems to be having him with him openly now, whereas formerly he kept him more or less under cover."[78]

However, economic indexes continued to show a gradual upward movement during the summer of 1938. Some observers were puzzled when they tried to account for it. While most attributed the improvement to a number of factors, including the resumption of deficit spending, the cause most frequently emphasized was renewed fear of inflation. *Banking* magazine referred to "a nervous inflationary psychology," while *Mill and Factory* wrote that "if you talk to hard-headed factory managers who are not concerned with the fancy theories of politicians, many will tell you that they have started up the plant because they do not want to get caught short by inflation."[79] Obviously, those who had been through the experience with the New Deal in 1937 wanted to be ready for the next round of it. But, economist Virgil Jordan warned, "the business blood count is still low, and the patient isn't getting much real nourishment out of the stomach-pump priming process any more."[80] Robert E. Wood, head of Sears, Roebuck, warned that although business was likely to be better in the fall as a result of the various governmental stimulants, "some time during the spring or summer of 1939, I believe we may run up against what happened in the spring of 1937."[81]

THE CONGRESSIONAL ELECTION

Politics began to loom increasingly important as the election year moved toward November. Walter Lippmann described the dilemma that faced Democrats during the 1938 congressional session as they decided whether to support or oppose Roosevelt's legislation. The dilemma, he suggested, arose "out of the conflict between the constructive idealism of the New Deal and the destructive animosities of the New Dealers." Roosevelt had, "with almost no important exception," pushed only legislation in the 1937 and 1938 sessions that tended "to reduce or discourage the production of wealth." Roosevelt had shown that he liked "his grudges more than ideals," would "rather punish his enemies than realize his promises," was "more devoted to his feuds than to his programs," and seemed to act like "a man who would rather destroy his opponents than save himself." The result was that Roosevelt seemed to be "literally jeopardizing the whole success of his Administration and risking a political catastrophe, in order that he may stand implacably against the business men he so much dislikes." This policy of "rule or ruin" had caused worry among friends of the Roosevelt administration. Lippmann observed that "for months the strange thing about Mr. Roosevelt's famous brain trust is that its brains have stopped working, the curious thing about his vaunted leadership is that he does not lead."[82]

Columnist Joseph Alsop found conditions in Washington "exceedingly black" as the primary elections approached. The advisers who had sold Roosevelt on the purge attempt, he observed, were the same ones who were counseling him to continue his war against business. The purge attempt could, at best, succeed in one or two states, and those who survived would be even more opposed to Roosevelt. Alsop concluded that Roosevelt and his Brandeisian advisers were "suffering from an attack of dizziness from success brought on by the Pepper election."[83] The *Economist* noted in early July that the qualities and policies of the Roosevelt administration had "unquestionably deteriorated," and every week saw "an increase in the number of former friends of the Administration who have retired to the side-lines or gone into actual opposition, until now it is very difficult to name more than a handful of eminent Americans who, without actually being in the service of the Administration, are known to be its supporters."[84]

Former New Dealer Adolf Berle regarded the purge attempt as aiming toward making the Democratic Party "a private club limited to the rather narrow academic progressivism, not too far dissociated from the class war."[85] The *American Banker* viewed it as an attempt "to hold Congress in line against business."[86] The revelations during the summer concerning the political uses to which the WPA was being put in behalf of the purge attempt aroused anger even from pro-Roosevelt columnists like Raymond Clapper, Joseph Alsop, and Robert Kintner.[87] Such blatant hypocrisy on the part of an administration whose attacks on business, finance, and banking had been pervaded by an attitude of "holier than thou" was not lost on observers.

Despite such tactics as the use of WPA, however, the attempt to purge the senators who had opposed Roosevelt in the court packing fight was a failure. In one case, unrelated to the court fight, the Roosevelt administration opposed the reelection of Democratic Congressman John J. O'Connor of New York, who had been a thorn in Roosevelt's side from his vantage point as chairman of the House Rules Committee. In that election, O'Connor was narrowly defeated. In all other contests Roosevelt's candidates lost.[88] Business welcomed Roosevelt's defeat in the purge effort as likely to make Democratic senators and congressmen more independent.[89] A writer in *Forbes* saw the result giving the anti-New Deal coalition "new strength and drive," since the "dissenters" now had a "mandate."[90]

In mid-October *Newsweek* polled 45 correspondents and 8 politicians (4 from each party) and found them predicting a 50-seat gain in the House for the Republicans, and a 4-seat gain in the Senate.[91] Mark Sullivan concluded that if the Republicans did not pick up at least 50 seats in the House it would be difficult to make a strong case for slippage in Roosevelt's popularity.[92] Arthur Krock predicted that a significant loss of seats by the Democrats would profoundly affect the New Deal legislative program, especially any attempt by Roosevelt to reinstate the undistributed profits tax. Krock concluded that "if the House increase [of Republicans] goes above fifty, the Senate as much as four, and the present seven Republican governors are joined by fellow-partisans in certain States, the political consequences to the Administration will be serious."[93]

In fact, the Republican gains in the 1938 elections exceeded the expectations of the most optimistic Republicans and other New Deal critics. Republicans gained 81 seats in the House of Representatives, 8 in the Senate, and added 13 governorships.

CHAPTER 14

The Second Roosevelt
Depression, III, 1939

REACTIONS TO THE ELECTION

Arthur Krock pronounced the widely held judgment on the 1938 election results when he wrote:

One-party government, under the domination of the President as leader of that party—a domination often exercised through young doctrinaires who never faced a poll—was emphatically abolished after trial by the voters of the United States last Tuesday. The average taxpayers who form what is loosely called the "middle class," shifted their allegiance from the President and the post–1936 New Deal to accomplish this.[1]

Generally, the election results were viewed as a defeat for Roosevelt and the New Deal rather than a victory for the Republicans.[2] As the Omaha *World-Herald* put it: "It was not the Republican Party that won the victories, rather it was the Administration that suffered defeats. Millions who had supported Roosevelt and his party turned to Republican candidates because there was no other available way of making evident their distrust and alarm."[3]

Viewed in the context of the war that Roosevelt had been waging against business since 1933, the defeat of the New Deal in 1938 was clearly a victory for business. The U.S. Chamber of Commerce *Washington Review* wrote:

As business sees it, this expression of public sentiment indicates a loss of faith in planned economy and vast public spending as a means of restoring prosperity; an increasing antipathy toward coercive and compulsory legislation; and a desire to remove some of the legislative handicaps which are preventing a broader expansion of business and employment.[4]

Raymond Moley regarded the election results as giving a "not guilty" verdict to business despite the attempts by the Roosevelt administration to blame businessmen for the new recession.[5] *Nation's Business* agreed that the election results showed "that the average voter recalls that what helps business helps him, and after a dizzy, giddy whirl of business hating and baiting, he'd like to see what a real breathing spell would do for prosperity and employment."[6]

Postmaster General James Farley found his correspondence with regular Democrats blaming the "brain trust," particularly Ickes, Corcoran, and Hopkins, for the defeat, but the message was lost on the New Dealers themselves.[7] Columnist Joseph Alsop, a Roosevelt relative, wrote his mother that the election had been a "fearful blow" for the administration, and added: "New Dealers rather defiantly refuse to recognize its full significance, but I don't see how you can get around the fact that . . . the election is a repudiation of precisely the intellectual liberalism for which the New Dealers stand."[8] If Roosevelt were smart, Walter Lippmann wrote, he would now

bring into his councils more men who represent the prevailing temper of the people; and he will get rid of those advisers who do not appreciate what has happened; he will propose, before they are forced upon him, such changes in the laws and their administration as responsible and progressive men have been urging. He will, in short, respond to the popular will so clearly expressed on Tuesday.'[9]

Few, however, expected that Roosevelt would surrender quite so readily to the verdict against the New Deal.[10]

Those who considered that there might still be life in the New Deal, despite the blows Roosevelt had suffered in 1937 and 1938, overestimated the president's political ability to somehow reverse his fortunes. But the record of 1937 and 1938 showed either that those political abilities had been exaggerated during his first term, or that they had departed him. The New Deal had, in fact, died with the beginning of Roosevelt's second term in 1937. Its final twitch late in the 1938 congressional session, with the passage of the much-weakened wages and hours bill and the monopoly study bill, was the result of the misleading suggestion from the Florida primary election that New Deal popularity remained high. That the Florida result was contrary to opinion in the country at large was soon demonstrated by the failure of Roosevelt's purge efforts and then by the resurgence of the Republicans in the general elections. The election results—both primary and general—had answered the question of whether the New Deal was alive or dead by a verdict for the latter. The only question that remained for 1939 was whether Roosevelt and his advisers would accept the verdict and change course, as Lippmann hoped, or would they continue to delay recovery by struggling against history.

As had almost always been the case during the New Deal years, those who anticipated the worst behavior from Roosevelt were closest to the mark. When the National Association of Manufacturers held its annual convention the month after the elections, it adopted a conciliatory platform calling for cooperation between all elements of the economy to promote recovery, and advocating action by the federal government to promote the use of capital by investors in expanding production. This could be done, the NAM pointed out, by providing relief from excessive taxation and by limiting the scope of the activities of administrative agencies.[11] Roosevelt's response was predictable. He used a press conference to lash out once again at business, apparently in the belief that it was still "good politics" to do so. Raymond Moley observed that the NAM had accepted much of the New Deal, but Roosevelt apparently still considered the industrialists criminals because they had

stoutly stood by a contention that can weather the examination of every reasonable man: that if American management is to be expected to produce enough national wealth—that is, goods and services—to raise the living standards of our people, it has the right to expect its government to permit it to do so. It has the right to consider the great and expensive mechanism in Washington as a common possession of all the people, not a competitor in business and an enemy in politics.[12]

Walter Lippmann thought he sensed a change, however, in the "fundamental prejudices" of the New Dealers— "from a prejudice against business as such to a prejudice which makes them wish free business to flourish."[13] Certainly that transition was taking place within the administration, but more slowly among some of the New Dealers than others, and slowest of all, it seemed, in Roosevelt himself.

THE HOPKINS APPOINTMENT

In December 1938 Roosevelt launched what a writer in *Barron's* called "one of the boldest experiments of a bold career—an attempt to bring the New Deal and business together on common ground through the medium of a man whose very name is now anathema to conservatives." This was Roosevelt's appointment of Harry Hopkins as secretary of Commerce, replacing Daniel Roper, a move that would inevitably be regarded by some as a "deliberate affront" to business. Indeed, the appointment seemed as calculatedly controversial as the appointment of Hugo Black to the Supreme Court—and just as inappropriate. Edson Blair of *Barron's* argued, however, that business should withhold such judgments since Roosevelt's move could very well turn out to be "a drastic and dramatic stroke in the field where his Administration has most noticeably failed—that of mutual understanding between Government and industry." If business could convince Hopkins of its needs, the new Commerce secretary presumably had enough influence with Roosevelt that he would be able to convince the president.[14] Other business organs agreed that Hopkins should be met half-way or more.[15] Others, however, would have agreed with the observation of Interior Secretary Harold Ickes who carped that he did not think "a social worker and a distributor of largesse is particularly qualified to be Secretary of Commerce."[16]

Reaction to Roosevelt's State of the Union message on January 4, 1939, was likewise divided. On the one hand, the president had seemed to move the emphasis of his administration away from reform and toward recovery, but at the same time he had introduced a new ingredient in the New Deal "stew"—national defense. While some business organs were cheered by the apparent change in emphasis, which one found "geared fairly closely to the pulse of prevailing public opinion in this country," and obviously influenced by the results of the 1938 elections, others wondered if Roosevelt might not be preparing to reintroduce a "third New Deal hiding behind defense needs."[17]

There were hopeful signs, however, of a new attitude on the part of the Department of Commerce. Members of the Business Advisory Council came away from their first meeting with new Secretary of Commerce Hopkins reporting "a better feeling of true optimism over the future relations between government and business than they have had for many years."[18] Meanwhile, Undersecretary of Commerce John Hanes was assuring businessmen that there was, indeed, a new mood in Washington.[19] To such assurances from the Commerce Department was added new evidence of congressional independence from White House control. Late in January the Senate joined the House in slashing $150 million from the amount Roosevelt had requested for the WPA until the end of June.[20]

Despite such hopeful signs, there was little evidence of a real change in Roosevelt's own attitude. The administration, Arthur Krock observed, seemed to have "a congenital inability to exist in an orderly and deliberative atmosphere." The White House seemed continually to feel a need to keep Congress and the nation "stirred up." Krock concluded:

Everything the President has said or done lately points to the conclusion that he intends to go on fighting with Congress or any group which offers him less than he asks. It seems unlikely this condition will disappear until Mr. Roosevelt has left office; that therefore the desired breathing spell will not be granted.[21]

Columnist Ray Tucker found many of Roosevelt's advisers convinced that he could "recover popular confidence and support only by cooperation with the very forces which he has so long assailed." But while this was the view being expressed by a number of Roosevelt's advisers, Tucker admitted that there had been only "a few, faint signs" that the president himself had converted to this view.[22] Indeed, one journalist observed: "The President's bad temper is getting to be annoying. It is doing us no national good at all. He seems to be furious at any serious opposition, and at the worst time for such a state of emotions. He ought to take a vacation."[23] Postmaster General Farley expressed his concern to Morgenthau early in February over Roosevelt's bad temper, especially toward Congress, to which Morgenthau replied: "Well, if you're asking me who's advising him, I can't tell you."[24]

Harry Hopkins had, however, proved a pleasant surprise in the Commerce Department. The Business Advisory Council welcomed working with him after years of trying to deal with Roosevelt through a "nonconductor"—Secretary Roper. One of the leading figures in the BAC thought he found Hopkins convinced that "the welfare of business and the welfare of the nation are synonymous."[25] Curiously, Hopkins had no idea why he had been named to his new post, since Roosevelt had never told him the reason for his appointment. He had decided on his own that his principal task was to eliminate bad feeling between the administration and business. He admitted to Raymond Clapper that some of his "left-wing friends" would not approve of this course of action, and that before the year was over he expected to be unpopular with some people (Clapper assumed that he meant Corcoran), but said that the prospect didn't bother him.[26]

Late in February, Hopkins delivered the speech that was an attempt to commit Roosevelt to a cooperative course. In it, Hopkins took what the *Wall Street Journal* called "a sympathetic attitude toward concrete problems of the day," including "a definition of the boundaries of future governmental power development, of further revision of the capital gains tax, of modification of the Wagner Act, of early action on means of taking steps to simplify and coordinate the railroads." If Hopkins delivered on these four problems alone, the *Journal* said, he would validate his declaration that "with the emphasis shifting from reform to recovery this Administration is now determined to promote that recovery with all the force at its command." While it assumed that the speech could not have been given without Roosevelt's approval, it nevertheless reserved judgment until it saw actions from the administration to match Hopkins' words.[27] *The Economist* found Hopkins' speech "remarkable" from one who had "always been considered one of the more extreme—and has certainly been, to business men, the most distrusted—of the New Dealers." Yet it found that in his speech Hopkins had come "close to an admission that the Administration had been wrong in mixing so much reform with its recovery and [had] promised better behavior for the future."[28]

Other cabinet members had begun to share a consciousness of the need, finally, for a genuine economic recovery. Early in February, Agriculture Secretary Henry A. Wallace wrote Morgenthau of his concern with the "problem of tapering off of government expenditures in 1940 and the possibility that in 1940 we might have a repetition of what we had in 1937." The urgent task, he now realized, was to get private capital energized so that this time it could take up the slack when government expenditures were cut back.[29] Wallace sent a copy of the letter to Hopkins and added: "It may be necessary to get the enthusiastic cooperation of business with the government and the utilization of both private and governmental capital if we are to prevent 1940 from being a repetition of 1937."[30]

THE MORGENTHAU CONVERSION

Late in the same month, Morgenthau pointed out to a press conference that Roosevelt had recently told business it need have no fear of increased taxes.

I am very glad that the President made that statement. Speaking only for myself the thing that bothers me is that businessmen I see have what I would call a "what's the use" attitude about going ahead. I feel that attitude is holding back normal business, that it is preventing businessmen from expanding their businesses and taking normal business risks. I sincerely hope that Congress will take a careful look at the tax law and see whether there are any deterrents that are holding back business and holding back businessmen from making future commitments. Businessmen ought to feel that the administration wants them to go ahead and take risks and that the administration wants them to make money. Tax legislation should be of a nature that is not a deterrent to businessmen. We want them to make profits. . . . Of course we must have additional revenue, but in my opinion the way to make it is for businessmen to make more money.[31]

It sounded very much as if Morgenthau, like Hopkins, was addressing his remarks to Roosevelt as much as to Congress and businessmen.

Looking at the Hopkins speech and the Morgenthau press conference, Arthur Krock wrote:

Not since the President took office has American business received such assurances of reform, conciliation and cooperation from important members of his administration as it received this week through the Secretary of Treasury and the Secretary of Commerce. If Mr. Roosevelt truly and steadily supports the platforms laid down by two of his most intimate counselors—Mr. Morgenthau and Mr. Hopkins—business will enter what is, from its viewpoint, the borders of a true New Deal.[32]

On the day of his press conference, Morgenthau met with his advisers in the Treasury and told them that he had "made up my mind that from now on I'm going to say what I think." He had come to the conclusion that businessmen had legitimate complaints and legitimate reasons for being "scared." It was time, he said, for the Roosevelt administration to make it possible for business to "make an honest living." He added: "Everybody talks about the capitalistic system. I say, what is the capitalistic system except a chance to make a profit."[33] Morgenthau's tax comments continued to stir a positive response, but the Treasury secretary told Raymond Clapper that it was important now for Roosevelt to issue a statement himself, to "back up Hopkins' speech and his own tax thing in order to get business going this summer and next fall."[34]

Early in March 1939, Morgenthau phoned Hopkins to congratulate him on his maiden speech. He told the new Commerce secretary that "the country is raring to go . . . if they're only convinced that the number one fellow really means it." Hopkins replied that he was "not worried about him."[35] Morgenthau meanwhile had some desk signs printed up that read, "Does it contribute to recovery?" to indicate the extent to which he, and he hoped the administration, was committed to putting priority finally on recovery. But when he lunched with Roosevelt he found the president still viewing his relations with business in terms of warfare, and thinking primarily of politics rather than recovery. The siege mentality revealed itself when Roosevelt told Morgenthau that "business thought they had us on the run and if they got adjustments in the taxes they would want adjustments in other fields.'' When Morgenthau told him that ''business conditions were such that we could within a month, have a boom,'' he found Roosevelt's primary concern being, ''if you have a boom now, will it last through until 1940?''[36] Apparently, Roosevelt was willing to postpone recovery from the depression until an election year. The economic welfare of the nation must be subordinated to the political fortunes of the New Deal.

The next day Morgenthau phoned Hopkins to tell him that he had ''the feeling that Roosevelt thought all businessmen were against him,'' and to suggest that Hopkins ''pick out half a dozen business men who feel mildly disposed and . . . arrange that they should see the President as soon as possible.'' Hopkins promised to do so.[37] Yet all of this was clearly beside the point. What did it matter that most businessmen opposed the New Deal, if Roosevelt was seriously interested in promoting recovery rather than in prosecuting his war against business? Was it so important that Roosevelt's ego be massaged by exposure to ''friendly'' businessmen? If so, what did this say about the mind and personality of the man in the White House? In fact, might not such exposure to ''friendly'' businessmen be counterproductive in confirming Roosevelt in his resolve to remain rooted in his position if he were convinced that not all businessmen were opposed to his policies? Meanwhile, Morgenthau was busy ''merchandising'' his signs, sending them to cabinet members, heads of independent agencies, Democratic leaders in Congress, and promising to send one even to Roosevelt ''whether the President wants to put one on his desk or not.''[38]

The problem for the ''new conservatives'' like Morgenthau and Hopkins was that despite their palace revolt against Roosevelt's antibusiness policies, the president still found ideological support for his own prejudices from the Brandeis-Frankfurter element around him, particularly from Tom Corcoran. Observing the struggle within the administration in early March, Adolf Berle concluded that Roosevelt was gradually being driven away from his antibusiness policies by the influence of Vice-President Garner and the cabinet.[39] He detected a growing dislike within the administration for Corcoran and the other ''left-wingers.'' Even Eleanor Roosevelt did not think Corcoran's thinking came ''within miles of the real issue.''[40] Berle found ''the throat-cutting between the Corcoran gang and the conservatives is amusing; the speed with which they are out to cut Hopkins' throat is particularly amusing.'' But the throat-cutting would accomplish nothing, and in the end he expected Roosevelt to try to bring the two factions together inconclusively.[41] The reaction of the ''left-wingers'' to Hopkins' ''conversion'' can be gleaned from Ickes' diary. Of Hopkins' speech, Ickes wrote:

Ben Cohen talked to me the other day about Harry Hopkins' Des Moines speech. He, too, was disappointed. I think it is true that liberals generally have been rather shaken by this speech. They are wondering just how liberal Harry will be on a showdown. The President told me that Ben Cohen had been urging upon him more vigorous leadership on the liberal side but that he thinks the proper policy just now is to continue to give Congress a chance to demonstrate just what it can and will do.[42]

Apparently the Ickes-Cohen-Corcoran definition of liberal centered mainly on one's attitude toward business—a "liberal" was one who advocated unremitting war on business, even at the expense of recovery if need be.

Roosevelt was silent. At his press conference on March 8, the president ignored the opportunity to express support for the public statements of Hopkins and Morgenthau, although, as Arthur Krock observed, "pencils were poised, and wires, press and the radio were eagerly waiting." Krock concluded that "when it comes to public recanting of twice-told views and reiterated acts for the obvious reason that they have become politically unpopular, Mr. Roosevelt is a very hard man to persuade." To do so would lay him open to charges of "appeasement" of business, a label that irritated the sensitive Roosevelt. As Krock put it, the task before those who sought to move Roosevelt in the direction of recovery was to "find sugar with which to coat the pill they are offering the President and perfumed oil to ease it into his system."[43]

The day after the press conference, Morgenthau and Hanes met with Roosevelt and presented their recommendations for tax revision. They proposed: (1) repeal of the capital stock and excess profits taxes; (2) repeal of the limitation on the deduction of net capital losses from other income; (3) allowance of a three-year carryover of net losses; (4) repeal of the corporate income tax, replacing it with a new rate schedule setting a maximum 22 percent tax for those earning over $50,000; (5) reduction of the surtax on the top bracket of individuals to 60%; (6) allowance of a three-year carryover of net business losses to offset business income of later years. They found Roosevelt opposed only to the reduction of the surtax on the higher brackets. Roosevelt also told Morgenthau that he thought his "Does it contribute to recovery?" signs were "very stupid." Morgenthau replied: "I am sorry. I disagree with you." Morgenthau recorded that "all through the first part of our meeting the President displayed a most unpleasant attitude." Roosevelt insisted that, while the tax revisions might help recovery into 1940, they would lead to the election of a fascist president that year. As they talked, however, Roosevelt appeared to grow less antagonistic toward their tax proposals. At the conclusion of their talk, the president exhorted the two of them not to "mention what we have talked about here to a living soul."[44]

Indeed, Roosevelt might well have insisted further that no record of the conference be preserved for posterity, for the insight that his remarks provided as to the workings of his mind. It was a vivid illustration of what Raymond Moley described as Roosevelt's growing tendency to identify "political progress too completely with his own political fortunes."[45] It showed Roosevelt's primary concern with political considerations over recovery, reluctant to take actions that even he conceded would be helpful to recovery because they might lead to the defeat of a "liberal" candidate for the presidency in 1940. One might well question how any sane man could entertain the belief that economic recovery from the depression would lead to the election of a "fascist" president of the United States, unless, like the ancient Greeks and barbarians, all who were not New Dealers were "fascists." But for a man driven into a corner by the failure of his policies, and pathological in his determination not to admit error or to retreat in the face of his critics, no matter how much the logic of the situation dictated, this rationalization was perhaps as good as any.

CIVIL WAR WITHIN THE NEW DEAL

By early March it was apparent even to the man in the street that a battle was raging within the administration between the antibusiness "liberals" of the Brandeis-Frankfurter camp and the prorecovery liberals led by Morgenthau and Hopkins. Arthur Krock told his readers that

certain influential New Dealers are bitterly against the Morgenthau-Hopkins recovery tax program and are being active in their opposition at the White House. Their advantages in this civil warfare consist of these factors: they know how to raise the Presidential bristles; they have a steady entree to Mr. Roosevelt; and taunts about "surrender" from some of the President's critics are most timely for their purposes.

These men had been Roosevelt's "idea factory," writing his speeches, drafting his bills, and lobbying for his legislation. Now, aware that a change by the administration in the direction of the Morgenthau-Hopkins course would cause them to lose status, these unnamed intimates were "seeking to shake [Roosevelt's] faith in the loyalty and counsel of these Secretaries of the Treasury and of Commerce," and "since these men have eliminated Presidential intimates before, the inner circle is wondering whether they can do it again." Krock concluded:

It is discouraging to have to record petty instances of this sort. But the country may gain from the recital a better idea of the nature of the White House battle here to save face at whatever expense; of an intrigue to discredit loyal aides of the President who are willing to admit that they have learned something from experiments that went wrong.[46]

The New York *Herald-Tribune* described the conflict as an "extraordinary civil war, a battle to the death, which is taking place within the White House around the Presidential mind, between the Corcoran-Cohen wing of his advisers and the Morgenthau-Hopkins group."

The leftists who have always pushed for more and faster reform, refuse to yield an inch in favor of recovery. The moderates, being by nature more realistic, perceive the necessity for a shift of policy and are urging prompt action in behalf of recovery and a postponement of reform. The issue of the struggle is plainly still in doubt. The left-wing stand-patters of the New Deal have always won Mr. Roosevelt to their views before. They are battling desperately to prevail today.

We wonder if there has ever been a parallel—of a President who could not make up his mind, of a political civil war going on within the ranks of a government while recovery marked time and the whole country watched and suffered.[47]

A Gallup poll in mid-March showed that 67 percent of the American people believed that the Roosevelt administration's attitude toward business was delaying recovery either "a lot" (41 percent) or "a little" (26 percent).[48]

Obviously the major initial battleground over which the issue between the Corcoran-Cohen and Hopkins-Morgenthau camps would be fought was the proposed tax revisions. If Hopkins and Morgenthau prevailed in this instance there might be a change of attitude in the White House; if they failed it would symbolize that the Brandeis-Frankfurter disciples were still in command. When in mid-March both Senate Majority Leader Barkley and Speaker of the House Bankhead deprecated the need for further tax revision and discouraged expectations that any would pass, it appeared that the Hopkins-Morgenthau camp had lost.[49] At a press conference a few days later, Roosevelt referred sarcastically to "well-meaning persons" who thought they could aid recovery by revising taxes and promoting economy.[50] But Morgenthau and Hanes, at least, had not given up the fight, and they were not above using a favorite Corcoran-Cohen tactic— leaks to the press. In late March, Hanes reported to Morgenthau that he had visited with Frank Kent, Raymond Clapper, people with the New York *Times* and *Herald-Tribune*, and with the Scripps-Howard chain. In each case he had given them a memorandum stating the chronology of the tax issue.[51]

In a column obviously inspired by his discussion with Hanes, Frank Kent gave the Treasury's view of the struggle. Kent described the work of the Treasury in putting together a package of tax revisions designed to assist economic recovery, with the apparent approval of the president who, until a few weeks earlier, had seemed to share "with them a desire to encourage business so far as it could be done without stultification." The Hopkins speech and Roosevelt's statement that "he had no further reform or regulatory legislation to offer fitted in with the Treasury tax-revision program." Kent continued:

In fact, everything was lovely until the young radicals of the "inner circle" began to prod the President with the hideous suggestions that he was "letting the people down"; "betraying the common man"; "making concessions to capital"; and other of their stock barbs which always have so potent an effect upon Mr. Roosevelt. Efforts along this line were successful enough to renew in him a desire to demonstrate to the "intellectual liberals" that his "heart is still in the right place." Accordingly, at the press conference last week he staged a demonstration, caustically commented upon "well-meaning persons" who thought they could help recovery by revising taxes and promoting economy.

Kent pointed out that in so doing, Roosevelt had left the efforts of Morgenthau and Hanes out on a limb, but instead of resigning the two were sticking to their guns and were working with Senator Harrison in putting together a new tax bill, and neither would "change his position . . . until directly told to desist by the

President personally.'' Morgenthau, he wrote, was loyal to the president, but his "self-respect is involved and he is going ahead until Mr. Roosevelt assumes full responsibility for stopping what he started.''

Both [Morgenthau and Hanes] know that from now on the palace politicians will campaign against them, but they propose to assume that the President is a man of sincerity who does not go back on loyal friends because lies are told about them. In other words, they will stick until convinced that this assumption is not well based.[52]

The gauntlet was down in public. Morgenthau had declared war on the Corcoran-Cohen group and it was up to Roosevelt whether he would support his "loyal friends'' Morgenthau and Hanes, or see them (and perhaps Hopkins, too) depart from the administration.

If there was to be any meaningful tax revision it was clear by early May that it must come without the support of Roosevelt. At a meeting with Morgenthau and congressional leaders, Roosevelt expressed disapproval now of the Morgenthau-Hanes recommendations and forbade them to be presented as an administration proposal.[53] Morgenthau, however, reiterated his intention to press for the removal of tax deterrents to business recovery if called by Congress to testify.[54] The New York *Times* concluded that it was "up to Congress" to do something about taxation since Roosevelt had refused to lead. Morgenthau, it observed, could now only express his views to Congress as a private citizen, since Roosevelt would not allow him to advocate tax reform as an administration spokesman.[55] The Treasury secretary would, Arthur Krock wrote, be able to go before Congress only "as the rather unhappy bearer of a set of statistics, a couple of conditions and possibly of a weak substitute.'' Roosevelt's actions had the effect of putting "every possible political obstacle in the way of useful tax revision by Congress.''[56]

The problem, Walter Lippmann observed in mid-May, was that the New Deal was divided between reformers interested primarily in social reform, and radicals interested primarily in control of the economic system. The radicals, he wrote, were "not primarily interested in the reforms.'' Instead, they were interested in reducing the power of business, and at the heart of their program were "precisely those deterrent taxes and those restrictive regulations which limit private initiative. Though they do not often avow it publicly, the radicals are opposed to a large revival of private initiative because a revival of initiative would mean a restoration of control.'' The radicals, Lippmann wrote, would "rather not have recovery if the revival of private initiative means a resumption of private control in the management of corporate business.'' For them, "the essence of the New Deal is the reduction of private corporate control by collective bargaining and labor legislation, on the one side, and by restrictive, competitive and deterrent government action on the other side.'' The difference between reformers like Morgenthau and radicals like the Brandeisians over taxes was that "at bottom . . . Mr. Morgenthau thinks a deterrent tax is a bad tax whereas they think it is a good tax." Where government spending was concerned, the "reformers" regarded it as "an instrument of recovery and a means for improving the condition of the people," while the "radicals" regarded it, instead, "as a substitute for recovery and as a means for altering the balance of social power." If Roosevelt "had wholeheartedly accepted" the Morgenthau tax proposals, it would have "been a pledge that the reformers rather than the radicals were predominant in the New Deal."[57] But Roosevelt had not done so, which indicated that the Brandeis-Frankfurter group, those who were uninterested in economic recovery, were still predominant.

A Gallup poll in May indicated that if Roosevelt were running for reelection that month against Thomas E. Dewey he would lose to the Republican by a 55–45 margin.[58] In that month, Senator Pat Harrison pressed on with the Morgenthau-Hanes tax proposal in the Senate and so did Democrats in the House. Called to testify before the House Ways and Means Committee, Morgenthau suggested that various miscellaneous federal taxes due to expire or to be reduced in coming months be renewed, and that those features of the tax system that had been hindering business development and expansion be abolished. In this category he included the undistributed profits, capital stock, and excess profits taxes. He also suggested that a carryover of net business losses should be allowed as a deduction from future business profits. A few days later Hanes followed Morgenthau and supported the secretary's views. In mid-June the House Ways and Means Committee sent a bill to the full House that did permit a two-year carryover of net operating business losses, abolished the existing $2,000 limitation on deductible capital losses of corporations, and extended the temporary taxes that Morgenthau wanted renewed. The committee also suggested a flat 18 percent corporate tax and recommended that the undistributed profits tax be allowed to expire. The House passed the proposed bill without amendments. The Senate then passed a tax bill that incorporated substantially the same features. By the end of June, both houses of Congress had agreed upon a final bill and passed it.[59]

The passage of the tax bill over his objections not only confirmed that Roosevelt had lost control of Congress where his war on business was concerned, but also signified that the key economic officers in his cabinet were no longer to be counted upon as soldiers in that war. On the contrary, they had defected to the camp of the "enemy." By May 1939, the secretaries of the Treasury and Commerce were scarred from their encounters with the Brandeis-Frankfurter group, and could agree with the conclusion of Walter Lippmann and other New Deal critics that influential Roosevelt advisers, and perhaps the president himself, were not interested in economic recovery. In the middle of that month, Morgenthau recorded in his diary a conversation with Hopkins in which the secretary of Commerce "said the trouble is that he and I have been sold down the river by people close to the President on this tax program." Hopkins cited the Lippmann article above and told Morgenthau that "he agreed with Walter Lippmann that there are people in this town who don't want recovery."[60] If leading figures in Roosevelt's own cabinet doubted the commitment of Roosevelt's closest advisers to the pursuit of economic recovery, it is hardly remarkable that businessmen, investors, journalists, and other critics were reluctant to believe that any such commitment existed in the White House.

The conversion of Hopkins and Morgenthau to policies designed to aid business recovery, and the difficulties they encountered with the Brandeis-Frankfurter radicals around Roosevelt, are ironic in view of the very different role the two men played during Roosevelt's first term. Raymond Moley credited Hopkins and Morgenthau as being among those most adept at poisoning Roosevelt's mind against business during the early New Deal years. Describing a speechwriting session in October 1934, at which Moley wanted to produce a speech conciliatory toward business, he wrote:

At once Hopkins and Morgenthau began what has come to be known in political jargon as the "needling" process—that is, the process of recounting information or suspicions in a way likely to irritate or vex a man with respect to others. For over an hour they regaled F.D.R. with stories of business antagonism to him. The President listened, his face stiffening.[61]

On that occasion Moley succeeded, but over the long run he and the others who tried to steer Roosevelt away from his war on business and toward a commitment to economic recovery failed. And when Hopkins and Morgenthau awakened at last to the bankruptcy of Roosevelt's policies and joined the ranks of those who sought recovery, they found the same methods used on them by Corcoran and others to frustrate their attempts that they had practiced earlier against Moley. The faces of Roosevelt's antibusiness advisers changed, but the antibusiness course was never altered. Even the defection of key advisers to the opposing camp did not bring any change. Those advisers quickly learned how powerless they actually were when they tried to deflect Roosevelt from the course on which his pride and prejudices drove him.

But this time it would be different. The unity of the Brandeis-Frankfurter forces, which had been their major advantage, was shattered over the court fight in 1937, with Frankfurter and his proteges torn between their loyalty to Brandeis on the court and Roosevelt in the White House. Corcoran supported Roosevelt and attracted much of the blame. As his visibility and influence on Roosevelt increased, he drew more criticism. The failure of Roosevelt's legislative program to pass Congress in 1937 and its modification in 1938, combined with his highly visible role in the attempted "purge" of 1938, made Corcoran a definite liability for Roosevelt in his efforts to regain influence with congressional Democrats. By 1939, Corcoran, the most influential of the Brandeis-Frankfurter group, was moving into eclipse, to be gradually replaced by Hopkins in the role of key confidant to Roosevelt.[62] The war on business was ended, an international war was increasingly a prospect, and the Roosevelt administration quickly filled with advocates of recovery and preparedness, many of them from the business and financial world.

Conclusion

Every survey of American historians consistently finds Franklin Delano Roosevelt ranked as one of this nation's greatest presidents. Certainly, exposure to even a sampling of the literature on Roosevelt and the New Deal can lead one to no other conclusion. Conventional wisdom has it that Roosevelt was an opportune choice to lead the United States through the midst of the Great Depression, that his cheerful and buoyant disposition uplifted the American spirit in the midst of despair and perhaps even forestalled a radical change in the direction of American politics toward the right or the left. Roosevelt's landslide reelection victory in 1936, and the congressional successes in 1934, are cited as evidence of the popularity of both the president and the New Deal among the American people. Polls by both Gallup and the Democratic National Committee early in the 1936 campaign, however, give a very different picture, and suggest that the electoral victories can be as accurately accounted for in terms of the vast outpourings of federal money in 1934 and 1936, and the inability or unwillingness of Landon to offer a genuine alternative to the New Deal in the latter year. To this must be added the fact that after early 1936 two of the most unpopular New Deal programs—the NRA and the AAA—had been removed as issues by the Supreme Court.

Conventional wisdom, in fact, suffers many setbacks when the Roosevelt years are examined from any other perspective than through a pro-New Deal prism—from the banking crisis of 1933 and the first inaugural address, through the reasons for the renewed downturn in 1937, to the end of the New Deal in 1937–1938. The American present has been ill-served by the inaccurate picture that has too often been presented of this chapter in the American past by biographers and historians. Roosevelt's achievements in alleviating the hardship of the depression are deservedly well known, his responsibility for prolonging the hardship is not. His role in providing long-overdue and sorely needed social and economic legislation is in every high school American history textbook, but the costs for the United States of his eight-year-long war against business recovery are mentioned in none.

Such textbooks (and those in college, too) frequently contain a chapter on the Great Depression, followed by one on the New Deal, the implication being that somewhere early in the second of the chapters the depression was ended by Roosevelt's policies. Only careful reading reveals that despite Roosevelt's immense labors to feed the unemployed, only modest recovery from the lowest depths of the depression was attained before the outbreak of World War II. Roosevelt, readers are told, was too old-fashioned, too conservative, to embrace the massive compensatory spending and unbalanced budgets that might have produced a Keynesian recovery sooner. But World War II, the books tell us, made such spending necessary and the recovery that might have occurred earlier was at last achieved.

Generations of Americans have been brought up on this version of the New Deal years. Other presidential administrations have been reevaluated over the years, and have risen or fallen in grace as a result, but not the Roosevelt administration. The conventional wisdom concerning the Roosevelt administration remains the product of the "court historians," assessments of the New Deal period that could not have been better written by the New Dealers themselves. The facts, however, are considerably at variance with this conventional wisdom concerning the course of the depression, the reasons for the delay of recovery, and the causes of the recovery when it came, finally, during World War II.

From the uncertainty among businessmen and investors about the new president-elect that aborted a promising upturn in the fall of 1932, to the panic over the prospect of inflationary policies that was a major factor in the banking crisis that virtually paralyzed the nation's economy by the date of his inauguration, Roosevelt's entry into the White House was not an auspicious beginning toward recovery. The prejudices that were to guide the policies and programs of the New Deal for the next six years were revealed in Roosevelt's inaugural address, although the message was largely overlooked until it had become more apparent in the actions of the administration later. It was an attitude of hostility toward business and finance, of contempt for the profit motive of capitalism, and of willingness to foment class antagonism for political benefit. This was not an attitude that was conducive to business recovery, and the programs and policies that would flow from those prejudices would prove, in fact, to be destructive of the possibility of recovery.

There followed the "hundred days," when Roosevelt rammed through Congress a variety of legislation that only depressed business confidence more. The new laws were served up on attractive platters, with tempting descriptions— truth in securities, aid for the farmer, industrial self-regulation—but when the covers were removed the contents were neither attractive nor did they match the labels. By broad grants of power to the executive branch of the government, the legislation passed regulation of the U.S. economy into the hands of New Dealers whose aim was not to promote recovery but to carry out their own agendas for radical change of the economic system even at the expense of delaying recovery. Thus, truth in securities turned to paralysis of the securities markets, aid for the farmer became a war against profits by processors of agricultural goods, and industrial self-regulation became government control and labor-management strife. International economic cooperation as a device for ending the depression was abandoned for an isolationist approach, and throughout 1933 the threat of inflation added further uncertainty for businessmen and investors.

The grant of such unprecedented peacetime authority to an American president aroused concern, but these after all were only "emergency" powers, to be given up once recovery was on its way. Or were they? Gradually the evidence accumulated that the Tugwells and the Brandeisians intended to institutionalize the "emergency" powers as permanent features of American economic life. By the end of 1933, opposition to the New Deal was already sizable. Business alternated between the paralysis of uncertainty and a modest "recovery" born of purchases and production inspired by fear of higher costs owing to inflation and the effects of the AAA and NRA. The implementation of the latter two agencies in the fall of 1933 brought a renewed downturn that improved only slightly during the winter and spring. A renewed legislative onslaught by the New Deal in the 1934 congress, combined with labor strife encouraged by the provisions of the NIRA, brought a new collapse of the economy in the fall of 1934, which lowered economic indices once again to near the lowest levels they had reached in the depression.

The pattern had been established. The war against business and finance was under way, and there would be neither retreat nor cessation. Roosevelt's pride and prejudices, and the perceived political advantages to be gained from the war, dictated that his administration must ever be on the offensive and never in retreat. But the administration suffered defeats, nevertheless, and embarrassment. The Supreme Court proved a formidable foe, striking down both the NIRA and the AAA. Dire predictions from the administration about the implications for the economy of the loss of the NRA proved embarrassing when the economy began to show gradual improvement after its departure. But defeat did not mean retreat. Under the goading of Felix Frankfurter and his disciples, Roosevelt became even more extreme in his verbal and legislative assault against business. Their attempts to cooperate with the Roosevelt administration having been spurned, businessmen and bankers awakened to the existence of the war being waged upon them and moved into opposition. Roosevelt gloried in their opposition and escalated the war against them in the 1936 reelection campaign.

Reelected in 1936 on a tidal wave of government spending, and against a lackluster Republican campaigner who offered no alternative to the New Deal, Roosevelt appeared at the apogee of his power and prestige. His triumph was, however, to be short-lived, despite an enhanced Democratic majority in Congress. A combination of factors was about to bring the New Deal war against business to a stalemate and eventual retreat. One of these was his ill-advised attempt to pack the Supreme Court with subservient justices, which aroused so much opposition even in his own party that he lost control of the Democrat-controlled Congress. More important, perhaps, was the growing economic crisis that the Roosevelt administration faced in 1937, largely as a result of its own past policies. The massive spending of 1936, including the payment of the veterans' bonus, had generated a speculative recovery during that year from concern about inflationary consequences. Fears of a "boom" were increased as a result of the millions of dollars in dividends, bonuses, and pay raises dispensed by businesses late in 1936 as a result of the undistributed profits tax. The pay raises, especially, were passed on in the form of higher prices, as were the social security taxes that were imposed on businesses beginning with 1937. Labor disturbances, encouraged by the Wagner Labor Act and the Roosevelt alliance with John L. Lewis' Congress of Industrial Organizations in the 1936 campaign, added further to the wage-price spiral that threatened as 1937 unfolded. Massive liquidations of low-interest government bonds, and sagging prices of the bonds, fueled concern among bankers and economists, and within the Treasury, that a "boom" would imperil the credit of the federal government and the solvency of the nation's banks whose portfolios consisted mainly of low-interest government bonds.

In considering the two principal options for cooling the "boom"—raising interest rates or cutting federal spending—the Roosevelt administration chose to move toward a balanced budget. It was a cruel dilemma that the New Dealers faced. All knew that the economy had not yet recovered from the depression, yet they were faced with the necessity to apply brakes to an economy that was becoming overheated as a consequence of their policies. Moreover, the reduction in consumer purchasing power caused by the cuts in federal spending was occurring at the same time that purchasing power was already being eroded as a result of the higher prices that worried the administration. Private industry, it should have been obvious, could not "take up the slack," since the Roosevelt administration had done nothing to prepare for the transition from government to private spending that John Maynard Keynes and others had warned them was necessary. The New Dealers had been far too busy waging war against business to allow it the opportunity to prepare for any such transition.

In fact, far from confronting the emergency of 1937 by making long-overdue attempts to cooperate with business in generating recovery, Roosevelt was busy pressing a new legislative assault against them. Denied passage of his legislative package by Congress during its regular 1937 session, Roosevelt called a special session for November despite evidence that the economy had begun a new downturn. Even the collapse of the stockmarket, within days after his announcement of the special session, and the growing unemployment that soon followed, did not deter Roosevelt from his determination to drive the legislative assault through it. With the nation in the grips of a full-blown economic collapse, Roosevelt offered nothing to the special session but the package of antibusiness legislation it had turned down in the regular session. Once again he was rebuffed by Congress. The nation drifted, its economic indices falling, with its president unwilling to admit the severity of the situation or unable to come to grips with what it said about the bankruptcy of the New Deal policies and programs.

By early 1938, Roosevelt was faced with problems similar to those he had faced when he first entered the White House five years earlier, but without the political capital he had possessed earlier. In 1933 the Hoover administration could be blamed for the depression. In 1938 the American people blamed the Roosevelt administration for retarding recovery. Five years of failure could not be brushed aside. Five years of warfare against business and disregard of criticism and offers of cooperation had converted supporters of 1933 into cynics or opponents by 1938. Even now, however, pride, prejudice, and politics dominated Roosevelt, making it impossible for him to extend the needed olive branch to business. The best that he could offer in 1938 was a renewal of federal spending and more of the same New Deal that had brought the nation renewed misery. In the 1938 congressional session he continued to press for passage of the antibusiness legislation that had been rejected by both sessions of 1937.

But Congress was no longer the pliant body it had been in 1933, and in the 1938 congressional elections the people's reaction was registered when the Republicans gained 81 new seats in the House and 8 in the Senate—far more than even the most optimistic Republican had predicted. If the message was lost on Roosevelt, it was obvious to some in his administration, notably his new Secretary of Commerce Harry Hopkins and his Secretary of the Treasury Henry Morgenthau. Two of the earliest business-baiters in the circle of Roosevelt advisers, they now recognized the bankruptcy of that course and the necessity for the administration to at last strive for recovery by removing the obstacles to normal and profitable business operation that the New Deal had erected. This was not what Roosevelt wanted to hear, nor was it what his Frankfurter disciples wanted him to hear. These latter knew, as Hopkins and Morgenthau had learned earlier, just which Rooseveltian buttons could be pushed to trigger his antibusiness prejudices and spite. A battle raged within the New Deal between the Frankfurter radicals and the "new conservatives," Hopkins and Morgenthau, amid growing public suspicion that the former were not interested in economic recovery.

It was not a fair battle. Hopkins and Morgenthau knew how to play the game, including use of the press, and had too many allies. They did not hesitate to talk bluntly to Roosevelt, perhaps the bluntest talk he had heard since the death of Louis McHenry Howe. Moreover, Roosevelt could afford the loss of a Corcoran and/or a Cohen, against whom there was already a great deal of congressional opposition, but a break with both Hopkins and Morgenthau would have been devastating for an administration already on the defensive. Gradually the

Frankfurter radicals moved into eclipse, along with their policies, to be replaced increasingly by recovery and preparedness advocates, including many from the business and financial world.

Conventional wisdom has it that the massive government spending of World War II finally brought a Keynesian recovery from the depression. Of more significance, in comparisons of the prewar and wartime economic policies of the Roosevelt administration, is the fact that the war against business that characterized the former was abandoned in the latter. Both the attitude and policies of the Roosevelt administration toward business during the New Deal years were reversed when the president found new, foreign enemies to engage his attention and energies. Antibusiness advisers were replaced by businessmen, pro-labor policies became pro-business policies, cooperation replaced confrontation in relations between the federal government and business, and even the increased spending of the war years "trickled down" rather than "bubbling up." Probably no American president since, perhaps, Thomas Jefferson ever so thoroughly repudiated the early policies of his administration as Roosevelt did between 1939 and 1942. This, and not the emphasis on spending alone, is the lesson that needs to be learned from Roosevelt's experience with the depression, and of the legacy of the New Deal economic policies.

The judgment of historians concerning Roosevelt's presidential stature is curiously at odds with that of contemporary observers. One wonders how scholars of the Roosevelt presidency are able so blithely to ignore the negative assessments of journalists, for example, of the stature of Raymond Clapper, Walter Lippmann, Dorothy Thompson, and Arthur Krock, to name only a few. Can their observations concerning Roosevelt's pettiness and spitefulness, their criticism of the obstacles to recovery created by his anticapitalist bias, and their genuine concern over his apparent grasp for dictatorial power be dismissed so cavalierly? Is there any other example in U.S. history of an incumbent president running for reelection against the open opposition of the two previous nominees of his own party? Will a public opinion poll ever again find 45 percent of its respondents foreseeing the likelihood of dictatorship arising from a president's policies? Will a future president ever act in such a fashion that the question will again even suggest itself to a pollster? One certainly hopes not.

Perhaps the positive assessment of Roosevelt by American historians rests upon a perceived liberalism of his administration. If so, one must wonder at their definition of liberalism. Surely a president who would pit class against class for political purposes, who was fundamentally hostile to the very basis of a free economy, who believed that his ends could justify very illiberal means, who was intolerant of criticism and critics, and who grasped for dictatorial power, does not merit description as a liberal. Nor are the results of the Gallup poll mentioned above consistent with the actions of a liberal president. If the perception is based on Roosevelt's support for the less fortunate "one-third" of the nation, and his program of social legislation, then historians need to be reminded that such actions do not, in themselves, add up to liberalism, they having been used by an assortment of political realists and demagogues—of the left and the right—to gain and hold power.

There were certainly positive contributions under the New Deal, but they may not have outweighed the negative aspects of the period. The weight of the negative aspects would, moreover, have been much heavier except for the existence of a free and alert press, and for the actions of the Supreme Court and Congress in nullifying, modifying, and rejecting many of the New Deal measures. When one examines the full range of New Deal proposals and considers the implications of their passage in the original form, the outline emerges of a form of government alien to any definition of liberalism except that of the New Dealers themselves. Historians need to weigh more thoroughly and objectively the implications for the United States if Roosevelt's programs had been fully implemented. They need also to assess the costs in human misery of the delay in recovery, and of reduced U.S. influence abroad at a critical time in world affairs owing to its economic prostration. We can only speculate concerning the possible alteration of events from 1937 onward had the United States faced the world with the economic strength and military potential it might have displayed had wiser economic policies prevailed from 1933 to 1938. There is, in short, much about Roosevelt and the New Deal that historians need to reevaluate.

Notes

ABBREVIATIONS USED

BLHU:	Baker Library, Harvard University
COHC:	Columbia University Oral History Collection
HI:	Hoover Institution on War, Revolution & Peace
HML:	Hagley Museum and Library
HPL:	Hoover Presidential Library
LC:	Manuscript Division, Library of Congress
RPL:	Roosevelt Presidential Library
SU:	Syracuse University Library

PREFACE

1. See, for example, Shoichi Saeki, "Images of the United States as a Hypothetical Enemy," in Akira Iriye, ed., *Mutual Images* (Cambridge, MA, 1975), p. 113.

2. Overton H. Taylor, "Economics versus Politics," in Joseph A. Schumpeter et al., *The Economics of the Recovery Program* (New York, 1934), p. 160.

CHAPTER 1

1. *Newsweek*, 11–24–1935, p. 50.

2. Florence Kerr oral history, p. 37, COHC.

3. William W. Alexander oral history, p. 362, COHC.

4. New York *Herald-Tribune*, 10–15–1936.

5. *Barron's*, 3–27–1933.

6. *Fortune*, 12–1935, p. 103.

7. Raymond Clapper Diary, 12–11–1937, LC.

8. W. Ross Livingston to Joseph A. Broderick, 3–24–1933, Raymond Moley Papers, HI.

9. *American Mercury*, 11–1938, p. 339.

10. *Fortune*, 1–1938, p. 91.

11. Ross T. McIntyre, *White House Physician* (New York, 1946), p. 76; observation of Marie (Mrs. Mark) Sullivan in Mark Sullivan to Herbert Hoover, 1–29–1934, Mark Sullivan Papers, HI; Max Lowenthal to Samuel Rosenman, 8–8–1932, Moley Papers, HI.

12. Hugh Johnson, "Profile of a President," *Reader's Digest*, 4–1938, p. 44.

13. H. L. Mencken, "Commentary," *American Mercury*, 11–1932, p. 381.

14. Sullivan to Harold B. Johnson, 12–27–1937, Sullivan Papers, HI.

15. Malcolm W. Bingay, " 'We' and 'I,' " 1936, pamphlet reprinted from the Detroit *Free Press*, in ibid.

16. Ibid.

17. Raymond Moley journal, 5–2 and 5–3–1936, HI.

18. New York *Herald-Tribune*, 4–24–1938.

19. Johnson, "Profile of a President," p. 44.

20. For example, Henry Morgenthau Diary, 1–24–1938, RPL.

21. Clapper Diary, 5–2–1938, LC.

22. Ibid., 5–10–1938.

23. Sullivan to Thomas W. Lamont, 1–6–1935, Lamont Papers, BLHU.

24. Roosevelt, "Memorandum for the Secretary of the Treasury," 12–6–1934, Morgenthau Diary, RPL.

25. Morgenthau Diary, 1–4–1937, ibid.

26. Lewis Strauss to Herbert Hoover, "about 5–8–1933," Strauss Papers, HPL; Thomas H. Greer, *What Roosevelt Thought* (Lansing, MI, 1958), p. 45.

27. Frances Perkins, *The Roosevelt I Knew* (New York, 1946), p. 155.

28. Jackson E. Reynolds oral history, p. 42, COHC.

29. Chicago *Tribune*, 6–21–1934.

30. New York *Herald-Tribune*, 2–8–1936.

31. Chicago *Tribune*, 7–7–1934.

32. Rexford Tugwell, "The Experimental Roosevelt," *Political Quarterly* (London) 31 (Spring 1950), p. 239.

33. New York *Times*, 4–23–1933.

34. Sullivan to Elizabeth Emmett, 8–3–1933, Sullivan Papers, HI.

35. Quoted in New York *Times*, 5–10–1934; *Wall Street Journal*, 2–5–1935.

36. Arthur Schlesinger, Jr., *The Coming of the New Deal* (New York, 1957), p. 193.

37. James McGregor Burns, *Roosevelt: The Lion and the Fox* (New York, 1958), pp. 197–98.

38. Perkins, *The Roosevelt I Knew*, p. 163.

39. Walter B. Mahony to Pinchot, 8–16–1933, Pinchot Papers, LC.

40. Bingay, " 'We' and 'I,' ", Sullivan Papers, HI.

41. Washington *Post*, 6–5–1937.

42. New York *Herald-Tribune*, 11–28–1937.

43. Grosvenor H. Backus to Harlan F. Stone, 12–6–1937, Stone Papers, LC.

44. *American Banker*, 4–1–1939.

45. Samuel I. Rosenman oral history, 1–16–1969, COHC.

46. Samuel I. Rosenman to Rexford Tugwell, 1–16–1939, Rosenman Papers, RPL.

47. Marquis W. Childs, *I Write From Washington* (New York, 1942), p. 12.

48. James G. Mitchell in *Annalist*, 6–1–1934, pp. 847–48; New York *Herald-Tribune*, 4–11–1934.

49. Chicago *Tribune*, 3–17–1935.

50. *Magazine of Wall Street*, 3–4–1933.

51. H. L. Mencken, "Bringing Roosevelt Up to Date," *American Mercury*, 3–1939, p. 260.

52. Pierre S. DuPont to Alfred P. Thomas, 2–26–1934, Pierre S. DuPont Papers, HML.

53. John C. Cresswill, "The Crucial Years for the New Deal," *Magazine of Wall Street*, 2–17–1934, p. 434.

54. *Wall Street Journal*, 8–16–1934.

55. *Kiplinger Washington Letter*, 5–19–1934, p. 4.

56. *Nation's Business*, 9–1935, p. 19.

57. Baltimore *Sun*, 4–18–1934.

58. Two contemporary descriptions of the divisions within the brain trust are: Raymond Moley, "There are Three Brain Trusts," *Today*, 4–14–1934, p. 4, and John Boettiger article in the Chicago *Tribune*, 4–27–1934.

59. The Unofficial Observer (Lindley and Carter), "Big Bad Wolves vs. Little Hot Dogs," *Today*, 11–2–1935, p. 5.

60. *Barron's*, 11–23–1936, p. 4.

61. Rexford G. Tugwell, "The Principle of Planning and the Institution of Laissez Faire," Supplement to the *American Economic Review* 32 (March 1932), pp. 75–92.

62. Tugwell to George Soule, 10–22–1932, Tugwell Papers, RPL.

63. Harry Laidler file, Tugwell Papers, ibid.

64. Tugwell Diary, 1–23–1935, ibid.

65. Bernard Baruch to Samuel Rosenman, 1–6–1959, Rosenman Papers, RPL.

66. Quoted in *Kiplinger Washington Letter*, 1–26–1935; Tugwell, "America Takes Hold of its Destiny," *Today*, 4–28–1934, pp. 6, 23.

67. Tugwell Diary, introduction, RPL.

68. Ibid.

69. Harry Shulman, "Memorandum of Talk with L.D.B[randeis]—December 8, 1933," in Felix Frankfurter Papers, LC.

70. Frankfurter to Walter Lippmann, 4–27–1932, Frankfurter Papers, LC.

71. The correspondence between the two men is mostly easily read in microfilm at the Roosevelt Presidential Library.

72. See, for example, Frankfurter to Moley, 3–21–1933 and 3–28–1933, Moley Papers, HI; Michael Parrish, *Felix Frankfurter and His Times: The Reform Years* (New York, 1982), p. 205.

73. Joseph Alsop and Robert Kintner, *Men Around the President* (New York, 1939), pp. 53–66.

74. Frankfurter to Roosevelt, 10–1–1933, FDR-Frankfurter Correspondence (microfilm), RPL.

75. Alsop and Kintner, *Men Around the President*, p. 53.

76. Tugwell Diary, introduction, RPL.

77. Parrish, *Felix Frankfurter*, pp. 244–45.

78. Frankfurter to Roosevelt, 3–19–1935, FDR-Frankfurter Correspondence (microfilm), RPL.

79. See Frankfurter to Miss LeHand (FDR's secretary), 3–29–1935, in ibid.

80. Monica L. Niznik, "Thomas G. Corcoran: The Public Service of Roosevelt's 'Tommy the Cork' " (Ph.D. diss., University of Notre Dame, 1981), pp. 379–82; Henry H. Adams, *Harry Hopkins* (New York, 1977), p. 165.

81. New York *Times*, 12–6–1935.

82. Raymond Clapper Diary, 3–24–1933, LC.

CHAPTER 2

1. *Federal Reserve Bulletin*, 11–1932, p. 686.

2. For example, *Dun's Review*: 7–23–1932, p. 8; 7–30–1932, p. 6; 8–6–1932, p. 16; 8–20–1932, p. 12; 9–3–1932, p. 5; 9–10–1932, p. 5; *Commerce*: 9–1932, pp. 9, 14, 45; 11–1932, p. 9; *Investment Banking*: 11–9–1932, p. 15; 10–8–1932, p. 5; Thomas W. Lamont to William N. Duane, 7–13–1932 and 9–26–1932, Lamont Papers, BLHU.

3. Leonard P. Ayres, *The Economics of Recovery* (New York, 1934), pp. 61–62.

4. Robert W. Higbie to Mark Sullivan, 9–19–1932, Sullivan Papers, HI.

5. George Fort Milton to Harold Lasswell, 10–26–1932, Milton Papers, LC.

6. Lammot DuPont to J. T. Brown, 11–10–1932, Records of E. I. DuPont De Nemours & Co., Administrative Papers, HML.

7. Ayres, *Economics of Recovery*, pp. 138–39.

8. *Federal Reserve Bulletin*, 4–1933, pp. 210–11.

9. *Guaranty Survey*, 2–27–1933; *American Banker*, 2–25–1933; Washington *Post*, 3–3–1933; *Review of Economic Statistics* 15 (3–15–1933), pp. 45–46; Samuel Untermyer to Charles Taussig, 3–1–1933, wire, and 3–5–1933, and Untermyer to Raymond Moley, 3–5–1933, all in Charles Taussig Papers, RPL; Loren N. Wood to Roosevelt, 3–6–1933 (wire), in Roosevelt Papers, OF 320, RPL.

10. Chester Morrill oral history, pp. 215–23, COHC; New York *Herald-Tribune*, 8–13–1936.

11. Basil Rauch, *The History of the New Deal, 1933–1938* (New York, 1944), p. 52.

12. *Magazine of Wall Street*, 2–18–1933, p. 461.

13. Ibid., 3–18–1933, p. 585.

14. Albert U. Romasco, *The Politics of Recovery* (New York, 1983), p. 30.

15. Quoted in Herbert Feis, *1933: Characters in Crisis* (Boston, 1966), p. 117.

16. James P. Warburg, *The Money Muddle* (New York, 1934), pp. 91–92.

17. "Causes and Background of the Banking Holiday," *Annalist*, 8–16–1935, p. 220.

18. Walter E. Spahr, *An Appraisal of the Monetary Policies of Our Federal Government, 1933–1938* (New York, 1938), p. 64.

19. Tugwell Diary, 2–19–1933, RPL.

20. *Annalist*, 4–28–1933, p. 594.

21. *American Salesman*, 4–1933, p. 11.

22. Samuel I. Rosenman, ed. *The Public Papers and Addresses of Franklin D. Roosevelt*, II (New York, 1938), pp. 11–12 (hereafter cited as *Public Papers*, I, II, etc.).

23. Lindley to Raymond Moley, 5–23–1939, Moley Papers, HI.

24. New York *Times*, 3–11–1933.

25. Washington *Post*, 3–17–1933.

26. *Annalist*, 3–24–1933.

27. Baltimore *Sun*, 3–21–1933.

28. New York *Herald-Tribune*, 3–21–1933.

29. *Public Papers*, II, 202–6.

30. Baltimore *Sun*, 4–6–1933.

31. Ibid., 4–20–1933.

32. Washington *Post*, 4–20–1933.

33. Ibid.

34. *Commercial and Financial Chronicle*, 4–22–1933.

35. *Public Papers*, II, 155–58.

36. Ibid., 202–6.

37. See, for example, *Textile World*, 5–1933, p. 901; Arthur Krock in New York *Times*, 5–14–1933; *Annalist*, 5–19–1933.

38. *Commercial and Financial Chronicle*, 6–3–1933, p. 3830.

39. Washington *Post*, 5–19–1933.

40. *Commercial and Financial Chronicle*, 6–3–1933, p. 3781.

41. See, for example, *Nation's Business*, 5–1933, p. 14.

42. Donald A. Ritchie, *James M. Landis* (Cambridge, PA, 1980), p. 45.

43. Moley to Eugene Gary, 3–27–1935, Moley Papers, HI.

44. Raymond Moley, *The First New Deal* (New York, 1966), p. 312.

45. Warburg, *The Money Muddle*, pp. 196–97.

46. S. C. Mead to Roosevelt, 5–12–1937, Roosevelt Papers, OF 242, RPL; there are many letters and telegrams in this file objecting to the Securities Act.

47. Roosevelt to Otto Kahn, 5–22–1933, responding to Kahn's letter of 5–12–1933, both in ibid.

48. Donham to Margaret LeHand, 5–15–1933 (wire), and Roosevelt to Donham, 5–19–1933, both in ibid.

49. Donham to LeHand, 5–23–1933 (wire), in ibid.

50. Wallace B. Donham and R. S. Meriam, *Notes on Recovery* (Harvard School of Business Administration, 1934), pp. 7–8, 10.

51. Ayres, *Economics of Recovery*, p. 72.

52. O'Connor to Roosevelt, 5–10–1933, copy in Moley Papers, HI.

53. *Dry Goods Economist*, 7–1933, pp. 16–17.

CHAPTER 3

1. *Public Papers*, II, p. 150.

2. Baltimore *Sun*, 5–19–1933, 4–10–1933, 4–15–1933.

3. Walter Lippmann in New York *Herald-Tribune*, 7–5–1933.

4. Herbert Feis, *1933: Characters in Crisis* (Boston, 1966), p. 245.

5. John Maynard Keynes, "National Self-Sufficiency," *Yale Review* 22 (6–1933), pp. 755–69.

6. Frankfurter to Roosevelt, 7–6–1933, Roosevelt-Frankfurter Correspondence (microfilm), RPL; Brandeis to Frankfurter, 7–8–1933, Frankfurter Papers, LC.

7. Arthur Krock oral history, COHC.

8. *Business Week*, 7–15–1933, p. 5, and 8–26–1933, p. 7.

9. Washington *Post*, 7–15–1933.

10. R. J. Bender to Raymond Clapper, 7–8–1933, Clapper Diary, LC.

11. William F. Leuchtenburg, *Franklin D. Roosevelt and the New Deal* (New York, 1963), p. 65.

12. Baltimore *Sun*, 7–19–1933.

13. *Business Week*, 8–19–1933, p. 3.

14. *Wall Street Journal*, 7–20–1933.

15. *Federal Reserve Bulletin*, 3–1934, p. 617.

16. Moley Journal, 9–30–1933, HI.

17. Press release of Committee for the Nation, 7–24–1933 and 7–26–1933, in Newton Baker Papers, LC.

18. *Federal Reserve Bulletin*, 3–1934, p. 146.

19. *Wall Street Journal*, 7–27–1933.

20. New York *Herald-Tribune*, 7–27–1933.

21. *Iron Age*, 7–6–1933, p. 7.

22. *Manufacturer's Record*, 12–1933, p. 15.

23. *Commercial and Financial Chronicle*, 12–23–1933, p. 4398.

24. *Textile World*, 8–1933, pp. 1411–12.

25. *Nation's Business*, 9–1933, p. 11.

26. *Dry Goods Economist*, 8–1933, p. 19.

27. *Manufacturer's Record*, 9–1933, p. 13.

28. *The Economist*, 8–26–1933, p. 403.

29. Ibid., 9–2–1933, p. 439.

30. Ibid., p. 489.

31. Ibid., 9–16–1933, p. 526.

32. Ibid., 10–7–1933, p. 655 and 669.

33. New York *Herald-Tribune*, 10–5–1933.

34. Ibid., 10–12–1933.

35. Ibid., 10–13–1933.

36. *Review of Economic Statistics* 15 (10–15–1933), p. 170.

37. Brandeis to Frankfurter, 8–5–1933, Frankfurter Papers, LC.

38. Frankfurter to Eugene Meyer, 9–18–1933, Meyer Papers, LC.

39. Stimson to Frankfurter, 10–31–1933, Frankfurter Papers, LC.

40. Clapper Diary, 10–18–1933, LC.

41. *Investment Banking*, 11–18–1933, p. 60; *Proceedings of the 22nd Annual Convention of the Investment Bankers Association of America* (Chicago, 1933), pp. 10–11.

42. *Wall Street Journal*, 10–7–1933.

43. Stimson to Roosevelt, 10–31–1933, Roosevelt Papers, OF 242, RPL; Stimson to Frankfurter, 12–5–1933, Frankfurter Papers, LC.

44. Baltimore *Sun*, 9–7–1933, and New York *Herald-Tribune*, 9–7–1933.

45. *Annalist*, 9–8–1933, p. 306.

46. George Fort Milton to Homer Cummings, 9–30–1933, Milton Papers, LC.

47. John Dickinson to Milton, 10–9–1933, in ibid., and Frank Kent in Baltimore *Sun*, 9–13–1933.

48. Harold Ickes Diary, 10–17–1933, LC.

49. *Engineering News-Record*, 9–21–1933, p. 360; Ickes Diary, 11–6–1933, LC.

50. Washington *Post*, 12–7–1933 and 12–21–1933; Chicago *Tribune*, 12–29–1933.

51. Washington *Post*, 12–16–1933.

52. Baltimore *Sun*, 12–20–1933; a survey by the Conference for Progressive Labor

Action confirmed the CWA rates were higher than NRA codes, leading that group to argue for higher NRA wage schedules. See A. J. Muste and Louis F. Budens to Roosevelt, 12–26–1933, Roosevelt Papers, OF 466, RPL.

53. New York *Herald-Tribune*, 10–28–1933.
54. Washington *Post*, 10–29–1933.
55. *Commerce*, 11–1933, p. 19.
56. Milton to John Dickinson, 10–30–1933, Milton Papers, LC.
57. *United States News*, 10–21 to 10–28–1933.
58. *Kiplinger Washington Letter*, 11–4–1933.
59. *Business Week*, 11–11–1933.
60. *Review of Economic Statistics* 15 (11–15–1933), p. 184.
61. Harold Ickes, *The Secret Diary of Harold Ickes* (New York, 1954), I, p. 104 (10–5–1933).
62. *Baltimore Sun*, 10–1–1933.
63. *Public Papers*, II, p. 426.
64. *Literary Digest*, 12–9–1933, p. 8; Washington *Post*, 10–24–1933; New York *Herald-Tribune*, 10–25–1933.
65. New York *Herald-Tribune*, 10–26–1933; *Annalist*, 10–27–1933, p. 538; *United States News*, 10–21 to 10–28–1933.
66. *The Economist*, 10–28–1933, p. 799.
67. New York *Herald-Tribune*, 10–24–1933 and 10–27–1933; Baltimore *Sun*, 10–28–1933.
68. Washington *Post*, 10–31–1933.
69. New York *Herald-Tribune*, 10–31–1933.
70. *Business Week*, 11–4–1933.
71. Chicago *Tribune*, 11–20–1933.
72. Thomas Corcoran to Frankfurter, 12–30–1933, Frankfurter Papers, LC.
73. *Bankers' Monthly*, 9–1933, p. 597; *Newsweek*, 12–2–1933, p. 5.
74. New York *Times*, 11–22–1933.
75. Washington *Post*, 12–18–1933; New York *Herald-Tribune*, 12–20–1933; Baltimore *Sun*, 12–19–1933.
76. *The Economist*, 12–19–1933, p. 1174.
77. New York *Times*, 12–20–1933; *United States News*, 12–18–1933.
78. Milburn Lincoln Wilson oral history, p. 1108, COHC.
79. Chester Davis oral history, p. 319, COHC.
80. *Business Week*, 12–9–1933, p. 12.
81. New York *Times*, 12–18–1933; New York *Herald-Tribune*, 12–11–1933; Baltimore *Sun*, 12–12–1933.
82. Frankfurter to Roosevelt, 12–10–1933, Roosevelt-Frankfurter Correspondence (microfilm), RPL.
83. Roosevelt to Frankfurter, 12–22–1933, ibid.
84. Frankfurter to Roosevelt, 12–16–1933, ibid.
85. New York *Times*, 12–31–1933.
86. Baltimore *Sun*, 1–1–1934.
87. *Wall Street Journal*, 1–10–1934.
88. Quoted in New York *Times*, 1–2–1934.
89. *The Economist*, 1–6–1934.
90. See, for example, New York *Times*, 1–4–1934, 2–19–1934, and 3–1–1934.

91. Chicago *Tribune*, 2–6–1934.

92. Harold J. Laski, "The Roosevelt Experiment," *Harpers*, 2–1934, p. 143.

93. New York *Times*, 9–11–1934.

94. New York *Herald-Tribune*, 1–9–1934.

CHAPTER 4

1. C. J. Bullock, "The Securities Act of 1933," *Review of Economic Statistics* 16 (1–15–1934), pp. 17–18; Hugh Leffingwell to Roosevelt, 1–4–1934, Roosevelt Papers, PPF 866, RPL; *Wall Street Journal*, 1–13–1934.

2. Otis Graham, *An Encore for Reform* (New York, 1967), pp. 166–67.

3. New York *Herald-Tribune*, 1–12–1934.

4. Ibid., 3–28–1934.

5. Ibid., 4–6–1934.

6. Ibid., 5–25–1934.

7. Frankfurter to Roosevelt, 2–14–1934, Roosevelt-Frankfurter Correspondence (microfilm), RPL.

8. James G. Mitchell in *Annalist*, 3–2–1934, p. 371.

9. *Nation's Business*, 4–1934, p. 93.

10. *Barron's*, 2–19–1934.

11. *Wall Street Journal*, 2–16–1934.

12. New York *Herald-Tribune*, 2–16–1934.

13. New York *Times*, 3–17–1934.

14. Fred Kent to Roosevelt, 3–23–1934, Roosevelt Papers, PPF 744, RPL.

15. Washington *Post*, 3–28–1934.

16. Roosevelt to Kent, 3–27–1934, Roosevelt Papers, PPF 744, RPL.

17. New York *Herald-Tribune*, 3–21–1934.

18. William O. Douglas, "Protecting the Investor," *Yale Review* 23 (3–1934), p. 529.

19. Quoted in Ritchie, *Landis*, p. 58; see also Washington *Post*, 3–28–1934.

20. New York *Times*, 1–16–1934; Washington *Post*, 1–26–1934; Baltimore *Sun*, 1–16–1934 and 2–2–1934.

21. New York *Times*, 2–11–1934.

22. Baltimore *Sun*, 2–11–1934; Washington *Post*, 2–11–1934.

23. *Business Week*, 2–17–1934; R.R.M. Carpenter to John Raskob, 3–16–1934, copy in Pierre S. DuPont Papers, HML.

24. *Magazine of Wall Street*, 3–3–1934, p. 485.

25. New York *Herald-Tribune*, 3–20–1934.

26. New York *Times*, 2–25–1934.

27. Chicago *Tribune*, 1–23–1934.

28. *Textile World*, 2–1934, p. 237.

29. *The Foundry*, 2–1934, p. 9; *Iron Age*, 2–18–1934, p. 41C.

30. Baltimore *Sun*, 3–1–1934.

31. *Public Papers*, III, pp. 123–31.

32. New York *Herald-Tribune*, 3–6–1934.

33. Wilbur Forrest to Laurence Hills, 3–17–1934, Reid Family Papers, LC.

34. Washington *Post*, 3–13–1934.

35. Roosevelt to Frankfurter, 3–24–1934, Roosevelt-Frankfurter Correspondence (microfilm), RPL.

36. New York *Times*, 3–22–1934.

37. Ibid., 2–20–1934.

38. Henry I. Harriman to Roosevelt, 3–3–1934, Roosevelt Papers, OF 105, RPL.

39. New York *Herald-Tribune*, 3–9–1934 and 3–17–1934.

40. *The Economist*, 3–10–1934, p. 508.

41. Washington *Post*, 3–2–1934.

42. See the Rexford Tugwell Diary, 3–24–1934, RPL.

43. New York *Herald-Tribune*, 3–6–1934 and 3–26–1934; Chicago *Tribune*, 3–24–1934.

44. Washington *Post*, 3–26–1934; see also *Iron Age*, 4–12–1934, p. 9.

45. New York *Herald-Tribune*, 4–18–1934.

46. *Barron's*, 3–26–1934.

47. *Dry Goods Economist*, 4–1934, p. 15; Chicago *Tribune*, 5–15–1934.

48. *Magazine of Wall Street*, 3–31–1934, p. 594.

49. Berle to "Caesar" [Roosevelt], 4–23–1934, Berle Papers, RPL.

50. Tugwell Diary, 4–26–1934, RPL.

51. U.S. Department of Commerce, Bureau of Census, *Historical Statistics of the United States* (Washington, 1975), p. 179.

52. *Commercial and Financial Chronicle*, 4–21–1934, pp. 2644–45.

53. Kent to Roosevelt, 4–23–1934, Roosevelt Papers, PPF 744, RPL.

54. W. A. Sheaffer to Moley, 8–9–1934, Moley Papers, HI.

55. *Guaranty Survey*, 7–30–1934.

56. New York *Times*, 5–4–1934.

57. *Business Week*, 5–5–1934, p. 5.

58. Harriman to Roosevelt, 5–10–1934, Roosevelt Papers, OF 105, RPL.

59. New York *Times*, 5–20–1934.

60. *United States News*, 5–14–1934.

61. *Iron Age*, 5–3–1934, p. 38.

62. *Annalist*, 5–25, 1934, p. 809.

63. *Public Papers*, III, pp. 287–93.

64. Baltimore *Sun*, 6–11–1934.

65. Printed in ibid., 6–10–1934.

66. Washington *Post*, 6–17–1934; New York *Times*, 6–10–1934; Baltimore *Sun*, 6–19–1934.

67. Washington *Post*, 6–8–1934.

68. New York *Herald-Tribune*, 7–27–1934; New York *Times*, 7–27–1934; *United States News*, 7–30–1934.

69. Chicago *Tribune*, 7–12–1934.

70. *Textile World*, 9–1934, p. 1817.

71. Wadsworth H. Mullen, "NRA and Business Profits," *Barron's*, 7–2–1934.

72. *Annalist*, 7–13–1934.

73. Washington *Post*, 7–29–1934.

74. New York *Times*, 8–2–1934; New York *Herald-Tribune*, 8–2–1934.

CHAPTER 5

1. *Public Papers*, III, 370–75.

2. *Wall Street Journal*, 8–10–1934.

3. Washington *Post*, 8–11–1934.

4. *Kiplinger Washington Letter*, 8–11–1934 and 8–18–1934.

5. *Barron's*, 8–27–1934; *Commercial and Financial Chronicle*, 8–25–1934, p. 1125; *Annalist*, 9–7–1934, p. 321.

6. Carl F. Clarke to Roosevelt, 9–19–1934, Roosevelt Papers, OF 172, RPL.

7. Kayce Blackburn to Early, 8–10–1934, sent to Roosevelt 8–14–1934, Roosevelt Papers, OF 466, RPL.

8. New York *Herald-Tribune*, 9–28–1934.

9. New York *Times*, 9–25–1934.

10. Fisher to Roosevelt, 8–30–1934, Fisher Papers, RPL.

11. New York *Herald-Tribune*, 9–4–1934.

12. *Wall Street Journal*, 9–5–1934.

13. Irving Fisher memorandum of 9–6–1934, Fisher Papers, RPL.

14. New York *Times*, 9–8–1934.

15. Chicago *Tribune*, 9–12–1934.

16. Ibid., 8–27–1934.

17. Baltimore *Sun*, 9–17–1934.

18. Harriman to Roosevelt, 9–21–1934, Roosevelt Papers, OF 172, RPL.

19. Unsent letter of 9–23–1934 in ibid.

20. Chicago *Tribune*, 9–27–1934.

21. New York *Herald-Tribune*, 9–22–1934; Baltimore *Sun*, 9–21–1934.

22. Baltimore *Sun*, 9–22–1934.

23. Roper to McIntyre, 9–26–1934, enclosing R. W. Wantz to Roper, 9–18–1934, in Roosevelt Papers, PPF 1820, RPL.

24. Dudley Harmon to McIntyre, 9–26–1934, with enclosure, Roosevelt Papers, OF 172, RPL.

25. New York *Herald-Tribune*, 9–26–1934.

26. Washington *Post*, 9–27–1934.

27. *Business Week*, 9–29–1934, p. 36.

28. *Public Papers*, III, p. 413–22.

29. Baltimore *Sun*, 10–2–1934.

30. *Wall Street Journal*, 10–2–1934.

31. New York *Herald-Tribune*, 10–3–1934.

32. Ibid., 10–4–1934 and 10–11–1934.

33. Ibid., 10–18–1934.

34. Ibid., 10–25–1934.

35. Joseph B. Hubbard, "Review of the Third Quarter of 1934," *Review of Economic Statistics* 16 (11–15–1934), p. 223.

36. Morgenthau Diary, 10–10–1934, RPL.

37. Ickes, *Secret Diary* I, p. 217 (11–4–1934).

38. Moley to Frankfurter, 10–31–1934, Moley Papers, HI.

39. Washington *Post*, 10–21–1934; New York *Times*, 10–14–1934 and 10–24–1934; Jackson Reynolds oral history, COHC.

40. Raymond Moley, *After Seven Years* (New York, 1939), pp. 296–98.

41. *Public Papers*, III, pp. 435–40.

42. Washington *Post*, 10–25–1934; S. Parker Gilbert in New York *Times*, 10–25–1934; New York *Times*, 10–26–1934.

43. Quoted in Baltimore *Sun*, 10–26–1934.

44. *American Banker*, 10–26–1934; *Bankers' Magazine*, 11–1934, p. 457; *Commercial and Financial Chronicle*, 10–27–1934, p. 2557.

45. Moley, *After Seven Years*, p. 297.

46. Roosevelt to Frankfurter, 11–27–1934, Roosevelt-Frankfurter Correspondence (microfilm), RPL.

47. For example, Chicago *Tribune*, 11–3–1934.

48. Ickes, *Secret Diary*, I, p. 180 (8–22–1934).

49. Baltimore *Sun*, 9–29–1934.

50. Washington *Post*, 10–31–1934.

51. Ibid., 10–24–1934; also Chicago *Tribune*, 10–8–1934 and 11–16–1934; New York *Times*, 10–15–1934; New York *Herald-Tribune*, 11–1–1934, 11–3–1934, and 11–7–1934; *Forbes*, 11–1–1934, p. 20.

52. Washington *Post*, 10–30–1934.

53. Baltimore *Sun*, 11–8–1934.

54. Chicago *Tribune*, 11–18–1934; Washington *Post*, 11–19–1934; *Newsweek*, 11–24–1934.

55. Chicago *Tribune*, 11–18–1934.

56. Ibid., 11–19–1934.

57. New York *Herald-Tribune*, 11–26–1934.

58. *Commercial and Financial Chronicle*, 11–24–1934; *Wall Street Journal*, 12–21–1934.

59. New York *Herald-Tribune*, 11–21–1934.

60. Hook to Richberg, 11–23–1934, Richberg Papers, LC.

61. *Banking*, 12–1934, p. 1A.

62. Chicago *Tribune*, 11–23–1934.

63. *Magazine of Wall Street*, 11–10–1934, p. 55.

64. Washington *Post*, 12–4–1934.

65. *Magazine of Wall Street*, 12–22–1934, p. 241.

66. New York *Herald-Tribune*, 11–30–1934.

67. For example, *Guaranty Survey*, 11–26–1934; *Iron Age*, 11–29–1934, p. 13; *Annalist*, 11–30–1934, p. 746; *Dry Goods Economist*, 12–1934, p. 11.

68. Chicago *Tribune*, 12–4–1934; *Textile World*, 12–1934, p. 2387.

69. Chicago *Tribune*, 12–5–1934.

70. New York *Times*, 12–7–1934.

71. *Wall Street Journal*, 12–8–1934.

72. *Newsweek*, 12–15–1934, p. 28.

73. Chicago *Tribune*, 12–10–1934.

74. New York *Times*, 12–23–1934.

75. *Kiplinger Washington Letter*, 12–22–1934; *Business Week*, 12–22–1934, p. 5.

76. New York *Times*, 12–20–1934.

77. Raskob to A. W. Robertson, 12–27–1934, Raskob Papers, HML.

78. New York *Times*, 12–20–1934.

79. Ickes, *Secret Diary*, I, p. 244 (12–17–1934).

80. New York *Times*, 12–23–1934.

81. Baltimore *Sun*, 12–22–1934.

82. *Commercial and Financial Chronicle*, 12–22–1934, p. 3856–57; Frank Kent in *Wall Street Journal*, 12–24–1934.

CHAPTER 6

1. New York *Herald-Tribune*, 1–5–1935; *Wall Street Journal*, 1–3–1935; *Barron's*, 1–7–1935.

2. *The Economist*, 1–5–1935, p. 12; *Wall Street Journal*, 1–2–1935.

3. *The Economist*, 1–12–1935, p. 65.

4. *Wall Street Journal*, 1–7–1935.

5. Lionel Robbins, "World Recovery Prospects: Short-Term Revival vs. Long-Term Instability," *Annalist*, 1–18–1835, p. 71.

6. C. J. Bullock, "Reform, Recovery, and The Budget," *Review of Economic Statistics* 17 (2–15–1935), p. 49.

7. *Kiplinger Washington Letter*, 1–26–1935.

8. *Business Week*, 2–2–1935, p. 39.

9. Clipping of Clapper article for *Review of Reviews*, in Clapper Papers, LC.

10. *Commerce*, 3–1935, p. 8.

11. *Business Week*, 3–2–1935, p. 44.

12. Washington *Post*, 3–3–1935; New York *Times*, 3–17–1935.

13. Quoted in Norman Hapgood to Roosevelt, 6–16–1935, Roosevelt Papers, PPF 278, RPL.

14. Frankfurter to Buxton, 4–4–1935, and Buxton to Frankfurter, 4–5–1935, Frankfurter Papers, LC.

15. Quoted in *Investment Banking*, 4–23–1935, pp. 179–80.

16. Report of Business Advisory Council, 5–2–1935, Roosevelt Papers, OF 3q, RPL.

17. Quoted in New York *Herald-Tribune*, 2–10–1935.

18. *Commercial and Financial Chronicle*, 2–9–1935, p. 837.

19. See, for example, Thomas Jefferson Coolidge memorandum of 2–1–1935, in Coolidge file, Morgenthau Papers, RPL.

20. Chicago *Tribune*, 3–9–1935.

21. Coolidge memoranda of 2–15–1935 and 3–13–1935, in Coolidge file, Morgenthau Papers, RPL.

22. Chicago *Tribune*, 3–8–1935.

23. Ibid., 3–28–1935.

24. Rodgers to Amos Pinchot, 3–20–1935, Pinchot Papers, LC.

25. New York *Times*, 4–30–1935.

26. Ibid., 5–4–1935.

27. Ibid., 5–13–1935.

28. Ibid., 3–30–1935.

29. Business Advisory Council Report of 4–10–1935, Roosevelt Papers, OF 3q, RPL.

30. New York *Times*, 5–25–1935.

31. Harriman to Roosevelt, 12–28–1934, Roosevelt Papers, OF 105, RPL.

32. Quoted in New York *Times*, 12–27–1934.

33. Business Advisory Council Resolution of 3–13–1935, Roosevelt Papers, OF 3q, RPL.

34. Chicago *Tribune*, 4–23–1935; *Newsweek*, 4–27–1935, p. 30.

35. New York *Times*, 4–22–1935.

36. *Wall Street Journal*, 5–2–1935.

37. New York *Herald-Tribune*, 5–4–1935.

38. Quoted in Baltimore *Sun*, 1–16–1935.

39. Quoted in Chicago *Tribune*, 2–10–1935.

40. *Annalist*, 2–15–1935, p. 266.

41. *Engineering News-Record*, 1–24–1935, p. 136, and 1–31–1935, p. 177.

42. Ibid., 4–11–1935.

43. *United States News*, 4–22–1935.

44. Albert W. Melone to Pinchot, 4–22–1935, Pinchot Papers, LC

45. New York *Herald-Tribune*, 1–31–1935 and 5–23–1935.

46. New York *Times*, 5–26–1935.

47. Washington *Post*, 2–27–1935.

48. Clapper to Alf Landon, 4–10–1935, Clapper Papers, LC.

49. *Annalist*, 3–22–1935.

50. *Saturday Evening Post*, 4–27–1935, p. 22.

51. Frankfurter to Meyer, 3–23–1935, and Meyer to Frankfurter, 3–25–1935, Meyer Papers, LC.

52. New York *Times*, 5–1–1935.

53. New York *Herald-Tribune*, 4–30–1935.

54. New York *Times*, 5–2–1935; Washington *Post*, 5–2–1935.

55. Washington *Post*, 5–2–1935.

56. New York *Times*, 5–3–1935.

57. *Nation's Business*, 5–1935, p. 17.

58. New York *Times*, 5–3–1935.

59. Washington *Post*, 5–2–1935.

60. *Commercial and Financial Chronicle*, 5–4–1935, p. 2915.

61. *Wall Street Journal*, 5–6–1935.

62. *Kiplinger Washington Letter*, 5–4–1935.

63. See Roosevelt Papers, OF 105, RPL for letters both supporting and attacking the resolutions.

64. New York *Times*, 5–3–1935.

65. James W. Hook to Ralph Flanders, 5–3–1935, Flanders Papers, SU; *United States News*, 5–6–1935; Winthrop Aldrich to Henry P. Kendall, undated and unsent, and Aldrich to Harold Smith, 6–24–1935, both in Aldrich Papers, BLHU.

66. *United States News*, 5–13–1935.

67. New York *Herald-Tribune*, 1–9–1935.

68. *United States News*, 1–14–1935.

69. Morgenthau Diary, 1–14–1935, RPL.

70. Ibid.

71. Chicago *Tribune*, 2–2–1935.

72. New York *Herald-Tribune*, 2–19–1935.

73. *Wall Street Journal*, 3–1–1935.

74. For example, Washington *Post*, 4–3–1935.

75. Stanley Reed to Roosevelt, 4–11–1935, in Roosevelt-Frankfurter Correspondence (microfilm), RPL.

76. Thomas Corcoran to Roosevelt, 4–4–1935, wire, in ibid.

77. Arthur Schlesinger, Jr., *The Politics of Upheaval* (New York, 1960), p. 277.

78. Leuchtenburg, *Franklin D. Roosevelt and the New Deal*, p. 145.

79. See *Supreme Court of the United States, No. 854 and 864—October Term, 1934*, p. 7.

80. Ibid.

81. New York *Times*, 5–4–1935.

82. Tugwell Diary, 5—9–1935, RPL.

83. *Business Week*, 5–11–1935, p. 3.

84. Homer Cummings Diary, 5–27–1935, LC.

85. Washington *Post*, 5–28–1935.

86. Cummings Diary, 5–17–1935, LC.

87. Memorandum of meeting on 5–27–1935, Frankfurter Papers, LC.

88. Cummings Diary, 5–29–1935, LC.

89. Frankfurter to Roosevelt, 5–29–1935 and 5–30–1935, Roosevelt-Fraukfurter Correspondence (microfilm), RPL.

90. Tugwell Diary, 5–30–1935, RPL.

91. Ickes Diary, 6–4–1935, LC.

92. Washington *Post*, 5–28–1935.

93. New York *Herald-Tribune*, 5–28–1935.

94. *Wall Street Journal*, 5–29–1935.

95. *Foundry*, 6–1935, p. 17.

96. *Bulletin of the National Retail Dry Goods Association*, 6–1935, p. 5.

97. *Manufacturer's Record*, 6–1935, pp. 1, 19.

98. *Motor*, 6–1935, p. 35.

99. *Commercial and Financial Chronicle*, 6–1–1935.

100. *Editor and Publisher*, 6–1–1935.

101. *Guaranty Survey*, 6–24–1935.

102. *Wall Street Journal*, 6–3–1935.

103. New York *Times*, 6–1–1935.

104. Washington *Post*, 6–6–1935.

105. *Kiplinger Washington Letter*, 6–8–1935.

106. Washington *Post*, 6–5–1935.

CHAPTER 7

1. *Business Week*, 7–27–1935.

2. New York *Times*, 9–15–1935.

3. New York *Herald-Tribune*, 6–13–1935.

4. Chicago *Tribune*, 6–16–1935.

5. Washington *Post*, 6–25–1935.

6. Chicago *Tribune*, 5–30–1935.

7. Morgenthau Diary, 7–9–1935, RPL.

8. New York *Times*, 7–27–1935.

9. *Business Week*, 8–24–1935, p. 32.

10. Walter Crowder, "Evolution and Analysis of the Banking Act of 1935," *Journal of Business* (University of Chicago) 9 (1–1936), p. 51.

11. Davis to Newton Baker, 6–11–1935, Baker Papers, LC.

12. New York *Herald-Tribune*, 6–13–1935.

13. New York *Times*, 7–2–1935.

14. Washington *Post*, 7–3–1935.

15. New York *Herald-Tribune*, 7–4–1935.

16. New York *Times*, 8–24–1935.

17. Morgenthau Diary, 6–19–1935, RPL.

18. Bruce Murphy, *The Brandeis/Frankfurter Connection* (New York, 1982), pp. 159–62.

19. New York *Times*, 6–21–1935.

20. *Wall Street Journal*, 6–21–1935.

21. *Annalist*, 6–21–1935, p. 913.

22. Milo Perkins memorandum of 6–5–1935, in Tugwell Diary, 6–5–1935, RPL.

23. Chicago *Tribune*, 6–25–1935; New York *Herald-Tribune*, 6–21–1935; *Commercial and Financial Chronicle*, 6–22–1935, p. 4113.

24. Frankfurter to Roosevelt, 5–16–1935 and 5–30–1935, Roosevelt-Frankfurter Correspondence (microfilm), RPL.

25. New York *Herald-Tribune*, 6–26–1935.

26. New York *Times*, 6–27–1935.

27. Washington *Post*, 6–27–1935.

28. *Forbes*, 7–1–1935; *Commercial and Financial Chronicle*, 6–29–1935, pp. 4291–3; *Manufacturer's Record*, 7–1935, p. 16.

29. New York *Herald-Tribune*, 7–1–1935.

30. Ibid., 7–16–1935.

31. Ibid., 7–19–1935.

32. *Magazine of Wall Street*, 7–20–1935, p. 325.

33. *Forbes*, 7–1–1935, p. 23.

34. Quoted in Washington *Post*, 8–12–1935; see also *Guaranty Survey*, 7–29–1935; H. M. Powell, of the Associated Industries of New York, in New York *Times*, 8–1–1935; Benjamin A. Anderson, in Chicago *Tribune*, 8–6–1935; Report on the Tax Bill (HR 8974) of the Business Advisory Council, 8–13–1935, Roosevelt Papers, OF 3q, RPL.

35. New York *Herald-Tribune*, 7–12–1935; New York *Times*, 6–25–1935, 7–7–1935, and 7–12–1935; *Textile World*, 7–1935, p. 1443.

36. Homer Cummings Diary, 7–5–1935, RPL.

37. New York *Herald-Tribune*, 7–12–1935; *Commercial and Financial Chronicle*, 7–13–1935, p. 166. The Business Advisory Council's objections to the bill can be found in Daniel Roper to Roosevelt, 7–12–1935, Roosevelt Papers, RPL.

38. Breckinridge Long Diary, 7–5–1935, LC

39. New York *Times*, 5–18–1935, contains the criticism of the bill by the Business Advisory Council; most business criticism was over the timing of the bill rather than the bill itself, owing to the additional expense that it would impose on business while still mired in the depression. See, for example, *Manufacturer's Record*, 12–1935, p. 42.

40. Morgenthau Diary, 5–20–1935 and 5–22–1935, RPL.

41. *Guaranty Survey*, 9–30–1935.

42. Quoted by Raymond Clapper in Washington *Post*, 6–7–1935.

43. *Engineering News Record*, 6–13–1935.

44. New York *Herald-Tribune*, 6–19–1935.

45. Washington *Post*, 6–15–1935.

46. New York *Herald-Tribune*, 6–27–1935.

47. Morgenthau Diary, 7–10–1935, RPL.

48. Washington *Post*, 9–14–1935.

49. Morgenthau Diary, 12–21–1935, RPL.

50. Moley, *The First New Deal*, pp. 532–34.

51. Ibid.

52. For example, *Commercial and Financial Chronicle*, 9–7–1935, p. 1483; *Business Week*, 9–7–1935, p. 1; *Wall Street Journal*, 9–7–1935; New York *Herald-Tribune*, 9–7–1935.

53. *United States News*, 9–9–1935.

54. *Magazine of Wall Street*, 9–14–1935, p. 521; *Business Week*, 11–2–1935, p. 1.

55. *Newsweek*, 11–23–1935, p. 10.

56. New York *Times*, 8–8–1935.

57. New York *Herald-Tribune*, 11–7–1935.

58. *Business Week*, 7–20–1935; Howard Wood in Chicago *Tribune*, 7–21–1935, for example.

59. *Commercial and Financial Chronicle*, 7–20–1935, p. 317.

60. Chicago *Tribune*, 7–21–1935.

61. Washington *Post*, 9–10–1935.

62. For example, Winthrop Aldrich to Henry P. Kendall, 6–17–1935, Aldrich Papers, BLHU.

63. New York *Herald-Tribune*, 7–5–1935.

64. New York *Times*, 10–13–1935.

65. Washington *Post*, 10–27–1935.

66. Ibid., 11–3–1935.

67. Chicago *Tribune*, 11–12–1935.

68. Washington *Post*, 11–15–1935.

69. Chicago *Tribune*, 11–30–1935.

70. George W. Davidson to Eugene Meyer, 12–3–1935, Meyer Papers, LC.

71. New York *Times*, 12–4–1935.

72. New York *Herald-Tribune*, 12–15–1935.

73. *Guaranty Survey*, 11–25–1935.

74. New York *Times*, 12–4–1935.

75. Washington *Post*, 12–5–1935.

76. New York *Herald-Tribune*, 12–14–1935.

77. *Public Papers*, IV, 13–7.

78. New York *Herald-Tribune*, 1–3–1936.

79. Ibid., 1–4–1936.

80. *Bankers' Magazine*, 2–1936, p. 121.

81. For example, *Kiplinger Washington Letter*, 1–4–1936.

82. Quoted in Chicago *Tribune*, 1–5–1936.

83. For example, Washington *Post*, 1–5–1936.

84. *United States News*, 1–6–1936.

85. Orville Bullitt to Roosevelt, 1–6–1936, Roosevelt Papers, PPF 3231, RPL.

86. Roosevelt to Bullitt, 1–15–1936, ibid.

87. Chicago *Tribune*, 1–5–1936.

CHAPTER 8

1. Washington *Post*, 1–5–1936.

2. Cummings Diary, 1–6–1936, RPL.

3. *Business Week*, 1–11–1936, p. 5.

4. *The Economist*, 1–11–1936, pp. 57–58.

5. *Wall Street Journal*, 1–16–1936.

6. For example, *Commercial and Financial Chronicle*, 1–25–1936, p. 503; *Commerce*, 2–1936, p. 7.

7. In *Wall Street Journal*, 2–5–1936.

8. Quoted in New York *Times*, 2–17–1936.

9. Ibid., 2–4–1936.

10. *Public Papers*, V. p. 44.

11. New York *Times*, 3–1–1936.

12. See John Blum, *From the Morgenthau Diaries: Years of Crisis, 1928–1938* (Boston, 1959), pp. 305–8.

13. New York *Times*, 3–4–1936.

14. New York *Herald-Tribune*, 3–10–1936.

15. Quoted in Chicago *Tribune*, 3–31–1936; see also Adolf Berle to LaFollette, 4–27–1936, Berle Papers, RPL.

16. Brandeis to Frankfurter, 3–5–1936, Frankfurter Papers, LC.

17. Morgenthau Diary, 5–1–1936 and 5–4–1936, RPL.

18. Blum, *Morgenthau Diaries*, p. 311.

19. New York *Times*, 5–6–1936.

20. Quoted in Blum, *Morgenthau Diaries*, p. 311.

21. *Magazine of Wall Street*, 5–23–1936, p. 133.

22. Earle Baillie to Morgenthau, 5–28–1936, Morgenthau Papers, RPL.

23. Morgenthau Diary, 6–16–1936, RPL.

24. *United States News*, 6–22–1936.

25. *Today*, 7–4–1936.

26. *Bulletin of the National Retail Dry Goods Association*, 4–1936, p. 5.

27. New York *Times*, 5–21–1936.

28. New York *Herald-Tribune*, 3–21–1936.

29. Morgenthau Diary, 3–6–1936, RPL.

30. Franklyn Waltman in Washington *Post*, 3–20–1936.

31. *United States News*, 3–23–1936.

32. Moley Journal, 3–19–1936, HI.

33. New York *Herald-Tribune*, 3–5–1936.

34. For example, *Washington Post*, 3–6–1936, and New York *Times*, 3–6–1936.

35. *Editor and Publisher*, 3–21–1936.

36. New York *Times*, 4–19–1936; *Editor and Publisher*, 4–25–1936.

37. *Wall Street Journal*, 3–13–1936.

38. Chicago *Tribune*, 5–6–1936; David Lawrence, "The Last Right of Privacy," *American Mercury*, 5–1936, p. 12.

39. Morgenthau Diary, 2–6–1936, RPL.

40. Ibid., 2–7–1936.

41. John B. McMahon to Frank Walker, 1–27–1936, copy in Moley Papers, HI.

42. Lippmann to Newton Baker, 1–22–1936, Baker Papers, LC

43. Garfield V. Cox, "Some Distinguishing Characteristics of the Current Recovery," *American Economic Review* 26 (3–1936), supplement, *Papers and Proceedings of the Forty-Eighth Annual Meeting . . .*, pp. 5–9.

44. *Wall Street Journal*, 1–27–1936.

45. New York *Times*, 3–3–1936.

46. Washington *Post*, 3–9–1936.

47. Sloan to John Raskob, 4–22–1936, Raskob Papers, HML.
48. *Dry Goods Economist*, 4–28–1936, p. 7.
49. Moley Journal, 5–2–1936 and 5–3–1936, HI.
50. For example, *Forbes*, 5–1–1936, p. 10.
51. *Wall Street Journal*, 5–3–1936.
52. New York *Herald-Tribune*, 5–24–1936.
53. The Unofficial Observer, "Louis McHenry Howe," *Today*, 5–9–1936, p. 8.
54. Moley Journal, 5–26–1936, HI.
55. Quoted in Mark Sullivan, New York *Herald-Tribune*, 5–24–1936.
56. *The Controller*, 8–1936 through 10–1936.
57. Robert H. Montgomery, "The Tax on Undistributed Income," *Harvard Business Review* 15 (Autumn 1936), pp. 19–27.
58. New York *Times*, 3–1–1936.
59. Ibid., 5–19–1936.
60. *Dry Goods Economist*, 5–26–1936, p. 17.
61. New York *Herald-Tribune*, 6–15–1936.
62. *The Economist*, 8–15–1936, p. 301.
63. *American Banker*, 8–29–1936.
64. Morgenthau Diary, 4–20–1936, RPL.
65. Ibid., 4–27–1936.
66. Chicago *Tribune*, 7–21–1936.
67. *The Economist*, 9–5–1936, p. 432.

CHAPTER 9

1. Morgenthau Diary, 6–25–1936, RPL.
2. Ickes Diary, 7–23–1936, LC.
3. Moley Journal, 6–24–1936 to 6–26–1936, HI.
4. Washington *Post*, 6–29–1936.
5. Quoted in Chicago *Tribune*, 7–8–1936.
6. Baltimore *Sun*, 9–11–1936.
7. Quoted in Washington *Post*, 9–27–1936.
8. Ickes, *Secret Diary*, I, pp. 638–9 (7–18–1936).
9. *The Economist*, 6–27–1936, p. 725.
10. Lippmann to Newton Baker, 6–30–1936, Baker Papers, LC.
11. *American Mercury*, 8–1936, p. 478.
12. New York *Herald-Tribune*, 7–12–1936.
13. Ibid., 8–2–1936.
14. Ibid., 8–9–1936.
15. Ibid., 8–29–1936.
16. Washington *Post*, 8–22–1936.
17. New York *Herald-Tribune*, 8–23–1936.
18. Ickes, *Secret Diary*, I, pp. 648–49 (7–24–1936).
19. Morgenthau Diary, 8–25–1936, RPL.
20. Ibid., 9–24–1936.
21. Memo from Miss Lonigan to Morgenthau, 10–21–1936, in ibid.
22. New York *Herald-Tribune*, 9–13–1936.
23. See Blum, *Morgenthau*, pp. 159–73.

24. Morgenthau Diary, memorandum of 9–26–1936, RPL.

25. New York *Herald-Tribune*, 10–1–1936.

26. Ibid., 10–11–1936.

27. Ibid., 8–30–1936.

28. Albert Jay Nock, "A Little Conservative," *The Atlantic Monthly*, 11–1936, p. 484.

29. Chicago *Tribune*, 10–15–1936.

30. New York *Herald-Tribune*, 10–28–1936.

31. Chicago *Tribune*, 10–28–1936.

32. *American Mercury*, 7–1936, p. 348.

33. New York *Herald-Tribune*, 10–18–1936.

34. Ibid., 10–24–1936.

35. Ibid., 10–18–1936.

36. Ibid., 11–1–1936.

37. *Public Papers*, V, 568–69.

38. Chicago *Tribune*, 11–3–1936.

39. New York *Herald-Tribune*, 11–3–1936.

40. *United States News*, 11–9–1936.

41. *Business Week*, 11–7–1936, p. 13.

42. *Barron's*, 11–9–1936, p. 4.

43. Washington *Post*, 11–29–1936.

44. Franklyn Waltman in ibid., 11–19–1936; New York *Herald-Tribune*, 11–19–1936.

45. Moley Journal, 11–13–1936, HI.

46. Washington *Post*, 11–23–1936.

47. *Bankers' Magazine*, 12–1936, p. 493.

48. *Wall Street Journal*, 12–12–1936.

49. Ibid.

50. Ibid., 12–18–1936.

51. New York *Herald-Tribune*, 11–24–1936; Minutes of 11–19–1936 meeting of the executive committee of the open market committee of the Federal Reserve System, in Morgenthau Diary, RPL.

52. Chicago *Tribune*, 10–27–1936.

53. Ibid., 11–25–1936.

54. Ibid., 11–10–1936.

55. Ibid., 11–8–1936.

56. Ibid., 11–16–1936.

57. Ibid., 11–24–1936.

58. *Textile World*, 12–1936, p. 63.

59. Minutes of the 11–19–1936 meeting in Morgenthau Diary, RPL.

60. Minutes of the meeting of the Treasury group, 11–20–1936, in ibid.

61. New York *Herald-Tribune*, 12–8–1936.

62. *Commercial and Financial Chronicle*, 12–5–1936, p. 3729.

63. Reprinted in Chicago *Tribune*, 12–16–1936.

64. Morgenthau Diary, 12–29–1936, RPL.

65. Wayne C. Taylor memorandum to Morgenthau, 11–13–1936, Wayne C. Taylor file, Morgenthau Papers, RPL.

66. Cummings Diary, 11–15–1936 and 12–26–1936, RPL.

CHAPTER 10

1. Morgenthau Diary, 1–4–1937, RPL.
2. *Public Papers*, V, 638.
3. *Kiplinger Washington Letter*, 2–6–1937.
4. *Business Week*, 2–13–1937, p. 5.
5. *Commercial and Financial Chronicle*, 2–6–1937, p. 822.
6. *Business Week*, 2–13–1937, p. 56.
7. *Public Papers*, VI, p. 114.
8. Washington *Post*, 3–9–1937.
9. Ibid., 3–6–1937.
10. *Editor and Publisher*, 3–20–1937.
11. Morgenthau Diary, 1–4–1937, RPL.
12. Ibid., 1–8–1937.
13. *Business Week*, 1–16–1937, p. 60.
14. Morgenthau Diary, 1–5–1937, RPL.
15. *Barron's*, 1–4–1937.
16. Washington *Post*, 1–12–1937.
17. Chicago *Tribune*, 1–13–1937.
18. Ibid., 2–19–1937.
19. Washington *Post*, 3–12–1937.
20. *Wall Street Journal*, 3–12–1937.
21. Morgenthau Diary, 3–12–1937 and 3–13–1937, RPL.
22. New York *Herald-Tribune*, 3–14–1937.
23. Washington *Post*, 3–14–1937.
24. Edwin Kemmerer, for example, in Chicago *Tribune*, 3–28–1937.
25. Morgenthau Diary, 4–1–1937, RPL.
26. *Public Papers*, VI, pp. 140–41.
27. Morgenthau Diary, 4–2–1937, RPL.
28. *Engineering News-Record*, 4–8–1937, p. 530.
29. *Business Week*, 4–10–1937, p. 13.
30. Chicago *Tribune*, 4–5–1937.
31. Morgenthau Diary, 4–12–1937, RPL.
32. Ibid., 4–21–1937.
33. Ibid., 4–27–1937.
34. *Magazine of Wall Street*, 4–24–1937.
35. *Newsweek*, 4–10–1937, p. 44; *Manufacturer's Record*, 5–1937, p. 48.
36. Undated memorandum for Roosevelt, in Morgenthau Papers for 1937, RPL.
37. Clapper Diary, 5–16–1937, LC.
38. Morgenthau Diary, 5–17–1937, RPL.
39. Ibid., 5–18–1937.
40. Ibid., 5–21–1937 and 5–24–1937.
41. Ibid. 5–26–1937.
42. New York *Herald-Tribune*, 5–30–1937.
43. *Newsweek*, 6–12–1937, p. 44.
44. Clapper Diary, 6–21–1937, LC.
45. John Flynn, "Other People's Money," *New Republic*, 7–7–1937.

46. Homer Cummings Diary, 4–12–1937, RPL.
47. Herman Oliphant to Morgenthau, 4–12–1937, Morgenthau Diary, RPL.
48. Morgenthau Diary, 5–14–1937, RPL; Wheeler to Amos Pinchot, 5–8–1937, Pinchot Papers, LC.
49. Clapper Diary, 5–20–1937,LC.
50. *Business Week*, 5–29–1937, p. 5.
51. Clapper Diary, 6–14–1937, LC.
52. New York *Herald-Tribune*, 6–17–1937.
53. *Wall Street Journal*, 6–18–1937.
54. *Commercial and Financial Chronicle*, 6–19–1937, p. 4072.
55. Breckinridge Long Diary, 6–1–1937, LC; Frank Kent in *Wall Street Journal*, 6–18–1937.
56. New York *Herald-Tribune*, 7–20–1937.
57. Ibid., 7–24–1937.
58. *Wall Street Journal*, 7–26–1937.
59. *Commercial and Financial Chronicle*, 7–31–1937, p. 664.
60. For example, *Wall Street Journal*, 8–13–1937; *Commercial and Financial Chronicle*, 8–14–1937, p. 989.
61. *Newsweek*, 8–21–1937.
62. Chicago *Tribune*, 8–14–1937.
63. Clapper Diary, 8–13–1937, LC.
64. Ibid., 8–14–1937.
65. New York *Herald-Tribune*, 1–14–1937 and 5–6–1937.
66. Ibid.
67. Quoted in *Business Week*, 6–12–1937, p. 19.
68. Morgenthau Diary, 4–27–1937, RPL.
69. Frank Altschul to Morgenthau, 4–26–1937, Morgenthau Papers, RPL.
70. Morgenthau Diary, 4–29–1937, RPL.
71. Harriman to Roper, 5–20–1937, with attachments in Roosevelt Papers, OF 3q, RPL.
72. Clapper Diary, 1–20–1937, LC.

CHAPTER 11

1. Franklyn Waltman in Washington *Post*, 1–23–1937.
2. *Wall Street Journal*, 1–27–1937.
3. *Magazine of Wall Street*, 1–30–1937, pp. 656–57; *Textile World*, 2–1937, p. 251; *Motor*, 3–1937, p. 35; *Bankers' Magazine* 3–1937, p. 185.
4. *Magazine of Wall Street*, 2–27–1937, pp. 601–2; *Wall Street Journal*, 2–27–1937.
5. *American Banker*, 3–6–1937.
6. *Kiplinger Washington Letter*, 3–6–1937; *Newsweek*, 3–13–1937, p. 5.
7. *The Economist*, 3–13–1937, p. 585.
8. New York *Herald-Tribune*, 3–18–1837.
9. *The Economist*, 3–30–1937, p. 641.
10. *Barron's*, 3–22–1937, p. 3.
11. *Wall Street Journal*, 3–23–1937.
12. Thomas W. Lamont to Sullivan, 1–4–1937, Lamont Papers, BLHU.
13. *Commercial and Financial Chronicle*, 4–3–1937, p. 2189.

14. New York *Herald-Tribune*, 3–25–1937.

15. *Textile World*, 4–1937, pp. 108–9.

16. *Commerce*, 4–1937, p. 7.

17. *Barron's*, 3–29–1937, p. 12.

18. *Business Week*, 5–1–1937, p. 11.

19. *Barron's*, 5–3–1937, p. 12.

20. Ralph Flanders to Gorton James, 4–21–1937, Flanders Papers, SU.

21. *Dry Goods Economist*, 4–27–1937, p. 9.

22. New York *Herald-Tribune*, 5–6–1937.

23. Chicago *Tribune*, 5–23–1937.

24. Washington *Post*, 5–28–1937.

25. *Commercial and Financial Chronicle*, 5–29–1937, p. 3553.

26. Washington *Post*, 4–18–1937.

27. New York *Herald-Tribune*, 5–25–1937, 5–27–1937, and 6–1–1937; *Dry Goods Economist*, 6–8–1937, p. 15; Clapper Diary, 5–30–1937 and 6–5–1937, LC.

28. Washington *Post*, 6–4–1937; Chicago *Tribune*, 6–4–1937.

29. New York *Herald-Tribune*, 6–11–1937.

30. *Wall Street Journal*, 6–11–1937.

31. *Commerce*, 6–1937, p. 20.

32. Bailey to Newton Baker, 6–14–1937, Baker Papers, LC.

33. Landon to Clapper, 6–14–1937, Clapper Papers, LC.

34. *United States News*, 6–14–1937; Chicago *Tribune*, 6–14–1937; *The Economist*, 6–5–1937, p. 565.

35. *Nation's Business*, 6–1937, pp. 173–74.

36. Chicago *Tribune*, 6–21–1937; *Business Week*, 6–19–1937, p. 11; Washington *Post*, 6–19–1937; *Dry Goods Economist*, 6–22–1937, p. 13.

37. Washington *Post*, 6–22–1937.

38. *Wall Street Journal*, 6–23–1937.

39. Washington *Post*, 6–24–1937; Clapper Diary, 6–23–1937, LC.

40. New York *Herald-Tribune*, 6–23–1937.

41. Clapper to Landon, 6–28–1937, Clapper Papers, LC.

42. *Wall Street Journal*, 6–29–1937.

43. New York *Herald-Tribune*, 6–26–1937.

44. Washington *Post*, 7–1–1937.

45. *Magazine of Wall Street*, 7–17–1937, p. 402.

46. Homer Cummings Diary, 7–23–1937, RPL.

47. New York *Herald-Tribune*, 7–13–1937.

48. Pinchot to Roosevelt, 7–26–1937, copy in Pinchot Papers, LC.

49. New York *Herald-Tribune*, 7–26–1937.

50. *Magazine of Wall Street*, 8–14–1937, pp. 566–67.

51. *Wall Street Journal*, 8–17–1937.

52. *Business Week*, 8–21–1937, p. 13.

53. New York *Herald-Tribune*, 9–4–1937, 9–9–1937, and 9–11–1937; *Business Week*, 8–7–1937, p. 11.

54. *Business Week*, 8–7–1937, p. 11

55. *Editor and Publisher*, 8–28–1937.

56. Chicago *Tribune*, 9–2–1937.

57. Morgenthau Diary, 9–5–1937, RPL.

58. Ibid., 9–7–1937 through 9–9–1937.
59. Ibid., 9–12–1937; Chicago *Tribune*, 9–14–1937.
60. *Magazine of Wall Street*, 9–11–1937, pp. 644–45.
61. New York *Herald-Tribune*, 9–4–1937, 9–9–1937, and 9–11–1937.
62. *Kiplinger Washington Letter*, 9–11–1937.
63. *Magazine of Wall Street*, 9–11–1937, p. 646.
64. Berle Diary, 9–14–1937, RPL.
65. New York *Herald-Tribune*, 9–19–1937.
66. Ibid., 9–22–1937; Franklyn Waltman in Washington *Post*, 9–22–1937.
67. Ibid., 9–25–1937.
68. *Nation's Business*, 9–1937.
69. Bernard De Voto, "Desertion from the New Deal," *Harper's,* 10–1937, p. 558.
70. Berle Diary, 9–27–1937, RPL.
71. Baruch to Hopkins, 9–28–1937, Hopkins Papers, RPL.
72. *The Economist*, 10–2–1937, p. 17.
73. *Kiplinger Washington Letter*, 10–2–1937.
74. New York *Herald-Tribune*, 10–3–1937.
75. Ibid., 10–5–1937.
76. *Barron's*, 10–4–1937, p. 5.
77. *Public Papers*, VI, pp. 415–6.
78. *Wall Street Journal*, 10–7–1937.
79. New York *Herald-Tribune*, 10–7–1937.
80. Morgenthau Diary, 10–8–1937, RPL.
81. *Commercial and Financial Chronicle*, 10–9–1937, pp. 2275–76.
82. Berle to Peter Nehemkis, 11–10–1937, Berle Papers, RPL.
83. Berle Diary, 10–15–1937, RPL.
84. Morgenthau Diary, 10–12–1937, RPL.
85. Ibid.
86. *Wall Street Journal*, 10–13–1937.
87. Washington *Post*, 10–14–1937.
88. Fisher to Roosevelt, 10–14–1937, Roosevelt Papers, PPF 431, RPL.
89. Morgenthau Diary, 10–12–1937, RPL.
90. Meyer to Alf Landon, 10–15–1937, Meyer Papers, LC.
91. Stanley High, "The White House is Calling," *Harper's*, 11–1937, p. 589.
92. Berle Diary, 10–15–1937, RPL.
93. *Kiplinger Washington Letter*, 10–16–1937.
94. New York *Herald-Tribune*, 10–18–1937.

CHAPTER 12

1. Berle Diary, 10–19–1937, RPL.
2. Berle to Roosevelt, 10–19–1937, wire, Berle papers, RPL.
3. Morgenthau Diary, 10–19–1937, RPL.
4. New York *Herald-Tribune*, 10–19–1937.
5. Ibid., 10–20–1937.
6. Ibid., 10–21–1937.
7. Ibid., 10–22–1937.
8. *Wall Street Journal*, 10–22–1937.

9. Melchior Palyi, "The Liquidation of an Induced Prosperity," 10–19–1937, Roosevelt Papers, OF 172, RPL.

10. *Business Week*, 10–23–1937.

11. Congressman R. M. Atkinson to Roosevelt, 10–29–1937, wire, Roosevelt Papers, OF 172, RPL.

12. *Wall Street Journal*, 10–26–1937.

13. Washington *Post*, 10–30–1937; New York *Herald-Tribune*, 10–30–1937.

14. Morgenthau Diary, 11–4–1937, RPL.

15. Ibid.

16. Roswell Magill, "Conference with the President at Hyde Park on 10–29–1937"; "Memorandum of Conference with the President on November 9, 1937," both in ibid.

17. *The Economist*, 11–6–1937, p. 248.

18. W. H. Gehm to Roosevelt, 11–10–1937, Roosevelt Papers, OF 172, RPL.

19. Frederick H. Thomas to Roosevelt, 11–10–1937, in ibid.

20. Morgenthau Diary, 11–8–1937, RPL.

21. John J. O'Brien to Roosevelt, 11–9–1937, Roosevelt Papers, PPF 1871, RPL.

22. H. H. Burton to Matthew W. Ryan, 11–9–1937, Roosevelt Papers, OF 172, RPL.

23. Donald W. Baker to Roosevelt, 11–9–1937, in ibid.

24. Quoted in New York *Herald-Tribune*, 12–9–1937.

25. Ibid.

26. *Barron's*, 11–22–1937, p. 5.

27. *Newsweek*, 11–22–1937, p. 11.

28. *Wall Street Journal*, 11–29–1937.

29. New York *Herald-Tribune*, 11–27–1937.

30. Ibid., 11–12–1937.

31. *Public Papers*, VI, p. 519.

32. Morgenthau Diary, 12–7–1937 and 12–8–1937, RPL.

33. Washington *Post*, 12–12–1937.

34. Ibid., 11–21–1937.

35. New York *Herald-Tribune*, 12–16–1937.

36. Albert Penn to Roosevelt, 12–23–1937, Roosevelt Papers, OF 172, RPL.

37. R. E. McMartin to Roosevelt, 12–23–1937, in ibid.

38. Ralph West Robey in *Newsweek*, 12–27–1937, p. 35.

39. Philip H. Schaff to Roosevelt, 12–29–1937, Roosevelt Papers, OF 172, RPL.

40. New York *Herald-Tribune*, 12–28–1937 and 12–30–1937.

41. Berle Diary, 12–13–1937, RPL.

42. *The Economist*, 12–11–1937, p. 522.

43. *Commercial and Financial Chronicle*, 12–18–1937, p. 3859.

44. Washington *Post*, 12–18–1937.

45. Berle to Sumner Welles, 12–20–1937, copy in Berle Diary, RPL.

46. *Wall Street Journal*, 12–22–1937.

47. *Guaranty Survey*, 12–27–1937.

48. *Public Papers*, VII, pp. 10–13.

49. New York *Times*, 1–4–1938.

50. New York *Herald-Tribune*, 1–4–1938.

51. New York *Times*, 1–9–1938.

52. *Public Papers*, VII, pp. 32–33.

53. Franklyn Waltman in Washington *Post*, 1–15–1938.

54. Ibid.

55. *United States News*, 1–17–1938.

56. *Wall Street Journal*, 1–18–1938.

57. New York *Herald-Tribune*, 1–21–1938.

58. *United States News*, 1–24–1938.

59. Clapper Diary, 1–14–1938, LC; *Newsweek*, 1–24–1938, p. 44.

60. Memorandum of 12–24–1937 in Tugwell Papers, and Berle Diary, 12–13–1937 through 12–29–1937, both in RPL.

61. Berle Diary, 12–30–1937, RPL; memorandum from ETS to TWL[amont], undated, in Lamont Papers, BLHU.

62. Taussig to Marvin McIntyre, 1–7–1938, Taussig Papers, and Berle Diary, 1–10–1938, both in RPL.

63. Clapper Diary, 1–12–1938 and 1–14–1938, LC; *Newsweek*, 1–24–1938, p. 11.

64. Ibid., 1–14–1938.

65. Berle Diary, 1–20–1938, RPL.

66. Ibid., 1–31–1938 and 2–7–1938.

67. New York *Times*, 1–24–1938.

68. Press statement of W. Averell Harriman, 1–19–1938, in Roosevelt Papers, Of 3q, RPL.

69. Ernest G. Draper to Marvin McIntyre, 1–20–1938, in ibid.

70. Morgenthau Diary, 1–24–1938, RPL.

71. New York *Herald-Tribune*, 1–20–1938.

72. *Newsweek*, 1–31–1938, p. 40.

73. Breckinridge Long Diary, 1–29–1938, LC.

74. *Newsweek*, 2–7–1938, p. 9.

CHAPTER 13

1. Morgenthau Diary, 2–8–1938, RPL.

2. Ibid., 2–10–1938.

3. For example, Franklyn Waltman in Washington *Post*, 2–17–1938.

4. *Kiplinger Washington Letter*, 1–29–1938; *Manufacturer's Record*, 2–1938, p. 26; New York *Times*, 2–1–1938.

5. *United States News*, 2–7–1938.

6. New York *Times*, 2–6–1938.

7. *Business Week*, 2–12–1938; *Kiplinger Washington Letter*, 2–15–1938.

8. *Manufacturer's Record*, 2–1938, p. 26; Walter White to Ralph Flanders, 2–5–1938, Flanders Papers, SU; New York *Herald-Tribune*, 2–6–1938 and 2–13–1938.

9. Clapper Diary, 3–15–1938, LC.

10. Morgenthau Diary, 2–10–1938, RPL.

11. Ibid., 3–16–1938.

12. League of Nations, *World Economic Survey 1937/38* (Geneva, 1938), p. 195.

13. *Barron's*, 1–10–1938, pp. 9, 35.

14. *Guaranty Survey*, 1–31–1938.

15. Keynes to Roosevelt, 2–1–1938, Roosevelt Papers, PPF 5235, RPL.

16. *The Economist*, 2–19–1938, p. 387.

17. *Washington Review*, 2–14–1938.

18. Washington *Post*, 1–5–1938.

19. Currie, Henderson, and Lubin, ''Causes of the Recession,'' in Harry Hopkins Papers, RPL.

20. New York *Herald-Tribune*, 1–29–1938.

21. Leonard Ayres, ''This Business Relapse,'' *The Atlantic Monthly*, 2–1938, pp. 151–54.

22. For example, *Review of Economic Statistics* 20 (2–1938), p. 43.

23. New York *Herald-Tribune*, 3–5–1938.

24. Morgenthau Diary, 3–2–1938, RPL.

25. Berle Diary, 3–23–1938 and 3–26–1938, RPL.

26. *Commercial and Financial Chronicle*, 3–26–1938; New York *Herald-Tribune*, 3–24–1938.

27. Ibid.

28. Clapper to Landon, 3–30–1938, Clapper Papers, LC.

29. *Wall Street Journal*, 3–25–1938.

30. Morgenthau to Roosevelt, 4–12–1938, copy in Morgenthau Papers, RPL.

31. Morgenthau Diary, 4–18–1938, ibid.

32. Clapper Diary, 5–18–1938, LC.

33. *Public Papers*, VII, pp. 361–65.

34. New York *Times*, 5–28–1938, *Textile World*, 6–1938, p. 89.

35. New York *Herald-Tribune*, 5–30–1938.

36. *Barron's*, 3–21–1938, p. 4.

37. Clapper to Landon, 3–30–1938, Clapper Papers, LC.

38. *Public Papers*, VII, pp. 179–81.

39. *Kiplinger Washington Letter*, 4–2–1938.

40. New York *Times*, 4–10–1938.

41. Ibid., 4–9–1938.

42. Quoted in New York *Herald-Tribune*, 4–9–1938; see also *Business Week*, 4–16–1938, p. 64.

43. Morgenthau Presidential Diary, 4–11–1938, RPL.

44. Morgenthau Diary and Morgenthau Presidential Diary, both 4–12–1938, RPL.

45. Viner to Morgenthau, 4–14–1938, Morgenthau Diary, RPL.

46. *Barron's*, 5–9–1938, p. 11.

47. New York *Times*, 5–1–1938.

48. New York *Herald-Tribune*, 5–12–1938.

49. *Barron's*, 4–4–1938, p. 4.

50. Quoted in *Commercial and Financial Chronicle*, 4–9–1938, p. 2271.

51. Quoted in New York *Herald-Tribune*, 4–15–1938.

52. Ibid.; *Business Week*, 4–16–1938, pp. 2418–19; *Wall Street Journal*, 4–18–1938; *Magazine of Wall Street*, 4–23–1938, p. 5; *Guaranty Survey*, 4–25–1938.

53. *Barron's*, 4–18–1938, p. 4.

54. New York *Herald-Tribune*, 4–19–1938.

55. *Magazine of Wall Street*, 5–7–1938, p. 78.

56. *United States News*, 4–25–1938.

57. Ibid.

58. New York *Herald-Tribune*, 5–24–1938.

59. *Commercial and Financial Chronicle*, 5–14–1938, pp. 3065–66.

60. New York *Herald-Tribune*, 5–26–1938.

61. *Barron's*, 6–13–1938, p. 11.

62. New York *Times*, 6–3–1938.
63. Ibid., 6–12–1938.
64. New York *Herald-Tribune*, 5–13–1938.
65. Pinchot to Richard M. Hurd, 6–17–1938, Pinchot Papers, LC.
66. *Forbes*, 6–15–1938, p. 30; see also Ray Tucker, "Does Roosevelt Really Want Recovery?" *Magazine of Wall Street*, 7–2–1938, pp. 3322–24, and Harold Lord Varney, "Roosevelt Does Not Want Recovery," *American Mercury*, 11–1938, pp. 257–66.
67. Harold J. Fishbein to Roosevelt, 6–13–1938, wire, Roosevelt Papers, OF 172, RPL.
68. Marvin McIntyre to Fishbein, 6–15–1938, in ibid.
69. *Business Week*, 5–7–1938, p. 5.
70. *Wall Street Journal*, 6–16–1938.
71. *Commerce*, 8–1938, p. 13; also *Textile World*, 7–1938, p. 30.
72. *Wall Street Journal*, 6–16–1938.
73. *Forbes*, 7–1–1938, p. 7.
74. George H. Davis to Thomas W. Lamont, 9–29–1938, Lamont Papers, BLHU.
75. New York *Herald-Tribune*, 10–20–1938.
76. *Magazine of Wall Street*, 7–2–1938, p. 317.
77. Quoted in New York *Times*, 6–26–1938.
78. Ickes Diary, 7–3–1938, RPL.
79. *Banking*, 8–1938, p. 1; *American Banker*, 6–27–1938; *Mill and Factory*, 8–1938, p. 35.
80. *Newsweek*, 10–17–1938.
81. Quoted in James Farley to Roosevelt, 9–6–1938, Roosevelt Papers, OF 172, RPL.
82. New York *Herald-Tribune*, 3–12–1938.
83. Joseph Alsop to Wes Stout, 6–1–1938, Alsop Papers, LC.
84. *The Economist*, 7–2–1938, p. 3.
85. Berle Diary, 7–9–1938, RPL.
86. *American Banker*, 7–25–1938.
87. Clapper to Landon, 6–7–1938, Clapper Papers, and Robert Kintner to Martin Sommers, 6–14–1938, copy in Alsop Papers, both in LC.
88. New York *Times*, 9–14–1938.
89. *Wall Street Journal*, 9–17–1938 and 9–23–1938.
90. *Forbes*, 10–1–1938, p. 34.
91. *Newsweek*, 10–17–1938.
92. New York *Herald-Tribune*, 11–5–1938.
93. New York *Times*, 11–1–1938.

CHAPTER 14

1. New York *Times*, 11–13–1938.
2. For example, *The Economist*, 11–12–1938, p. 314.
3. Quoted in *United States News*, 11–14–1938.
4. *Washington Review*, 11–14–1938.
5. *Commerce*, 12–1938, p. 25.
6. *Nation's Business*, 12–1938, p. 11.
7. Homer Cummings Diary, 12–9–1938, RPL.
8. Joseph Alsop to his mother, 11–15–1938, Alsop Papers, LC.

9. New York *Herald-Tribune*, 11–10–1938.

10. For example, Amos Pinchot to Wesley Stout, 11–10–1938, Pinchot Papers, LC.

11. New York *Herald-Tribune*, 12–9–1938.

12. *Newsweek*, 12–12–1938, p. 44.

13. New York *Herald-Tribune*, 12–13–1938.

14. *Barron's*, 12–19–1938, p. 4.

15. For example, *Magazine of Wall Street*, 1–14–1939, p. 364; *Kiplinger Washington Letter*, 1–14–1939; *Textile World*, 1–1939, p. 30.

16. Ickes Diary, 11–19–1938, LC; New York *Herald-Tribune*, 12–26–1938 and 12–29–1938.

17. *Public Papers*, VIII, pp. 7–8; *Business Week*, 1–7–1939; *Magazine of Wall Street*, 1–14–1939; *Wall Street Journal*, 1–5–1939; *Forbes*, 1–15–1939; *Commercial and Financial Chronicle*, 1–7–1939, p. 2; *United States News*, 1–9–1939.

18. New York *Times*, 1–7–1939.

19. Hanes speech of 1–20–1939, in Hanes file, Morgenthau Papers, RPL.

20. New York *Times*, 1–28–1939.

21. Ibid., 2–8–1939.

22. *Magazine of Wall Street*, 2–25–1939, p. 538.

23. John W. Love to Moley, 2–7–1939, Moley Papers, HI.

24. Morgenthau Diary, 2–9–1939, RPL.

25. *Barron's*, 1–30–1939, p. 4.

26. Clapper Diary, 2–1–1939, LC.

27. *Wall Street Journal*, 2–27–1939.

28. *The Economist*, 4–3–1939, p. 436.

29. Wallace to Morgenthau, 2–3–1939, copy in Harry Hopkins Papers, RPL.

30. Wallace to Hopkins, 2–3–1939, in ibid.

31. Morgenthau Diary, 2–23–1939, RPL.

32. New York *Times*, 2–26–1939; *Commercial and Financial Chronicle*, 2–25–1939, p. 1061.

33. Morgenthau Diary, 2–23–1939, RPL.

34. Ibid., 2–25–1939; Clapper Diary, 2–28–1939, LC.

35. Ibid., 3–3–1939.

36. Ibid., 3–6–1939.

37. Ibid., 3–7–1939.

38. Ibid.

39 Berle Diary, 3–7–1939, RPL.

40. Ibid., 2–22–1939.

41. Ibid., 3–10–1939.

42. Ickes Diary, 3–12–1939, RPL.

43. New York *Times*, 3–8–1939 and 3–9–1939.

44. Morgenthau Diary, 3–8–1939, RPL.

45. Moley to Tugwell, 2–6–1939, Moley Papers, HI.

46. New York *Times*, 3–10–1939; *Commercial and Financial Chronicle*, 3–18–1939, p. 1525.

47. New York *Herald-Tribune*, 3–12–1939; Arthur Krock in New York *Times*, 3–12–1939.

48. New York *Times*, 3–17–1939.

49. Ibid., 3–15–1939.

50. New York *Herald-Tribune*, 3–23–1939.
51. Hanes to Morgenthau, 3–27–1939, Hanes File, Morgenthau Papers, RPL.
52. Copy with James Farley to Morgenthau, 3–28–1938, in ibid.
53. New York *Times*, 5–11–1939.
54. Ibid., 5–12–1939.
55. Ibid.
56. Ibid., 5–14–1939.
57. New York *Herald-Tribune*, 5–16–1939.
58. New York *Times*, 5–31–1939.
59. Randolph E. Paul, *Taxation in the United States* (Boston, 1954), pp. 215–18.
60. Morgenthau Diary, 5–16–1939, RPL.
61. Moley, *After Seven Years*, p. 296.
62. Niznik, ''Thomas G. Corcoran,'' pp. 329, 379; Adams, *Harry Hopkins*, p. 165.

Bibliography

The literature on Roosevelt and the New Deal years has reached such dimensions that it now requires a book-length bibliography to deal with it. Rather than list all manuscript collections and published sources consulted for this work, I have included only those actually cited in the notes. The reader who wishes to learn more about the specific personalities, programs, and events of the New Deal years is advised to consult James S. Olson, editor, *Historical Dictionary of the New Deal* (Westport, CT: Greenwood Press, 1985), which also contains an extensive bibliography.

MANUSCRIPT COLLECTIONS

Winthrop W. Aldrich Papers, Baker Library, Harvard University
Frederick Lewis Allen Papers, Library of Congress
Joseph Alsop Papers, Library of Congress
Newton Baker Papers, Library of Congress
Adolf Berle Papers, Roosevelt Presidential Library
Raymond Clapper Papers, Library of Congress
Bainbridge Colby Papers, Library of Congress
Homer Cummings Collection, Roosevelt Presidential Library
Pierre S. DuPont Papers, Hagley Museum and Library
Records of E. I. DuPont De Nemours and Company, Administrative Papers, Hagley Museum and Library
Irving Fisher Collection, Roosevelt Presidential Library

Ralph Flanders Papers, Syracuse University
Felix Frankfurter Papers, Library of Congress
Harry Hopkins Collection, Roosevelt Presidential Library
Harold Ickes Diary, Library of Congress
George F. Johnson Papers, Syracuse University
Thomas W. Lamont Papers, Baker Library, Harvard University
Breckinridge Long Papers, Library of Congress
Eugene Meyer Papers, Library of Congress
George Fort Milton Papers, Library of Congress
Raymond Moley Papers, Hoover Institution on War, Revolution and Peace
Henry Morgenthau Papers, Roosevelt Presidential Library
Amos Pinchot Papers, Library of Congress
John J. Raskob Papers, Hagley Museum and Library
Reid Family Papers, Library of Congress
Donald Richberg Papers, Library of Congress
Franklin Delano Roosevelt Papers, Roosevelt Presidential Library
Samuel Rosenman Papers, Roosevelt Presidential Library
Harlan F. Stone Papers, Library of Congress
Lewis Strauss Papers, Hoover Presidential Library
Mark Sullivan Papers, Hoover Institution on War, Revolution and Peace
Mark Sullivan Papers, Library of Congress
Charles M. Taussig Collection, Roosevelt Presidential Library
Rexford G. Tugwell Papers, Roosevelt Presidential Library
George Warren Papers, Cornell University

ORAL HISTORIES (in the Columbia University Oral History Collection)

Horace Albright
William W. Alexander
Paul H. Appleby
Louis H. Bean
William L. Clayton
Chester Davis
Jerome Frank
Marvin Jones
Florence Kerr
Arthur Krock
James Landis
Chester Morrill
Frances Perkins
Jackson E. Reynolds
Samuel I. Rosenman
Louis Taber
Rexford Tugwell
Milburn L. Wilson

PERIODICALS

Newspapers

Baltimore *Sun*, 1933–1936
Chicago *Tribune*, 1933–1938
New York *Herald-Tribune*, 1933–1938
New York *Times*, 1933–1939
Wall Street Journal, 1933–1938
Washington *Post*, 1933–1938

Business and Banking Periodicals, 1933–1938

American Banker
American Salesman
Annalist
Banker's Magazine
Bankers' Monthly
Banking
Barron's
Bulletin of the National Retail Dry Goods Association
Business Week
Commerce
Commercial and Financial Chronicle
The Controller
Dry Goods Economist
Dun's Review
The Economist
Editor and Publisher
Engineering News-Record
Federal Reserve Bulletin
Forbes
Fortune
The Foundry
Guaranty Survey
Harvard Business Review
Investment Banking
Iron Age
Journal of Business
Kiplinger Washington Letter
Magazine of Wall Street
Manufacturer's Record
Mill and Factory
Motor
Nation's Business

Review of Economic Statistics
Textile World

Other Periodicals, 1933–1938

American Economic Review
American Mercury
Atlantic Monthly
Harper's
Literary Digest
New Republic
Newsweek
Political Quartely
Reader's Digest
Today
Saturday Evening Post
United States News
Yale Review

BOOKS

Adams, Henry H. *Harry Hopkins*. New York, 1977.
Alsop, Robert, and Robert Kintner. *Men Around the President*. New York, 1939.
Ayers, Leonard P. *The Economics of Recovery*. New York, 1934.
Blum, John. *From the Morgenthau Diaries: Years of Crisis, 1928–1938*. Boston, 1959.
Burns, James M. *Roosevelt: The Lion and the Fox*. New York, 1958.
Childs, Marquis W. *I Write From Washington*. New York, 1942.
Conkin, Paul K. *The New Deal*. 2nd ed. New York, 1975.
Donham, Wallace B., and R. S. Meriam. *Notes on Recovery*. Harvard School of Business Administration, 1934.
Feis, Herbert. *1933: Characters in Crisis*. Boston, 1966.
Freidel, Frank. *Franklin D. Roosevelt: Launching the New Deal*. New York, 1973.
Graham, Otis. *An Encore for Reform*. New York, 1967.
Greer, Thomas H. *What Roosevelt Thought*. Lansing, MI, 1958.
Ickes, Harold. *The Secret Diary of Harold Ickes*. New York, 1954.
Iriye, Akira. *Mutual Images*. Cambridge, MA, 1975.
League of Nations. *World Economic Survey 1937/38* and *1938/39*. Geneva, 1938, 1939.
Leuchtenburg, William F. *Franklin D. Roosevelt and the New Deal*. New York, 1963.
McIntyre, Ross T. *White House Physician*. New York, 1946.
Moley, Raymond. *After Seven Years*. New York, 1939.
———. *The First New Deal*. New York, 1966.
Murphy, Bruce. *The Brandeis/Frankfurter Connection*. New York, 1982.
Niznik, Monica L. "Thomas G. Corcoran: The Public Service of Roosevelt's 'Tommy the Cork.' " Ph.D. diss. University of Notre Dame, 1981.
Parrish, Michael. *Felix Frankfurter and His Times: The Reform Years*. New York, 1982.
Paul, Randolph E. *Taxation in the United States*. Boston, 1954.
Perkins, Frances. *The Roosevelt I Knew*. New York, 1946.

Rauch, Basil. *The History of the New Deal, 1933–1938*. New York, 1944.

Ritchie, Donald A. *James M. Landis*. Cambridge, MA, 1980.

Romasco, Albert U. *The Politics of Recovery*. New York, 1983.

Rosenman, Samuel I., ed. *The Public Papers and Addresses of Franklin D. Roosevelt*. 9 vols. New York, 1937–1946.

Schumpeter, Joseph A. et al. *The Economics of the Recovery Program*. New York, 1934.

Schlesinger, Arthur, Jr. *The Coming of the New Deal*. New York, 1957.

———. *The Politics of Upheaval*. New York, 1960.

Spahr, Walter E. *An Appraisal of the Monetary Policies of Our Federal Government, 1933–1938*. New York, 1938.

U.S. Department of Commerce, Bureau of Census. *Historical Statistics of the United States*. 2 vols. Washington, DC, 1975.

Warburg, James P. *The Money Muddle*. New York, 1934.

Index

Benns, Sir Ernest: 90
Berle, Adolf: 7, 10, 16, 63, 169, 171,
173, 175, 184, 185, 186, 201, 209
Black, Hugo: 28, 29, 122–24, 152
Black-Connery 30 hour week bill: 118,
162
Blanket code (NRA): 39–40
Bone, Homer: 123
Borah, William: 10, 60
Boston Conference on Distribution: 73
Boyle, James: 118
Brain trust: 7
Brandeis, Louis: 10, 13, 14, 15, 17, 18,
38, 43, 58–59, 62, 87, 97, 104, 105,
120, 215
"Breathing spell": 109–11, 121
British Companies Act: 31–32
Brookings Institution: 49, 89, 102, 153,
164, 192
Brown, Douglas: 52
Brown, Lewis: 80, 186
*Bulletin of the National Retail Dry Goods
Association*: 98, 121
Bullock, C. J.: 55, 86
Burns, James McGregor: 6
Business Advisory Council: 57, 87, 89,
93, 102, 111, 154, 186, 206–7
Business Week: 39, 40, 47, 49, 50, 59,
64, 73, 86, 87, 101, 102, 110, 117,
137, 146, 148, 151, 161, 167–68, 178,
190
Buxton, Frank: 87

Carothers, Neil: 197
Carter, Jay: 11
Catledge, Turner: 81
Chester, Colby: 186
Chicago *Tribune*: 8, 62, 67, 79, 105,
139, 152
Childs, Marquis: 7
Civil Works Administration: 46, 64
Civilian Conservation Corps: 27
Clapper, Raymond: 3, 77–78, 79–80, 86,
91, 97, 99, 103, 105, 108, 111, 127,
149, 151, 152, 154, 163, 165, 186,
188, 194, 201, 207, 208, 212
Clement, M. W.: 186

Cohen, Benjamin: 10, 31, 57, 87, 97,
186, 209, 210, 211
Colby, Bainbridge: 136–37
Colm, Gerhard: 192
Commerce: 160
Commercial and Financial Chronicle: 30,
78, 83, 88, 93, 98, 140, 144, 151,
152, 160, 162, 171, 184
Committee for the Nation: 9
Communications Act: 66
Congress of American Industry: 80
Congress of Industrial Organizations: 145
Congressional election of 1934: 77–78
Congressional election of 1938: 202–4
The Controller: 127–28
Corcoran, Thomas: 10, 17, 18, 49, 57,
87, 97, 104, 131, 138, 151, 186, 200,
204, 207, 209, 210, 211, 215
Cox, Garfield: 124–25
Cummings, Homer: 18, 94, 96, 97, 106,
117, 141–42, 144

Davis, Chester: 50
Davis, John W.: 102, 136
Delano, Warren: 3
DeVoto, Bernard: 169
Dewey, Thomas E.: 214
Donham, Wallace: 32–33, 73
Douglas, Lewis: 136
Douglas, William O.: 58–59, 169, 190–
91
Dry Goods Economist: 35, 62, 125, 128,
161–62
DuPont, Pierre: 8
Durable Goods Industries Committee
(NRA): 72–73

Early, Stephen: 70
Eccles, Marriner: 102, 128–29, 131, 134,
141, 146, 147, 148, 183, 186, 187,
192, 200, 204, 206, 209–10
Eccles banking bill: 87–88, 102
The Economist: 42, 48, 52, 85, 117, 128,
133, 158, 170, 180, 184, 192, 201,
207
Economy bill: 26
Edie, Lionel: 141, 146, 177
Editor and Publisher: 98, 123

About the Author

GARY DEAN BEST is Professor of History at the University of Hawaii at Hilo. He is the author of *The Politics of American Individualism* (Greenwood, 1975), *To Free A People* (Greenwood, 1982), and *Herbert Hoover: The Postpresidential Years*, 2 volumes (1983), as well as numerous essays for scholarly books and journals. He has held fellowships from the American Historical Association and the National Endowment for the Humanities, and was a Fulbright Scholar in Japan, 1974–1975.